DEFEATING
POLITICAL
ISLAM

DEFEATING POLITICAL ISLAM

THE NEW COLD WAR

Moorthy S. Muthuswamy

Foreword by Steven Emerson

 **Prometheus Books**

59 John Glenn Drive
Amherst, New York 14228–2119

Published 2009 by Prometheus Books

Inquiries should be addressed to
Prometheus Books
59 John Glenn Drive
Amherst, New York 14228–2119
VOICE: 716–691–0133, ext. 210
FAX: 716–691–0137
WWW.PROMETHEUSBOOKS.COM

13 12 11 10 09   5 4 3 2 1

Library of Congress Cataloging-in-Publication Data

Muthuswamy, Moorthy.
   Defeating political Islam : the new Cold War / by Moorthy S. Muthuswamy.
      p. cm.
   Includes bibliographical references.
   ISBN 978–1–59102–704–1 (cloth : alk. paper)
   1. Jihad. 2. Terrorism—Religious aspects—Islam. 3. Islam and politics. 4. Terrorism—Prevention—International cooperation. 5. World politics—21st century. I. Title.

BP182.M874 2009
363.325'15610973—dc22

                                                                          2008054560

Printed in the United States of America on acid-free paper

CONTENTS

FOREWORD

*D*efeating Political Islam is one of those rare books on radical Islam that is not afraid to pull any punches in its analysis and proscription on how to deal with the growing menace of radical Islam, or as Dr. Muthuswamy calls it "political Islam." This is a book that will provoke you. It will fascinate you. It will push your thinking way past the limits of the politically correct discourse about militant Islam in the United States today. This is also a book that may anger you. Dr. Muthuswamy has written a book that contains some of the best analysis I have ever read about the roots of contemporary Islamic violence stemming from the Koran and *sharia*, but it also contains recommendations and opinions that I strongly disagree with. Even so, this book will make you think out of the box about the problems of radical Islamic proliferation in the world today.

It is a book that covers the entire spectrum of thought about how to stop the spread of political Islam, which includes not only the violent Islamic terrorist groups but also the "peaceful" ones—the ones that pretend to be moderate in public but in fact represent radical Islamic theology. Dr. Muthuswamy, in authoring *Defeating Political Islam*, has tackled problems that the West refuses to acknowledge. In their denial and cognitive dissonance, Western regimes, commentators, reporters, and intellectuals have tried to portray all Islamic movements and groups, with the exception of the manifestly violent ones, as organizations the West can have reasonable dialogue with and that can be integrated into the pluralism of the West. These are the same government officials and journalists who now refuse to even utter the term "radical Islam," instead insisting on using the sanitary and meaningless terms "radical" or "extremist" without any modifiers, as if Islamic extremism or Islamic terrorism does not exist. This raises the question as to whether we should drop the terms "white racists" or "eco-terrorists" and instead just use the terms "racists" and "terrorists," making them indistinguishable from Islamic terrorists. Of course, this attempt to sanitize the term "Islamic terrorism" is but part of a much grander effort to whitewash Islamic extremism and take away the onus of responsibility from the Muslim world for producing such extremists. In the end, if we are not allowed to identify our enemy, how can we hope to defeat it?

Dr. Muthuswamy has produced a truly original piece of intellectual thinking and analysis that stands as a counterweight to the politically correct and dangerously misleading analysis produced by the empty vessels at the *New York Times*, the US State Department, the Brookings Institution, and the Carnegie Endowment for International Peace, to name just a few of the high priests in Washington, DC, who pretend they know what they are talking about.

As I said before, I don't agree with all of Dr. Muthuswamy's analysis and recommendations. I do believe in the existence of genuine moderate Islam, although obviously in the minority but authentic just the same. I don't believe that Muslim populations should be expelled from Europe for the violence their communities are producing, although that leaves me without an answer to the growing threat to free speech by those radicalized Muslim populations who deem any criticism of Islam as an insult deserving of death, not to mention the proliferation of localized *sharia* law invocations in Europe that threaten the basic foundation of the West, the separation of church and state, as well as the rights of women not to be killed or beaten. I don't believe that the Koran is intrinsically violent: I believe that the interpreters of the Koran, who have never undergone a reformation and have been in control of the Islamic religious establishment, are the ones who instill the violence in those that are inspired by the verses in the Koran that call for killing Jews and Christians. For the Koran also has verses that say you have to make friends with Jews and Christians. Regrettably, the dominant interpreters of the Koran and the writers of the Hadith have been radical from day one. So in the end, the Koran is what you want it to be. Dr. Muthuswamy, however, has made a cogent argument, backed up by impressive statistical analysis, that diverges from my belief. Am I being naïve or is he wrong? Only one who reads his book can tell.

Dr. Muthuswamy is a brilliant writer and analyst who has written an opus that needs to be read by the public and policymakers as well. You will find yourself tremendously enlightened by the genuinely original analysis Dr. Muthuswamy has done in examining Islamic texts. You may find yourself disagreeing with some of what he writes or recommends (as I do), but I was fascinated to read his findings. He brings genuine scholarship to the debate that is sorely missing in Western circles. His book is designed to make you think out of the proverbial box that is rampant in current circular and insular thinking about how to contain radical Islam. This is a book that needs to be read by anyone concerned with understanding the full scope of the problem Western societies face from a growing radical Islamic movement that seeks to shut down debate, claim all critics are racists, intimidate writers, and challenge our most valuable freedom—that of free speech.

Steven Emerson
Executive Director of the Investigative Project on Terrorism
and author of *Jihad Incorporated: A Guide to Militant Islam in the US*

We can't be consumed by our petty differences anymore
We will be united in our common interests
You will once again be fighting for our freedom—not from tyranny, oppression,
or persecution, but from annihilation
We are fighting for our right to live—to exist!
We are going to survive!

Portions of a speech delivered before launching the
decisive battle to defeat and destroy alien invaders
(from *Independence Day*—a 1996 Hollywood blockbuster movie)

PREFACE

A smoldering Iraq and reverses in Pakistan and Afghanistan signify that war on terror is far from over. Left alone, radical Islam is not a containable problem. It will stop at nothing less than destruction of civilization as we know it. Radicals have a clear focus: the anchor state of civilization—America—must be brought to its knees; its economic and military capability must be destroyed. Pressure is mounting on America and its military with the economic toll of the war on terror already close to a trillion dollars thus far and about ten thousand civilians and military personnel killed and several tens of thousands injured.

The quick and unprecedented victory of the America-led coalition forces over Iraq has shown that Islamic states are lacking in conventional military might. However, through proxies, radical Islamic states have imposed a strategically effective terror war. Now more of them are at the threshold of acquiring nuclear weapons capability.

This is a serious threat. Having weathered Nazis and countless invaders, portions of Europe face the probability of being overrun demographically by Muslim radicals. Among the states at the border of Islam, the lands of Israel and India are staring at the possibility of an Islamic conquest.

The up-to-date and extensive information required for conducting research—the so-called virtual library—is just a touch of a key away on the Internet. Indeed, the advent of the Internet has made it possible to develop a multidisciplinary approach to solving these problems, or even to win the war on terror.

There is a need for a scientific point of view in discrediting doctrines that tell believers to kill unbelievers. When so many nations' or societies' survival is at stake, especially when the enemy is a proven genocidal one who obeys no rules, problem solving should take center stage. This is something that traditional policy-advising institutions—used to thinking in terms of diplomacy, military, or a combination thereof—find difficult to understand. The need to solve the radical Islamic problem is not lost on world leaders. President George W. Bush, for one, noted this issue as the "inescapable calling of our generation."[1]

I have moved away from using the term "radical Islam" to identify the enemy. The enemy is really the political Islamic movement; radical Islam is one subset of this political movement, one that has the objective of conquering the unbelievers. Contrary to the conventional belief that the radical Islamic movement, represented by the likes of al Qaeda, is an independent, stateless entity, this book develops the view of a movement that is thriving due to the continued sponsorship of mainly three nations and their citizens. These nations are Saudi Arabia, Pakistan, and Iran; they are introduced in this book as the "axis of jihad."

Incriminating data on axis nations is discussed here with the aim of developing a sense of grievance in victim nations. It is argued that the main reason for the limited headway that has been achieved thus far in the war on terror is due to America's and its allies' inability to effectively go after the axis of jihad nations and the nodes of social network in Muslim communities spawning terror.

With America and its allies yet to engage the axis militarily and given the ideological nature of this conflict, this book's subtitle, "The New Cold War," seems appropriate. Accordingly, many of the strategies discussed here are similar to the ones deployed to fight the old cold war with the former Soviet Union–inspired communist movement, but with one main difference: we must acknowledge the fact that the political Islamic movement fights in the name of Allah, unlike secular communism.

This book discusses the ways in which America could execute an innovative multinational terror war policy without directly occupying terror-sponsoring nations. For a successful counteroffensive against political Islam, there is a need to build and pursue crimes-against-humanity charges against the axis of jihad nations and to discredit the standing of Saudi Arabia—the nation most responsible for creating and sustaining the terror unleashed on unbelievers. We must identify political Islam's theological weaknesses and exploit them. As a professional physicist, I give arguments based upon science and common sense to discredit the theology that Islamists use to justify jihad—a religious war waged on unbelievers.

As an America-trained nuclear physicist, I can inform readers that nuclear bomb-making physics and technology is a thing of yesteryear. Determined Muslim states will acquire nuclear bombs, as Pakistan has already demonstrated. In the near future, America, Israel, and India will be their primary targets. It is going to require more than military capability to dissuade Muslim radicals from using nukes on us.

The extent to which America and its allies could go after the sponsors and foot soldiers of political Islam has to be justified by data that show how jihad develops and what its dire consequences are, if not confronted effectively. Not widely known or realized, the data presented here unequivocally show that a growing Muslim population can be a genocidal threat to the local unbeliever population. Such data is provided here through a detailed look at the ongoing jihad in India, a nation that has long been ravaged by waves of Muslim invasions and that had been ruled by Muslim kings for over five hundred years. It is also a nation that was divided on the basis of Islam only about sixty years ago—and is yet seen by Islamists as having escaped Islamic control.

All available evidence points to a concerted and ongoing effort to systematically destroy India and bring it under the Islamic fold. This is a daring, high-risk adventure against a nation of more than one billion people, of which 850 million are non-Muslims. Amazingly, Islamists are making headway—and the siege of India by political Islam is intensifying, despite the current economic resurgence. The project conquest-India has some big-name backers—nation-states whose passion is Islamic conquest. A cornered India and its majority non-Muslim population offer an overstretched America the unprecedented possibility of taking war to the jihadists and their sponsoring states.

Having fallen behind Western societies in civilizational advancement (which rules out using Muslim "achievement" to impress and convince unbelievers to embrace Islam) but endowed with vast natural resources and a passion for conquest, political Islam's goal of worldwide conquest could be achieved only by access to power through legitimate means in many areas of the world with non-Muslim majority populations. This approach to "conquest" is over and above that of terrorism conducted in the name of Allah.

Any such politico-terror war requires committed adherents and an ideology that is perceived by many as being all encompassing. The reader may be surprised to discover in these pages that nations with a medieval outlook could wage a fairly sophisticated jihad on unsuspecting and powerful nations. The approach presented in this book—compartmentalizing the problem and identifying the enemy's weaknesses—could be considered a general outline for neutralizing violent, religion-based political movements.

This book doesn't call for full-scale war on Muslims or for restriction of their individual rights. But it suggests how this war could be fought predominantly on ideological and political grounds and in the context of human rights and religious freedom. A survival problem of this magnitude requires an involved public. With that in mind, it is hoped that this book will engage nonexperts.

NOTE

1. Rudi Williams, "Terror War 'Inescapable Calling of Our Generation,' Bush Says," *American Forces Press Service*, March 20, 2004.

ACKNOWLEDGMENTS

A project of this magnitude needs the involvement of many people. Over the years I have benefited immensely from discussions with many people. Due to circumstances I am forced to be discreet in acknowledging their contributions.

I am indebted to scholars Bill Warner, Andrew G. Bostom, and Robert Spencer for their inspiration and support. I am also grateful for their help in finding reference material.

Whatever virtues this book may possess is mainly due to the editorial guidance and involvement of Prometheus's extraordinary Steven L. Mitchell. What is good here is his, and the errors are only mine.

Chapter One

WHAT WENT WRONG?

E ven the most sanguine optimist couldn't deny that the war on terror, as manifested by extensive American and allied military engagements abroad (i.e., in Iraq and Afghanistan), is not proceeding well.[1] With recruitment apparently robust, radical Islam appears to be as strong as ever. This means that the numbers of America-hating Islamic terrorists are continuing to grow. This may point to the reality of the situation: the so-called pro-American regimes in some Islamic nations are not effective in countering jihad. Clearly, America needs a coherent new strategy to win the war on terror.

Six years in, the military expenses associated with the terror war alone may have cost at least as much as the Vietnam War—about $500 billion.[2] There have been extensive other economic costs and internal security expenses as well.

There are also other pressing short-term and long-term challenges. Islamic Iran is relentlessly pushing toward developing nuclear bombs, the nuclear-armed jihad factory called Pakistan has become highly unstable, and a truly strategic and economic challenge to America has emerged from China. This China challenge far exceeds the one posed by the former Soviet Union.

RESURGENT POLITICAL ISLAM

America was the most dominant nation of the past century, especially after the Second World War. Understandably, until the last part of the twentieth century, Western politicians and strategic experts viewed Islamic civilization as a struggling one, not a strategic threat at all.

Until recently many Islamic nations had been under the control of Western colonizers. Due to this fact, little effort had been made by the Westerners to understand the religious and political underpinnings of Islam. Yet Islam had been an expanding power until at least the eighteenth century, with a long history of conflict with Christianity, the majority religion in the West.

From a classical Western view, in order for Islam to become a strategic threat, Muslim nations would have to first build their economies and industrial infrastructure to the point that they are comparable to those of the West, which would take many decades. For instance, Nazi Germany and Imperial Japan had become threats in the 1930s because they had economies and industrial know-how that were comparable to those of the Allies. But radical Islamists have shown that, by influencing a vast majority of Muslim civilians globally and by converting many of them into foot soldiers, they can become a strategic threat to Western civilization. In other words, they can overcome the deficiency of not being classical military powers. The proliferation of AK-47 assault rifles and bomb-making technology has made terror acts easier to execute and costlier to prevent.

Political Islam holds that Islam should have a prominent if not dominant say in governing the affairs of those nations in which Muslims are the majority or a significant minority.[3] Seen through the context of the Islamic trilogy—consisting of the Koran, the Hadith, and the Sira—political Islam dominates over spiritual Islam (see chapter 2, "Conquest by Design").[4] Hence, Islam itself has a dominant political flavor to it. There is an internal component of political Islam, as it governs the kind of life and political system to which Muslims should adhere. But the internal politics of Islam and its legal code, called *sharia*, do not provide a way of setting up a modern state, for the obvious reason that it reflects the customs of societies that existed several hundreds to thousands of years ago. The economic and social aspirations of Muslims have therefore gone unfulfilled, with rising expectations fueled by television and movies from the West and the East. However, the needed focus or a missing mission in the internal component is provided by the external one: conquest of "unbelievers," or non-Muslims. Conquest of unbelievers is either taken to mean their embrace of Islam or their reduced status under Muslim control as the non-Muslim *dhimmis*. Political Islam concerns those of us who do not believe in its tenets because it commands Muslims to conquer the world for Islam.

With other religions, when disciples' aspirations went unfulfilled, introspection resulted and it led to a reform of religious practices. However, as is discussed in the next chapter, one aspect of Islam that is unique is that whenever Muslims felt they had fallen behind, the most vocal among them were calling for Muslims to embrace even more retrogressive practices of political Islam. These retrogressive practices were identified as fueling the drive toward regenerating the "glory" days of Islamic civilization—defined by the conquering of large swaths of unbeliever land in the aftermath of the death of Muhammad. These practices include literal interpretations of the Islamic trilogy and the importance of conquest through jihad, rather than reform (i.e., the reinterpretation of Muslim scriptures in a contemporary way and the downgrading of the importance given to them). The fundamentalists assert that once the whole world is Islamized, everyone will feel fulfilled and be at peace with one another. Of course, fundamentalists may or may not realize the inconvenient reality that even in Islamic nations, different schools of religious thought are in conflict with each other.

In other words, inner political Islam is keeping Muslims from providing a better future for themselves and their families, and external political Islam commands them to wage jihad. Thus the increasingly accepted view is that the agenda set by political Islam is spawning terrorism.

The doctrine of jihad is the most important tool political Islam uses to assert its influence and achieve its vision. In general, the term *jihad* can be used to describe two concepts: there is an inner struggle, called "greater jihad," within each Muslim, whose aim is to please the almighty God; and then there is "lesser jihad," which is external warfare aimed at conquest of land belonging to unbelievers and the imposition of Islam on its inhabitants. On the primary meaning of jihad, from the Koran, the most important of the Islamic doctrines:

> Jahada, the root of the word Jihad, appears 40 times in the Koran—under a variety of grammatical forms. With 4 exceptions, all the other 36 usages [in specific Koranic verses] are variations of the third form of the verb, i.e., Jahida. Jahida in the Koran and in subsequent Islamic understanding to both Muslim luminaries—from the greatest jurists and scholars of classical Islam [including Abu Yusuf, Averroes, Ibn Khaldun, and Al Ghazzali], to ordinary people—meant and means "he fought, warred or waged war against unbelievers and the like," as described by the seminal Arabic lexicographer E. W Lane.[5]

Hadiths signify the oral traditions recounting events in the life of Islam's founder, Muhammad, who lived during the time period 570 to 632 CE. Of the six traditions of the Haiths, the one by Muhammad al-Bukhari is considered to be the most trusted. Al-

Bukhari is said to have lived between the years 810 and 870 CE.[6] In Bukhari Hadith, 97 percent of the jihad references are about war and 3 percent are about the inner struggle, showing that from a practical perspective lesser jihad is more important.[7]

Typically, it is the institutions in unbeliever nations who misinterpret jihad. The United States Commission on International Religious Freedom (USCIRF) states, while ignoring the statistical dominance of lesser jihad in the doctrines, "While there are various meanings of the term jihad, including an internal struggle of the soul, none are given in this brief discussion [in Saudi school texts], which also includes an emphasis on the importance of power or force over one's enemies and discusses 'martyrdom' with approval."[8] However, American scholar Bernard Lewis disagrees:

> Conventionally translated "holy war" [jihad] has the literal meaning of striving, more specifically, in the Koranic phrase "striving in the path of God" (fi sabil Allah). Some Muslim theologians, particularly in more modern times, have interpreted the duty of "striving in the path of God" in a spiritual and moral sense. The overwhelming majority of early authorities, however, citing relevant passages in the Koran and in the tradition, discuss jihad in military terms.[9]

The celebrated *Dictionary of Islam*, published in the year 1895 by Thomas Hughes, characterizes jihad along these lines:

> [A] religious war with those who are unbelievers in the mission of Muhammad. It is an incumbent religious duty, established in the Koran and in the traditions as a divine institution, enjoined especially for the purpose of advancing Islam and of repelling evil from Muslims.[10]

Well-known American ex-prosecutor of jihadists Andrew McCarthy uses the above quotes and further articulates:

> It is no wonder that this should be so. The Koran repeatedly enjoins Muslims to fight and slay non-Muslims. "O ye who believe," commands Sura 9:123, "fight those of the disbelievers who are near you, and let them find harshness in you, and know that Allah is with those who keep their duty unto him." It is difficult to spin that as a call to spiritual self-improvement. As it is, to take another example, with Sura 9:5: "But when the forbidden months are past, then fight and slay the pagans wherever ye find them. And seize them, beleaguer them, and lie in wait for them in every stratagem (of war)," relenting only if they have accepted Islam.[11]

The Hadith, lengthy volumes recording the words and traditions of the prophet, are even more explicit, as in Muhammad's teaching that "[a] single endeavor (of fighting) in Allah's cause in the afternoon or in the forenoon is better than all the world and whatever is in it."[12]

The most significant modern interpretation of jihad is revealed in what Muslim entities and institutions tell their fellow Muslims. Consistent with the overwhelming importance given to the lesser jihad in the doctrines, a Saudi text books says: "In these verses is a call for jihad, which is the pinnacle of Islam. . . . Only through force and victory over the enemies is there security and repose."[13] The emphasis of lesser jihad, including the armed one in Pakistan's textbooks, too has been noted.[14]

Throughout the discussion, the word *jihad* is taken to mean the dominant form, the lesser jihad. This is the jihad that Muslim extremists, radicals, or jihadists—practitioners of jihad—mean in their discourse. Armed warfare imposed on unbelievers is one form of jihad. More generally, jihad should be understood as a struggle that uses every means possible to achieve the goal of Islamic conquest. The doctrine of jihad is used by political Islam to achieve conquest. Muslims who pursue political Islam's goals include activists—jihadists, radicals, extremists—and nonactivist ordinary Muslims who identify with and sponsor actual activists. With this in mind, we can see that even though many ordinary Muslims are busy eking out a living, without their support political Islam's vision of Islamic conquest would be a nonstarter. In this context the main goal of winning the war on terror can be defined as the negation of the support political Islam receives from the Muslim public and sponsoring nations.

We will use the term "political Islam" to denote the ideology we are fighting. This ideology has spawned a worldwide movement whose intent is a violent conquest of unbelievers. This may be the first necessary step toward identifying the enemy correctly and coming up with a coherent policy response.

The majority of Muslims associate the trilogy with all of the necessary information for leading a complete life.[15] This interpretation has made it difficult for Muslim nations to adapt to new ideas and to evolve, and especially to compete with the Western world, which in the last several hundred years led the industrial and technological revolutions that have been considered the basis for the modern world. These revolutions shifted wealth and power to the nations with industrial know-how. This put most Muslim nations at a disadvantage until huge deposits of petroleum were found in many Middle East nations, including Saudi Arabia, the birth nation of Islam's founder, Muhammad.

Regardless of how predisposed a theology or an ideology is toward a certain outlook, such as conquest, it has to have committed and resourceful backers to become influential. In Saudi Arabia, political Islam has found a passionate backer. The enormous oil wealth of the country gave the Saudis an opportunity to reinvigorate the expansionist designs of political Islam. By many accounts, since the mid-1970s, Saudi Arabia alone is said to have spent well over $85 to 90 billion (strictly through official channels) on spreading the Wahhabi version (see chapter 2, often described in the West as an "extremist" version of Islam) of political Islam to Sunni (the other major denomination is Shia Islam) Muslim populations around the world.[16] Added to this is the tradition for Saudis in all walks of life to fund the propagation of Islam. As new groundbreaking research discussed in the next chapter shows, statistically, jihadist politics form a significant component of Islamic doctrine. Hence, one has to wonder whether the Wahhabi interpretation of Sunni Islam is indeed a fair and accurate representation of Islamic doctrine as defined in the trilogy.

There is every reason for Saudi Arabia to promote Wahhabism, because along with Wahhabism, as part of a package, the Saudis could also promote their political and strategic agenda to unsuspecting nations and populations. Also, as Islam originated in Saudi Arabia, a nation under the Wahhabi ideological spell creates a civilization subservient to Saudi Arabia.

There are other reasons for the Saudis to support the Wahhabi version. Islamists of various hues have a common goal of an Islamic caliphate. A caliphate is the political leadership of the Muslim *ummah* (community of Muslims in the whole world) in classical or medieval Islamic history and juristic theory. The head of state's position or the caliph is based on the notion of a successor to the prophet Muhammad's political authority.[17] Who can lead the caliphate? According to the so-called Islamic law, it has to be an Arab from Quraysh tribe (the tribe the prophet Muhammad belonged to—now found in Saudi Arabia and Jordan).[18] During the early 1900s when India was a British colony, the Hyderabad Nawab (or the king) in India, out of religious reasons, had periodically sent allowances to the cash-strapped Saudi royal family—the custodian of the Muslim holy sites. With oil yet to be found, these allowances were an important source of funding for the Saudi royals.[19] Hence, it is not unreasonable for Saudi Arabia to invest in conquest and the spread of Wahhabism and to expect a payoff later—in the form of subsidies from better-off Wahhabi-influenced Muslim nations (such as Turkey or Malaysia), once oil revenues dry up in about a hundred years.

With a long and successful history of conquest and being deeply Wahhabi, Saudi Arabia is unlikely to put to good use (such as providing a broad-based modern education system internally—a must for overall development and empowerment) the free wealth it got in the form of oil revenues. From a traditional Wahhabi view, all important knowledge is in the Islamic trilogy. By implication, there is really no important knowledge in modern science; besides, science is associated with the *infidel* or "Christian" Western world. Even within Saudi Arabia, education is tilted toward Islamic history and less toward modern literature or science.[20] Saudi Arabia has more than enough wealth to buy or pay for both skilled and unskilled guest workers, and their population in Saudi Arabia reflects this reality. When the call for jihad came from Soviet-occupied Afghanistan, to free the country from non-Muslim "oppressors," the Saudi Arabian regime and society were more than prepared to assist a popular jihad.

An alternate and competing Islamic school of thought is Shiite Islam. The Sunni and Shiite sects have bloody political differences dating back almost to the immediate aftermath of Muhammad's death. Iran, the most populous Shiite-dominant country, found itself awash with petroleum reserves. It also joined the movement of Islamic conquest in the 1980s by spending its wealth to influence Shiite groups around the globe toward jihad.

Pakistan is the first Muslim nation to be carved out of a non-Muslim majority nation, since it was partitioned from British-ruled India in 1947. As the torchbearer for Islam in South Asia, Pakistan sees the largest nation in the region, non-Muslim-majority India, as the stumbling block for extending Islamic boundaries. Although Sunni-majority Pakistan was frustrated by its smaller size and lack of resources, it has an extensive track record of jihad dating back to 1947. Even without Saudi funding, between 1947 and 1980 Pakistan was a standout nation in terms of the selective killings of non-Muslims or their displacement as part of a jihad.[21] Generous jihad funding from Saudi Arabia (which is also predominantly Sunni) since the mid-1970s has made Pakistan even more powerful.

Perhaps more than any other Islamic nation, Pakistan has acted as a collaborator for Saudi Arabia and a translator of jihad plans into action; it has provided logistics, training, and know-how for jihadist movements around the world. For instance, aided by Saudi Arabia, the Afghan Taliban was Pakistan's creation. There is also a suspicion that Saudi Arabia has been heavily financing Pakistan's nuclear program for mutual benefit.[22]

The Soviet occupation of Muslim-majority Afghanistan was used to build jihad fervor in many Islamic nations. This occupation also attracted holy warriors from many Islamic nations, including Egypt; this also includes Pakistan, the eventual base for anti-Soviet jihad. The Soviets found their occupation untenable because political Islam was entrenched in the minds of the Afghans and because a relentless and resourceful enemy kept coming at them from Pakistan. After the Soviet retreat in

1989, the Afghan faction known as the Taliban consolidated power. The Taliban consisted of former students from Pakistani *madrassas* (Muslim religious schools) and was the brainchild of Pakistani intelligence—specifically, the Inter-Services Intelligence (ISI).[23]

One unfortunate side effect of the Soviet-Afghan war was the jihadist training of nationals from many Islamic nations. Although most of the regimes ruling these nations invariably sided with the radicals on the Afghan jihad, they failed to measure up to the radical expectation of complete dedication to jihad and unadulterated enforcement of *sharia* or the medieval Islamic law. More important, the Muslim ruling establishment's embrace of Western culture had appalled the radicals. Upon returning home, many of these jihadists set about establishing terror cells with the aim of overthrowing existing home governments that they saw as un-Islamic. As a result, instabilities were being created in many Muslim nations, such as Egypt, Saudi Arabia, and Pakistan. A band of Arab Islamic radicals, including Osama bin Laden and his cohorts, decided to use Afghanistan as a base for jihad against unbelievers. Bin Laden's group, al Qaeda, operated in Taliban-ruled Afghanistan.

The attack on the World Trade Center in 1993 by Islamic radicals associated with al Qaeda should have served as a wake-up call for America. In retrospect, we understand why it didn't. There were no easy options in dealing with the Taliban or al Qaeda, and Pakistan was not helpful. The Soviet imbroglio in Afghanistan was fresh in American minds. Also, Bin Laden's vision of imposing Islam on the entire humanity by waging a war on unbelievers either was not clearly understood or was seen as being overly ambitious. An American attack on the Taliban was seen as having the potential for creating further instabilities in the Islamic world and making America even more unpopular. However, the dominant reason for the muted American response was that Bin Laden's group was seen as lacking the ability to strategically hurt America. "Militant or radical Islam" was seen as a transient phenomenon, one that had been created by the Afghan war and that was soon to die out.

But attacks on American interests that were attributed to al Qaeda were increasing in sophistication. Bin Laden was systematically escalating his rhetoric as well. His edict justifying the killing of American civilians was made in 1998. Just before the African embassy (in Kenya and Tanzania) bombings of the same year, the CIA looked into the possibility of capturing Bin Laden in Afghanistan, but it eventually dropped the plan because it was unsure of success and worried about the casualties and their implications both in America and in the Islamic world.[24] The simultaneous American embassy bombings in Africa did wake the Clinton administration up. It responded with cruise missile strikes on Bin Laden's camps but failed to kill him. According to the 9/11 Commission, officials in Washington suspected that Bin Laden or the Taliban might have received advance warning from Pakistani officials.[25] Then came the attack on the destroyer USS *Cole* in 2000 that killed seventeen American sailors. Al Qaeda operatives carried it out when the destroyer docked in the Yemeni port of Aden.[26] Soon after the attack the George W. Bush administration took office and was notified of the evidence implicating al Qaeda. Condoleezza Rice, who at the time was national security advisor, told the 9/11 Commission that the president did not want to respond to al Qaeda one attack at a time. Instead, the administration apparently began to work on a "new strategy" to eliminate al Qaeda completely.[27]

American efforts were not successful for one main reason: the United States did not understand the new enemy. America had defeated the former Soviet Union, the old enemy, in a protracted struggle that was spread over four decades. The new enemy, political Islam, is very different from the old one; the new one fights in the name of God and the former abhorred the very concept of God. A godless enemy such as the Soviet Union was easy to ostracize in an America led to believe that religion and God are constructive influences. For a nation founded on the principle of religious freedom, America seems to view religion as a constructive influence, and this has created significant complications in policymaking and in understanding the new enemy. There was another problem: America helped to create the jihad fervor through recruitment and training against the Soviet Union's occupation of Afghanistan. The United States had encouraged all movements that would oust the Soviet occupiers.

For decades, the established American strategy had been tuned to dealing with Soviet communism. Hence, there was little institutionalized knowledge of political Islam that the policymakers could rely upon. Also, heavy dependence on imported oil from nations that have long sponsored political Islam has not helped. A nonreligious Soviet Union was amenable to rational discussion and accommodation, however difficult it might be. But jihadists blindly follow ancient scriptures and their outdated interpretations and are not open to accommodation. More important, jihadists want nothing less than the submission and conversion of America to Islam. Many radical Muslim leaders, such as Iran's Mahmoud Ahmadinejad, are even openly apocalyptic.

When it quickly became apparent that al Qaeda was behind the 9/11 attacks, the Afghanistan invasion was inevitable. There was also considerable empathy and worldwide support for America in this invasion endeavor. A vastly superior American military invaded Afghanistan and quickly drove away both the Taliban and al Qaeda from power, with the help of the anti-Taliban Northern Alliance. It now appears that poor military tactics allowed the toppled al Qaeda and Taliban leadership to escape to Pakistan.[28] There is no question that the capture or death of Bin Laden at American hands would have instilled fear in the minds of jihadists.

But Bin Laden, al Qaeda, and the Taliban are just symptoms or proxies of a resurging political Islamic movement sponsored and nurtured by powerful entities in Saudi Arabia and Pakistan. Similarly, the militant Muslim group Hezbollah is sponsored by Shiite Iran. The problem with the American strategy in the war on terror is its focus on the proxies and a relative lack of focus on confronting and neutralizing its sponsors.

TALIBAN OR AL QAEDA WERE PROXIES

Throughout the 1990s, jihadists had strong backing in the Middle East. Indeed, funds flowed generously, with most there viewing the Afghan Taliban regime as a virtuous Islamic government. In addition to Pakistan, the Taliban-controlled Afghanistan was recognized also by Saudi Arabia and the United Arab Emirates. A Canadian intelligence report concluded that Saudi charities funnel $1 to 2 million per month to al Qaeda, while the Council on Foreign Relations task force described Saudi individuals and charities as "the most important source of funds for al Qaeda" and deplored the Saudis' turning "a blind eye" to this activity. Several principal financial backers of al Qaeda, most of them wealthy Saudis, were described as "the check writers."[29] While al Qaeda may not have been directly controlled by Saudi Arabia, it no doubt shared many Saudi aspirations. Hence it found a certain level of acceptance among the Saudi ruling elite and the public.

The Saudi government had been the principal financial backer of Afghanistan's fundamentalist Taliban movement since at least 1996. The Taliban not only had strong backing among the public in Pakistan but the Pakistani intelligence service was at the forefront of sponsoring and aiding the Taliban. It provided fuel, arms, ammunition, and even advice.[30] The *madrassa*-educated, semi-illiterate Taliban leadership didn't have the experience to run the nation, so Pakistanis did it for them. When the Afghan Taliban blew up Bamiyan Buddhas, the expertise was provided by Pakistani and Saudi engineers.[31]

Throughout the nineties, when American targets were being attacked in many parts of the world by al Qaeda, many, if not most, of its members used the Pakistani port city of Karachi as a transit point to fly in and out of Pakistan and to reach

Afghanistan by road. There is every reason to believe that the Pakistanis could have easily tracked and stopped them had they wanted to do so. The inconvenient conclusion: whether directly or indirectly, Pakistan was aiding al Qaeda. Therefore, it is hardly surprising that, even after its defeat at the hands of America and its allies, the Afghan Taliban—brainchild of Pakistani intelligence—is now back in force, again emerging from Pakistan.[32]

Even if Pervez Musharraf, the former Pakistani leader, was personally sincere about ending Pakistan's support for the Taliban, the establishment in Pakistan—especially the ISI, a deeply political Islam-influenced institution—obviously had other ideas. In December 2006 a captured Taliban spokesman told Afghan investigators that the Taliban would never have been able to challenge the Afghan military and NATO forces without the direct assistance of Pakistan's ISI.[33] This goes to prove that the most influential entity in Pakistan is political Islam.

The writ of Hamid Karzai's government is now mostly restricted to Kabul and its surrounding areas. This does not bode well for the possibility of a democratic or a pro-Western regime in Afghanistan in the future. Now Pakistani officials are urging NATO countries to accept the Taliban and to work toward a new coalition government in Kabul that might exclude the Afghan president Hamid Karzai. Pakistan's foreign minister, Khurshid Kasuri, has said in private briefings to foreign ministers of some NATO member states that the Taliban are winning the war in Afghanistan and NATO is bound to fail. He has advised against sending more troops.[34]

AXIS OF JIHAD AND THE NEW COLD WAR

We have now come to realize that political Islam and jihad have spread throughout the world due to the ideological and financial sponsorship of many Islamic nations. However, as discussed before, three nations stand out through their leadership in this unsavory endeavor: Saudi Arabia, Iran, and Pakistan—the "axis of jihad." Of these nations, Iran and Saudi Arabia are regional rivals, as are Iran and Pakistan. Nonetheless, this axis has a common vision—that of conquest of unbelievers and their lands, and the use of terror as a long-standing instrument of this vision. Evidence is put together here to show the axis nations' sponsorship of terror in many parts of the world where Muslims exist in sizable numbers. This has continued even after the 9/11 attacks. Once more, this goes to show that America and its allies need a new policy vis-à-vis the so-called allies: Saudi Arabia and Pakistan.

Why only these three nations? Why not Syria, Bangladesh, or other Muslim-majority states? The secular Syrian regime uses terrorism as part of its military and foreign policy strategy (e.g., by backing the militant Islamic group Hezbollah in Lebanon).[35] But by definition of being secular, the ruling regime in Syria has little to gain by sponsoring Islamic conquest through jihad. Bangladesh has been influenced into jihad by Saudi Arabia and Pakistan.[36] In terms of scale, as well as ideological, financial, and physical commitment toward jihad sponsorship, the axis nations can be seen as the leaders—and many other Islamic states as the followers.

Saudi Arabia funds mosques, trains preachers, and builds schools across the globe that teach virulent Wahhabi Islam, which views the outside world and modernity with hatred. This is part of an integral strategy to infect Muslim populations with jihadism and get them to identify with Saudi interests. Jihadism is the necessary instrument for conquest of *infidel* lands; therefore, it is given importance in Saudi society because political Islam is, by far, the dominating force in Saudi Arabia. In other words, jihad is a Saudi Arabian passion. Therefore, this book rejects the widely held notion that Saudi Arabia supports jihad as a way of deflecting and diverting internal jihadist pressure.

Saudi Arabia has allowed private individuals and charities to donate to terrorist causes in Kashmir, Chechnya, Bosnia, and Afghanistan. Over two decades, the Saudi royal family has spent between $85 and 90 billion of its oil wealth to finance some 1,350 new mosques, 210 Islamic centers, and hundreds of universities in Europe, the Americas, Asia, and Africa.[37] These Saudi-funded organizations have been hotbeds of anti-Western and particularly anti-American indoctrination. The schools, for example, not only indoctrinate students in a virulent and autocratic form of Islam but also teach them to hate secular Western values. They are taught to view America as the center of *infidel* power in the world and the enemy of Islam.[38] Graduates of these schools are frequent recruits for Bin Laden's al Qaeda terror network, as well as other extremist groups.

In a 2001 article in the *Spectator* of London, American journalist Stephen Schwartz points out that people who have embraced Wahhabism have conducted every major terrorist attack against the West in recent years. "Bin Laden is a Wahhabi. So are the suicide bombers in Israel. So are his Egyptian allies, who exulted as they stabbed foreign tourists to death at Luxor.... So are the Algerian terrorists.... So are the Taliban-style guerrillas who murder Hindus in Kashmir.... None of this extremism has been inspired by American fumbling in the world, and it has little to do with the tragedies that have beset Israelis and Palestinians."[39]

It is clear that Saudi Arabia now exports two products around the globe—oil and religious fanaticism. In 2005 Saudi Arabia's secretary-general of the official Muslim

World League's Koran Memorization Commission, Sheikh Abdallah Basfar, urged Muslims everywhere to fund terrorism. He declared, "The Prophet said: 'He who equips a fighter—it is as if he himself fought.' You lie in your bed, safe in your own home, and donate money and Allah credits you with the rewards of a fighter. What is this? A privilege."[40]

The Saudi investment in jihad is paying off. A Pew June 2006 Global Attitudes poll showed that a majority of Muslims in Jordan, Egypt, and Nigeria, as well as roughly a third of Muslim residents in France, Spain, and Great Britain, felt violence against civilians can be justified in order to defend Islam.[41] Of course, it is left to medieval clerics, who are invariably jihad sympathizers, to define when and where Islam needs to be defended. Thus, from a practical perspective, this poll indicates that a majority of Muslims in many Muslim nations support terror against non-Muslim civilians.

From a *Reader's Digest* article detailing Saudi sponsorship of terror worldwide:

> It has been pointed out that Saudi officials have, at minimum, a clear pattern of looking the other way when funds are known to support extremist purposes. Even after 2001, Saudi officials continue to support organizations that finance international terrorism. It has also channeled funds to Hamas and other groups that have committed terrorist acts in Israel and other portions of the Middle East. The Bosnia and Herzegovina offices of Al-Haramain Islamic Foundation, for example, are accused by the US Treasury Department of funneling money earmarked for orphanages and mosques in Mogadishu, Somalia, to a local terrorist group linked to Al Qaeda. Al-Haramain is active in more than 50 countries. Officials of the Saudi Arabia–based International Islamic Relief Organization (IIRO) have also been implicated in terrorism around the world, according to testimony to the US Congress from Mr. Levitt, a former FBI agent....
>
> The IIRO's Manila office was headed for eight years by Osama bin Laden's brother-in-law, Muhammad Jamal Khalifa, "through which he sent funds to terrorist groups affiliated with al Qaeda, including Abu Sayyaf," said Levitt. "IIRO is part of the Muslim World League, which is funded and supported by the Saudi government." Saudi Arabian officials claim that any involvement of these organizations with terrorism is the work of "rogue elements." But few people believe this claim. "All individuals running overseas charities are government appointed and the government watches every penny," a Saudi academic told *Reader's Digest* in the country's capital, Riyadh....
>
> Much of the money comes directly from the Saudi king himself, Fahd bin Abdul Aziz Al Saud....In Pakistan, Kashmir, the newly independent Central Asian republics, and Chechnya, Saudi religious and charitable agencies have encouraged

radical Islamists and armed rebellion against secular governments. "It's hard to know where the line is drawn between funding charity and weapons for insurgents or money for terrorists," says Ahmed Rashid, a leading Pakistani expert and author of a best-selling book about the Taliban....

Saudi money has also financed thousands of religious seminaries in Pakistan, Afghanistan, Central Asia, and Africa. Professor Vali Nasr, a US-based expert on Islamic extremism, characterizes many of the seminaries as "Islamic West Points mixing a dosage of Islam with a lot of military training.... Many members of Bin Laden's al Qaeda network are graduates of these Saudi-funded schools.... In Western Europe, from Edinburgh to Lisbon, from Brussels to Moscow, a large number of mosques, Islamic centers, and schools are now under Saudi control.[42]

Excerpts from terrorism expert Steven Emerson's statement before the 9/11 Commission on Saudi sponsorship of terror:

Nazir Qureshi is assistant Secretary-General of WAMY [the World Association of Muslim Youth]—a Saudi charity. He has been accused by the Indian government of supplying money to Kashmiri terrorist groups headed by Syed Ali Shah Geelani. The Pakistani paper *The News* reported on March 25, 2001, that the Pakistani youth organization *Jamiat Taleba Arabia* is the only Pakistan-based member organization of WAMY. The article continued, "WAMY is also involved in religious and jihadist training for its member organizations...."

According to *The News, Jamiat Taleba Arabia*, the WAMY member-organization, was: "involved in Afghanistan from the very beginning. It joined the jihad in Kashmir as soon as the Kashmiris started their armed struggle in 1990 and was fully involved by 1993. The members of the *Jamiat Taleba Arabia* fought under the umbrella of Gulbadin Hakmatyar's *Hizbe Islami* in Afghanistan and, in Occupied Kashmir, under the discipline of the *hizbulMujahideen*....Jihad has become the focus of the *Jamiat's* activities in the last two decades...."

According to the Indian magazine *Frontline*, Muhammad Ayyub Thukar, president of the World Kashmir Freedom Movement, was a financier of *Hizbul Mujahideen*, a Kashmiri terror organization. During his exile in Saudi Arabia, Thukar was affiliated with MWL, WAMY, and the Muslim Brotherhood. Sardar Ija Afzal Khan, Amir of *Jamait-e-Islami* since early June 2002, "highlighted [the] freedom struggle of the Kashmiris at the forums of World Assembly of Muslim Youth...." The Indian government contends that "90 percent of the funding [for Kashmir militants] is from other countries and Islamic organizations like the World Association of Muslim Youth."[43]

Only after the May and November 2003 attacks on its own mainland did the Saudis crack down on homegrown extremists. Nonetheless, unofficial Saudi financial support for political Islam, represented by Wahhabism, continues. One Saudi document found in a Palestinian office demonstrated that the Saudis were aiding Palestinian families involved in suicide attacks on Israel.[44]

"Funds are available for the asking for LeT (Lashkar-e-Taiba, an India-specific terror outfit based in Pakistan) not only from Pakistan, but also from Wahhabi fundamentalists in Saudi Arabia and the UAE," says an ex-activist of the Student Islamic Movement of India (SIMI)—potential evidence of jihad directed at non-Muslim Indians.[45]

A report on terrorism in Southeast Asia notes that Saudi Arabia and Pakistan are working together to fund jihad:

> In recent years, said Rohan Gunaratna, who heads a Singaporean research center on terror, Saudi Arabia has financed much of the terror in Southeast Asia. Until 2003, funds went from the Saudis, supposedly U.S. allies, to al Qaeda and through Pakistan to Southeast Asia. After the Pakistan channel was disrupted, funds have been sent directly from Saudi Arabia....
>
> Mr. Gunaratna said terrorists in Southeast Asia are increasingly driven by ideology, which calls for setting up an Islamic state centered on Indonesia, the world's most populous Muslim nation. It would include the southern Philippines, Malaysia, and southern Thailand, which have large Muslim populations. "Asian groups," he said, "are becoming Arabized."[46]

According to the Indian scholar Ramashray Upadhyay terror sponsorship in Bangladesh is originating from the Middle East:

> Direct funding to the terrorist outfits in Bangladesh from international NGOs [nongovernmental organizations] like Kuwait-based Revival of Islamic Heritage, Saudi Arabia–based Al Haramain Islamic Institute, Rabita Al Alam Al Islami, Qatar Charitable Society...[were] primarily responsible for fomenting extremism, training, and recruiting of youths to carry out jihadist activities.[47]

Iran's sponsorship of jihad is not as extensive as Saudi Arabia's; it is mostly specific to Shiite communities. Hezbollah received tactical guidance from Iranian diplomats, fundamentalist ideology from Iranian clerics, and training in Iran. A state subsidy of about $100 million was also given to Hezbollah in the 1980s for "humanitarian and social work."[48]

In 1992 terrorists who were suspected of being sponsored by Iran bombed a synagogue in Argentina. Finally, in 1998, a telephone call intercepted from the Iranian embassy in Argentina demonstrated Iran's involvement. Argentina immediately expelled six of the seven Iranian diplomats in the country.[49] Still, even today, this bombing remains unsolved.

Israel's 2006 thrust into Lebanon to retrieve its soldiers captured by Hezbollah was met with fierce rocket attacks, indiscriminately aimed at civilian areas in Israel. Many of these rockets were said to have been given to Hezbollah by Iran.[50]

According to terrorism expert Daniel Byman, Pakistan is funding, arming, training, and providing diplomatic support for varied terrorist groups that are active in Indian Kashmir. So close is the tie between the Pakistani state and these outfits that Pakistani intelligence unit ISI "selects targets, including civilian ones, and knows about major attacks in advance."[51] Pakistan also inserted foreign fighters from the Taliban and al Qaeda into India.[52] A Pakistan-based jihad commander named Syed Salahuddin said in a 2006 interview, "We can hit any soft target in India at any time."[53]

Exposing the focus of Pakistan's India-directed jihad is a 2005 study by Rubina Saigol, country director of Action Aid, Pakistan:

> About 8,000 Pakistani Punjabis, about 3,000 from the northwest Frontier Province and about 500 from Sindh, are estimated to have died as jihadists in Indian Kashmir since 1989. In comparison, only 112 Balochs have died as jihadists, mostly in Afghanistan.[54]

At a 2006 conference on terrorism in Mumbai, a number of non-Muslim activists from Islamic Bangladesh spoke. Alleging Islamic militant organizations' involvement in a large number of rapes and murders in the region, Prajnalankar Bhikku, an activist from Bangladesh, said: "A silent genocide and ethnic cleansing (of non-Muslims) is taking place in the hills of Bangladesh without the knowledge of the outside world." Journalist and activist Shahriar Kabir cites the rise of militant organizations as the reason. "On the one hand, the West asks [Pakistani president] General [Pervez] Musharraf to take action against fundamentalists in that country. On the other, it supports the four-party fundamentalist coalition in Bangladesh. The United States and other nations must ask Pakistan and Saudi Arabia to stop funding these fundamentalist organizations."[55]

Pakistan's track record of butchering and terrorizing the non-Muslim population is well recorded. In 1971 it launched a military strike in what was then East Pakistan (now known as Bangladesh) by selectively choosing non-Muslims to murder or to expel to India, in order to cleanse the region of *infidels*. Before the Indian Army finally subdued the Pakistani Army and its local collaborators, they had slaughtered up to 3 million Bengalis in nine months of unabated killings throughout the summer of 1971.[56] Of the three million, at least two million are estimated to be Hindu Bengalis.[57]

The Pakistani army moved methodically from village to village, leaving a trail of destruction in its wake. Sydney Schanberg of the *New York Times* described the systematic subjugation and killing of Bengalis:

> Army trucks roll through the half-deserted streets of the capital of East Pakistan these days, carrying "antistate" prisoners to work-sites for hard labor. Their heads are shaved and they wear no shoes and no clothes except for shorts—all making escape difficult. Street designations are being changed to remove all Hindu names as well as those of Bengali Moslem nationalists as part of a campaign to stamp out Bengali culture. Shankari Bazar Road in Dacca is now Tikka Khan Road, after the lieutenant general governor of East Pakistan, whom most Bengalis call "the Butcher."
>
> Since the offensive began the troops have killed countless thousands of Bengalis—foreign diplomats estimate at least 200,000 to 250,000—many in massacres. Although the targets were Bengali Moslems and the 10 million Hindus at first, the army is now concentrating on Hindus in what foreign observers characterize as a holy war.... Of the more than six million Bengalis who are believed to have fled to India to escape the army's terror, at least four million are Hindus. The troops are still killing Hindus and burning and looting their villages.[58]

In the summary of a 1971 report to a US Senate Judiciary Committee investigating the problem of refugees and settlement in South Asia, Senator Edward Kennedy wrote of the situation:

> Field reports to the US Government, countless eyewitness journalistic accounts, reports of International agencies such as World Bank and additional information available to the subcommittee document the reign of terror which grips East Bengal (East Pakistan). Hardest hit have been members of the Hindu community who have been robbed of their lands and shops, systematically slaughtered, and in some places, painted with yellow patches marked "H." All of this has been officially sanctioned, ordered and implemented under martial law from Islamabad.[59]

From Pakistan's own Hamoodur Rahman Commission report on 1971 war:

> There was a general feeling of hatred against Bengalis amongst the soldiers and officers, including Generals. There were verbal instructions to eliminate Hindus. The

statements appearing in the evidence of Lt. Col. Aziz Ahmed Khan (Witness no 276) who was Commanding Officer 8 Baluch and then CO 86 Mujahid Battalion are also directly relevant. "Brigadier Arbbab also told me to destroy all houses in Joydepur. To a great extent I executed this order. General Niazi visited my unit at Thakurgaon and Bogra. He asked us how many Hindus we had killed. In May, there was an order in writing to kill Hindus. This order was from Brigadier Abdullah Malik of 23 Brigade."[60]

Since Pakistan was never held accountable for these crimes against humanity, it was predictably emboldened to do more of the same in the coming decades. Indeed, this was to repeat again in the 1980s, 1990s, and in this century (see more details in chapter 3, "Siege of India").

We see throughout this discussion the mounting evidence of a political ideology masquerading as a religion to create conditions ranging from terrorism to unbeliever genocide for the purpose of conquest. Axis of jihad nations are the prime movers and shakers behind Islamic terrorism and the resulting war on terror. These nations have learned little from the 9/11 attacks on America. This is because they have not been held accountable. American efforts to engage "moderate" rulers of these nations have failed, as evidenced by unabated jihad still emanating from these nations. Unfortunately, hostile relations have limited American influence over Iran.

There is no doubt that, on least at a limited level, American policymakers and lawmakers have been aware of Saudi Arabian or Pakistani roles in sponsoring worldwide jihad. Dependence on oil and Pakistan's status as a nuclear power have limited American options, as has America's limited understanding of the enemy's ideology.

Any direct attacks on Saudi Arabia or Iran will likely lead to massive disturbance to the flow of oil throughout the world—a critical and scarce engine of modern economies. Attacking Pakistan could lead to unsecured nukes being fired across the world, especially at its archenemy, India. Besides, compelling justification for attacking these states has yet to be articulated.

Due to the conventional and nuclear might of America, none of the Islamic states are likely to directly engage America militarily. All of these limitations have turned the war on terror into a new cold war! In this cold war, America and its Western allies are squared off against the political Islamic movements primarily based in Saudi Arabia, Iran, and Pakistan. Alternate ideas on managing the new cold war are taken up in the last chapter, which addresses policy response issues. Yet, there is no a priori reason to believe that this cold war may end peacefully, like the previous one. In chapter 4 we will discuss why it may not and how to prepare for this eventuality.

The "democracy approach" to neutralizing radical Islam was taken soon after the 9/11 attacks.[61] Regrettably, the project to democratize Iraq has diverted attention from the axis of jihad. Although American efforts in Iraq now stand discredited, there are many in the legislative and executive branches and in the American bureaucracy who still think of democracy as the antidote to terror. The coming section discusses why this democracy hypothesis is flawed and points out what factors lead to functional democracies and terror disengagement.

THE DEMOCRACY ANGLE

In response to the 9/11 attacks on America, some neoconservatives close to centers of power in Washington had felt that if a successful democracy could be introduced in the heart of the Middle East, then perhaps democracy would retard growth of radical Islam in the host nation. It was thought that this success would encourage the flowering of democracy in nearby nations and eventually triumph over radical Islam. Iraq seemed to be a good candidate, with the semisecular dictatorship of Saddam Hussein already keeping radical Islam at bay. Iraq also had a fairly well-educated population, and more important, al Qaeda didn't seem to have any following there. With Iraq having the world's second-largest oil deposits, financing this democracy project appeared feasible. Iraq was already under a UN-sponsored sanctions regime, and any apparent violation subjected it to external intervention. Also justifying the armed American intervention in Iraq was the following explanation (from an American view): Never allow an enemy with a track record of violence directed at American interests to develop the ability to launch strikes (a lesson learned from the surprise 9/11 attacks on America).

When the Bush administration claimed to be in possession of data indicating that Hussein was developing weapons of mass destruction—in violation of the sanctions regime and potentially threatening the national security of the United States—the die was cast and an opportunity presented itself for an invasion. If this data were indeed true, there would have been some justification for invading and removing Hussein on the grounds of preemption. However, there is much controversy now as to whether this data were genuine or exaggerated to justify the intervention.

Years after the swift removal of Saddam's Baathist regime, despite the ongoing American occupation, the democracy project is clearly not succeeding in Iraq. It now appears, as analyzed in Bob Woodward's book *State of Denial*, that there was really no plan to build a functional democracy in Iraq after the initial takeover.[62] The army's own report released in June 2008 confirms Woodward's assertions.[63] Clearly, meddling by Iraq's neighbors has not helped the allied effort. Bush administration officials seem to have thought that once the Baathist regime was taken out of power, democratic institutions would somehow fall into place.

"Nation building" refers to the process of constructing or restructuring a nation with the aid of armed forces. The armed forces in such a situation are used with the aim of unifying peoples within the state and of making the situation politically stable and viable in the long run. Nation building also involves the use of propaganda or major infrastructure development to foster social harmony and economic growth. The nation-building process helps empower the populace to practice democracy by building institutions for governance.[64] But the Bush administration appears not to have thought through two critical questions: whether the Iraqi Muslim majority population—although no ally of al Qaeda—would embrace a largely Christian and white occupying force, and whether this population had any desire for nation building. A lack of affinity for jihad, even a desire to participate in free elections, doesn't necessarily translate into the desire for nation building. This is an observation that was made painfully obvious by the failed American effort to establish a robust democracy in Haiti.[65]

It is useful to discuss under what conditions American efforts at nation building had succeeded in the past. In the immediate aftermath of World War II, along with its allies, the United States stationed its army in both Germany and Japan. America then helped to rewrite the constitutions of these nations, brought stability, and helped build these devastated nations into leading economies. In the case of Germany, Nazi ideology was roundly defeated, its former rulers were vanquished, and an elaborate denazification program was put in place.[66] Emperor Hirohito of Japan ordered surrender to the Americans and told his people to cooperate. With the imperial army adjusting to the emperor's wishes, there was hardly any insurgency by the locals. In addition, a sustained program was put in place in Japan to neutralize religion-based imperialism, as explained by historian John Lewis:

> Over the next five years, under stern American guidance, and with zeal as great as that with which they had once armed for battle, the Japanese reformed their nation. They adopted a new constitution, purged their schools of religious and military indoctrination, and abandoned aggressive warfare. Imperial subjects became citizens; "divine" decrees were replaced with rights-respecting laws; rulers became administrators; feudal cartels became corporations; propaganda organs became

newspapers; women achieved suffrage; and students learned the principles of self-reliance and self-government. Hiroshima, formerly the headquarters of a fanatical military force, became a world center for nonviolence. Those who had once marched feverishly for war now marched passionately for peace.[67]

In the end, the American occupation was a win-win for all parties. What also helped was that the citizens of these countries had an outlook similar to that of America; they had the desire and know-how for nation building, even before the war.

American efforts at nation building had also succeeded in South Korea, which unlike Germany and Japan had no prior experience with wealth creation or democracy. South Korea, which was economically comparable to India in the 1950s, latched on to the opportunity provided by America to become a high-power economy. Here the South Koreans had the right "outlook"—that of being willing to learn and follow America and not mount insurgencies. One could argue that, threatened by communist North Korea and China, South Koreans had limited options. In all of these cases—Germany, Japan, or Korea—there existed no ideology or institutions with a strong grassroots base that was opposed to American involvement.

DEMOCRACY AND ISLAM

The situations in Afghanistan and Iraq are different. After swift military victories in both countries, not knowing any better, American policymakers allowed political Islam to fill the power vacuum.

Thinking they were doing a good deed, the Americans gave spiritual "access" to the Iraqi public who they had liberated from Saddam's oppressive yet secular Baathist regime. This was not a smart move, since political Islam in Iraq is ideologically opposed to a Western-styled democracy. This shouldn't be a surprise; as we will see later, political Islam as practiced in most Muslim nations believes in jihad building, not nation building. Muslim religious institutions form nodes of social networks among Muslim communities and are well positioned to spawn insurgencies against an occupying power. By allowing mosques and their clerics to occupy center stage, America may inadvertently have laid the foundation for a no-win situation.

In Afghanistan, the United States was more careful. But years of Saudi funding and Pakistani involvement had helped install hard-line clerics in its many mosques. Subsequent to the American invasion, after the initial restraint, many clergy, especially among the Pashtun majority, have turned up the anti-American rhetoric. This has undermined the allied effort to build reliable local security forces and the whole effort of building democracy there. The other major problem is a resurgent Taliban infiltration from Pakistan—also home to a Pashtun population.

The ways in which political Islam is undermining America and its allies' good-faith effort in both Iraq and Afghanistan are explained in an analysis by Edward Luttwak, an American military strategist, historian, and scholar at Center for Strategic and International Studies (CSIS):

> Since the 2003 invasion, both Shiite and Sunni clerics have been repeating over and over again that the Americans and their "Christian" allies have come to Iraq to destroy Islam in its cultural heartland and to steal the country's oil. The clerics dismiss all talk of democracy and human rights by the invaders as mere hypocrisy— with the exception of women's rights, which the clerics say are only propagandized to persuade Iraqi daughters and wives to dishonor their families by imitating the shameless nakedness and impertinence of Western women.
>
> The vast majority of Afghans and Iraqis naturally believe their religious leaders. The alternative would be to believe what for them is entirely unbelievable: that foreigners are unselfishly expending blood and treasure in order to help them. They themselves would never invade a foreign country except to plunder it, the way Iraq invaded Kuwait, thus having made Saddam Hussein genuinely popular for a time when troops brought back their loot. As many opinion polls and countless incidents demonstrate, the Americans and their allies are widely considered to be the worst of invaders, who came to rob Muslim Iraqis not only of their territory and oil but also of their religion and even their family honor. Many Muslims around the world believe as much, even in Turkey, whose most successful recent film depicted an American Jewish military doctor who was operating on Iraqis not to save their lives but to remove their kidneys, which of course he was sending back to the U.S. for transplantation and his personal profit (he was Jewish after all). It is the same in Afghanistan, where the American-imposed quota of women parliamentarians has caused widespread resentment, not least because most Afghans are scandalized by the spectacle of a woman contradicting a man in public—as in, for example, televised parliamentary debates.[68]

In this new cold war against political Islam some costly mistakes have been made and others will be made; the Iraq occupation may well be one of them.[69] The issue of whether it is possible to bring functional democracy to Islamic nations with a history of repression and dominance of political Islam is worthy of study. Below is a letter I wrote that was published in the *Washington Times* on November 22, 2002:

PAKISTAN'S UNDEMOCRATIC UNDERPINNINGS

The conclusions found in "Studies say elites spurred to terror" (Business, November 20, 2002) are incomplete. The question should be what causes political repression?

Pakistan and India were created in 1947 in British-ruled India. When the British left, both of these nations inherited democracy. Hindu-majority India has remained secular and democratic, but Muslim-majority Pakistan couldn't sustain democracy and is now a dictatorship. Pakistan also has become a dominant source and sponsor of Islamic terrorism.

Pakistan couldn't sustain democracy because the retrogressive political indoctrination taught in its mosques does not allow the separation of church and state. This has led to political repression amid a flowering of Islamic fundamentalism.

This conclusion tells us that if the United States wants to make any Islamic state a model nation for democracy, it must first address the issue of the hateful and retrogressive preaching in its mosques.[70]

I explored these ideas further in another letter published in the *Washington Times*, on December 8, 2003 (excerpted here):

A NEW PARADIGM FOR THE WAR ON TERROR

I am writing to request that the Bush administration revisit the idea of pulling troops out of Iraq, where the general tide is going against America. I would like to give an alternate view to William Taylor's column ("War and impatience," Commentary, December 6, 2003).

The virtual absence of democracy in the Islamic world points to fundamental flaws in Islam that must first be fixed before democracy can take root. Political and retrogressive preaching by most Muslim clerics [such as emphasis on jihad on unbelievers and *sharia* and a throwback into the tribal culture of the prophet Muhammad] does not allow for the separation of mosque and state, and leads to repressive regimes such as Saddam Hussein's in Iraq. America is already a target of these clerics in Iraq, who are doing everything to undermine America's desire to bring democracy there.

A pullback now from Iraq will probably lead to a takeover by another repressive regime hostile to American interests. But such a regime inherits an Iraq with weakened infrastructure—and a much less developed ability to create weapons of destruction. However, it is much better than the no-win situation America now finds itself in in Iraq.[71]

Apart from religion, India and Pakistan share history, language, dietary habits, and culture. Hence, the difference in outlook should have been shaped by the respective majority religions. It should be noted that the outlook of Pakistan had been predisposed toward radicalism well before the 1970s infusion of petrodollars. Chapter 2 will discuss the reasons for this outlook in greater detail.

Since Muslim religious institutions work at the grassroots level, with the resources and the freedom of a democratic environment, they are best placed to bring about jihadization of Muslim communities. We are seeing this occurring in just about all Muslim communities around the world, even under democracy. This is bad news for those who claim that democracy is an antidote to radical Islam! In the last chapter, some ideas will be presented to demonstrate how political Islam can be repelled even within a democratic regime.

The power and influence attained by mosques, derived from their political sermons, is well known. As discussed in my letter previously, these sermons, with their emphasis on jihad and *sharia*, and their intense focus on Islamic history and doctrines, disrupt the functioning of a state and nation building. This must be seen as the hallmark of political Islam in modern times. This has made even non-Islamist regimes in the Middle East unable to make progress, in terms of development and in the process of democratization. This is true in Egypt and it was in Saddam's Iraq, where the state in many ways regulated what was said in influential mosques. Also, retrogressive sermons discourage modern education, which is a must for wealth creation and progress. This eventually creates conditions of dissatisfaction and impoverishment, setting the stage for Islamic radicals, pushed to the front by political Islam, to gain power through the ballot box.

Like the fundamentalist Muslim Brotherhood in Egypt, its offshoot in the West Bank, Hamas, has understood the importance of providing social services. Before coming to power, this fundamentalist group had managed to come across as caring and as a "defender" of the people, through suicide attacks directed at Israel, in sharp contrast to the dysfunctional Palestinian authority—which failed to provide even basic social services and "secure" Palestinians. This shows how political Islamic organizations can use the ballot box and "service" to reach power. Once such a politico-religious organization comes to power, the first order of business becomes exporting jihad externally and consolidating the internal process of Islamization through repression—by persecuting its opponents and by limiting the rights of others.

Not surprisingly, in representing political Islam, organizations such as Hamas have no vision for development—due to the focus on medieval *sharia* and jihad as the instruments of internal and external policy framework, respectively. Iran is another example of a country in which Islamists gained power through the ballot box and then pursued jihad-spreading policies. Once radicals get set in power, it is hard to get rid of them through internal political mechanisms such as voting them out or attempting a type of referendum. Due to their control of the military and the mosques, the two strong institutions that would be capable of challenging them, the radicals can maintain control over the reigns of power. In all likelihood, such a nation, whether or not it is nominally democratic, will become a fountainhead for jihad.

Not just America, but even Israel has underestimated the power and influence of a religion-based ideology married to military power to keep control. After using force to wrest control of Gaza Strip from its Palestinian rival Fatah, a year into power, Hamas is now seen to be fully in charge, despite a blockade by Israel and the West.[72]

What is more interesting is the dynamics of Islam within India, a secular democratic nation where Muslims are a clear minority. Contrary to general perception, all the available evidence indicates political Islam's dominance of the Indian Muslim community. At the moment, India is reeling under an escalating surge of homegrown Islamic terrorism. Because its democracy is under an effective siege by Islamist radicals who convince Muslims to vote as a bloc, India finds itself unable to undertake decisive steps to deal with this threat (which will be discussed further in chapter 3). A successful siege of India by political Islam may be discounted if India is viewed as a developing nation that may not be well governed.

Homegrown Islamic terrorism in England has shown how political Islam can recruit activists even in a developed multiethnic functional democracy. Clearly, it has taken radical Islamic elements decades to indoctrinate young Muslims, typically of Pakistani ethnicity. In the name of religious freedom, clerics were imported from Pakistan or from other Middle Eastern nations. Knowing little English and reared in repressive Islamic countries with a strong political Islamic base, most of these clerics had one qualification—their ability to indoctrinate impressionable young minds toward jihad.

Several important conclusions can be drawn thus far. Muslim populations can be radicalized under varying conditions; in Muslim majority countries with a strong political Islamic presence, it is hard to establish functional democracies; and the ballot box will likely be controlled by radicals, who take the opportunity to gain power in order to sponsor jihad through the state apparatus.

DEMOCRACY THROUGH WEALTH CREATION

Given the ongoing debacle in Iraq, many would consider security, rather than democracy building, to be the primary objective of the United States vis-à-vis the war on terror. But as we will see in this section, the components that converge to make functional democracies also tend to lead to nations that focus on nation building and trade. In short, such nations' primary or secondary passion would not be the jihadist conquest of unbelievers but the development of egalitarian social and political institutions.

How can functional democracies be built? Providing the conditions to create wealth will go a long way toward developing functional democracies.

Wealth creation is about manufacturing technically sophisticated products that can be used for trade and for internal consumption. This is what distinguishes "developed" nations from "developing" nations. For the manufacturer, the ability to trade generates wealth, which is the most important requirement for survival. Wealth creation also requires an entrepreneur-oriented capitalistic system that allows healthy competition, a system of laws protecting property rights, a world-class education system, and rigorous enforcement of law and order.

A church that heavily mixes politics with religion will interfere with that of governance. Hence, separation of church and state is necessary to enact and enforce laws that are appropriate for contemporary global relationships and economic interactions.

Wealth creation is a win-win situation, producing not just wealth itself but also a capable and creative population. Wealth creation can also be seen as the intended consequence of nation building, the necessary process for achieving a functional democracy.

To create wealth, people have to learn to work together—the very same requirement needed to make a democracy function. Once the fruits of wealth creation begin to reach the masses, they, too, embrace the philosophy of a free market economy, rather than manipulating the system through corrupt practices designed to garner wealth for themselves and their families. Hence, the required conditions for creating wealth indirectly undermine corruption, which is a common and debilitating problem in developing nations new to democracy.

During the last sixty years, many formerly developing nations have achieved prosperity and, eventually, functional democracies on the basis of the free market system and the wealth and stability they create for the most part, in spite of nondemocratic modes of governing. The East Asian nations of Taiwan, Singapore, and South Korea have shown that economic growth can be achieved through policies that encourage wealth creation, although some rights are sacrificed in the short term. This can lead to long-term dividends of economic prosperity, stability, and, more important, a natural transition to functional democracy. The nondemocratic mode of governing ensures stability and order during the economic transition period. Also notable in these nations is the near absence of strong retrogressive institutions and ideological agendas.

Without stability, a regime's energy, time, and scarce resources may be wasted. This is the case with India. Although the Indian economy is growing, as we will see in chapter 3, escalating instabilities are threatening to unravel a largely nonfunctioning Indian democracy.

In the past fifty years, there is almost no example of a nation evolving from a developing to a developed country through democratization. It is not hard to see why. When a country is developing, its citizens generally have yet to develop skills to work together to solve problems. When such people are given a voice, governing becomes almost impossible. The lack of problem-solving skills is then reflected in the leadership. The press and media also become very vocal and tend not to be particularly constructive, lacking vision and abilities, as is so common among their colleagues in developed countries.

The African nation of Malawi has had free elections, a multiparty system, and a free press since 1994, and can arguably call itself a democracy. Yet democracy in Malawi is now considered to be a failure due to poor governance that has worsened the poverty levels there.[73] Democracy is clearly failing in Africa's largest nation, Nigeria, and in several more African nations—in Gambia, Uganda, Ethiopia, and Zambia.[74] American efforts to bring democracy to Haiti after the departure of the dictator Jean-Claude Duvalier ("Baby Doc") have also been considered a failure in many ways.[75] In all of the above cases quality educational institutions and the resulting educated population who could provide governance and help create wealth were missing.

In developing democracies, a destabilizing force can arise in the form of insurgencies mounted by minorities (as is the case in India—see chapter 3) or by a strong institution that does not believe in the separation of religion and state and that is jihad building in its outlook (e.g., political Islam in Pakistan). These destabilizing forces in developing nations often become too hot to handle, as elected politicians, answerable to the public, cannot afford to be seen as ruthless in dealing with these problems. Many of these democracies never end up resolving their problems, which often have devastating consequences as a result.

But developing nations ruled by undemocratic regimes often can deal with destabilizing forces ruthlessly and effectively, since the regime's leaders are not answerable to the public. Chinese leaders have understood the importance of stability in economic development and wealth creation.[76] The student democratic movement in the early nineties was ruthlessly crushed. Among the reasons given by the Chinese leadership was the instability that the ongoing movement would bring. Investments in China really took off after that, encouraged by the ruling regime's determination to enforce stability. Western leaders, who overwhelmingly supported this nascent democratic movement, probably never took home the lesson of the importance of stability in nations embarking on wealth creation.

Even democratic nations, faced with certain forms of destabilization, find themselves using undemocratic means, such as violating human rights, in order to be effective. This was true of the American approach to dealing with Native Americans and the institution of slavery.

Noted author and *Newsweek* editor Fareed Zakaria, in a live talk, stated: "Dictatorships are great for economic growth when they have the right ideas and implement them well. China has grown faster than any country in the world for this reason. Trouble is, how do you make sure you get a dictator like Lee Kuan Yew and not Mobutu (Seko) or (Ferdinand) Marcos?"[77]

One strong man or woman cannot dictate a system unless the system is receptive to him or her. Make no mistake! Kuan Yew's visionary leadership was critical for Singapore. However, he still had to rely on a system to get the job done. Kuan Yew would be hard pressed to repeat his efforts in Zaire, where Mobutu ruled. Looking at it in a different way, if Zaire ends up having a dictator, in all likelihood it will be someone like Mobutu, a thug who is only interested in lining his and his cronies' pockets.

A nation's leader typically reflects the nation. If a developing nation decides against the suitability of a democratic mode of governing with regard to warding off instabilities, and opts for authoritarian rule, the system in the country, defined by culture, outlook, and religion, will likely determine the nature of the authoritarian rule. It doesn't happen randomly, as Zakaria implies.

We have arrived at an important conclusion: wealth creation, rather than democracy, is the basis for building modern civilizations. A well-developed and functional democracy is the eventual consequence of such an economic process.

There is another bonus: an educated and informed population, shaped by wealth creation, is not going to be brainwashed by medieval and regressive religious priests. One can now understand why it is not in the best interests of political Islam to create conditions for generating wealth. We have already seen—in Iraq, Afghanistan, Pakistan, and even in Palestinian territories—that trying to create a functional democracy, without neutralizing political Islam, is a ticket to nowhere. Yet the establishment in

Washington, in a bipartisan way, continues to preach the establishment of democracy in the Muslim world—without neutralizing political Islam—as the answer to winning the war on terror.

Where does this hypothesis, that wealth creation is the necessary precursor to a functional democracy, put nations endowed with natural wealth such as massive deposits of high-in-demand petroleum reserves? The reality is that exceptional levels of inherited wealth at the individual level or the societal level discourages further wealth creation in a developing nation. When combined with entrenched, expansionist, and regressive ideologies such as political Islam, this can lead to terror sponsorship as a channel for using the newfound wealth.

Yet inherited wealth is a one-trick pony. It does not ensure wealth for most, nor is this natural wealth likely to sustain. Most Saudis and Iranians know this only too well, when high birthrates and falling oil prices lead to a significant drop in per capita income. The Saudi Arabian oil economy can provide only one job per three young men coming into the work force.[78] Although Iran has increased its oil production over the years, increased consumption has led to a net decrease in oil exports. Some of its bigger and older oil wells are also showing signs of drying up. For a nation deriving about 85 percent of its export income from oil sales, these are not good signs.[79]

9/11 COMMISSION'S RECOMMENDATIONS

The commission was an independent and bipartisan entity, created by congressional legislation and receiving the signature of President George W. Bush in late 2002. It was chartered to prepare a full and complete account of the circumstances surrounding the September 11, 2001, terrorist attacks, including American preparedness for and immediate response to the attacks. The commission was also mandated to provide recommendations designed to guard against future attacks.

The commission has made several valuable suggestions on how a coalition, especially one comprising non-Muslim states, can be put together against what it calls "radical Islam." It also evaluated funding for terrorism and provided good ideas on curtailing financial support for terror organizations.

But the commission, in the views of many, has underestimated the strength of radical Islam, calling it a "minority tradition," and has downplayed the importance of jihad as a tool for political Islamic conquest. American scholar Andrew Bostom made an admirable but futile appeal to the commission: "Although time grows dangerously short, it is not too late for the 9/11 commissioners and, more importantly, those who share their assessment, to broaden their understanding of the depth of the ideological threat posed by jihad."[80]

How can the United States and its friends help moderate Muslims to combat extremist ideas? Here is the 9/11 Commission's recommendation:

> The US government must define what the message is, what it stands for. We should offer an example of moral leadership in the world, committed to treat people humanely, abide by the rule of law, and be generous and caring to our neighbors. America and Muslim friends can agree on respect for human dignity and opportunity. To Muslim parents, terrorists like Bin Laden have nothing to offer their children but visions of violence and death. America and its friends have a crucial advantage—we can offer these parents a vision that might give their children a better future. If we heed the views of thoughtful leaders in the Arab and Muslim world, a moderate consensus can be found.[81]

As will be pointed out in the chapters to follow, extremism—not moderation—is the mainstream among Islamic traditions. This distinction means a great deal in terms of outlining effective strategies. For instance, the commission observes that "cures" or reform must come from within Muslim societies themselves and that the United States must support such developments.[82] This book contends that when extremism is mainstream, moderates are simply not empowered enough to reform Islamic society from within; hence, outsiders must step in. Some ideas on accomplishing this are discussed in the last chapter.

The misdiagnosis by the commission, which is not realizing that extremism among Muslims in certain nations is mainstream, means several of the grand strategies outlined in its report—in particular, the idea of constructive engagement with Pakistan or Saudi Arabia—are limited in scope. The deterioration in both Afghanistan and Iraq and the adverse meddling by its neighbors point to two inevitable realities: (1) these societies do not have a progressive streak worth nurturing, and (2) Muslim states neighboring Afghanistan or Iraq have no interest in seeing these states become progressive democratic societies. Hence, coalition building between America and Muslim states, as suggested by the commission, will not really be a viable option for some time to come.

The major blunder of the 9/11 Commission may have been to let the Saudis off the hook. The 1993 World Trade Center bombing and other attacks directed at the United States by al Qaeda should have given more than ample warning to the Saudi ruling class (and Pakistan) that continued funding—directly or through government-linked charities—of either the Taliban or al Qaeda would do harm to American interests—and that corrective measures must be put in place to roll back extremism. But the fact that Saudi Arabia and Pakistan pursued these old policies till 2001 makes them significantly responsible for the 9/11 attacks on America.[83] American Scholar Alex Alexiev of the Center for Security Policy comments on the commission's findings on Saudi Arabia:

> I firmly believe that the 9/11 Commission did a pitiful job of explaining to the American people what actually happened and its greatest failure by far was its conclusion that the Saudis had nothing to do with Al Qaeda and 9/11. If you look at what the Saudis do when accused of enabling terrorism, as for example in an ongoing lawsuit against them in Philadelphia, they invariably use this 9/11 Commission finding as their key defense. Yet, anybody that is halfway familiar with how Al Qaeda came into being and with the involvement of Saudi charities...would have to consider such a conclusion as bordering on outright disinformation....I think what needs to be done and I trust that sooner or later it will be done, is a congressional investigation of the 9/11 Commission findings and who made it possible for the Saudis to engage in openly subversive behavior against this country and get away with it.[84]

The 9/11 Commission's report reflects the then–American establishment's limited understanding of the new enemy, political Islam; its recommendations should be treated accordingly.

Regardless of who rules nations such as Saudi Arabia or Pakistan, the national pastime remains jihad. Indeed, jihadists and other Muslim radicals have consistently claimed that their vision of unbeliever conquest is derived from theology. The next chapter deals with what the unbelievers of the world can learn about the theology or ideology behind political Islam.

NOTES

1. John Lehman, "We're Not Winning This War," *Washington Post*, August 31, 2006, http://www.washingtonpost.com/wp-dyn/content/article/2006/08/30/AR20060830027 30.html (accessed May 1, 2007); Harlan Ullman, "Divided 'They' Fall," *Washington Times*, April 4, 2007, http://www.washingtontimes.com/op-ed/hullman.htm (accessed May 2, 2007).

2. "Rising Price of the War on Terror," *Christian Science Monitor*, November 21, 2006, http://www.csmonitor.com/2006/1121/p01s03-usmi.html (accessed July 20, 2008).

3. "What Is Political Islam?" *Alliance For Security*, http://www.allianceforsecurity.org/islamism (accessed December 5, 2007).

4. "The Study of Political Islam," *FrontPage Magazine*, February 5, 2007, http://www.frontpagemag.com/Articles/ReadArticle.asp?ID=26769 (accessed May 2, 2007).

5. Andrew Bostom, *The Legacy of Jihad: Islamic Holy War and the Fate of Non-Muslims* (paperback) (Amherst, NY: Prometheus Books, 2008), preface; Edward Lane, *An Arabic English Lexicon* (London, 1865), p. 472; Paul Stenhouse, "Muhammed, Quranic Texts, the Sharia and Incitement to Violence," *Jihad Watch*, August 31, 2002, http://www.jihadwatch.org/archives/Muhammad%20and%20Incitement%20to%20Violence.pdf (accessed September 30, 2008).

6. "Sahih al-Bukhari," *Wikipedia*, http://en.wikipedia.org/wiki/Sahih_Bukhari (accessed October 31, 2008).

7. "The Study of Political Islam."

8. "USCIRF Confirms Material Inciting Violence, Intolerance Remains in Textbooks Used at Saudi Government's Islamic Saudi Academy," *USCIRF*, June 11, 2008, http://www.uscirf.gov/index.php?option=com_content&task=view&id=2206&Itemid=1 (accessed July 8, 2008).

9. Bernard Lewis, *The Middle East: A Brief History of the Last 2,000 Years* (New York: Scribner, 1995), p. 233.

10. Thomas Hughes, *The Dictionary of Islam* (Ottawa: Laurier, 1996), p. 243.

11. Andrew Bostom, ed., "Collecting Qur'anic verses Commanding Warfare," in *The Legacy of Jihad: Islamic Holy War and the Fate of Non-Muslims* (Amherst, NY: Prometheus Books, 2005), pp. 125–26.

12. Andrew Bostom, "Jihad in the Hadith—Vol. 4, bk. 52, nos. 42 & 48," in *The Legacy of Jihad: Islamic Holy War and the Fate of Non-Muslims* (Amherst, NY: Prometheus Books, 2005), pp. 136–37; Andrew McCarthy, "The Jihad in Plain Sight," *Hudson Institute*, June 4, 2008, http://www.hudson.org/files/pdf_upload/2008_Bradley_Symposium_McCarthy_Essay.pdf (accessed July 20, 2008).

13. "USCIRF Confirms Material Inciting Violence, Intolerance Remains in Textbooks Used at Saudi Government's Islamic Saudi Academy."

14. Paul Watson, "In Pakistan's Public Schools, Jihad Still Part of Lesson Plan," *Los Angeles Times*, August 18, 2005, http://articles.latimes.com/2005/aug/18/world/fg-schools18 (accessed July 20, 2008).

15. Mary Habeck, *Knowing the Enemy: Jihadist Ideology and the War on Terror* (New Haven, CT: Yale University Press, 2006), pp. 42–43.

16. Rachel Ehrenfeld, "Saudi Dollars and Jihad," *FrontPage Magazine*, October 24, 2005, http://www.frontpagemag.com/Articles/ReadArticle.asp?ID=19938 (accessed March 2, 2007).

17. "Caliphate," *Wikipedia*, http://en.wikipedia.org/wiki/Caliphate (accessed November 3, 2008).

18. *Reliance of the Traveller: The Classic Manual of Islamic Sacred Law Umdat Al-Salik* (Beltsville, MD: Amana, 1997), pp. 640–42.

19. Shine Dighe and Charisma Murari, "The Life and Times of HEH," *Times of India,* July 3, 2006, http://timesofindia.Indiatimes.com/articleshow/msid-1702680,prtpage-1.cms (accessed March 2, 2008).

20. Steven Stalinsky, "Saudi Arabia's Education System," *FrontPage Magazine,* December 30, 2002, http://www.frontpagemag.com/Articles/ReadArticle.asp?ID=5243 (accessed July 20, 2008).

21. "Hindus in Bangladesh, Pakistan and Kashmir: A Survey of Human Rights," *Hindu American Foundation,* 2004, http://www.hinduamericanfoundation.org/HHR2004.pdf (accessed March 2, 2007).

22. Arnaud de Borchgrave, "Pakistan, Saudi Arabia in Secret Nuke Pact," *Washington Times,* October 22, 2003, http://www.washtimes.com/world/20031021-112804-8451r.htm (accessed March 2, 2007).

23. Arnie Schifferdecker, "The Taliban-Bin Laden-ISI Connection," American Foreign Service Association, December 1, 2002, http://www.afsa.org/fsj/Dec01/schiff.cfm (accessed May 2, 2007).

24. Lawrence Right, *The Looming Tower: Al-Qaeda and the Road to 9/11* (New York: Knopf, 2006), p. 291.

25. Condoleezza Rice, "National Commission on Terrorist Attacks upon the United States: Ninth Public Hearing," April 8, 2004, http://govinfo.library.unt.edu/911/archive/hearing9/9-11Commission_Hearing_2004-04-08.htm (accessed March 2, 2007).

26. "USS Cole Bombing," *Wikipedia,* http://en.wikipedia.org/wiki/USS_Cole_bombing (accessed November 3, 2008).

27. Rice, "National Commission on Terrorist Attacks upon the United States."

28. Gary Berntsen, *Jawbreaker: The Attack on Bin Laden and Al-Qaeda: A Personal Account by the CIA's Key Field Commander* (New York: Crown, 2005).

29. Mathew Levitt, "The Political Economy of Middle East Terrorism," *Middle East Review of International Affairs,* December 2002, http://meria.idc.ac.il/journal/2002/issue4/jv6n4a3.html (accessed May 1, 2007).

30. John Burns, "How Afghan's Stern Rulers Took Hold," *New York Times,* December 31, 1996.

31. Khalid Hasan, "Swiss Documentary on Afghanistan: Pakistani, Saudi Engineers Helped Destroy Buddhas," *Daily Times,* March 19, 2006, http://www.dailytimes.com.pk/default.asp?page=2006%5C03%5C19%5Cstory_19-3-2006_pg7_38 (accessed November 3, 2008).

32. Peter Bergen, "Afghanistan Testimony Before the House Committee on Foreign Affairs," *New American Foundation,* April 7, 2007, http://www.newamerica.net/publications/resources/2007/peter_bergens_afghanistan_testimony_before_the_house_committee_on_foreign_affairs (accessed April 28, 2007).

33. Aryn Baker, "A Taliban Spokesman's Confession," *Time*, January 17, 2007, http://www.time.com/time/world/article/0,8599,1579979,00.html (accessed March 2, 2007).

34. Ahmed Rashid, "Accept Defeat by Taliban, Pakistan Tells NATO," *Telegraph*, November 30, 2006, http://www.Telegraph.co.uk/news/main.jhtml?xml=/news/2006/11/29/wafghan29.xml (accessed March 2, 2007).

35. "Hezbollah," *Wikipedia*, http://en.wikipedia.org/wiki/Hezbollah (accessed November 4, 2008).

36. K. Krishnakumar, "A Silent Genocide Is Taking Place in Bangladesh," *Rediff.com*, November 21, 2006, http://www.rediff.com/news/2006/nov/21rights.htm (accessed May 1, 2007).

37. Brian Eads, "Saudi Arabia's Deadly Export," *Australian Reader's Digest*, February 2003, pp. 119–25.

38. Ted Carpenter, "Terrorist Sponsors: Saudi Arabia, Pakistan, and China," Cato Institute, November 16, 2001.

39. Stephen Schwartz, "Ground Zero and the Saudi Connection," *Spectator*, September 22, 2001.

40. Rachel Ehrenfeld, "The Cure for the Wahhabi Virus," *FrontPage Magazine*, October 24, 2005, http://www.frontpagemag.com/Articles/ReadArticle.asp?ID=19853 (accessed March 2, 2007).

41. "The Great Divide: How Westerners and Muslims View Each Other," Pew Global Attitudes Poll, June 22, 2006, http://pewglobal.org/reports/display.php?ReportID=253 (accessed May 24, 2008).

42. Eads, "Saudi Arabia's Deadly Export."

43. Steven Emerson, "National Commission on Terrorist Attacks upon the United States: Third Public Hearing," *U.S. Govt. Press*, July 9, 2003, http://www.9-11commission.gov/hearings/hearing3/witness_emerson.htm (accessed March 2, 2007).

44. Levitt, "The Political Economy of Middle East Terrorism."

45. S. Balakrishnan, "Attacks Retaliation for Gujarat Riots?" *Times of India*, July 13, 2006, http://timesofindia.Indiatimes.com/articleshow/1742854.cms (accessed March 2, 2007).

46. Richard Halloran, "SEA Terror," *Washington Times*, April 21, 2007, http://www.washingtontimes.com/commentary/20070420-080426-8307r.htm (accessed April 25, 2007).

47. Ramashray Upadhyay, "Islamic Terrorism in Bangladesh—A Threat to Regional Peace," *SAAG*, May 10, 2007, http://www.southasiaanalysis.org/papers23/paper2242.html (accessed March 2, 2007).

48. Daniel Byman, *Deadly Connections: States That Sponsor Terrorism* (Cambridge: Cambridge University Press, 2007).

49. Ibid.

50. "Hizballah Rockets," *GlobalSecurity.org*, http://www.globalsecurity.org/military/world/para/hizballah-rockets.htm (accessed May 2, 2007).

51. Byman, *Deadly Connections: States That Sponsor Terrorism*, p. 156.

52. "Kashmir Militant Extremists," Council on Foreign Relations, July 12, 2006, http://www.cfr.org/publication/9135 (accessed April 3, 2007).

53. Hamid Mir, "'We Can Hit any Soft Target in India,'" *Rediff.com*, January 9, 2007, http://ushome.rediff.com/news/2007/jan/09inter.htm (accessed March 13, 2007).

54. B. Raman, "India & Pakistan: Can Mindsets & Perceptions Change?" *SAAG*, December 10, 2006, http://www.southasianalysis.org/papers21/paper2057.html (accessed March 2, 2007).

55. Krishnakumar, "A Silent Genocide Is Taking Place in Bangladesh."

56. Mashuqur Rahman, "The Demons of 1971," *Rediff.com*, January 4, 2007, http://www.rediff.com/news/2007/jan/04spec.htm (accessed March 2, 2007).

57. Richard Benkin, "No Outrage Over Ethnic Cleansing of Hindus," *Analyst-network.com*, October 16, 2008, http://www.analyst-network.com/article.php?art_id=2500 (October 18, 2008).

58. Rahman, "The Demons of 1971."

59. Edward Kennedy, "Crisis of South Asia," *U.S. Govt. Press: Senate Judiciary Committee*, November 1, 1971, p. 66.

60. "Hamoodur Rahman Commission Report: Annexure," Govt. of Pakistan, 1972, http://www.bangla2000.com/bangladesh/Independence-War/Report-Hamoodur-Rahman/Annexure.shtm.

61. Bob Woodward, *State of Denial: Bush at War, Part III* (New York: Simon & Shuster, 2006).

62. Ibid.

63. "On Point II: Transition to the New Campaign," Combat Studies Institute, June 2008, http://usacac.army.mil/CAC2/CSI/OP2.asp (accessed March 2, 2007).

64. Noah Feldman, *What We Owe Iraq: War and the Ethics of Nation Building* (Princeton, NJ: Princeton University Press, 2006).

65. Philippe Girard, *Paradise Lost: Haiti's Tumultuous Journey from Pearl of the Caribbean to Third World Hotspot* (New York: Palgrave Macmillan, 2005).

66. "De-nazification," *Wikipedia*, http://en.wikipedia.org/wiki/Denazification (accessed July 8, 2008).

67. John Lewis, "'Gifts from Heaven': The Meaning of the American Victory over Japan, 1945," *Objective Standard* (Winter 2007–2008), http://www.theobjectivestandard.com/issues/2007-winter/american-victory-over-japan-1945.asp (accessed July 29, 2008).

68. Edward Luttwak, "Dead End: Counterinsurgency Warfare as Military Malpractice," *Harper's*, March 5, 2007, http://www.harpers.org/archive/2007/02/0081384 (accessed March 15, 2007).

69. Moorthy Muthuswamy, "Bring Democracy to Iraq," *Washington Times,* July 19, 2003.

70. Moorthy Muthuswamy, "Pakistan's Undemocratic Underpinnings," *Washington Times,* November 22, 2002.

71. Moorthy Muthuswamy, "A New Paradigm for the War on Terror," *Washington Times,* December 8, 2003.

72. Ethan Bronner, "A Year Reshapes Hamas and Gaza," *New York Times,* June 15, 2008, http://www.nytimes.com/2008/06/15/world/middleeast/15gaza.html (accessed July 20, 2008).

73. Joshua Hammer, "Freedom Is Not Enough," *Newsweek,* November 14, 2005.

74. Lydia Polgreen, "Africa's Crisis of Democracy," *New York Times,* April 23, 2007, http://www.nytimes.com/2007/04/23/world/africa/23nigeria.html (accessed July 20, 2008).

75. Girard, *Paradise Lost.*

76. "Freedom in the World—China (2006)," *Freedom House,* http://www.freedom house.org/inc/content/pubs/fiw/inc_country_detail.cfm?year=2006&country=6941&pf (accessed March 2, 2007).

77. Fareed Zakaria, "India Rising," *Newsweek,* March 2, 2006, http://www.msnbc.msn .com/id/11564364/site/newsweek (accessed March 2, 2007).

78. Fareed Zakaria, *The Future of Freedom: Illiberal Democracy at Home and Abroad* (New York: Norton, 2003), p. 154.

79. Bill Spindle, "Crude Reality: Soaring Energy Use Puts Oil Squeeze on Iran," *Wall Street Journal,* February 20, 2007.

80. Andrew Bostom, "The 9/11 Commission and Jihad," *FrontPage Magazine,* July 30, 2004, http://www.frontpagemag.com/Articles/ReadArticle.asp?ID=14439 (accessed January 15, 2007).

81. "National Commission on Terrorist Attacks upon the United States: Chapter 12," U.S. Govt. Press, http://www.9-11commission.gov/report/911Report_Ch12.htm (accessed March 2, 2007).

82. Ibid.

83. "Profile: World Muslim League," *History Commons,* http://www.historycommons .org/entity.jsp?entity=muslim_world_league (accessed July 20, 2008); "Saudi 'Charities' and the War against America," *Frontpage Magazine,* July 16, 2008, http://frontpagemag .com/Articles/Read.aspx?GUID=B164102B-EAB6-4407-9263-D2C34C43D838 (accessed July 20, 2008); see also Eads, "Saudi Arabia's Deadly Export."

84. Ibid.

Chapter Two

PASSION FOR CONQUEST

In the aftermath of 9/11, questions were raised whether the attacks were in response to American policies in the Middle East. Specifically, America's siding with Israel in the ongoing Israel-Arab conflict and the perceived American economic and cultural domination of Arabs have been cited as factors that came into play. Now a growing number of analysts have come to the conclusion that America had to be attacked, because it is seen as the bulwark against the spread of Islam or Muslim conquest of *infidel*. Well-known American scholar of Islam Bernard Lewis notes:

> America is now perceived as the leader of what is variously designated as the West, Christendom, or more generally the "Lands of the Unbelievers." In this sense the American president is the successor of a long line of rulers—the Byzantine emperors of Constantinople, the Holy Roman emperors in Vienna, Queen Victoria and her imperial colleagues and successors in Europe. Today as in the past, this world of Christian unbelievers is seen as the only serious force rivaling and obstructing the divinely ordained spread of Islam, resisting and delaying but not preventing its final, inevitable, universal triumph.[1]

As well, the American mode of governing, its separation of church and state, and its democracy are seen as antithetical to the jihadist outlook of a regime, in which people are "subservient" to Allah and follow precisely the extremist interpretation of what is discussed in the Islamic trilogy.[2]

The jihadist desire and action for conquest can't be accommodated with our own desire to live in peace. This chapter, after briefly discussing the evolution of political Islam, articulates some ideas on how its theological underpinnings could be discredited. Undercutting theology is one important way of weakening the nodes—the mosques and *madrassas*—of the social network that spawns jihad.

CONQUEST BY DESIGN

If an individual wants to capture, control, and rule a land and its people, it is hard to think of a better way than to declare oneself so close to the almighty God as to be the sole purveyor of his "revelations." This gives the leader enormous legitimacy in the eyes of the followers. There is another added advantage to mixing religion with the desire for conquest: the fight for conquest can be enduring, the cause taken over by communities and nations long after the founder is gone.

If this individual had lived over a thousand years ago, how can we know whether he truly received "revelations" from God that he wanted to pass along for the goodness of humankind or that he designed these "revelations" for extending his power base as an absolute ruler? The answer to the above question lies in a scientific analysis of these "revelations," his life story, and the track record of his followers in ancient and, more important, in contemporary, times.

If conquest is the primary purpose of the individual, these revelations and the story of his life would betray the intent.[3] Indeed, the words of Allah are only about 17 percent of the Islamic trilogy, but the words and actions of Muhammad comprise 83 percent of the trilogy.[4]

Statistics can be uniquely useful in deciphering the true intent of an individual or an ideology.[5] An important statistic that betrays the underlying theme of conquest or political intent while giving lip service to spirituality comes in the form of glorifying the founder of Islam.[6] The following quotation is from American scholar Bill Warner published in 2007:

> But the Trilogy is clear about the doctrine. At least 75% of Sira (life of Muhammad) is about jihad. About 67% of the Koran written in Mecca is about the [condemning of] unbelievers, or [external] politics. Of the Koran of Medina, 51% is devoted to the [violent conquest and subjugation of] unbelievers. About 20% of Bukhari's Hadith is about jihad and [external] politics.... There are 146 references to Hell in the Koran. Only 6% of those in Hell are there for moral failings—murder, theft, etc. The other 94% of the reasons for being in Hell are for the intellectual sin of disagreeing with Muhammad, a political crime.[7]

How much of the Koran tries to be good to humanity as a whole? The answer to this question, together with the above statistics that speak negatively of unbelievers, sheds light into the characterization of Islam as a "religion of peace." The Koran is given special attention here because it is seen to consist of revelations from God. At my urging, Bill Warner conducted further analysis:

[H]ow much of the Koran represents good for humanity as a whole? What is the good Koran? This question turns out to have a simple answer based upon the scientific method. We need to examine the data, the "good verses" from the Koran.

The Koran addresses three audiences—Muslims, kafirs [unbelievers or *infidels*], and humanity as a whole. In looking for the good, we cannot use verses that advocate good for Muslims.... Every [Koranic] verse that deals with kafirs is negative and/or violent. So we can't use any verse that is about kafirs.... We are left with one category to examine—humanity as a whole....

There are 4,018 words in the verses that seem to offer goodness to all of humanity (there are 153,207 words in the Koran, this varies upon which translation). Of course, this goodness is denied later in the chapter, but even at that, we have only 2.6% of the Koran that speaks well of humanity initially....

Even the 2.6% vanishes under the threatened violence if kafirs don't accept Islam's offer of goodness. Violence and suffering are promised to 100% of those who do not believe Muhammad....

Based upon a detailed analysis, there is no unmitigated benevolence toward or good for kafirs in the Koran.[8]

Until now, many Western leaders, including George W. Bush, have described Islam as a "religion that preaches peace (toward unbelievers)."[9] Now, utilizing this new statistical analysis we can assert that Islam's (doctrinal) outlook toward unbelievers is definitely *not* one of peace (61 percent of the Koran speaks ill of unbelievers versus, at best, 2.6 percent speaks well of humanity).[10] I have estimated from Bill Warner's figures listed in this section that fully 19 percent of the Koran calls for violent conquest and subjugation of unbelievers. From the position of power and strength, the Medina Koran speaks even more insistently along these lines.

More important, the above statistical analysis forms the basis not just for contesting but even for comprehensively discrediting the often quoted description of Islam as a "religion of peace." In fact, an appropriate and statistically acceptable characterization is that Islamic doctrines overwhelmingly preach dislike, hatred, and conquest of unbelievers and that this material constitutes the majority of the content in the Koran and the Sira. Using this statistical basis, one may also interpret that the token "goodness" toward unbelievers is present in the Koran in order to camouflage the true intent of subjugating and conquering them. When this anti-unbeliever-rich Islamic doctrine is preached through mainstream mosques, one could justifiably claim that neither the mosques nor the people who deliver the sermons there nor those who listen to them are likely to have a moderate outlook toward unbelievers. Furthermore, the above statistics may explain why the overwhelming numbers of terrorists are Muslims, and why their conflicts over power sharing with fellow local unbelievers find resonance and sponsorship among the much larger *ummah* (community of Muslims in the whole world). These attributes, by and large, are not shared by any other faith or religion. Throughout this work, the reader would find a remarkable correlation between the extent of Muslims' identification with jihad (and *sharia*) and the degree of their exposure to Islamic doctrines.

What is notable is the irrational and absurd nature of overwhelming hostility to unbelievers in Islamic scriptures. They do not appear to give the possibility for Muslims to coexist with non-Muslims, to learn, and to trade with them. Of course, such levels of hostility can be readily understood if Islam was designed just to extend the power base of its founder enduringly—and at the expense of its followers.

Admittedly Bill Warner's groundbreaking statistical analysis is rather new—and is yet to be independently verified. However, there is no a priori reason to discount it. The reader might wonder why this type of an analysis hasn't been carried out until now. This analysis requires someone with a modern scientist background who also has a keen interest in theology (like Bill Warner). Such an analyst is a rarity indeed, as those trained in theology do not normally have a solid scientific background.

Muhammad had left behind four very close students or companions—the so-called righteously guided caliphs. These caliphs reflect the vision and aspiration of the founder himself.[11] They carried his teaching forward into history, where their actions were recorded. The actions constitute murderous campaigns against Muslims who wanted to leave Islam—also known as apostates—and extensive conquest of *infidel* lands and their subjugation to Islam.

Another revelation of the conquest intent comes in the form of adverse treatment of unbelievers.[12] Bill Warner defines the Golden Rule of unitary ethics and outlines why violations of this ethic have made it impossible to coexist with political Islam:

> On the basis of the Golden Rule—the equality of human beings—we have created democracy, ended slavery and treat women and men as political equals. So the Golden Rule is a unitary ethic. All people are to be treated the same. All religions

have some version of the Golden Rule except Islam.... The term "human being" has no meaning inside of Islam. There is no such thing as humanity, only the duality of the believer and unbeliever. Look at the ethical statements found in the Hadith. A Muslim should not lie, cheat, kill or steal from other Muslims. But a Muslim may lie, deceive or kill an unbeliever if it advances Islam.

There is no such thing as a universal statement of ethics in Islam. Muslims are to be treated one way and unbelievers another way. The closest Islam comes to a universal statement of ethics is that the entire world must submit to Islam.... By the way, this dualistic ethic is the basis for jihad. The ethical system sets up the unbeliever as less than human and therefore, it is easy to kill, harm or deceive the unbeliever.

The dualism of Islam is more deceitful and offers two choices on how to treat the unbeliever. The unbeliever can be treated nicely, in the same way a farmer treats his cattle well. So Islam can be "nice," but in no case is the unbeliever a "brother" or a friend. In fact, there are some 14 verses of the Koran that are emphatic—a Muslim is never a friend to the unbeliever. A Muslim may be "friendly," but he is never an actual friend. And the degree to which a Muslim is actually a true friend is the degree to which he is not a Muslim, but (considered) a hypocrite.[13]

If Islamic ideology was cleverly designed for violent conquest, most of the material in the Islamic trilogy should talk about jihad as war. Indeed, over 50 percent of the Medina Koran deals with hypocrites and jihad against unbelievers. Nearly 75 percent of the Sira deals with jihad, signifying the dominance of conquest outlook over spirituality. About 97 percent of the references to jihad in the Hadith recorded by Bukhari are about war.[14] The trilogy commends Islam as the perfect political system, destined to rule the world for all time. Starting with the Medina, Islam has spread mostly by the sword in many continents. In the lands Islam has occupied, indigenous cultures, religions, and in many instances, languages, have disappeared.

Bill Warner notes:

Islam has been waging civilizational war for centuries. Before Muslims arrived, Egypt and North Africa, and the southern coast of the Mediterranean were Christian. There was a Buddhist monastery in Alexandria, Egypt. Turkey was Buddhist and Christian. Persia—now Iran—was Zoroastrian. The Hindu culture covered an area of the world twice as large as it is now. Languages disappeared to be replaced by Arabic. When Napoleon invaded Egypt, he had discovered that the Muslim population knew nothing about the pyramids or temples. The 5,000-year-old culture of the Pharaohs had been annihilated.[15]

The view that the Islamic doctrines emphasized conquest of unbelievers can be further consolidated by their interpretation in the subsequent centuries. American Islamic scholar Robert Spencer points out: "[A]ll the schools of Islamic jurisprudence [of the four traditional schools: *Hanbali, Shafii, Hanafi, and Maliki*] teach that the *infidels* must be subjugated through jihad."[16] These schools of thought form the foundation of the modern interpretation of the all-important Muslim law—the *sharia*.

Even the modern interpretation of jihad and its association with conquest of unbelievers continues to be inspired by Islamic doctrines. The foremost Shiite scholar of the modern era, Ayatollah Ruhollah Khomeini of Iran, made these remarks in 1942: "[T]hose who study jihad will understand why Islam wants to conquer the whole world. . . . The sword is the key to paradise, which can be opened only for holy warriors!"[17] Muslim Brotherhood is a Middle East–based mainstream mass movement. On a Web site devoted to Ramadan, the Muslim Brotherhood posted a series of articles by Dr. Ahmad 'Abd al-Khaleq about an Islamic doctrine called Al-Walaa Wa'l-Baraa, in which the writer "argues that according to this principle, a Muslim can come closer to Allah by hating all non-Muslims—Christians, Jews, atheists, or polytheists— and by waging jihad against them in every possible manner."[18]

Institutionalized mistreatment and repression of Muslim women has long puzzled many observers. But this is readily understood in the context of the conquest model and with the observation that the prophet Muhammad, by historical accounts, was a strong male and that his conduct was fully consonant with long-established cultural precedents.[19]

At a fundamental level, Islam appears to be dominated by the politics of its founder, with its external focus on conquest—and not coexistence. The conclusion that Islamic doctrines are the root cause of terror conducted against unbelievers is no longer escapable and is backed by statistics—not subjective opinions!

Clearly, America and other non-Muslim nations need to understand the religious motives and the vision of jihadists. This "vision" should be derived from the trilogy of Muslim holy books, as these books in the eyes of jihadists represent the only complete knowledge people need. Since the original Islamic literature is in Arabic and is not particularly transparent, it is difficult for unbelievers to comprehend. Fortunately, in recent years several scholars have managed the difficult job of translating or deciphering the Islamic trilogy.

Of the three, the Koran is the oldest and is considered to consist of revelations God sent through Islam's founder, Muhammad. The Muslim legal code of *sharia* law's origins is in the Koran and in the Hadith. The Hadith is a collection of the sayings and actions of Muhammad. The Sira is the biography of Muhammad by Ibn Ishaq. Since Islamic doctrines view Muhammad as the role model for all Muslims, his biography is considered very important for them.

Muhammad first preached in the Saudi Arabian city of Mecca for thirteen years. The portion of the Koran revealed in Mecca is called the Meccan Koran. During this period, Muhammad had only a few followers and had to live peacefully among the predominantly non-Muslim Meccans. Accordingly, the Meccan Koran is peaceful, although it considers non-Muslims inferior.[20] An example from the Meccan Koran (73:10): "Listen to what they [unbelievers] say with patience, and leave them with dignity."[21]

Following the death of his protector uncle, Muhammad was run out of town by wealthy Meccans who did not appreciate his sermons. Muhammad took refuge in a nearby town called Medina. This is where Muhammad started building an army of his own, obtaining a huge following and military power. This was achieved by sending his followers, as many say, to rob trading caravans from Mecca, thereby obtaining wealth for himself and his followers.[22] An example from the more aggressive Medina Koran is (8:12):

> Then your Lord spoke to His angels and said, "I will be with you. Give strength to the believers. I will send terror into the unbelievers' hearts, cut off their heads and even the tips of their fingers!"[23]

These two Koranic verses, the earlier one from Mecca and the later one from Medina, appear to contradict each other. The Medina Koran commands violent conquest and subjugation of unbelievers. According to the Koran, the later verse replaces the earlier verse.[24] That is, whenever there is a contradiction, the Koran of Medina abrogates the Koran of Mecca. Yet these Mecca Koran verses couldn't be done away with completely, because they are considered "God's revelations."

Bill Warner calls this contradiction symptomatic of the inherent duality of political Islam and points out: "Both sides of the contradiction are true in dualistic logic."[25] He then goes on to discuss situations in nature where duality holds true, such as in quantum mechanics. For instance, the quantum mechanical description of subatomic particles such as electrons, which makes up an atom (along with the nucleus consisting of protons and neutrons), consists of a dual role in which the electron acts as a well-defined single entity (like a ball) or as a dispersed wave entity (as in an ocean wave). Unfortunately, this analogy by Bill Warner could be taken by Islamists as a scientific justification for political Islam's glaring and hard-to-justify contradictions!

Here we take a simple alternate view. In an ideology designed by an earthly power intent on conquest, depending upon the situation encountered (militarily weak Meccan versus militarily strong Medina times of Muhammad and his followers), the ideology should adjust its tactics toward its adversaries in order to survive and to eventually succeed in its search for conquest. Hence, inconsistencies in the treatment of adversaries are a hallmark of a human-made ideology of conquest.

The political foundations of Islam, especially jihad, have had a profound impact in the later years. American scholar Mary Habeck observes:

> The ideas supported by the jihadists didn't spring from a void, nor are all of them the marginal opinion of a few fanatics. The principle dogmas they assert—that Islam is the one true faith that will dominate the world; that Muslim rulers need to govern by *sharia* alone; that the Koran and Hadith contain the whole truth for determining the righteous life; that there is no separation between religion and the rest of life; and that Muslims are in a state of conflict with the unbelievers—have roots in discussions about Islamic law and theology that began soon after the death of Muhammad and that are supported by important segments of the clergy (ulema) today.[26]

Bassam Tibi, a well-respected contemporary European Muslim scholar of jihad, had this to say in 1996 about jihad within the context of Islamic theology—noted by Andrew Bostom:

> At its core, Islam is a religious mission to all humanity. Muslims are religiously obliged to disseminate the Islamic faith throughout the world. "We have sent you forth to all mankind" (Quran 34:28). If non-Muslims submit to conversion or subjugation, this call can be pursued peacefully. If they do not, Muslims are obliged to wage war against them. In Islam, peace requires that non-Muslims submit to the call of Islam, either by converting or by accepting the status of a religious minority and paying the imposed poll tax, *jizya*. World peace, the final stage of the *da'wa* [Islamic proselytizing], is reached only with the conversion or submission of all mankind to Islam.... Muslims believe that expansion through war is not aggression but a fulfillment of the Koranic command to spread Islam as a way to peace. The resort to force to disseminate Islam is not war (*harb*), a word that is used only to describe the use of force by non-Muslims. Islamic wars are not *hurub* (the plural of *harb*) but rather *futuhat*, acts of "opening" the world to Islam and expressing Islamic jihad. Relations between *dar al-Islam*, the home of peace, and *dar al-harb*, the world of unbelievers, nevertheless take place in a state of war, according to the Koran and to the authoritative commentaries of Islamic jurists. Unbelievers who stand in the way, creating obstacles for the *da'wa*, are blamed for this state of war, for the *da'wa* can

be pursued peacefully if others submit to it. In other words, those who resist Islam cause wars and are responsible for them. Only when Muslim power is weak is "temporary truce" allowed (Islamic jurists differ on the definition of "temporary").[27]

Political Islam's demand of following just the trilogy alone, when the trilogy deals only with the Arabic way of life as it was over one thousand years ago, can be interpreted as an attempt to impose a tribal Arabic way of life on non-Arabs. Hence it is legitimate and probably correct to see political Islam as a tool for conquest for Muhammad during his times, and for his extended tribe of Arabs beyond his time. It can thus be seen as an alien ideology whose purpose is to bring the world population under Arab control.

Osama bin Laden, the leader of al Qaeda, outlines conditions for attacks on America to cease: "There are two solutions to stopping it [terror attacks on America and Americans]. One is from our side, and it is to escalate the fighting and killing against you. This is our duty, and our brothers are carrying it out.... The second solution is from your side. I invite you to embrace Islam."[28] Hence one may view jihadists as the contemporary activists of the old conquest.

The perception of the trilogy as the complete manual that defines the righteous way of life meant that Muslims were reluctant to embrace new ideas. This implies that the religion of Islam was not easy to reform. Indeed, whenever external forces challenged Islamic nations, the cry for embracing "true" Islam as defined in the trilogy dominated. This situation continues today, with the likes of Bin Laden calling for the establishment of "true" Islam internally and invoking jihad to Islamize the world. This is unlike other major religions—Christianity, Buddhism, or Hinduism—where external influences can be credited with creating reform.

In the next few pages the practice and evolution of Islam is analyzed to determine how we should deal with political Islam.

ISLAM IN THE MIDDLE AGES

A fourteenth-century influential Islamic scholar named Ibn Taymiyya had shaped the idea of what jihad meant and put it in the context of Islamic law. He belonged to the *Hanbali* school of jurisprudence. He lived at a time when Mongol invaders from central Asia had conquered the core of the Muslim world. He elevated the importance of waging jihad, making it even more important than some of the customary five obligatory duties of Islam: profession of faith, prayer, paying of alms, fasting during the month of Ramadan, and pilgrimage to Mecca.[29] For him the purpose of jihad was to fight until all religion was for God alone. He also suggested fighting and killing Muslims (the heretics) who tried to avoid participating in jihad and those who failed to fully and dutifully implement God's commandments as laid out in the Koran. He declared that unbelievers had to be fought and killed.[30]

Even the Sufi movement, heralded for its tolerance and mysticism, is not immune to the call for jihad. This is even seen in the twelfth-century writings of al-Ghazali, who is considered the paragon of the Sufi movement. American scholar Andrew Bostom quotes al-Ghazali: "[O]ne must go on jihad (i.e., warlike razzias or raids) at least once a year.... One may use a catapult against them [non-Muslims] when they are in a fortress, even if among them are women and children. One may set fire to them and/or drown them."[31]

During the time the Ottoman Islamic empire was entering a period of military reverses, in the middle of eighteenth century, Abd al-Wahhab started articulating his vision of Islam. An adherent to the *Hanbali* school of thought, he was clearly influenced by Ibn Taymiyya. Like his predecessor Taymiyya, Wahhab also prescribed jihad against fellow Muslim heretics as the solution to their evil. He suggested that only God is worthy of worship, and in his view any Muslim worshipping images, idols, tombs, or shrines should be treated as a heretic or an unbeliever and should be fought and killed.[32] The Wahhabi Islam is still in practice and is identified as the dominant form of Islam practiced in Saudi Arabia.

In India, toward the twilight of Mughal rule in the sixteenth century, scholar Shah Wali-Ullah called for forcing Islam on Hindus for their own well-being.[33] The Australian Islamic scholar Sayyid Athar Abbas Rizvi writes in his book *Shah Wali-Ullah and His Times* that in Wali-Ullah's view the modern interpretation of jihad or Islamic holy war overemphasized its defensive character:

> To the 'ulema [clerics], jihad was the *fard kifaya* (collective duty) and it remained a duty as long as Islam was not the universally dominant religion in any area.... If it was done forcefully it was quite acceptable but if someone mixed it with kindness it was even better. However, there were people, said the Shah who indulged in their lower nature by following their ancestral religion, ignoring the advice and commands of the Prophet Mohammad. If one chose to explain Islam to such people like this it was to do them a disservice. Force, said he was the much better course—Islam should be forced down their throat like bitter medicine to a child.... This, however, was only possible if the leaders of the non-Muslim communities who failed to

accept Islam were killed; the strength of the community reduced, their property confiscated and a situation was created which led to their followers and descendants willingly accepting Islam. The Shah pleaded that the universal domination of Islam was not possible without jihad.[34]

In Africa, political Islamists Muhammed al-Jaylani, Usman dan Fodio, and Shehu Ahmadu promoted jihad aimed at restoring "true" Islam—stricter enforcement of *sharia* and the conquest of *infidels*.[35]

ISLAM IN THE MODERN AGE

Toward the end of nineteenth century, the Muslim elite felt weak compared to the European powers. They were determined to extricate themselves from European domination and to return to their former military "glory." At first, in the beginning of the twentieth century, nationalist, socialist, and liberal Muslims helped form modern Muslim nations. But overcome by centuries of underdevelopment, the progress was slow in achieving military parity with the Christian-majority West. This frustrated the Muslim public. Extremist Muslim scholars stepped in to fill the vacuum by asserting that a deeper embrace of the way of life defined in the trilogy would help Muslims to regain Muslim glory (it is not often pointed out what this glory is; it usually means conquest of unbelievers and their land). These scholars were: Muhammad Rashid Rida, Hassan al-Bana, Sayyid Abdul A'la Mawdudi, and Sayyid Qutb. Other than the South Asian scholar A'la Mawadudi, all of the others were based in the Middle East. Muhammad Rida, born in 1865, was one generation ahead of the other three. Their scholarship forms the modern basis for waging jihad by extremist groups all over the world—including al Qaeda and regional ones such as the Muslim Brotherhood (Egypt) and Jamait-e-Islami (South Asia). In Mary Habeck's opinion:

> During the mid-twentieth century three ideologues (al-Banna, Mawdudi, and Qutb) would take the ideas of Ibn Taymiyya, Wahhab, and Rida and transform them into a coherent set of beliefs about Islam, politics, and warfare. Their thought is by far the most significant [modern] source of jihadist ideology as well as for other, less radical, expressions of Islamism.[36]

There are reasons for the near absence of reform or moderation in Islam. Throughout history, even during modern times, those who articulated views on the moderate side of Islam faced violence from entrenched mainstream schools of Islamic thought. As discussed before, many Islamic scholars, including Ibn Taymiyya and Abd al-Wahhab, proposed waging war on fellow Muslim "heretics." Minority sects, such as Ahmadiyya Muslims, have faced persecution or even death at the hands of the majority Sunni sect of Islam. The Ahmadiyya's view of their nineteenth-century founder, Mirza Ghulam Ahmad, being a prophet or that jihad can be used only in circumstances of extreme religious persecution made them heretics in the view of mainstream orthodox Sunnis.[37]

The emphasis of jihad in the trilogy and the constantly reinforced view that the trilogy is the complete source of all useful knowledge meant that internal wealth creation was not among the priorities. Hence, conquest or jihad building is an important means of acquiring new wealth and status within the community. In the modern context, this means using terror and the threat of nuclear weapons to extract aid and arms from wealthy nations. This is the Pakistani model, for unlike Saudi Arabia or Iran, it lacks free wealth in the form of oil. But the modern age is characterized by materialism, which requires significant wealth creation. In essence, this defines the fundamental incapacity of Islamic states in the global order.

In past centuries, just about all religions waged wars on people they considered unbelievers; Islam was no different. But today, no religion other than Islam uses violence, expulsions, and discrimination to marginalize unbelievers and to create conditions for conquest (see chapter 3). Most Western nations have a Christian majority and yet practice secularism. In nations where followers of other major faiths (such as Buddhism or Hinduism) live, the societies are, by and large, secular. This may be no coincidence; unlike all major religions of the world—Christianity, Buddhism, Hinduism, or Judaism—Islam was founded by just one individual who was also its absolute ruler.

In many nations where Muslims are a majority, political Islam is the dominating power and exerts strong influence over daily governance. In most Islamic nations, non-Muslims are given second-class treatment (examples would be Saudi Arabia, Pakistan, and Iran). The origin of this outlook is traced to the core of Islamic doctrine—devotion to the trilogy.[38]

In Malaysia, a barely Muslim majority nation at the time of independence has since systematically worked to marginalize its non-Muslim citizens. When they can, ethnic Chinese and Indians have been steadily leaving the country. In Egypt, Coptic Christians, who have been resident natives for a thousand years and are often targeted by the Muslim Brotherhood, are moving out.

When Muslims are a minority in non-Muslim nations, conquest through warfare or constitution-based discrimination of the unbelievers is unlikely due to the Muslims' minority status. Hence, from a conquest point of view, the percentage of Muslims in the population must be raised by increased birth rates and by immigration. This is happening in many nations—France, Britain, India, Russia, and even Israel. But Muslim clerics have cooperated with the regimes in power in Muslim-majority states to help convince their followers to have smaller families.[39] This has not been the case in nations such as India, for obvious reasons.

As discussed in the next chapter, South Asia is a region of particular focus of political Islam's conquest through jihad. In every area of South Asia, once Muslims obtained power through majority status, be it in Pakistan, Bangladesh, or the Kashmir valley, massive ethnic cleansing and marginalizing of non-Muslims has been observed.[40] In fact, most of Pakistan has been cleansed of non-Muslims, and the same has happened in the Kashmir valley. Bangladesh is well on its way (see chapter 3, "Siege of India"). One objective and important conclusion can be made on the basis of this data: South Asian Muslim populations don't believe in coexisting with unbelievers even in modern times. With about a third of the worldwide Muslim population residing in the countries of South Asia, the above damning conclusion can't be set aside as an anomaly! This data, unique in exposing the outlook of political Islam–influenced Muslim populations, indicates a bleak future for non-Muslims, as Muslim populations increase faster than the non-Muslim populations in non-Muslim-majority nations.

Most of the expulsions and genocides in South Asia occurred before 1972 (and after 1947), well before the large-scale infusion of petrodollars and Wahhabism. This observation discredits the notion that oil money, Muslim "grievance," or "freedom fighting" are somehow responsible for the terror. As noted earlier, political Islam's fundamental emphasis on conquest, and the resulting influence on Muslims, can be traced to Koranic scripture.

CONVERSION, CONQUEST, AND THE CRUSADES

Missionary activities aimed at converting people to Christianity are well known. These conversions are directed not only at non-Christians but also at those belonging to different Christian denominations. Religious conversion can be seen as the adoption of a new religious identity. This typically entails the sincere avowal of a new belief system, but may also present itself in other ways, such as adoption into an identity group or spiritual lineage.[41] The conversion of a person from Islam to Christianity or Hinduism can be seen to fall in the former category; the embracing of a different Christian denomination (e.g., Baptism) by a person belonging to another denomination (e.g., Catholicism) falls in the latter category.

Unlike other religions, conquest seems to be a more appropriate term than conversion to define the embracing of Islam—as nations and communities who have embraced Islam have been gradually Arabized. This is probably due to the unique nature of the Islamic trilogy that reflects an Arabic tribal system and due to the perception that the trilogy has all the useful information needed to lead a righteous life.[42] Indeed, the vastness of the lands where Arabic is spoken and the continuing process of Arabizing of Muslim communities in Asia and in Africa is a testament to this.

Among the primary reasons driving violent Islamic conquest is the reward given for slaying unbelievers in the Koran (the only absolute guarantee of a place in paradise). However, there is no equivalent doctrine in Christianity.[43] Still, until recently, Christianity also viewed nonbelievers as heretics and the pagans were seen deserving of poor treatment and subjugation as a form of saving them.

Christianity, too, has been at the receiving end of Islamic conquest almost from the time of Islam's inception. Scholar Robert Spencer observes:

> The crusades were a late and small-scale response to Islamic jihad conquests that began 450 years before the First Crusade and overwhelmed what had been up to the time of these conquests over half of Christendom. Three of the five principle centers of early Christianity—Alexandria, Antioch, and Jerusalem—were conquered and Islamized before the First Crusade, and a fourth (Constantinople) would fall in 1453, 150 years after the Islamic conquest of the last crusader kingdom.[44]

SCIENCE TO THE RESCUE

As condemned unbelievers in the eyes of adherents of political Islam, we have every reason to scientifically investigate the origin and the contents of the Islamic trilogy.[45] As a full-fledged investigation is outside the scope of this work, we give here few examples.

- The Koran was the first book of the trilogy to be put together, and that was accomplished several decades after the death of Muhammad.[46] In the Hadith it is said that Koranic verses were collected from bits of bone, stone, parchment, date palm leaves, and also from the memories of those who had memorized it.[47]

- This is evidence that it is very likely that the Koran was not accurately put together, nor is it complete.
- It is mentioned in the Hadith that at least one verse was missed. It was found in "Khuzaima's" possession.[48]
- One wonders how many more Koranic verses went missing. This is proof that the Koran is not complete. If it is not complete, how valid is the interpretation that the Koran is the word of God?
- Muhammad himself was prone to forgetfulness. Muhammad listened to a man reciting the Koran, and he says: "May Allah bless that man. He has reminded me of verses and chapters I had forgotten."[49]
- This brings up the legitimate argument that Muhammad could have forgotten the original "God's revelations" as well.
- When Muhammad conquered Mecca while riding with an army from Medina, he gave a specific order to kill a man. He was a former secretary. He had earlier accused Muhammad of letting him enter a better speech when he was recording Muhammad's Koranic revelations.[50]
- This narrative in the Hadith gives the impression of portions of the Koran being doctored even during the time of Muhammad. Besides, it also gives an impression that the Koran was not being accurately documented.
- In many situations when Muhammad made "revelations," as described in the Koran, Hadith, or Sira, careful note takers did not appear to be present.
- This means the revelations were written down later. This raises concern about the verses' authenticity.

Mistreatment by God, the Merciful:

- On the treatment of Muslim women, the 34th verse of the fourth chapter of the Koran, *An-Nisa*, or Women: "[A]nd (as to) those on whose part you fear desertion, admonish them and leave them alone in the sleeping-places and beat them."[51]
- The second-class status and treatment of Muslim women instituted through *sharia* is also well documented: "A woman counts as half a man in giving evidence in a court of law, or in matters of inheritance. Her position is less advantageous than a man's with regard to marriage and divorce.... A woman does

not have the right to choose her husband, or her place of residence, to travel freely or have freedom in her choice of clothing. Women have little or no autonomy and are deemed to need the protection of their fathers, husbands or other male relatives throughout their lives. Any conduct that undermines the idea of male supremacy will fall foul of the *sharia*."[52]

- Koranic verses such as *At-Tauba* ("The Repentance") 9:5, state that Muslims should "slay the pagans wherever ye find them."[53]
- On how Muslims should treat Christians and Jews: *Al-Mâ'idah* ("The Table Spread with Food") 5:51 states: "Take not the Jews and Christians as friends."[54]

All of the above reveal the conquest-based and political emphasis of the Islamic ideology: death for non-Muslims such as Buddhists or Hindus, dislike of Christians and Jews, and double standards for fellow Muslims—the mothers and daughters of today's and tomorrow's Muslims. These are not just ancient writings; they are a way of everyday life that is practiced by communities and nations. Taliban-ruled Afghanistan was one such nation.

Even if "God's revelations" had been made to Muhammad, based on the information presented in the trilogy, there is an open question as to how accurately these revelations were taken down, preserved, and converted in the form of books or any other form of information storage. We know from archaeological studies that as recently as a thousand years ago humans lacked credible technology for processing and storing information. Clearly, leaves, stones, bits of bone, and people's memory are not reliable forms of note taking or information storage when Muhammad delivered his "revelations." This is common sense! This approach raises serious doubts about the credibility of *sharia*, which is considered Muslim personal law and is partly derived from the Koran.

Muhammad may have delivered a revelation from his deathbed calling for reconciliation, along the lines described in the Meccan Koran, in order to make permanent peace with unbelievers. However, his immediate followers may have concealed it to keep their power base. The point is, where does one draw the line regarding the accuracy or completeness of the Koran, and on what grounds? For something as profound as God's "revelations," there shouldn't be an iota of doubt about their authenticity. This is clearly not the case here.

Another relevant issue is whether the Arab tribes Muhammad belonged to had the ability to identify phony messengers of God. After all, many in ancient history claimed to possess God's revelations. But most were ignored. Probably for the right reasons. "Messengers" of God distinguished themselves by their claim of supernatural abilities, such as receiving God's revelations or possessing supernatural powers.

Modern science provides an understanding of nature and explanations for natural phenomena that would have been considered supernatural or "Godly" just a few centuries ago. This implies that as a society increases its scientific awareness, it can more easily distinguish phony messengers of God.

How good was the scientific understanding of the tribes Muhammad belonged to? To build an extensive understanding of nature or science requires a sophisticated experimental ability at verification. This is common sense—a scientific explanation must be verified in real life. An understanding of our solar system may require a powerful telescope, but it requires industrial know-how to build one. The more we want to understand the science of the solar system, the more sophisticated are the needed instruments—radio telescopes, rockets, satellites, and so on. Building them requires considerable infrastructure. The conclusion is that to conduct a thorough verification, a society requires an increasingly complex technological infrastructure.

But we know from archaeological studies and history that the Saudi tribes Muhammad was part of didn't have sophisticated infrastructure, which meant that their understanding of nature or science was limited. The conclusion that follows is that Arab tribes at the time of Muhammad were not well placed to identify phony messengers of God.

The inability of political Islam to coexist with other religions or their followers is traced to the Islamic trilogy, which is probably designed to ensure conquest.

Still, the proof is in the pudding.

How do most Muslim societies that have embraced the trilogy deal with unbelievers? They wage jihad (chapter 3 will shed light on jihad waged on unbelievers).

NOTES

1. Bernard Lewis, *The Crisis of Islam* (Waterville, ME: Thorndike Press, 2003).

2. Ali Sina, "Yes, Study the Quran!" FaithFreedom.org, January 21, 2004, http://www.faithfreedom.org/oped/sina40121.htm (accessed March 2, 2007).

3. Robert Spencer, *The Truth about Muhammad: Founder of the World's Most Intolerant Religion* (Washington, DC: Regnery, 2006).

4. *A Simple Koran: Readable and Understandable* (Nashville, TN: Center for the Study of Political Islam, 2006), p. 395.

5. Bill Warner, in discussion with the author, March 2007.

6. According to Bill Warner, the percentages stated above are not based upon verses, but are a measure of ideas, topics, and concepts; http://frontpagemagazine.com/Articles/Read.aspx?GUID=A00F3895-42BB-4A7D-9FA5-4A19F3286EAD (accessed July 19, 2008).

7. "The Study of Political Islam," *FrontPage Magazine*, February 5, 2007, http://www.frontpagemag.com/Articles/ReadArticle.asp?ID=26769 (accessed May 2, 2007).

8. Bill Warner, "The 'Good' in the Koran," *PoliticalIslam.com*, November 13, 2008, http://www.politicalislam.com/blog/the-good-in-the-koran/ (accessed November 13, 2008).

9. "Interview of the President by Al Arabiya," White House press release, October 4, 2007, http://www.whitehouse.gov/news/releases/2007/10/20071005-5.html (accessed November 5, 2008).

10. "A New Koran," *FrontPage Magazine*, April 18, 2008, http://frontpagemagazine.com/Articles/Read.aspx?GUID=A00F3895-42BB-4A7D-9FA5-4A19F3286EAD (accessed July 20, 2008).

11. "Fictional Muhammad," *Frontpage Magazine*, March 7, 2008, http://www.frontpagemag.com/Articles/Read.aspx?GUID=5A39DDF5-9CA9-4543-8B6E-6C83B92AB59E (accessed July 20, 2008).

12. Bill Warner, in discussion with the author, March 2007.

13. "The Study of Political Islam."

14. Ibid.

15. "An Ethical Basis for the War against Political Islam," *Center for the Study of Political Islam*, 2006, p. 13 (booklet distributed by Bill Warner at the 2007 Human Empowerment Conference, Los Angeles).

16. "Confronting Islamization of the West," *Frontpage Magazine*, July 11, 2008, http://www.frontpagemag.com/Articles/Read.aspx?GUID=3EBBF3CD-1F0C-4455-B2AD-E0C25C3AAEDC (accessed July 20, 2008).

17. Ruhollah Khomeini, "Islam Is Not a Religion of Pacifists," *Danielpipes.org*, 1942, http://www.danielpipes.org/comments/95189 (accessed December 30, 2008).

18. "Muslim Brotherhood Website: Jihad against Non-Muslims Is Obligatory," *MEMRI*, October 17, 2008, http://www.memriiwmp.org/content/en/report.htm?report=2877 (accessed October 19, 2008).

19. "Islam and the Submission of Women," *Frontpage Magazine*, October 10, 2007, http://www.frontpagemag.com/Articles/Read.aspx?GUID=2ACCD764-5177-4D05-9186-4B9EFE442849 (October 10, 2007).

20. "The Study of Political Islam."

21. Ibid.

22. Spencer, *The Truth about Muhammad*.

23. "The Study of Political Islam."

24. Ibid.

25. Ibid.

26. Mary Habeck, *Knowing the Enemy: Jihadist Ideology and the War on Terror* (New Haven, CT: Yale University Press, 2006), p. 17.

27. Andrew Bostom, "Confused Islamic Apologetics," *FrontPage Magazine*, August 10, 2004, http://www.frontpagemag.com/Articles/ReadArticle.asp?ID=14578 (accessed July 20, 2008).

28. "Bush: Bin Laden's Video Underscores Threats," *MSNBC.COM*, September 8, 2007, http://www.msnbc.msn.com/id/20640658 (accessed July 20, 2008).

29. "Five Pillars of Islam," *Wikipedia*, http://en.wikipedia.org/wiki/Five_Pillars_of_Islam (accessed July 8, 2008).

30. Habeck, *Knowing the Enemy*, pp. 20–22.

31. Bostom, "Confused Islamic Apologetics."

32. Habeck, *Knowing the Enemy*, p. 24.

33. Ibid., pp. 20–22.

34. Sayyid Rizvi, *Shah Wali-Ullah and His Times* (Canberra, Australia: Ma'rifat, 1980), pp. 285–86.

35. Habeck, *Knowing the Enemy*, pp. 6–7.

36. Ibid., pp. 28–29.

37. "Ahmadiyya," *Wikipedia*, http://en.wikipedia.org/wiki/Ahmadiyya (accessed November 8, 2008).

38. "The Study of Political Islam."

39. "Pakistan Mosques to Preach Family Planning," *Times of India*, December 18, 2006, http://timesofindia.indiatimes.com/NEWS/World/Pakistan/Mosques_in_Pakistan_to_preach_family_planning/articleshow/839925.cms (accessed March 2, 2008).

40. "Hindus in Bangladesh, Pakistan and Kashmir: A Survey of Human Rights," *Hindu American Foundation*, 2004, http://www.hinduamericanfoundation.org/HHR2004.pdf (accessed March 2, 2007).

41. "Religious Conversion," *Wikipedia*, http://en.wikipedia.org/wiki/Religious_conversion (accessed July 8, 2008).

42. Habeck, *Knowing the Enemy*, pp. 42–43.

43. Robert Spencer, *Religion of Peace? Why Christianity Is and Islam Isn't* (Washington, DC: Regnery, 2007), p. 90.

44. Ibid., p. 99.

45. Moorthy Muthuswamy, "Certain Koran Verses Threaten World Safety," *Washington Times*, October 2, 2001.

46. Spencer, *The Truth about Muhammad*.

47. *The Political Traditions of Muhammad: The Hadith for the Unbelievers* (Nashville, TN: Center for the Study of Political Islam, 2006), p. 143.

48. Ibid.

49. Ibid., p. 144.

50. *Muhammad and the Unbelievers: A Political Life* (Nashville, TN: Center for the Study of Political Islam, 2006), p. 126.

51. Asra Nomani, "Islam and Women: Clothes Aren't the Issue," *Washington Post*, October 22, 2006, http://www.washingtonpost.com/wp-dyn/content/article/2006/10/20/AR2006102001261.html (accessed March 2, 2007).

52. "Women's Rights and the *Sharia*," *NTPI.org*, September 22, 2004, http://www.ntpi.org/html/womensrights.html (accessed November 9, 2008).

53. Nomani, "Islam and Women: Clothes Aren't the Issue."

54. Ibid.

Chapter Three

MANY A FACE OF JIHAD

In Muslim nations under a strong political Islamic influence, the citizens' aspiration appears to be one of conquest for Islam. The primary national agenda is waging jihad on non-Muslim nations by indoctrinating their resident Muslims and sending homegrown jihadists or proxies from other Muslim nations to fight these non-Muslim nations. Indeed, across the globe, many nations with sizable minority Muslim populations have been victimized by jihad. In this chapter, three select nations or regions—Israel, Europe, and India—where Muslims are a minority are studied in order to understand how various forms of jihad are executed.

American gangster Al Capone was found guilty on a relatively minor tax-evasion charge, not on the many heinous crimes he had allegedly committed. The gangster nations of the world—the axis of jihad nations—may have been more circumspect in the acts of terror they have directed at powerful nations of the world, but with soft or weak states such as India, they could be both more direct and more overt. In fact, India has been a perennial victim of political Islam. These soft-victim nations of jihad may possess some of the most incisive data implicating the gangster nations and proving the genocidal intent of the political Islamic movement. Due to this incentive, I will take a critical look at India in order to provide a wealth of jihad-related data and analysis that is not yet widely known or realized.

ASSAULT ON ISRAEL

Among the nations bordering Islamic states, Israel, along with India, is the nation most targeted by political Islam. As a developed nation and a close ally of America, Israel has been effective in warding off military attacks from neighboring Islamic states and their proxies. But the emergence of Nasrallah's Hezbollah and Iran's effort to acquiring nuclear weapons have likely made Israel more vulnerable than it has been since its birth.

There are compelling reasons to view the warfare imposed by Israel's Arab neighbors as an extension of the war started by Muhammad nearly fourteen hundred years ago. The trilogy talks about Jewish settlements in the heart of Saudi Arabia and in nearby lands, and Muhammad's verbal and armed conflicts with them.[1] In fact, for quite some time, Saudi Arabia has had virtually no Jewish population. It can be argued, based upon the trilogy, that political Islam didn't have any particular liking for the Jews. A widely quoted hadith below that calls for killing of Jews has created much controversy in the United States:

> The prophet, prayer and peace be upon him, said: The time [of judgment] will not come until Muslims will fight the Jews and kill them; until the Jews hide behind rocks and trees, which will cry: O Muslim! There is a Jew hiding behind me, come on and kill him![2]

American scholar Andrew Bostom has provided an interesting account of how he came to suspect that Islamic antisemitism must have a theological basis. In the seventeenth century, ruled by a Mughal king named Akbar, India had an influential Sufi theologian by the name of Sirhindi. Bostom notes:

> In the midst of an anti-Hindu tract Sirhindi wrote, motivated by Akbar's pro-Hindu reforms, Sirhindi observes, "Whenever a Jew is killed, it is for the benefit of Islam." The biographical information I could glean about Sirhindi provided, among other things, no evidence he was ever in direct contact with Jews, so his very hateful remark suggested to me that the attitudes it reflected must have a theological basis in Islam—contra the prevailing, widely accepted "wisdom" that Islam, unlike Christianity, was devoid of such theological anti-Semitism.[3]

Clearly, centuries ago the Jewish community had suffered grievously in Saudi Arabia. For instance, during the prophet Muhammad's stay in Medina in the year 627 the Quraiza Jewish tribe was vanquished. "Charged with collaboration with the enemy, the tribe's six to eight hundred men were brought in small groups to trenches dug the previous day, made to sit on the edge, then beheaded one by one and their bodies thrown in. The women and children were sold to slavery and the money fetched, together with proceeds from the tribe's possessions, was divided among the Muslims."[4] In addition to a substantial presence in Palestine, Jews had lived in many Middle Eastern nations for centuries. This, along with various historical documents and archaeological studies, points to the reality that Jews belong in the Middle East. In the aftermath of the Nazi Holocaust, it is only natural that Jews would want a land and nation in the Middle East to call their own.

The establishment of a modern Jewish state in the 1940s led to the displacement of a large number of Palestinians. There was also another side of the story not widely noted—the ensuing Israel-Arab conflict led to a large number of Jews leaving Arab countries for Israel.[5]

Very few Arab Muslim states have recognized Israel's right to exist thus far. Even Egypt's recognition, in light of its otherwise unfriendly outlook, can be seen as more of an act of convenience, designed to secure large handouts from America, than one of conviction. Muslim nations' denial of Israel's right to exist, the continued one-sided harping of displaced Palestinians while ignoring the displacement of Jews from Arab lands, and the funding of a large number of suicide bombers who have wrecked thousands of Jewish families give the impression of systematic war crimes committed on a large scale. Going by the nature of these crimes and their massive scale, these appear to be crimes against humanity whose intention is to drive Jews out from the land of Israel and to expand or recapture the land for political Islam, as is described in the trilogy.

Political Islam's grip on Palestinians is evident by the power and influence of hateful and regressive Muslim clergies. The clerical preaching does not appear to emphasize the need for Palestinians to focus on modern education or on learning to work with Israelis. Instead, the emphasis has been on building feelings of grievance in impressionable minds. This means nation building is on the backburner, while jihad building is emphasized. These are among the primary reasons that the enormous aid given to the Palestinians by the Europeans, Americans, and even Arabs has not been utilized constructively. The extent of political Islam's influence can be ascertained by the 2006 election results, in which Hamas, an offshoot of the Muslim Brotherhood, was voted to power in the West Bank and the Gaza Strip. Hamas's manifesto is extremist, dedicated to the destruction of Israel, and not surprisingly, is derived from Islamic doctrine (Hadith).[6] The bulging population, which is due to a high Palestinian birthrate, creates a steady stream of jihadists to sustain the conflict with Israel.

Israel's very own restive Arab Muslim population is also a source of worry. Increasingly, Israeli Arabs are identifying with al Qaeda and Hamas.[7] Arabs in Israel constitute about 20 percent of the population, of which 82 percent are Muslims. Muslims in Israel have the highest birthrate of any group: 4.0 children per woman, as opposed to 2.7 for Jewish Israelis.[8] Through voting, the Arab population participates in the political process in Israel. The long-term demographic challenge brought by this restive Muslim population in Israel can be understood by studying the fate of Christians in neighboring Lebanon. American author and former Lebanese resident Brigette Gabriel notes in *Because They Hate*:

> Power shifted in Lebanon in 1970, Christians became the minority and the Muslims the majority.... These demographic changes created political pressure to modify the structure of the Lebanese government. When Muslims became the majority, they started demanding more power in executive, legislative, and administrative branches of the government.... The Christians in Lebanon always had differences and problems with the Muslims, but we never thought our [Muslim] neighbors would turn on us to kill and blow up our cities, towns, and villages.[9]

THE EUROPEAN SURVIVAL THREAT

Wealthy European nations, which are among the most advanced in the world, found themselves slow to react to the emerging threat from political Islam. Not only do Muslims in Europe have much higher birthrates compared to the natives, but they appear to be firmly in thrall to political Islam. Among the most vulnerable nations are France and the Netherlands, with Britain, Belgium, and Germany following closely behind. Muslims in France constitute about 12 percent of the total population. However, in terms of newborns, the Muslim birthrate is probably close to 30 percent, aided by a low birthrate among the white natives. In the nearby Netherlands, the Muslim population is at 6 percent and probably has a much higher birthrate compared to the native whites.[10] Overall, among newborns, the Muslim percentage in Europe is estimated to be anywhere between 15 and 20 percent.[11]

Colonial connections and the need for cheap labor led to the initial wave of immigration from Muslim nations to Europe. Later on, Muslims' close family relatives, including relatives by marriage, were allowed to settle in Europe. The Middle Eastern funding for Wahhabi preaching in European mosques aggravated assimilation problems for the Muslim immigrants and even their European-born children. Clerics hardly proficient in native European languages were allowed to be imported from Islamic nations with strong political Islamic bases of influence. Clearly, these clerics must have had little or no idea of community building in Western nations, but as torchbearers of political Islam they sure know one thing: jihad building.

In his best-selling book *While Europe Slept: How Radical Islam Is Destroying the West from Within*, author Bruce Bawer provides a fascinating account of the political Islamic buildup in the Netherlands that led to the gruesome murder of journalist Theo van Gogh by a Dutch Islamist.[12] Van Gogh's murder was the final straw for many Dutch families who were concerned about the growing Islamic extremism. Many of them have left for Canada, Australia, or New Zealand. A survey conducted in April 2005 showed that every third Dutchman wanted to leave the country.[13] A July 2005 poll found 22 percent of British Muslims saying that the past summer's rush-hour bombings of London's metro system, which killed fifty-two people, were justified because of Britain's support for the war on terror. This included 31 percent of young British Muslims.[14] In France, the interior ministry accused Muslims of waging an undeclared "intifada" against police, with attacks that injured an average of fourteen officers a day.[15] The large-scale riots by French Muslims pointed out not just their inability to assimilate but also the jihadist outlook and intentions of large sections of the French Muslim population.[16]

A study conducted by the right-wing think tank Policy Exchange has found that 40 percent of Muslims between the ages of sixteen and twenty-four said they would prefer to live under *sharia* law in Britain, a legal system based on the teachings of the Koran. The figure among the over-fifty-five age group, in contrast, was only 17 percent. Munira Mirza, a broadcaster and one of the authors of the report, was quoted as noting that multicultural policies pursued by the government had succeeded in making things worse rather than better. "The emergence of a strong Muslim identity in Britain is, in part, a result of multi-cultural policies implemented since the 1980s which have emphasized difference at the expense of shared national identity and divided people along ethnic, religious, and cultural lines."[17]

Why jihad is a thriving enterprise among Muslim communities even in Britain, let alone in Saudi Arabia or Pakistan, is exemplified in this interview with a former British jihadist, Hassan Butt:

> He became one of the network's star fundraisers.... [Former British jihadist Hassan] Butt says he openly told them [his audience] he was raising funds for jihad. ... Over the next couple of years, he says he raised $300,000.... His biggest contributors? Doctors. People who were businessmen. Professional people, basically, who wanted to donate substantial amounts of money.[18]

Before blaming the locals for not helping Muslims to assimilate, one should study other transplanted communities. This apparent "negative influence" of multicultur-alism has not occurred in Hindu or Sikh communities, whose members started arriving from India in 1950s as blue-collar workers to work in British textile mills. These émigrés shared language, food habits, history, and some culture with Muslims from Pakistan who also arrived at about the same time to find work. Yet almost thirty to forty years later, Hindus and Sikhs have income levels either comparable to or sur-passing those of native whites; their children have excelled in education, at times even surpassing the majority.[19] Muslims of Pakistani origin have exactly the opposite record; they tend to be poorer, less educated, and tend to have high crime rates.[20] In fact, the Muslim population (of which Muslims of Pakistani origin constitute about 40 percent) in British prisons is about twenty times that of Hindus, although the Muslim population in Britain is only about three times the Hindu population—and British Muslims are three times more likely to be unemployed.[21] Three of the four bombers associated with the 7/7 London bombings were from ethnic Pakistani Muslim communities.[22] The reason has now become transparent: political Islam rules these Muslims, just as it does in Pakistan.

Living the "European dream"—a comfortable, gadget-oriented life—requires wealth creation that, in turn, requires time and effort. The addition of any children to this equation, who are dependent by default, meant that, for a resident, children have become an expensive responsibility both in terms of time and resources. Understand-ably, the European socialist system has given generous subsidies to the poor and espe-cially to those who have many children. This policy was a godsend to political Islam. Not material minded but conquest minded, clerics encouraged Muslims to have more children and to receive government subsidies. In Denmark, 5 percent of the Muslim population receives 40 percent of the total welfare outlays.[23]

European Muslim families are told by the clerics to reject the European dream and instead embrace a tribal Arabic way of life. This has led to high Muslim birthrates and parents who have looked to imported radical clerics for guiding their children, instead of executing their parental responsibilities as good citizens. This has resulted in a new generation of homegrown European jihadists under clerical control.

Why did European societies, especially the ruling class, fail to wake up to this growing genocidal threat decades ago? As former rulers of the Islamic nations from which most of the Muslims emigrated, the European ruling class never saw them as posing a challenge at any point. Bruce Bawer explains how the emerging Islamist threat went unnoticed for decades in western Europe. Those who reach high office have been active in party politics since they were very young. "You learn to fit in. You learn not to rock the boat.... Those who are most lavishly rewarded tend to be those who play the strongest loyalty to the party and its platforms. Original thinkers are not welcome. People who might shake things up are closed out."[24] The normally liberal press gave a sympathetic ear to Muslim leaders who made claims of harassment and of being disadvantaged—a classic tactic of political Islam, calling itself a victim even as it victimizes unbelievers. While there is some basis to Muslim claims of discrimination in Europe, the examples of successful assimilation of other ethnic groups such as the Chinese or Hindus from South Asia and how they got there were not given adequate coverage by the European press. Highlighting the Chinese and Hindu successes vis-à-vis Muslims would have shed light onto why Muslims were falling behind in Europe.

Not many had understood that political Islam was experiencing resurgence due to the free wealth in the form of oil; nor was it understood just how conquest-oriented political Islam is. Some clearheaded politicians—Pim Fortuyn of the Netherlands, for instance—who boldly pointed out the "Muslim problem" found themselves in an unenviable position, in fear of being unfairly criticized by the media with descriptions such as "racist," "bigot," and the rest.

In an operation that is typical of the way political Islam is making inroads into Europe, Belgian journalist Paul Belien analyzes how extremists are taking control of the Muslim population in Belgium:

> About three years ago, young men dressed in black moved into the [Antwerp, Belgium] neighborhoods. They had been trained in Saudi Arabia and Jordan and adhere to Salafism, a radical version of Islam. They set up youth organizations, which gradually took over the local mosques. "The Salafists know how to debate and they know the Koran by heart, while the elderly running the mosques do not," she [a civil servant of Antwerp] said they also have money. "One of them told me that he gets Saudi funds." Because they are eloquent, the radicals soon became the official spokesmen of the Muslim community, also in dealing with the city authorities.... [T]he reason why the Socialists, who run the city, allow the Islamists to do as they please is because they want to get the Muslim vote, which is controlled increasingly by the Salafists who are in the process of taking over the mosques.[25]

Many European nations, including France and the Netherlands, are struggling to come up with an effective policy framework to deal with what they see as a "radical" Islamic threat. Not knowing any better, they have continued to move in the direction of allowing political Islam to influence the government and help regulate their Muslim residents, by establishing councils dominated by clerics. France has its French Council of the Muslim Faith and in Britain the government has funded the Board of Islamic Theologians, while in Germany there is the Coordination Council of Muslims.[26]

A major victory in the consolidation of political Islam in Britain was achieved when the government sanctioned powers for *sharia* judges to rule on cases ranging from divorce and financial disputes to those involving domestic violence. The government established a network of five *sharia* courts whose rulings are enforceable with the full power of the judicial system, through the county courts or High Court.[27]

The only legitimate ground (in the eyes of the British establishment) for granting power to the *sharia* courts is due to the view that most Muslims see *sharia* as a "divine" law (in reality, there is considerable evidence pointing to human-made origins of the *sharia*).[28] However, portions of *sharia* also call for second-class treatment of non-Muslims by Muslims.[29] Yet, by definition, these portions couldn't be ignored because they, too, are part and parcel of the "divine" law. Hence, in my view, by legitimizing *sharia*, the British may be legitimizing a law that violates the equal rights provisions of the British constitution.

Given the circumstances, the European Union's unease regarding Turkey's inclusion is entirely understandable. Allowing Turkey with its Muslim majority to become part of Europe could be one of the fastest ways to empower and even ensure political Islam's dominance of Europe. Turkey is an overwhelmingly Muslim-majority nation, with a large and growing population. I published a letter on December 18, 2002, in the *Washington Times* that gives the EU's perspective:

WHY THE EU DOES NOT WANT TURKEY

In their column "Road Map to a Western Turkey" (Commentary, yesterday), John C. Hulsman and Brett D. Schaefer have glossed over an important concern many Europeans have about Turkey's inclusion in the European Union: namely, giving Turkey's Muslim population easier access to settling in Europe.

European Muslims, including second-generation ones, have difficulty assimilating and are among the largest recipients of welfare. They also have high crime rates and poor education levels. While the native white population in the European Union is barely reproducing itself, European Muslims have among the highest birthrates.

If Turkey were admitted to the union, Europe's Muslims could jump from about 4 percent to 20 percent of the population. Furthermore, there is the obvious issue of pan-Islamic extremism sweeping the world, including Europe, with the burgeoning of the immigrant Muslim population. It also must be acknowledged that, given its deep Islamic roots, Turkey is at best an experiment in democracy and modern development. Its admission into the European Union could portend the devastation of Western Europe through a massive influx of Muslims who have little in common with Europeans.[30]

Enhanced exposure to Islamic doctrine, brought by Middle East–funded gleaming new mosques may be seen to aid the European Muslims' embrace of jihad and *sharia*. As the resident Muslim population under the control of political Islam rapidly increases vis-à-vis the native population in western Europe, the democracies of these countries are coming under an increasing Islamic siege, making it difficult for them to fight back.[31] The situation in India, discussed in the following section, gives a grim picture of how such a siege could evolve and what it could mean for Europe.

SIEGE OF INDIA

It is no exaggeration to note that India stands today as an advanced laboratory for Project Jihad. Supported by Saudi Arabia and many other Islamic states, Pakistan has made deep inroads into the fabric of Indian society. This section offers insights into how a political Islamic siege of a non-Muslim developing nation is carried out. Incisive data on the impact of jihad is presented here. This description of what is happening to India in the hands of political Islam and of the fate of non-Muslims in India's neighbors should be eye opening.

All available evidence suggests that India is engulfed by a multifront jihad. To understand this assault on India, one has to look at the larger picture associated with Islamic conquest in South Asia itself. South Asia is one of the regions where political Islam's border ends and pluralism, as represented by secular Indian democracy, begins.

The Islamic thrust into ancient India started within a few hundred years after the death of Muhammad. Muslim victories led to the establishment of kingdoms in vast portions of ancient Hindu-majority India; this continued until the advent of colonial British rule. Despite ruling most of India for several hundred years, Muslim conquerors from the Middle East or their descendents could manage to convert only a small fraction of the native Hindus to Islam. This is due to the fact that Hinduism is divided into disparate groups, each with its own ideologies, and to the small number of the Muslim ruling elite compared to the vast Hindu population in extended areas. It also made little economic sense to exterminate Hindus, when as slaves they could well serve the small Muslim ruling class. Still, history records millions of Hindus and Sikhs killed by Muslim invaders and kings in India; their temples deliberately and systematically destroyed.[32]

> My principle object in coming to Hindustan . . . has been to accomplish two things. The first was to war with *infidels*, the enemies of the Mohammadan religion; and by this religious warfare to acquire some claim to reward in the life to come. The other was . . . that the army of Islam might gain something by plundering the wealth and valuables of the *infidels*: plunder in war is as lawful as their mother's milk to Musalmans who war for faith.[33]

So said Amir Timur, a Muslim commander who had invaded India in the fourteenth century.

There is much misunderstanding about the role played in India by the Sufi (more mystical) Muslim saints centuries ago. They have been falsely portrayed as promoters of peace and harmony between Hindus and Muslims and wonderful symbols of spiritualism. Former high-ranking Indian security official R. Ohri has published an analysis of Sufi contributions in the Indian context:

> It needs to be assessed how did the Sufis conduct themselves during reckless killings and plunders by the Muslim invaders? Did they object to the senseless mass killings and try to prevent unremitting plunder of Hindu temples and innocent masses? Did the Sufis ever object to the capture of helpless men and women as slaves and the use of the latter as objects of carnal pleasure?
>
> Most Sufis came to India either accompanying the invading armies of Islamic marauders, or followed in the wake of the sweeping conquests made by the soldiers of Islam. At least the following four famous Sufis accompanied the Muslim armies which repetitively invaded India to attack the Hindu rulers, seize their kingdoms and riches and took recourse to extensive slaughtering of the commoners. Almost all Sufi masters were silent spectators to the murderous mayhem and reckless plunder of temples and cities by the marauding hordes across the subcontinent. Taking advantage of the fact that the Hindu masses are deeply steeped in spiritual tradition and mysticism, the Sufis used their mystic paradigm for applying sort of a healing balm on the defeated, bedraggled, and traumatized commoners with a view to converting them to the religion of the victors.
>
> [The Sufi] task was to apply the balm of spiritual unity on the traumatized Hindu population and then gradually persuade them to convert to Islam. Not a single Sufi, the so-called mystic saints, ever objected to the ongoing senseless manslaughter and reckless plunder, nor to the destruction of temples, and nor for that matter to the ghoulish enslavement of the so-called *infidel* men and women for

sale in the bazaars of Ghazni and Baghdad. Operating from the sidelines of spiritualism they even participated in the nitty-gritty of governance to help the Muslim rulers consolidate their authority in the strife-torn country. And significantly, their participation in the affairs of the State was not conditional upon the Muslim rulers acting in a just and evenhanded manner. On the contrary, the Sufis invariably tried to help the Sultans in following the path shown by the Prophet and the *sharia*. Another important objective of the spiritual and mystic preaching of the Sufi masters was to blunt the edge of Hindu resistance and prevent them from taking up arms to defend their hearth and home, their motherland and their faith, through the façade of peace and religious harmony.[34]

Andrew Bostom has studied the outlook and deeds of Sufis worldwide. He has this to say:

> Consistent with this nexus between Sufism and orthodox Islam, Sufis have supported (fervently) the corollary institution of dhimmitude, replete with all its oppressive and humiliating regulations for non-Muslims.[35]

Many do not know that Sikhism itself was baptized at the end of the medieval period into a warrior mode in order to withstand the onslaught of the ruling Muslim (Mughal) kings in India. Sikhism was originally founded by Nanak Dev, who was born in 1469. Unable to defend its followers from the relentless Mughal kings, in 1969 Sikhism's tenth *guru* (leader), Gobind Singh, converted his people into a warrior order (*Khalsa*).[36] This order requires the mandatory strapping of a sword by a Sikh male.

When the British East India Company entered the Indian subcontinent several hundred years ago, the long Muslim rule was in its twilight. Resurgent Hindu and Sikh kings were in the process of successfully transplanting Muslim kingdoms. Among the reasons was that, immersed in conquest and in their elevated sense of superiority and power, and more important, repressed by an ideology that allows little room for evolution, Muslims simply fell behind in India, as they did in other parts of the globe.

After a series of decisive battles, the powerful British established supremacy. Still, even during British rule, the Muslim elite saw themselves as rulers of Hindus. However, Indian Muslims were falling behind, because of their reluctance to embrace modern education. Indian sociologist Balbir Punj notes: "When the British authorities announced a program in 1835 to introduce English in schools, a huge majority of Muslim clerics signed a petition to oppose the move; they claimed the philosophy of such education imparted in English was at variance with the tenets of Islam.... On the other hand, when in 1829 the British set up a Sanskrit College in Kolkata, orthodox

Hindus strongly opposed the decision, asking the British to set up English medium schools instead. Obviously, this contrasting attitude resulted in more Hindus learning English and moving forward with it while the reverse held true for Muslims."[37] Apart from their comprising over 25 percent of the manpower in the Indian military under the British, Muslims had dismal representation in most government sectors.[38]

When the ruling British colonizers decided to leave India, not wanting to be dominated by a Hindu majority, some Muslims demanded a land where Muslims were the majority. The founder of Pakistan and the most prominent Muslim leader of that time, Muhammad Ali Jinnah, articulated the reason for dividing India in the name of Islam: "So far as I have understood Islam, it does not advocate a democracy which would allow the majority of non-Muslims to decide the fate of the Muslims. We cannot accept a system of government in which the non-Muslims merely by numerical majority would rule and dominate us."[39]

Not only was Jinnah unable to digest the basic premise of democracy, but he was also suggesting that the structure of Islam is such that it may not tolerate Muslims living under majority non-Muslim rule—a popular pet theme of Islamists around the world today. Jinnah then went on to set the stage for India's partition by noting, "[A] constitution must be evolved that recognizes that there are in India two nations, who both must share the governance of their common motherland."[40] This evolved into an outright demand for the partitioning of India along religious lines, through the Lahore Resolution, passed in the Pakistani city of Lahore in 1940.[41] When the demand was resisted by nationalists, Jinnah's party, the Muslim League, initiated violent "Direct Action Day" against non-Muslim Indians to achieve its objectives.[42]

In an election conducted before Indian independence in 1947, Indian Muslims overwhelmingly voted for a separate nation.[43] British India was therefore partitioned in 1947 into Hindu-majority India and Muslim-majority Pakistan. The 25 to 30 percent Muslim portion of the population in British India got 25 percent of the land, in the form of East and West Pakistans.[44] Minorities were expected to stay in their respective lands even after the partitioning. It is illustrative to note what Jinnah said just days before Pakistan was formed in 1947:

> I shall not depart from what I have said repeatedly with regard to minorities. The minorities, to whichever community they may belong, will be safe-guarded. Their religion or their faith or belief will be protected in every way possible. Their life and property will be secure. There will be no interference of any kind with the freedom of worship. They will have their property and culture. They will be in all respects treated as citizens of Pakistan without any distinction of caste, religion or creed.[45]

Still, Jinnah was setting up Pakistan to become an Islamic state. After Pakistan was established, in 1948, Jinnah spoke to the bar association in the Pakistani city of Karachi and said: "Why this feeling of nervousness that the future constitution of Pakistan is going to be in conflict with *sharia* Laws? Islamic principles today are as applicable to life as they were 1,300 years ago."[46]

What the leader had declared regarding minority safety was neither respected by the Pakistani government nor by the political leadership. The Muslim League Jinnah commanded formed militia to kill, convert, or drive out the minorities from Pakistan. In 1949, one year after the death of Jinnah, the Constitutional Assembly of Pakistan passed a resolution making it clear that Muslims would have higher status than non-Muslims.[47] Within the next three years, spearheaded by mosques, most non-Muslims—primarily Hindus and Sikhs who constituted anywhere from 16 to 20 percent of the population—were driven out of West Pakistan (it is now called Pakistan) and hundreds of thousands were possibly killed.[48] Now the non-Muslim population there stands at less than 2 percent.[49] This was achieved once the Muslim majority in Pakistan acquired political power by obtaining independence from the British. Also, some non-Muslim Pakistanis converted to Islam in order to keep their property and not live as hounded *infidels* in this new Islamic nation.

Indian Punjab, which shares a border with Pakistani Punjab, retaliated by driving out Muslims from its region. However, in the rest of India, most Muslims were allowed to stay. According to the Indian census report of 1951, 10 percent of the Indian population consisted of Muslims.[50]

At that time Saudi Arabia was a poor nation and was in no position to influence these events. Here is evidence indicating that even without the help of oil-based resources or the support of a wealthy and influential Saudi Arabia, political Islam in the modern age can be genocidal.

Prior to 1947, East Pakistan—now called Bangladesh—had at least a 29 percent Hindu and Buddhist population. This has now been reduced to less than 10 percent.[51] These minorities, in the aftermath of the partitioning, while certainly not violently kicked out as in West Pakistan, were finding conditions slowly deteriorating for them in the Muslim-majority nation. There has been a steady outflow of non-Muslims from East Pakistan into India.

The government of both West and East Pakistan was located in West Pakistan. Urdu, a language spoken mostly in the West and based upon Arabic script, was the official language, although East Pakistanis were more numerical and spoke Bengali, which is a language based on Sanskrit and is considered a Hindu or an *infidel* language. The West

Pakistanis dominated the military and the government bureaucracy. The cultural and power-sharing disagreements between the two Pakistans resulted in West Pakistan sending its troops to crush the East Pakistani rebellion and, more important, to eradicate what it saw as an *infidel* Hindu influence on East Pakistan, due to the presence of a large Hindu minority. While being brutal to the Bengali Muslims whom they saw as being less Muslim, the West Pakistani troops selectively chose Hindus to rape and murder, and drove out millions of Hindus and Bengali Muslims into India (see chapter 1, "Axis of Jihad and the New Cold War"). This led to the Indo-Pak war of 1971; as a result of this, East Pakistan gained its independence to eventually become Islamic Bangladesh.

Since 1947, Hindu minorities in Bangladesh have faced violence from Islamic elements that have been both passively and actively supported by the state. Using the Enemy Vested Property Act, the state took over the properties of millions of Hindus by simply declaring them as "enemy of the state."[52] If one or more minority family members left Bangladesh for any reason (due to economic or political reasons, such as violence directed at them), the state could simply declare them as enemies and confiscate their properties.

This act has been in place since 1948. A study has shown that "members of the Hindu community have lost 26 million acres of land from 1965 to 2006, while an estimated one crore [ten million] Hindus were forced to leave the country from 1964 to 2001 because of the communal conflicts and deprivation caused by the Enemy (Vested) Property Act."[53] This scheme has proved to be an important avenue for rapidly achieving Islamic conquest of *infidel* and their lands within Muslim-majority regions of South Asia. American activist Richard Benkin has noted that "when Bangladesh won its independence from Pakistan in 1971, Hindus made up almost one in five of its citizens. Today, they are less than one in ten. Demographers and others estimate that approximately 20 million Bangladeshi Hindus have disappeared."[54] In a book released in 2008, *Empire's Last Casualty: Indian Subcontinent's Vanishing Hindu and Other Minorities*, US-based political scientist Sachi Dastidar puts out a figure of 49 million Hindus "missing" from Bangladesh based upon decade-wise census.[55]

In recent years, more Hindus and Buddhists have left Bangladesh for India. Their community leaders have consistently complained of violence directed at them by Islamic parties and groups, especially by Jamait-e-Islami, which was originally established by none other than the well-known jihadist scholar of South Asia Abdul A'la Mawdudi (see chapter 2, "Islam in the Modern Age"). At a 2006 terrorism conference in Mumbai, a minority leader from Bangladesh implicated both Pakistan and Saudi Arabia in funding extremist organizations.[56]

Many powerful people in these nations have been eyeing India's northeastern region for an Islamic conquest. To achieve this vision, they have been sending Muslim Bangladeshis through the porous Indian borders for some time. By some estimates there are at least some 10 million illegal Bangladeshi Muslims in India.[57]

What about Muslim growth within India? The Indian Muslim population has increased from 10 percent in 1951 to 13.5 percent in 2001.[58] The Kashmir valley, a Muslim-majority region within non-Muslim-majority India, has seen massive non-Muslim ethnic cleansing. In 1989, more than 300,000 Hindus were driven out to the rest of India.[59] Even towns that have a Muslim majority but that lie within regions having over 90 percent non-Muslim populations in India are not immune from the desire for jihad. The Thondi and Rasathipuram municipalities of the Ramanatha-puram and Vellore districts, respectively, are in the southern Indian state of Tamil-nadu. They are located within predominantly non-Muslim-majority districts. These Muslim-ruled municipalities denied the minority-Hindu areas civic amenities, funding for schools, garbage clearing, and so on, and sent notices in Urdu bluntly telling them to convert to Islam if they wanted civic facilities. Non-Muslims have found themselves driven out of the Muslim-majority cities of Meerut and Mau in northern India.[60]

These statistics, hardly known to the outside world, show political Islam's crimes directed at humanity, especially in modern times. What is striking is the deadly influence of a political ideology masquerading as a religion. Indeed, about 25 percent of what was known as British India has now become almost exclusively Muslim, or is on its way to becoming so. Non-Muslims are now squeezed into densely populated present-day India. As a result of this non-Muslim ethnic cleansing in all Muslim-majority areas of South Asia, India had to accommodate an excess number of people in the land it inherited after the partitioning.

The statistics showing how Muslims are unable or unwilling to coexist in modern times in *all* Muslim-majority areas of South Asia—where they share ethnicity, language, food, and culture with unbelievers—point to an underlying conquest outlook and strongly discount benign notions of Muslims. Furthermore, it appears that this devastating data implying Muslim inability to coexist is traceable to only one source: dislike and hatred of unbelievers dominantly present in Islamic scriptures (see chapter 2, "Conquest by Design"). If a necessary requirement of a religion is the ability to coexist with other faiths, it is certainly not evident in the case of Islam, as is practiced in South Asia. One could argue that because they are a minority, perhaps Indian Muslim traits are camouflaged unlike their counterparts in other Muslim-majority regions of South Asia. Hence, due to the faster-growing Muslim population, it is no exaggeration to say that non-Muslim Indians face a bleak future—in the form of terrorism and subversion through an intensifying multi-front jihad, which is what we are seeing now in India (see the later pages). Conclusion: political Islam grows in power along with the Muslim population, and it will increasingly destabilize the host non-Muslim-majority nation and, if left unchecked, eventually threaten the integrity of the nation and the very existence of its non-Muslim citizens. These are exactly the kinds of power relationships that need to be exposed if non-Muslims are to undertake decisive and long-term policy measures and mobilize. This is particularly true of regions with fast growing and restive Muslim minority populations, including Europe.

The proliferation of *madrassas* in Pakistan is well known. It started occurring only in the late 1970s, when Middle Eastern petrodollars started flowing into Pakistan. Nevertheless, as was noted earlier, Pakistan's preference for Islamism goes all the way back to its inception. Since 1947, Punjab University, based in Lahore, has granted over 60 percent of its doctoral degrees in subjects related to Islam; in contrast, only a few percent of its doctoral degrees have been given in engineering.[61] It was only in March 2006 that Pakistan decided to establish premier engineering institutions.[62] In contrast, India went on to form several Indian institutes of technology and regional engineering colleges in 1950s and 1960s. Undoubtedly, this education initiative has played a crucial role in India's economic resurgence and wealth creation, and is particularly related to India's computer software successes.[63] From a *Los Angeles Times* report:

> The current [Pakistani] social studies curriculum guidelines for grades 6 and 7 instruct textbook writers and teachers to "develop aspiration for jihad" and "develop a sense of respect for the struggle of [the] Muslim population for achieving independence." [T]he federally approved Islamic studies textbook for eighth grade teaches students they must be prepared "to sacrifice every precious thing, including life, for jihad."
>
> "At present, jihad is continuing in different parts of the world," the chapter continues. "Numerous mujahedin [holy warriors] of Islam are involved in defending their religion, and independence, and to help their oppressed brothers across the world."
>
> The textbook for adolescent students says Muslims are allowed to "take up arms" and wage jihad in self-defense or if they are prevented from practicing their religion. "When God's people are forced to become slaves of man-made laws, they are hindered from practicing the religion of their God," the textbook says. "When all the legal ways in this regard are closed, then power should be used to eliminate the evil. "If Muslims are being oppressed," the book says, "then jihad is necessary to free them from this cruel oppression...."

But Pakistani critics of the public school system maintain that jihad's softer sense is easily lost in lessons that emphasize that Muslims are oppressed in many parts of the world, and that encourage fellow Muslims to fight to free them.

"All of that shows that somehow the schooling system has fed intolerance and bigotry," said [Husain] Haqqani, who has written a new book on the links between the Pakistani military and radical Muslims.

A study of the public school curriculum and textbooks by 29 Pakistani academics in 2002 concluded that public school "textbooks tell lies, create hatred, inculcate militancy and much more."[64]

Being the new nation created for the Muslims of India, it was increasingly accepted by influential sections of the Pakistani society that Islam should "guide" it. Here again is evidence that the dominance of jihadist politics in Islamic doctrines (chapter 2) was always going to favor the extremist religious right. Indian journalist Praveen Swami, in an article tracking the evolution of Pakistan, observes: "Ever since the birth of the Pakistani state, Islamists and secular democrats became locked in an irreducible ideological war for its soul. Each important battle, tragically, the religious right won."[65] Pakistani physicist Pervez Hoodbhoy points out how the "Saudization" of Pakistan came about:

For three decades, deep tectonic forces have been silently tearing Pakistan away from the Indian subcontinent and driving it towards the Arabian Peninsula. This continental drift is not physical but cultural, driven by a belief that Pakistan must exchange its South Asian identity for an Arab-Muslim one. Grain by grain, the desert sands of Saudi Arabia is replacing the rich soil that had nurtured a magnificent Muslim culture in India for a thousand years.... This change is by design. Twenty-five years ago, the Pakistani state used Islam as an instrument of state policy. Prayers in government departments were deemed compulsory, floggings were carried out publicly, punishments were meted out to those who did not fast in Ramadan, selection for academic posts in universities required that the candidate demonstrate a knowledge of Islamic teachings and jihad was declared essential for every Muslim. Today, government intervention is no longer needed because of a spontaneous groundswell of Islamic zeal.[66]

With this emphasis on Islamism, its history, and its focus on conquest, it is not hard to see why Pakistan's primary goal is one of expanding political Islam's boundaries, rather than nation building. Indeed, the extent of Pakistan's commitment to jihad extends to its armed forces. The motto of its army reads: "*Imaan, taqwa, jihad fi sabilillah*" or "faith, piety, and holy war in the path of Allah."[67] No stone is left unturned in an effort to kindle the passion for conquest. A map distributed to the Pakistani military by the ISI "targets north India, and projects a desire to convert that region into 'Islamic Republic of Pakistan' by 2020. It mentions South India as disputed territory and treats Bangladesh, Sri Lanka, and Nepal as its neighboring countries. The other map indicates a drastic change of Mumbai's topography, turning the metropolis into 'Muslimabad' by 2012."[68]

Having managed to get rid of most of its unbeliever population quickly by 1950, Pakistan had carried out the first stage of Islamic conquest. The Muslim-oriented constitution undermined and marginalized the leftover non-Muslims in the country, and laws were enacted that discriminated against non-Muslims in the hope that they would either convert to Islam or leave the country. With the Muslims of old India holding power in Pakistan, it is also a natural base for regaining the past glory of Muslim efforts to conquer a "Hindu" India. Outmatched by India economically and militarily, Islamic Pakistan has turned to a multifaceted jihad to weaken its neighbor, using Indian Muslims as foot soldiers and sending into India its homegrown jihadists nurtured through a farm system of *madrassas*.[69] It has been bankrolled by several Middle Eastern nations, Saudi Arabia in particular, to indoctrinate Indian Muslims with political Islam.

With Middle Eastern aid and Pakistan's logistics, Muslim populations in neighboring Nepal, Bangladesh, and even in Sri Lanka have come under the spell of political Islam through newly established mosques and *madrassas*.[70] This has made Muslim-majority Bangladesh increasingly accepting of extending political Islam's frontiers. Faced with less penetrable borders with India, according to Indian reports, Pakistan has used Islamic Bangladesh's porous borders to infiltrate terrorists into India.[71]

Pakistan's crowning strategic jihadist success lies in establishing a terror base within India through the Muslim Kashmir insurgency. What is notable is Pakistan's support for "self-determination" of Muslims in Indian Kashmir, even as the Pakistani part of Kashmir is almost completely cleansed of non-Muslims—with most being driven away to India. This approach is consistent with trying to expand political Islam's frontiers at the expense of non-Muslims.

Even under a "moderate" leader like Pervez Musharraf, Pakistan-influenced terrorists have killed scores of Hindu families and have successfully created a Hindu exodus out of certain parts of Kashmir.[72] To put more pressure on India to cede Kashmir to Pakistan, under Musharraf, Pakistan-sponsored terrorists are suspected of having escalated acts of terror in the rest of India. These attacks have imposed a huge economic cost on India's economy. These attacks have grown in number and in frequency despite Musharraf's promise in the following joint statement released on January 6, 2004, in India: "[H]e [Musharraf] will not permit any territory under Pakistan's control to be used to support terrorism in any manner."[73]

Seen in the above context, Musharraf's consistent declaration that "it [Pakistan] has a political and moral right to support what it calls a struggle for self-determination in Indian-controlled Kashmir" has become an immoral and genocidal framework for extending Islam's frontiers.[74] This is through a combination of non-Muslim ethnic cleansing—a form of genocide—and support for self-determination of Muslims, which in reality has turned out to be terror sponsorship. Having already worked to indoctrinate Kashmiri Muslims with a hatred of Hindu-majority India, Pakistan hopes that, given the right to self-determination, Muslim-majority Indian Kashmir will vote to become part of Pakistan.

There is more to the Kashmir Muslim insurgency than a violent confrontation between political Islamists and the Indian state. This insurgency appears to be part of a much larger operation to indoctrinate the local Muslim population in order to extend political Islam's boundaries. Jamait-e-Islami operates several hundred *madrassas* in Indian Kashmir, with funds coming from Saudi Arabia and other Muslim nations. The Kashmiri Jamait is an extension of the party operating under the same name in Pakistan. Jamait managed to instill virulent hatred of *infidel* India in the minds of young children in order to initiate indoctrination at a young age. Below is a portion of a school poem prescribed for Class III (or third grade):

> Little children, be very calm
> I will tell you what is Islam.
> You may be a few and without army,
> But you must fight for Islam.[75]

Kashmir has become the primary terror base for political Islam within India; its Muslim population has been strategically indoctrinated to feel sympathy for political Islam's cause in order to sponsor terrorists infiltrating from Pakistan. Understanding jihad in Kashmir is important, because jihad in the rest of India is developing along similar lines.

Geographically and demographically, the part of Kashmir that sits within India is divided into three regions. The fertile Kashmir valley consists mostly of Sunni Muslims, who make up roughly 50 percent of the total Kashmir population. The area known as Jammu is mostly Hindu, and the Ladakh region has a ratio of about 55 percent Buddhist to 45 percent Muslim residents.[76] Using the bogey of India's only Muslim-majority state, the Kashmir ruling elite extracted a special status for Kashmir through Article 370 of the constitution. Under this deal, the constitution and laws are not applicable in Kashmir. In addition, people from the rest of India cannot buy property in Kashmir, but Kashmiris can own property in the rest of India.[77] Although Article 370 was meant to be a temporary provision, it is still in effect.

New Delhi's undemocratic means of excluding radical or secessionist leaders from power contributed to Muslim Kashmiris' grievances. However, the religion-based grievances nurtured by the Muslim leaders of Kashmir for several decades comprised the primary ingredient needed for Pakistan to implement the Afghan model of jihad in Kashmir. Starting in the 1980s, this involved setting up *madrassas* or mosques inside Kashmir to instill elements of Wahhabism or Deobandism (an early Indian version of Wahhabism—founded by a group of *Hanafi* Islamic scholars) and a hatred of *infidel* India in the minds of the local Muslim population. This could be accomplished because Kashmir had its own laws and its administration was in the hands of Kashmir valley Muslims, who were known for their sympathy to the cause of political Islam. Just as in Afghan jihad, many Middle Eastern nations were involved in funding this endeavor. Apparently, the goals of the Kashmir jihad are threefold: to cleanse the region of non-Muslims, to use Kashmir as a staging post to destabilize the rest of India, and to merge Kashmir with the greater Islamic world by attaching it to Pakistan.

As a natural first step toward Islamizing Kashmir, the conditions were being created to cleanse the Kashmir valley of its entire Hindu population. Newspapers and mosques in the Kashmir valley openly exhorted Hindu *infidels* to leave Kashmir. Many mainstream mosques posted a list of local *infidel* Hindus to be killed or driven away. Sure enough, with the killings of Hindus increasing and their businesses being destroyed, more than 300,000 Hindu minorities were forced to leave the Kashmir valley in 1989.[78] Many of their abandoned properties have now been illegally appropriated by the Muslim leaders. Below is the story of a Kashmiri Hindu family driven away by political Islamists (note the role played by mainstream mosques):

> Janaki Rani [the mother] was all of 48 years when the family had to flee Kashmir, from their home in [the town of] Delina in Baramullah district. It was in the year 1990 [when Islamic] militancy had begun in the valley. "There was a sudden surge of Islamization. Men I grew up with suddenly started wearing a beard, keeping aloof, frequenting the mosques," he [the son] recalls. Then when the assassination of prominent Kashmiri Hindus started, panic surged inside their home. [He said:] "We

stopped venturing out of our homes, except [when going] to work." The Jammu and Kashmir Liberation Front [a Muslim militant outfit] took out a full-page advertisement in the daily newspaper *Al-Safa*, calling for Hindus to leave the valley within 48 hours. Ultimately, the family's resilience broke. "We had to flee, there were warnings over the loud-speakers in the mosques, asking us to convert or leave. But worst, they asked us, the men, to leave without our womenfolk, who were to stay behind. We could not take that." The family of seven—Janak Rani, her husband, two sons, and three daughters—made their way to [the] safe [Hindu-majority] Jammu [region]. Along the way, Janak Rani's husband died of a heart attack."[79]

Slow to react to the jihad buildup in Kashmir, New Delhi finally struck back forcefully after most Hindus had already been driven out of the Kashmir valley. This conflict almost escalated into an Indo-Pak war in 1989. Since then, Muslim insurgency has spread to other parts of Kashmir. Predictably, indiscriminate killings of Hindu civilians are now under way in the Doda region of the southern part of Kashmir—thirty-five Hindu children, women, and men were massacred by suspected Pakistan-based Lashkar-e-Taiba (LeT) terrorists on May 1, 2006—to create a Hindu exodus.[80]

Kashmir is now held together by several hundred thousand soldiers of the Indian army—a huge drain on India's limited resources. India does not appear to have a long-term plan to deal with political Islam's successful efforts to cleanse the region of non-Muslims. While the ruling Kashmir valley Muslims claim grievances against India, it is pertinent to discuss how they treat non-Muslim areas within Kashmir. There is also the issue of the extent of the grants they extract from the central government in New Delhi.

Indian journalist Arvind Lavakare, a columnist for the well-known Indian news portal Rediff.com, has pointed out in a detailed analysis that until 2005, for almost sixty years, the chief minister of Kashmir came only from Muslim-majority Kashmir valley. Through a pseudo-preference system, Kashmir valley Muslims, who constitute 50 percent of the population, have grabbed about 75 percent of the positions in government, semi-governmental organizations, and educational institutions throughout the state of Kashmir. In Muslim-controlled Kashmir, admissions to educational institutions are not merit-based but are decided preferentially for Muslims. While Jammu and Ladakh contribute over 90 percent to the state's finances, only a small portion of these revenues are spent on the underdeveloped Jammu and Ladakh regions. Since the Kashmir valley is classified as a "disturbed" or insurgency-intensive area, its residents do not pay taxes. This out-of-proportion preference for Kashmir valley Muslims, as well as the almost one-way collection of tax revenues, comes at enormous expense to Hindu-majority Jammu and Buddhist-majority Ladakh.[81] It is important to note that, due to their marginalized status, non-Muslim Kashmiris are unable to counter the ever-expanding political Islamic influence in the region.

Rajeev Srinivasan, another columnist for Rediff.com, notes in an extensive analysis that the Kashmir valley Muslim ruling class has managed to extract enormous no-strings-attached grants, totaling ten times the state's fair share, from New Delhi: "J&K (Kashmir) is the least poor state in the country, with a rate of poverty of about 3.4 percent, compared to 26 percent for India as a whole."[82] These grants constitute economic hemorrhaging of an impoverished India, in addition to the enormous cost of providing security in Kashmir. It must be kept in mind that despite the recent economic resurgence, by and large, India has remained largely poor. For instance, the per capita gross domestic product (GDP) for the year 2007 stands at about $2,600, with 25 percent of the population below the poverty line.[83] By comparison, for China these figures for the same year were $5,400 and 8 percent, respectively.[84]

We note that the Kashmiri Muslims use the bogey of "discrimination" to marginalize non-Muslim Kashmiri residents and they expect India to subsidize their lifestyle. This is a classic behavior of a Muslim population under the grip of political Islam.

The former chief minister of Kashmir, Mufti Muhammad Syeed, is the head of the People's Democratic Party (PDP) that represents jihadist interests in the state. True to the base it represents, the Syeed-led government granted subsidies to the families of killed jihadists, without being challenged by India's central government led by Prime Minister Manmohan Singh.[85] Mr. Singh himself is a big proponent of aiding families involved in terrorism; India probably became the first nation in the world in which families of killed Islamic terrorists are aided both by terror groups and by the government—giving a new meaning to the phrase "terrorism pays."[86]

The push toward further Islamizing Kashmir continued when the Muslim-dominated Kashmir assembly passed a bill in 2007 bringing India's only Muslim-majority state under the ambit of *sharia*.[87] This move is certain to institutionalize extremist hold over the Kashmiri Muslim population and further distance them from non-Muslim Kashmiris. The failure of successive regimes in Delhi rests with their inability to expose Kashmir valley Muslims' exaggerated portrayal of themselves as victims of religious persecution while marginalizing non-Muslim Kashmiris, extracting unfair handouts, and still sponsoring terror.

Amarnath Hindu Temple is located in Kashmir. It has historically attracted a large number of Hindu devotees from the rest of India. It has been a select site of Islamic terrorist attack, due to its religious symbolism, despite extensive security cover provided by the Indian army. This site is managed by Kashmiris and provides employment to a large number of Kashmiri Muslims. In the summer of 2008, the state government led by a Muslim chief minister agreed to transfer about forty acres of barren land nearby to set up temporary shelters for the visiting pilgrims.[88]

However, this land deal was seen as an *infidel* intrusion into the newly "*infidel-free*" land of Islamic Kashmir. Kashmiri mosques were soon at the forefront of the effort to whip up the Kashmiri Muslim passions in order to revoke the land transfer deal. Kashmir saw mass demonstrations by Muslims as a result. As noted earlier, the political interest of jihadists in the state is represented by the PDP.[89] Pressured by its supporters who opposed the land deal, the PDP took itself out of the ruling coalition. Prodded by the weak Singh regime in New Delhi, the state government caved in and revoked the decision on the land transfer. Now, the jihadists are demanding that the Indian army vacate the facilities it uses in Kashmir.[90]

A Hindu backlash in response to the Kashmiri Muslim opposition to the temple project and government bungling led to large-scale and sustained demonstrations in the nearby Jammu region where Hindus are the majority and also elsewhere in India.[91] At the same time, separatist elements in Kashmir led by Syed Ali Geelani of Jamait-e-Islami took control of the Kashmir Muslim opposition to the land deal and redirected it toward "liberation" of Kashmir from India.[92]

Slow to react, by the end of August of 2008, the Indian government saw its options increasingly limited and had to resort to force to quell separatist uprising. The Indian regime was facing a two-front confrontation—with Islamists in Kashmir and Hindu nationalists in Jammu. Finally, the Indian government did another about-face and signed a deal with the Hindus in Jammu to allocate the land for erecting temporary facilities for Amarnath pilgrimage.[93] This victory for the Hindu movement may be the most significant in modern India vis-à-vis Islamic forces, because this is the first time a Hindu-based mass movement stood up to protect its interests.

Now we move on to the Muslim outlook in the rest of India. The Afghan Taliban's ideological underpinnings are said to have come from the Deoband Islamic seminary, located in the town of Deoband, situated ninety miles northeast of New Delhi. The Taliban connection underlines the critical importance played by this seminary in pushing the Indian Muslim population ever more into radicalism. This Wahhabi-influenced Sunni Islamic institution was established in 1866. Over the years it has spread a vast network of *madrassas* under its administrative and ideological guidance all over India, making it the biggest Islamic institution in the country.

Apparently, either through official or *hawala* (illegal or unofficial money exchange) channels, Middle East money and fake Indian currency continue to flow into India and to Islamic radicals. A high-level meeting attended by government officials was convened to address this issue by better tracking the alarming flow of funds into the country.[94] According to an estimate by Indian officials, about $4 billion in fake Indian currency, most likely printed in Pakistan, is in circulation.[95]

Spearheading the jihadist movement in India are descendents of invaders or settlers from the Middle East, who call themselves "Muslim Indians." They are natural allies of Saudi Arabia, Pakistan, and a whole host of other nations trying to complete the violent "conquest" of *infidel* India for Islam.

Terror is one of the advanced stages of a process called jihad buildup. The initial stage involves the indoctrination of Muslim populations. Not just in Kashmir, but in the rest of India too, jihad buildup started in the early 1980s. The Kuwait-based World Association of Muslim Youth and the Saudi Arabia–funded International Islamic Federation of Student Organizations were among the prominent West Asia–based charity organizations involved in this unsavory endeavor. This led to financing a welter of magazines—*Islamic Movement* in Urdu, Hindi, and English; *Iqra* in Gujarati; *Rupantar* in Bengali; *Sedi Malar* in Tamil; and *Vivekam* in Malayalam—that propagated the idea of an Islamic revolution in which India will be transformed to a *sharia*-based Islamic state through jihad.[96]

These magazines increased Muslim exposure to Islamic doctrines and imparted their significance. In the meantime, Indian mosques received funding from the Middle East and many new ones were constructed. With jihadist politics statistically dominating the doctrines (see chapter 2, "Conquest by Design"), it was inevitable that the stage was set in the coming decades for the political Islamic siege of India and escalating terror sponsored by Indian Muslims against their fellow non-Muslim compatriots and the state.

A retired joint director of the Indian Intelligence Bureau Maloy Dhar notes, in his book *Fulcrum of Evil: ISI, CIA, Al Qaeda Nexus*: "It is understood that the Saudi Wahhabi Sunnis and Al Azhar trained purists of Egypt have been using the Pakistani collaborators in spreading militancy amongst Indian Muslims and Muslims of southeast Asia."[97] Also, with the connivance of the local governments, the Indian Muslims working in the Middle East are getting indoctrinated to wage jihad in India. Indian security agencies have implicated some of these individuals in terrorist blasts conducted in the nation.[98]

Still, to mobilize the Indian Muslim population, the expertise of educated Muslims and the continued involvement and inspiration of the clergy is going to be needed. This is where the Student Islamic Movement of India (SIMI) and the

Deoband Islamic seminary come into play. SIMI was founded in 1977 in Aligarh Muslim University in northern India. Historically, Aligarh Muslim University has played a leadership role for the Muslims in British India, as the first university established by Syed Ahmed Khan for Muslims in British-ruled India, dating back to 1875.[99]

Deeply inspired by Mawdudi, the founder of Jamait-e-Islami, SIMI's vision was to make Islam the supreme organizing entity in Muslim social and political life. From a practical perspective, this goal translated into making Indian Muslims more fundamentalist and intent on converting the whole of India into an Islamic state under the rule of *sharia* law through violence.[100] In this context, the Middle Eastern funding to establish magazines directed at Indian Muslim populations can be seen to aid SIMI's goal—that is, the so-called West Asian charities knew exactly what they were doing; they were building up jihad in India!

By the time of SIMI's 1999 convention in the central Indian city of Aurangabad, the ground-level manifestations of this radicalism were only too evident. Many of the speeches delivered by delegates were considered inflammatory and hostile. When twenty-five thousand SIMI delegates met in Mumbai in 2001, at what was to be its last public convention, the organization, emboldened by its growing strength, for the first time called on its supporters to turn to jihad.[101]

SIMI's pro-Taliban stance, including support for the destruction of the Bamiyan Buddhas in the Taliban-ruled Afghanistan, and in the wake of the 9/11 terrorist attacks, anti-US demonstrations in the Indian states of Madhya Pradesh, Uttar Pradesh, Maharashtra, Gujarat, and Rajasthan—and its glorification of Bin Laden prompted the Indian government to impose a ban on it being allowed to operate as an officially registered entity. But despite the ban, SIMI has continued to expand its base among the Indian Muslim populace. SIMI's outlook, growth, and actions have followed along predictable lines. The Indian government claims that despite the ban SIMI pursued subversive activities relentlessly. This has also included giving local support to Pakistan-based radical groups, such as Lashkar-e-Taiba, Jaish-e-Mohammad, or Hizbul Mujahadeen members sent to India to create mayhem and terror.[102]

Due to political pressure (driven by Muslim voting-bloc politics) Indian security agencies often developed a go-slow attitude in dealing with Muslim organizations such as SIMI and overlooked their subversive activities. Another major reason for SIMI's growth has been tacit support by Deoband and Indian Muslim clergy. Indian scholar on Islam Ramashray Upadhyay elaborates:

> The Islamic priestly class condemned terrorism during the All India Anti-Terrorism Conference at Deoband in February last (2008), but instead of condemning the

activities of SIMI some of the speakers defended it and said no court has ever convicted a single member of it while in fact some of the SIMI activists were convicted
by POTA courts in 1996. They also maintained that the case has been blown out of
proportion by the media while the common Muslim students were ignorant of this
organization. Like all the Islamist terrorist outfits, SIMI has also considered the USA
as an enemy of Islam and supported the jihad call of Osama bin Laden against the
"Western Crusader."

The Deoband conference too used the same language of Osama bin Laden
against America. The stand of Deoband on Islamic issues is highly appreciated by
the Sunni Muslims of the country and therefore similarity of its language with
Osama has reduced the chances of isolating SIMI from the Muslim community.
Defense of the SIMI by Islamic clergies is therefore the main reason behind the
growth of SIMI.... In fact, its success in brainwashing a sizable section of even
modern educated Muslim youths in terror ideology was not possible without the
support of the [Muslim] priestly class [in India].[103]

Upadhyay further explores the outlook of the Indian Muslim leadership at the
Deoband "anti-terrorism" conference attended by about ten thousand Indian clerics
and the mainstream Indian media coverage of it:

A close look at the [conference] printed materials including the presidential speech,
speakers' deliberations, and the final declaration suggests that the objective of the
whole exercise was not to combat terrorism but to keep Deoband at a safe distance
from it by projecting Islam as "a religion of peace and mercy" and also to put the
entire blame for terrorism on "anti-Islamic forces," particularly the "tyrant and colonial master of the West." Another agenda of the conference was to defend the Muslims arrested in terrorism-related cases by law enforcing agencies in India. What has
been more worrisome was that instead of a threadbare discussion of the violent face
of terrorism, like the September 11 incident at the World Trade Centre, the attack
on the Indian parliament, train bombings in Mumbai, explosions in crowded markets in Delhi and Hyderabad, and attacks on Hindu temples like Akshardham in
Ahmadabad and Sankatmochan in Varanasi, the conference devoted over eighty
percent of its time to a high-voltage campaign that "Islam is a religion of mercy and
peace" as if this forum was not for discussing terrorism but for propagation of the
faith. Of the remaining twenty percent, ten percent of the time was used in passing
the entire burden on "anti-Islamic forces," particularly "Western Crusaders" and
"Zionists," nine percent on defending the arrested Muslims in terrorist-related cases
by law enforcing agencies as well as putting the blame on the government of India,
and only one percent on denouncing terrorism. The total absence of any discussion

either of the ongoing violence in the name of Islam or of specific terrorist groups like the Taliban, al Qaeda, and others gave an impression that the main concern of the conference was to defend the declining image of the Muslims and not to formulate any strategy to combat terrorism.

The focused attention of the conference was seemingly to erase the adverse image of Dar-ul-Uloom [Deoband Islamic seminary] due to its ideological link with all the prominent terrorist groups without passing any stricture on them or on neighboring countries, namely, Pakistan, known for the mother of all terrorism, and Bangladesh, which provides bases for terrorist training camps.

The conference condemned terrorism as "anti-national" but did not mention Pakistan, which has continuously sponsored terrorism in Kashmir and various other parts of India. It discussed the plight of Muslims in Iraq and Palestine at the hands of "anti-Islamic forces" but did not speak even a word against the continued resurgence of the Taliban along the Pak-Afghan border and its violent activities all over Afghanistan affecting mostly Muslims. The conference asked the Muslims "to spend their lives in the country following Islamic *sharia* and teachings with full confidence." Does it mean that Muslims should launch jihad against the secular laws in India? In support of the Koranic concept of peace, which was the main highlight of the conference, it [the conference communiqué] quoted a number of verses to justify the point but there was no word about the number of verses of the Holy Book quoted by the various authors on the Koranic concept of war.

In his presidential address [Maulana Margoobur] Rahman expressed his grave concern over the destructive action of terrorists and described it as anti-Islamic. However, he neither disclosed the name of any terrorist outfit nor explained the Islamic ideology of Deoband, which is the ideological inspiration for the Taliban and other terrorist groups. Instead he criticized the government for putting the innocent Muslims behind bars. "Now the situation has worsened so far that every Indian Muslim, especially those associated with *madrassas*, who are innocent with a good record of character, are always gripped by the fear that they might be trapped by the administrative machinery anytime. And today countless numbers of innocent Muslims are spending their lives behind bars and are forced to bear many intolerable tortures."

Giving a certificate of innocence to those arrested in terror-related cases suggests that the rector of Deoband does not have faith either in the investigating agencies or in the judiciary. His criticism of the government for maligning the image of Islam and its followers is also not convincing as almost all the political parties either in the government or in opposition are in a mad race to keep the Muslims pleased in order to gain their votes. Defending the role of *madrassas* in guiding the Indian Muslims, he said that in spite of the suffering the community has been facing since independence, they remain faithful to the country and its constitution. He did not elaborate on the suffering of the community, but if he meant its economic backwardness, Deoband is more responsible for their plight since *madrassas* are not imparting modern education, which is the key for economic elevation....

He raised the question of the plight of Muslims but did not discuss anything about its modernization. Since Dar-ul-Uloom cannot provide job opportunities to its graduates, a large number of them are frustrated. He did not even spell out the root cause behind the inhuman acts of terrorism in the name of Islam and the remedy to combat it. He expressed greater concern over "state-sponsored terrorism not only in Palestine, Iraq, and Afghanistan but also in Bosnia and various South American countries," but no such specific concern was shown by him over the killings of Hindus in Kashmir, Pakistan, and Bangladesh and their forced eviction from these countries.

Speaker after speaker parroted the viewpoints expressed by the president and blamed the government for not taking any action against the forces responsible for maligning the image of the *madrassas* and Indian Muslims.... They talked in detail of the killing of Muslims by America in Iraq and by Israel in Palestine but did not refer to the killings of innocent people including Muslims by the terrorists in other parts of the world, particularly India. They devoted more time in campaigning about the Islamic philosophy of peace, justice, and mercy but did not speak a word on the mechanism for implementation of such philosophical speculations to counter terrorism.

A speaker narrated the story of the arrival of the Prophet in Medina and his treaty with the Jews for the establishment of friendly relations and peaceful coexistence between the Muslim and Jewish communities. He, however, did not narrate the extinction of Jews in Medina. Another speaker quoted the Koranic verse— "Allah does not forbid you to deal justly and kindly with those who fought not against you on account of Religion and did not drive you out of your homes" (Surah Mumtahanah 60:8). However, he ignored the plight of Hindus, Christians, and Buddhists at the hands of the followers of Allah in Pakistan, Afghanistan, and Bangladesh, where those helpless and hapless non-Muslim minorities were either forcibly converted to Islam or killed or forced to migrate to India as refugees.

Were they not aware before quoting holy verses that protracted atrocities on the Hindus reduced their population from 22 percent at the time of partition to the nearly 1 percent in Pakistan and from 29 percent to 8 percent in Bangladesh? A digitalized voice of Osama bin Laden calling for the murder of UN Secretary General Kofi Annan and US Iraq Administrator Paul Bremer with ten kilograms of gold as the prize to the assassin does not justify what the speakers propagated during the conference. They described the massive killings of Muslims in Iraq, Afghanistan, and Palestine by Western powers time and again but remained curiously silent on the massacre of Muslims during the regime of fellow Muslim rulers like the late

Saddam Hussein in Iraq and others in Muslim countries like Afghanistan and Sudan.

Unfortunately, no speaker [at the conference] mentioned the name of any [Islamic] terrorist group let alone any condemnation of its violent deeds. Maulana Arshad Madani, the president of Jamait-e-Ulema-e-Hind, known as custodian of Dar-ul-Uloom, used the occasion for criticizing the government of India for its alleged discrimination of Muslims for the last sixty years. He accused President George Bush of being the greatest terrorist in the world but did not speak a word against Osama bin Laden. Similarly, Maulana Mahmood Madani, another senior leader of the Jamait-e-Ulema-e-Hind, while accusing George Bush of being "the world's biggest terrorist," blamed America and other Western powers for "spreading hatred against Muslims and Islam."

"Secular" [Indian] politicians and media widely hailed the declaration of the [Deoband] conference condemning terrorism but they left out the claims of the speakers, who associated the entire burden on Western Imperialism and Zionism as the major factors behind global [Muslim] "terrorism."

"Secular press" had no space to critique the Ulema [clerics] who used the occasion to criticize the alleged hounding of Muslim youth and mounting Islamophobic offensives across the world, including in India, in the name of countering terrorism. However, these issues found wide space in papers mostly read by Muslims to ensure that the followers of Islam may not revise their thinking about Islamist terrorist groups and their supporting countries, Pakistan and Bangladesh. Thus, the role of media in presenting only a one-sided and imbalanced picture [at the conference] was also disappointing.[104]

Finally, in May 2008, Deoband clergy came out with a *fatwa*, or a religious injunction, condemning terrorism. They didn't, as usual, single out any Muslim nation, leader, or group for sponsoring terrorist acts. Instead, subtly America and Israel were identified as the terror perpetrators! The clergy denounced terrorism, while praising jihad.[105] In a nutshell, Indian Muslim clergy were associating only non-Muslim-nations' military responses directed at Muslim states or groups as "terrorism." Any armed response, including terrorism, perpetrated by Muslim groups on non-Muslim states or populations was justified or praised as "jihad"!

One has to wonder whether the February 25, 2008, Deoband conference and the issuance of the *fatwa* were orchestrated as the broad-based clerical sanctioning of jihad directed at India—the necessary precursor to the escalating bomb blasts that started in many Indian cities in July of 2008. This was followed by another two-day conference starting on November 8, 2008, in the Muslim bastion southern Indian city of Hyderabad, attended by about six thousand mostly Deoband-educated clerics from all over India. This conference also endorsed the previous Deoband *fatwa* on "terrorism."[106] These conferences provide unprecedented opportunities for jihadists to network and to coordinate their activities as jihad in India intensifies. It is of interest to know who had funded these very expensive conferences; of particular interest is whether Saudi Arabia was involved in their funding.

Intense and prolonged regressive political preaching is bound to adversely affect the Muslim population; the "supremacy" of Islam and the privilege of being a Muslim are emphasized in sermons, while *infidel*-majority Hindus are degraded. From *Where Indian Muslims Have Gone Wrong* by Aakar Patel, we found the following information:

> A recent poll revealed that just under 90 percent of Mumbai's Muslims, presumably the most progressive in the country, rejected a secular civil code—preferring instead *sharia* law, favoring polygamy, triple *talaq* [Muslim verbal divorce], and Islam's unequal inheritance laws which allow women half as much property as they allow men. The views of most younger and educated Muslims and of women were also the same, in almost the same proportion."[107]

The above data can be seen as representative of the Muslim outlook in all of India, since other data associated with the Muslims in the rest of India are consistent with this. The preference for regressive *sharia* over a modern secular uniform code can be seen as associating with radical ideas at the expense of a moderate outlook. The above poll, taken together with other information, including extremists invariably representing Muslims, does not appear to contradict the inconvenient reality: most Indian Muslims identify with political Islam and, as a result, are not moderates at all. Writing on the role of Muslim institutions in *Islamic Institutions in India—Protracted Movement for Separate Muslim Identity?* Ramashray Upadhyay concludes:

> Instead of providing value-based education based on modern, proper, and scientific teachings to create good citizens for the overall development of Indian society, the Islamic institutions produced clergies for driving the Muslim mass to a medieval era as a part of their movements for Muslim separatism.[108]

The above conclusion implies that even within secular, democratic, and largely Hindu-majority India, there exist no major reformed or moderate versions of Islam. This is not good news for those who insist that it is possible to reform Islam anytime soon. In any case, which (non-existing) Muslim religious institution is going to give its stamp of approval and work toward the reform of Islam?

Former president George W. Bush's March 2006 visit to India was almost exclusively opposed by Indian Muslims, who undercut national interests by demonstrating in favor of pan-Islamism and radicalism and by carrying posters of Osama bin Laden.[109] There were a number of Muslim-Hindu clashes related to this visit. Anti-Bush demonstrations brought into the open the diverging outlook, priorities, and uneasiness of Indian Muslims' dealings with the rest of the population. Here is one example: when in the 1990s hundreds of thousands of non-Muslim Indians were driven out of Kashmir by jihadists, Indian Muslim groups were busy raising funds for displaced Kosovar Muslims, while doing almost nothing to aid their fellow Indians, who were under attack by their religious compatriots. In fact, increasingly, recruitment for the Kashmir jihad was occurring within the rest of India![110]

According to the Indian government, there are more than eight hundred terrorist cells operating with "external support" within the nation.[111] These cells are spread all over India, in locations with a sizable Muslim population. It is important to realize that these cells are a consequence of the deliberate process of jihad buildup that went on unchallenged for decades (see previous pages), spearheaded mainly by Pakistan and Saudi Arabia. The south central Indian city of Hyderabad with a significant concentration of Muslims is suspected to have become a base of terrorist recruitment:

[S]cores of young Muslim men have disappeared from the central Indian city of Hyderabad, suspected of leaving for Pakistan to be trained by the country's Islamist terror groups. As many as 40 potential recruits are reported to have left the city— which has a large Muslim minority—under extremist guidance, while many other young men cannot be traced. Police efforts to track the youths have floundered in the wake of the Mumbai attacks last month. A wall of community silence has protected the activities of teachers and other shadowy figures working inside fundamentalist Islamic schools and mosques. "We have tried to establish where the city's youth has gone but we don't know," said Hyderabad's police commissioner, Prasada Rao. "We know they have gone to other places, either Indian states or abroad. We are checking but the parents or the others will not let us into what's going on."

Two Islamic movements based in Hyderabad, *Darsgah Jihad-o-Shahadath* (DJS) and *Tahreek Tahfooz Shaer-e-Islam* (TTSI), have been accused by local police of allegedly acting as "feeder" groups for militants seeking to recruit armed fighters. They have denied the allegations.... Officials at the DJS madrassahs— religious schools—in Hyderabad were not willing to discuss the disappearance of the city's young men.... DJS carries a message on its website that is explicit about the right of Muslims to resort to violence. "The DJS has trained and are training thousands of Muslim youths to defend themselves and to help, protect, and defend the other Muslims," it states, before adding that once trained in "self defence" members can leave to join any other Muslim group. It continues that "the long term goal of the DJS remains to achieve the supremacy and prevalence of Islam in practice in its entirety".[112]

It is illustrative to analyze the views of a Muslim who was born and bred in India but was educated in the West and who makes a living specializing in foreign affairs. Fareed Zakaria, the well-known author, commentator, and international editor of *Newsweek*, was born to a practicing Muslim family. He describes the Islam he had encountered in India growing up as, "the rich, colorful, pluralistic, and easygoing Islam of my youth."[113] Yet he was oblivious to the reality that in his youthful days, in every Muslim-majority area of South Asia, non-Muslims had been marginalized, were fearful, and were leaving for parts of India with Hindu majorities.

In an interview, Zakaria notes that "[the Indian Muslim] faces discrimination and exclusion. A good part of the problem is their lack of real political power."[114] In another interview, he has taken the line on Kashmir that is often taken by the likes of hard-core Islamists, accusing India of "a military occupation of people [in Kashmir] who do not want to be occupied" and "suppressed popular movements."[115]

Given the nature of jihad waged on India, with a growing and significant support base among the Indian Muslim populace and the unfortunate fate of non-Muslims in *every* Muslim-majority area of South Asia, it would be surprising if Indian Muslims did not face discrimination and exclusion. Muslims are simply feared and distrusted in this part of the world. As discussed earlier, political power for Muslims in South Asia has invariably turned into state-sponsored jihad on non-Muslims. What is also notable is Zakaria's convenient neglect of non-Muslim ethnic cleansing in the Pakistani part of Kashmir and Kashmiri Muslims' widespread support for jihad directed at the Indian state, which resulted in a military crackdown.[116] Pakistan could simply solve the Kashmir conflict by absorbing Muslims from the Indian part of Kashmir and by settling them in the Pakistani part of Kashmir and in the rest of Pakistan. Pakistan should do that; after all, it kicked out most non-Muslims from the portion of Kashmir it controls and from its mainland to India.[117]

Zakaria's apparent inability to identify political Islam's influence in making Muslims advocates of conflict extends to his analysis of Iraq. He blames America for the chaos in Iraq, saying, "We gave them a civil war," when all America did—at an enormous cost to itself—was to try to help Iraqis build a democratic nation.[118]

Using Zakaria's terminology, given the extent of the radicalization among the Muslim populace, Muslim-sponsored terrorism in Britain could be called a "popular movement." Yet, in reality, this is a jihadist movement directed at the destruction of Britain, not much different from the "popular movement" in Muslim-majority Kashmir. If the British government doesn't suppress or neutralize this movement, it will put the future of Britain in jeopardy.

For all his writings on Islamic terrorism, Zakaria either doesn't understand or chooses not to understand the extent of political Islam's manipulation of Muslims and the grave danger it poses to civilization. That Zakaria comes from a Konkani Muslim community in India, who are descendents of Arab traders, should be taken note of.[119]

Zakaria is not alone when it comes to misreading the dynamics of Islam or populations adhering to it. I have noted similar misconceptions when it comes to policy-making for peace in South Asia, especially vis-à-vis the Indo-Pak conflict. In discussing the work of Ambassador Teresita Schaffer of the Center for Strategic and International Studies (CSIS) or scholar Stephen Cohen of the Brookings Institution, I have noted the following:

> Almost none of these scholars appear to have adequately understood the dynamics of Islam that is very intolerant in South Asia—the massive non-Muslim ethnic cleansing conducted in every Muslim majority area of South Asia.... I was among the first to point this out and study the implications of this tragic dynamic of Islamization of South Asia. However, from what I can tell, almost all American scholars specializing in this area have yet to realize this or to understand its implications.... By missing out on this crucial pattern of behavioral dynamics of Islam in South Asia, it seems these scholars have undermined their ability to provide solid policy-making advice to the US government and others.[120]

In this context, it is worthwhile to spend some time discussing the thrust of a work considered definitive on Hindu-Muslim relations in India, by Indian American political scientist Ashutosh Varshney, titled *Ethnic Conflict and Civic Life: Hindus and Muslims in India*.[121] Using the data on Hindu-Muslim riots during the period 1950–55, Varshney's team compared three riot-prone Indian cities—Aligarh, Ahmedabad, and Hyderabad—with three "peaceful" cities having equal Hindu-Muslim population ratios—Calicut, Lucknow, and Surat. In his analysis, Varshney makes the point that cities with developed social, economic, and political integration were less prone to conflict. Such a conclusion shouldn't be surprising; due to the economic interdependence of both communities, they have vested interest in avoiding riots.

What stands out is the role played by mosques in provoking riots. Hindus, unlike Muslims, do not have the system of political sermons delivered to them in temples. Varshney notes that, in Aligarh, the government-funded Aligarh Muslim University, with its Muslim focus (taken to mean that it is allowed to hire a disproportional number of Muslim faculty, give preferential admission to Muslim students, and offer extensive courses in Arabic and Islamic history), plays a significant communal role in the riots. Specifically, its faculty and students have consistently participated in these riots, unlike local colleges with Hindu majorities.

The point missed by Varshney, his supporters, and his critics is that in regions where Muslims are a majority in South Asia, there are hardly any Hindu-Muslim riots—because Hindus have been systematically "cleansed" from these regions. This is the case in Pakistan and in many areas of Bangladesh. In fact, Varshney doesn't even appear to be aware of the data that when Muslims are the majority and control political power in any region of South Asia—without exception—Hindus have been driven out of these regions in large numbers.

But the more fundamental question, not adequately answered by Varshney, is why Muslims engage in riots in the first place in regions where they are a minority. This is a major weakness in his analysis. Hindus driven away from Pakistan, Bangladesh, or even Kashmir valley within India were from the upper echelons of the society, both through education and financial means, and can be considered well integrated into the society; but that didn't save them. However, the Muslim minority in the secular India didn't face these sorts of expulsions. This data and the major role played by mosques and even Muslim-specific universities in these riots give a clear indication that these riots are the symptom of the underlying Muslim frustration of being a minority and not being able to impose their will on the *infidels*. This mind-set can be traced to Islamic doctrines (see chapter 2, "Conquest by Design").

Not surprisingly, escalating terror attacks in India are now increasingly supported by its Muslim population. This escalation is rooted in the increased funding from the Middle East. When an ideology continues to drive Muslims into conflict with Hindus, peace can only be temporary. Indeed, in recent years, "the peaceful cities" of Lucknow in northern India and Surat in western India have seen Hindu-Muslim riots and so has the southern Indian city of Calicut, in 1992. Hence, Varshney's prescription for avoiding Hindu-Muslim riots in India through enhancing links between communities, at best, is to temporarily suppress the symptom of the underlying conflict—and is no long-term solution. Obviously, the long-term solution requires addressing the ideologies that make Muslims so prone to conflict. This is what I am trying to uncover.

Indeed, the core political Islamic strategy for escalating jihad lies in falsely characterizing the Hindu majority as "oppressors" of Indian Muslims through virulent clerical sermons to create hatred of Hindus. This sets the stage for increased confrontation and separation and, eventually, dissolution of the Indian state with a fast-growing Muslim population. As discussed earlier, with most Indian Muslims already under the influence of political Islam, the stage is set for an intensifying jihad.

The arrival of 2006 saw a quantum leap in attacks by suspected Islamists against majority Hindus and their religious institutions and organizations. In Assam, an Indian state bordering Islamic Bangladesh that is reeling from a massive illegal influx of Bangladeshis, a Deoband-educated cleric formed a Muslim party, the Assam United Democratic Front (AUDF), and won many seats in local elections with an all-too-familiar theme—that of addressing Muslim "grievances." One such grievance is the "need" for a separate autonomous region for Muslims in lower Assam (adjacent to Bangladesh).[122] The United Front for the Liberation of Assam, a group funded and sponsored by Islamic Bangladesh and Pakistan, has escalated attacks to drive out "Indians." This is translated to mean Hindus from the rest of India, and the effort is designed to speed up the process of Islamization of the state and the northeast region. One of the biggest serial blasts occurred in Assam in October of 2008.[123] In its latest intelligence, American think tank Stratfor forecasts that "New Delhi is facing a 'bleak situation' [in the Indian northeast] in which the ISI's [Inter-Services Intelligence, Pakistan] maneuvers and Bangladesh's political troubles are sure to further constrain India's ability to dig itself out of the [Islamic] militant trap that Pakistan has set for India with the help of Bangladesh."[124]

It is not unusual for Muslim mobs to become violent after fiery Friday sermons in Indian mosques. In almost all these instances, public property, law enforcement, or the majority Hindu community bears the brunt of this violence. In India's largest state, Uttar Pradesh, whose Muslim population is about 20 percent of the total, clerics overwhelmingly rejected attempts in 2002 to introduce job-oriented state-financed modern education in about twenty thousand *madrassas*.[125] Such a religious configuration creates and sustains a base for terror. Indeed, an Indian Intelligence official admitted in 2006 to the Indian Internet newsmagazine *Newsinsight*: "[W]hat has exceptionally moved the government is that UP [the state of Uttar Pradesh near New Delhi] is becoming a big Lashkar (LeT) [terror] base."[126] There is widespread Indian Muslim clerical resistance to expelling illegal immigrants from Islamic Bangladesh. This resistance fits in with the idea of enhancing the Islamic thrust into India.

In a statement that shocked even officials of the state health department, Ahmad

Hasan, the family planning minister of Uttar Pradesh, urged Muslim women to produce as many healthy children as they want, stating that the state government would give Rs 1,000 (about $25, a big sum by Indian standards) toward the care of each child.[127] Notably, Muslim leaders have been taking strategic cabinet positions in order to carry out their jihadist agenda; unfortunately, these agendas are often diametrically opposed to what is needed. This is seen almost without exception in India. In Kerala, a southern Indian state where Muslims are a minority, a Muslim party kept the education cabinet position in the ruling coalition governments for decades to promote Muslim and Islamic interests almost exclusively at the expense of others. Kerala academic C. Issac has stated: "In all the 25 years the Muslim league followed the policy of filling up of all posts in the educational department with Muslims." Arabic (not an indigenous language) was promoted at the expense of indigenous Sanskrit. Muslims were appointed exclusively as engineers in the public works department.[128] It is no stretch to say that one of the rare nationalist Muslims in a position of power was former president Abdul Kalam, who was financially helped by Hindus in his younger days and who as a result has kept away from the pan-Islamic agenda.

Fundamentalist Muslim pressure against the Indian government is intensifying. A staunch supporter of the Afghan Taliban and a top Indian cleric Shahi Imam Bukhari, representing a coalition of Indian Muslim clerics, demanded across-the-board preferences for Muslims at a meeting with Prime Minister Singh on April 18, 2006. He also issued a veiled threat: "We do not want to chart a different path, but would be forced to do so if our demands are not met."[129] This is also the man who has proclaimed at least once before: "We were rulers here [in India] 800 years. By God willing, we shall return to power here once again."[130]

With Muslims constituting only about 15 percent of the population, in comparison to the Hindu majority's 80 percent, and due to Muslim underrepresentation in decision-making positions that require education, efficient and fast Islamization of India has not occurred. This has frustrated jihadists. Given their inclination toward political Islam, Indian Muslims are unlikely to embrace modern education wholeheartedly anytime in the near future; hence, a different way has to be found. If across-the-board job preferences could be enacted for Indian Muslims, including positions in military and law enforcement agencies, the goal of placing jihadists and jihadist sympathizers in positions of influence and power could be achieved.

Muslim underrepresentation in professional jobs is most likely due to discouragement by clerics regarding modern education and joining the mainstream. Hence, instituting preferences for Muslims does nothing to address this self-induced deficiency. The well-rounded education deficiency of Muslims, it can be argued, is a must for clerics in order to control Muslim masses and channel their energies toward the conquest of unbelievers. With Pakistan and Bangladesh already standing out as a 25 percent permanent and almost exclusive preference of land, wealth, and opportunities for Muslims (as a result of the partitioning of British-ruled India in the name of Islam in 1947, with 25 percent of the original land mass forming Pakistan and Bangladesh) and most non-Muslims from these regions already driven away to present-day India, it is hard to justify further preferences for Indian Muslims. If any justification can be given at all, it is clearly non-Muslim Indians who need preferences in India.

Islamists see proportional Muslim preferences in jobs and education as part of an integral strategy to extend Islam's boundaries. A proportional Muslim preference, given the Muslim population growth rate of over 1.5 times the majority Hindu or non-Muslim growth rate, is indeed a convenient way of marginalizing non-Muslims in the long run.[131] Unfair preference for Indian Muslims takes wealth away from the deserving majority and others, granting them instead to undeserving Muslims. Under this scheme, even the Muslims who choose to focus on jihad instead of academics will receive taxpayer-funded education and jobs through preference. The result is an India with an increasingly poor and illiterate majority, whose Muslim population will be wealthier, better placed, and sympathetic to Islamists. A case in point: it was noted in this section that the jihadist movement in Kashmir strengthened over the years through an unfair pseudo-preference system in favor of Kashmir valley Muslims.

Omar Khalidi has interesting credentials for an American Muslim scholar of Indian origin. Khalidi obtained his doctorate in 1994 from the University of Wales in Islamic studies. He is currently on staff at the Agha Khan Institute at Massachusetts Institute of Technology. Khalidi is relatively unique among South Asian Muslims in that he understands the importance of Muslims obtaining political power, as well the role of modern education and occupying decision-making administrative positions in the society. While such a goal can be seen as a normal aspiration of any community activist, his one-sided portrayal and selective use of data to favor his Muslim community at the expense of others is notable for a scholar. Indeed, Islamic doctrines encourage Muslims to deceive (*Taqiyya*) unbelievers as part of waging jihad.[132]

In his writings, he has consistently portrayed Indian Muslims as being victimized, attacked, and discriminated, while saying little or nothing about the ongoing jihad in South Asia—which includes massive non-Muslim ethnic cleansing conducted with the active support of Muslims. Khalidi clearly understands the need to reach out to non-Muslim Indians and to create a feeling of guilt about the dismal state of Indian

Muslims in order to extract unfair concessions that would eventually doom these non-Muslims.

Khalidi is a proponent of reconfiguring districts in many Indian states to create "compact Muslim zones" where Muslim culture and rights could be "safeguarded."[133] It doesn't matter to him, as some have pointed out, that India has more than safeguarded Muslim interests at a constitutional level, even at the expense of social cohesiveness and national security.[134] Looking at this suggestion from a jihadist angle is revealing: Khalidi is devising new ways by which Muslims can achieve political power within certain areas in a secular and democratic India. This is a clever ploy. As pointed out earlier, in every Muslim-majority area of South Asia, including ones within India, non-Muslims have been marginalized and ethnically cleansed in a massive way. Also, once Muslims in these regions achieve power, the regions have become jihad bases for further destabilizing India.

Khalidi published a book in 2005 titled *Muslims in Indian Economy*.[135] This book discusses the shortcomings of Muslims in India—the lack of proportional representation in government, private jobs, law enforcement agencies, the armed forces, and education, as well as the prevalence of poverty and illiteracy. The blame was squarely placed on the majority Hindu community and the government. An objective analysis would have concluded otherwise: most Indian Muslim problems, including the ones under discussion, are self-inflicted. Besides, most Indian Muslims appear to be under the spell of extremists. Since India is currently being targeted by neighboring Islamic nations for conquest, and as these nations are finding ready recruits among Indian Muslims, no sane government could afford the luxury of proportional representation of Muslims in law enforcement and in the armed forces.

In the category of "other workers" listed in the 2001 Indian census report, Muslims enjoyed a 49.1 percent representation, while the Hindu majority had only a 35.5 percent share. Thus, a higher percentage of Muslims are in these kinds of jobs as compared to majority Hindus. In another category of household industry workers, Muslim representation was 8.1 percent—double the national average of 4.2 percent (and only 3.2 percent for majority Hindus). These statistics are indicative of Muslims shunning education and embracing low-skill professions. This implies that the bulk of Muslims who drop out of school seek gainful employment and start earning at a younger age.[136] Another independent study by the National Council of Applied Economic Research published in the Indian newspaper *Economic Times* found that "Hindus and Muslims are not only very close when it comes to average household income, expenditure, and savings, they match each other even in terms of ownership of select consumer goods."[137] The conclusion that follows is that Muslims in a largely impoverished India are economically comparable to Hindus, once their reluctance to embrace modern education is taken into account.

Yet for Prime Minister Manmohan Singh's United Progressive Alliance, which was elected to power through a Muslim voting bloc controlled by jihadists, Khalidi's book had the "ingredients" necessary to reverse the "injustice" done to Indian Muslims. Islamist interests in this regime are well served by the presence of several Muslim cabinet ministers. The ruling regime established a committee headed by retired justice Rajinder Sachar to produce a report largely based upon Khalidi's work.

Not surprisingly, the Sachar Committee, stocked with Muslims and led by Rajinder Sachar, who has supported the ceding of Muslim-majority Kashmir from India through "self-determination,"[138] called for a sweeping and far-reaching system of giveaways allotted to Muslims, from preferred student admissions in Indian elite schools to job allotments.[139] The committee called for allotting an increased number of loans to Muslims and for evaluating the contents of school texts, presumably to ensure that Muslims and Islam are portrayed in the best manner possible and to make the unbelievers least prepared to counter jihad. On one of the most important national interest issues, that of Kashmir, Sachar's views are similar to that of Pakistan's and many other Indian Islamists. That the ruling Singh regime would convene a commission consisting of individuals who may neither have national interests at heart nor are likely to have a neutral (and therefore, objective) outlook toward Muslims should be noted.

A coordinated jihadist pressure was following through. In a significant development, after the tabling of the Sachar report, Muslim parliamentarians cut across party lines to hand over a wish list of sorts. It called for establishing exclusively Muslim schools, colleges, and professional institutions across the nation. In addition, the parliamentarians demanded two hundred thousand scholarships, most of which would be funded through taxes collected from struggling and law-abiding non-Muslim Indians (most tax revenues come from the salaried class and big business in India, staffed or owned mostly by non-Muslims).[140]

With a per capita income of just $530 dollars per year (based on 2003 figures), Indians are among the most impoverished people on the planet. A 2006 family health survey conducted in India found that 46 percent of its children under the age of three were underweight, even surpassing 28 percent for children under the age of five in sub-Saharan countries. Anemia, a condition reflecting malnutrition, was found among 79 percent of Indian children in the six- to thirty-five-months age group, up from 74 percent only seven years ago.[141] The extent of malnutrition is such that nearly two million Indian children every year—that is, about six thousand children every day—die from it.[142] Yet, as a result of the Islamist siege of the country, the regimes in power are giving away exclusive Muslim-specific subsidies at the expense of the taxpayers, such as the one for hajj trips to Saudi Arabia. The 2009 budget has earmarked a whopping $130 million for the airfare part of the hajj subsidies alone![143]

That the elected Muslim leaders in India would make such an unconscionable demand shouldn't be surprising. Sermons by Muslim clergies are designed to unfairly put the blame for self-induced Muslim ills on the beleaguered majority. Indeed, Indian Muslim leaders are making their intentions increasingly transparent. Indian security analyst B. Raman notes in an article:

> A Delhi-based intellectual who attended the meeting convened by one of the ministries of the government of India to discuss the implementation of the Sachar Committee report on the condition of Muslims in India said that at the meeting some Muslim leaders threatened that there would be more jihadi terrorism in India if the report was not implemented in toto.[144]

Having managed to market the flawed idea successfully—with no entity of influence countering the flawed analysis behind the Sachar report and Khalidi's book—that Muslims in India are facing "injustice," the die was cast. Faced with the prospect of mass demonstrations and full-fledged terrorism that would result from fiery Friday sermons all over Indian mosques, exhorting Muslims to rise up against "injustice," Manmohan Singh's regime, propped up by jihadists, has predictably played into their hands—when this regime decided to implement all of the recommendations of the Sachar report.[145]

With Muslim leaders controlling the Minority Affairs ministry, it is all too easy to issue circulars to central government employers to increase Muslim representation—a key recommendation of the Sachar report. Since January 2007, through circulars, this ministry has managed to increase Muslim recruitment to about 20 percent in two paramilitary forces.[146] These forces are used to quell internal disturbances and guard the nation's infrastructure against sabotage. As a result of this Muslim reservation scheme, in just one year after its implementation, Muslim employment in central government shot up significantly when the minority representation increased by about 25 percent—from 6.9 percent to 8.7 percent![147] Also, in what may be seen as a reckless decision by the Singh regime with national security implications, the regime allowed accelerated Muslim recruitment in the Indian armed forces in a substantial manner (incredibly, many thousands from the Kashmiri Muslim population, which has a strong track record

record of sympathy for jihad directed at India). As a result, in just one year, Hindu representation in the armed forces declined from 94.5 to 91.1 percent.[148] To summarize, the infiltration of Indian institutions by potential Islamists and jihadists has occurred at an unprecedented level during the last few years of the Singh-Gandhi regime.

The Manmohan Singh regime has even gone to the extent of instituting the Muslim claims of marginalization (the core grievance strategy of jihadists), by introducing a chapter, "Muslims and Marginalisation" in a Class-VIII Social Sciences textbook. It speaks about how the Muslims have not received proper benefit in the social and economic development of the country.[149]

Political Islamists are extracting their pound of flesh at every opportunity available. The summer of 2008 saw the Left pull out of the coalition government, making the Manmohan Singh–led regime a minority in the Indian parliament. Majlis-e-Ittehadul Muslimeen, a local party in southern India representing a Muslim-dominated constituency, extracted a promise of an additional $1.2 billion to establish "four centers of the Aligarh Muslim University and Maulana Azad National Urdu university" for its support of the minority regime in New Delhi.[150] Recall that Aligarh Muslim University can be seen as the intellectual base of jihad in India.

In summary, the Sachar Committee's unfair and unjustified recommendations had the ingredients—by design—to achieve sinister ends politically and undermine the majority in India. This is a sophisticated form of jihad waged on an unsuspecting population.

There is a growing impression among majority Hindus that with Indian democracy under siege by political Islam, justice will not be served and their interests not protected. The most violent and early manifestation was expressed in 2002 when Hindu devotees in a train compartment were burned alive by a Muslim mob in Godhra in the western Indian state of Gujarat. In the ensuing riots, Hindu mobs retaliated by taking law into their own hands, resulting in scores Muslims and Hindus killed.[151]

With Islamists appearing to control the Muslim voting bloc, and with the Hindu-majority vote divided, most parties are finding themselves having to placate political Islam. According to Newsinsight.net: "[E]xcept the BJP (considered a Hindu nationalist party) terrorist links are showing up in leaders connected to several mainline parties."[152] Manmohan Singh's Congress Party, which was indirectly shown by India's own intelligence agency to be infiltrated by jihadists, has taken a number of steps within the past three and a half years to placate Islamists. India's antiterrorism law, Prevention Of Terrorist Activities Act (POTA), was rescinded, because it was considered "anti-Muslim."[153] The Indian Supreme Court's verdict to identify and expel illegal immigrants from Bangladesh was circumvented, since its proposal was considered too troublesome for Bengali-speaking Indian Muslims.[154] Clearly, the ruling Congress-led regime was putting political expedience ahead of the rule of law, national security, and governance.

For years now, Indian democracy has been caving in to the effective Muslim voting bloc politics of jihadists. Successive Indian regimes have been unable to take steps to resettle more than three hundred thousand Hindus driven out of the Muslim-majority Kashmir valley. A Muslim minister in the Uttar Pradesh (UP) cabinet issued a *fatwa* to kill the creators of the now-well-known Danish cartoons that lampooned prophet Muhammad.[155] Even though this was in violation of the constitution he had sworn to uphold, no action was taken against him, presumably because he has a wide following among local Muslims. The icing on the cake was a 2005 unanimous resolution passed by the southern Indian state of Kerala's elected assembly that called for the release of Abdul Nasser Madani, jailed in neighboring state Tamilnadu's prison. A proven hardcore Islamist, the prime suspect accused in terrorist bombings, and the founder of the People's Democratic Party, Madani has a large following among Kerala's 26 percent Muslim voting bloc.[156]

Prime Minister Singh seemed to outdo even jihadists for the cause of political Islam when he stated in December 2006: "We will have to devise innovative plans to ensure that minorities, particularly the Muslim minority, are empowered to share equitably in the fruits of development. They [Muslims] must have the first claim on resources."[157] Sonia Gandhi, the Congress Party president and Singh's boss, went a step further. She wrote a letter as part of a 2007 election campaign in the northern Indian state of UP, specifically pleading to over fifteen thousand Muslim leaders, including clerics, in the state to "help me generously to fight against caste and communalism [read majority Hindus, already targeted by jihadists] so that I can build a society of your dreams."[158] With most clergy in UP representing political Islam, this is nothing less than a promise to work for a jihad-sponsoring Islamic India!

Hindu temples do not stage political sermons by religious leaders, unlike most other religions in India. The overall Hindu literacy rate is only about 60 percent and tens of millions are impoverished.[159] The extent to which the Hindu majority is undermined and discriminated against by its own government is revealed through the following statistics. During the five-year period from 1997 to 2002, the overwhelmingly Hindu-majority southern Indian state of Karnataka was ruled by a Congress Party–led regime. In this period revenue collected from more than a quarter million Hindu temples was controlled by the ruling regime, unlike mosques or churches (that were left to manage their own revenue collection, which included huge sums from abroad).

In 1997, of the total revenue of $12 million collected from Hindu temples, about 9 percent was used as a subsidy for hajj trips (i.e., a round-trip airfare plus expenses from India to Saudi Arabia to visit Muslim holy sites) for local Muslims and the funding of *madrassas*, and 6 percent was allotted for church maintenance. But only 30 percent of this temple revenue was used for their upkeep and maintenance, while another 44 percent was allocated for rural women development. By 2002, the hajj and *madrassa* subsidy took out a whopping 70 percent of the total temple revenue, and the temple upkeep and maintenance share dropped to 15 percent, while church maintenance more than doubled to 15 percent—and there was no money left for social programs for the poor, let alone the Hindus. As a result, five thousand temples have already been shut down due to a lack of maintenance.[160]

In terms of sheer percentages, according to the 2001 census, Hindus, Muslims, and Christians constitute 84 percent, 12 percent, and 2 percent, respectively, of Karnataka's population.[161] Yet, while the literacy rates of Hindus and Muslims are comparable in Karnataka, they are much lower than the Christians' in the state.[162] As we will see later, the much higher Christian literacy rate is due to the disproportional number of education institutions controlled by the church and to certain provisions in the Indian constitution that allow even state-funded minority-controlled institutions to discriminate in favor of their religious compatriots. This is clearly the case of the Indian state practicing religious apartheid on the majority. In fact, this is a case of robbing the majority in order to unwittingly advance jihadism in India, by driving Indian Muslims into extremism through subsidized hajj trips to Wahhabi-ruled Saudi Arabia and through *madrassa* funding.

As mentioned in the previous paragraph, some provisions of the Indian constitution are stacked against the majority, while aiding jihadists and others. The constitution and the Indian court system were modeled after the British system that remained after 1947. Even then, due to a dismal literacy rate, it can be argued that the young nation did not have much of an intellectual base from which to draft a robust and functional constitution.

Article 30 of India's constitution confers special status to religious minorities. The term minority refers to a group's status as it relates to the whole of India—for example, by this standard Muslims are considered a minority in Kashmir, even though they are the majority there and hold the reins of power; Hindus are considered a majority in all of India, even in Kashmir, irrespective of their relatively smaller number in the region. As a community enslaved for almost six hundred years, first by the Muslim invaders and later by the British colonizers, the majority Hindus in India obviously lacked the ability to protect their interests at the time of India's independence in 1947. The majority community leaders did not realize that it was their own community that needed protection, especially from minorities who represent the remnants of their past masters—namely, Muslims and Christians. Yet, not knowing any better, in what appears to be an act of majority magnanimity, the majority leaders gave minority-only preferences through Article 30 that have formed a platform for the minorities to marginalize the majority.

> Article 30 of the constitution of India defines [the] rights of [a] minority to establish and administer educational institutions.... [T]he minority community may reserve up to 50 percent of the seats [student, enrollments, and staff or faculty employment opportunities] for the members of its own community in an educational institution established and administered by it even if the institution is getting aid from the State.[163]

Below are samples of taxpayer-funded Muslim/Christian-controlled educational institutions that give preferential employment in staff/faculty positions and in student admissions to minorities. These samples are in general representative of minority-controlled or -operated educational institutions in India. No such preferences are given to Hindu-controlled taxpayer-funded educational institutions. This discrimination is sanctioned by Article 30.

Taxpayer-funded Muslim institution in India	Muslim faculty percentage	Local Muslim population percentage[164]
Jamia Millia Islamia University, New Delhi	88[165]	12
Aligarh Muslim University, Aligarh	90[166]	19
New College, Chennai	84[167]	6

Taxpayer-funded Christian institution in India	Christian faculty percentage[168]	Local Christian population percentage[169]
American College, Madurai	66	6
Union Christian College, Aluva	83	19
St. Xavier's College, Mumbai	42	1

These preferential positions also extend to student admissions in taxpayer-funded schools and colleges. For instance, Muslim-controlled Jamia Hamard University in New Delhi can allow up to 50 percent of its admission to be reserved for Muslim students.[170] St. Stephen's College in New Delhi, a missionary-controlled elite Christian institution, now has 50 percent of its enrollments reserved for Christians.[171]

Education provides not only critical opportunities for economic well-being and personal development but also empowerment. The religious apartheid practices permitted by Article 30 of India's constitution have devastated the majority community in certain regions of India by marginalizing their educational opportunities. Indian academic C. Issac has analyzed below the impact of Article 30 in the southern Indian state of Kerala, where the minority population percentages are substantial (the Christian and Muslim minorities together constitute almost 50 percent of the population there). Article 30 has given minorities in Kerala legal power to discriminate and to regulate educational access at the expense of the taxpayers:

> The education is one of the major sectors where the organized strength of the minorities in Kerala [where Christians and Muslims constitute around 19% and 25%, respectively] is used in a covert manner. In this sector the majority [Hindu] community as well as the government together control only 11.11 percent, on the other hand, the church controls 55.55 percent and Muslim religious organizations 33.33 percent of all institutions. At present the professional education sector of Kerala is almost under the full control of the minorities. About 12,000 engineering enrollments and 300 medicine enrollments are in the minority institutions and they are fully controlling the admissions. At present 60 percent of the enrollments in paramedical courses are controlled by the organized minority religious leadership.... In this situation the successive governments are functioning as mere onlookers.[172]

The local government in Kerala continued to make decisions unfairly favorable to Muslims, by allotting, in 2008, exclusive scholarships to Muslim girls and pensions to *madrassa* teachers. These decisions were recommended by a committee headed by the Muslim Kerala cabinet minister Paloli Mohammed Kutty.[173] These schemes to reserve enrollment for minority students and preferentially hire minorities in taxpayer-funded staff positions may be in violation of Articles 23 and 26 of the United Nations' Universal Declaration of Human Rights to which India is a signatory.[174] Specifically, the right to "free choice" of employment mentioned in Article 23 is violated by an unfair denial of employment opportunities for the Hindu majority in minority-controlled and taxpayer-funded educational institutions in India. A similar argument applies regarding the "equal accessibility" of educational opportunities mentioned in Article 26 for majority community students.

> Article 23 (relevant section): Everyone has the right to work, to free choice of employment, to just and favorable conditions of work and to protection against unemployment.
>
> Article 26 (relevant section): Everyone has the right to education. Education shall be free, at least in the elementary and fundamental stages. Elementary education shall be compulsory. Technical and professional education shall be made generally available and higher education shall be equally accessible to all on the basis of merit.

Christian missionaries in India have a history of serving the community by controlling a disproportionate number of hospitals and educational institutions. But they also have a tradition of aggressive proselytizing activities. Article 30 of the Indian constitution gives missionaries an unfair advantage; a large part of an impoverished majority is easier to proselytize than an empowered one whose members know how to protect their interests.

With churches or missionaries controlling over forty thousand educational institutions in India that are most likely supported by taxpayers, these unfair practices of preferential treatment to Christians are denying the empowerment of millions of Hindu children, youths, and adults every year in one of the most impoverished nations in the world.[175] The figure of millions can be arrived at by assuming a conservative number of at least fifty Hindu children and adults being denied admission and employment, respectively, every year due to their religion in a Christian-controlled education institution, and instead, the opportunities are unfairly given to less deserving Christians. These unfair denials of the right to employment and education constitute violations of Articles 23 and 26 of the Universal Declaration of Human Rights. The sheer size and scale of these human rights violations by the Church in India make them egregious.

The egregious human rights violations of the Church in developing nations in order to facilitate the political agenda of its flock is neither surprising nor is it unprecedented. In the recent past in the white-ruled South Africa, the Afrikaner church supported racist apartheid policies of the ruling minority regime.[176] This contrasts with the Church's outlook in developed democracies where, by and large, it acts as a strong sponsor of human rights.

Having a very high percentage of the Muslim faculty in Muslim-controlled but taxpayer-funded institutions is consistent with the intent to conquer India by marginalizing *infidels*. This institutionalized marginalizing of the majority community through selective implementation of Article 30 and the practical effect of Sachar committee recommendations discussed earlier will continue to act to weaken India's ability to counter jihadist efforts in the coming years and decades.

Many advanced democracies have enacted laws to discourage discrimination. The United States enacted the Civil Rights Act of 1964 precisely to penalize discrimination of any kind and to adhere to the Universal Declaration of Human Rights. Title VII of the act prohibits employment discrimination on the basis of race, color, religion, sex, or national origin.[177] However, the affirmative action program in the United States was instituted to correct for the past discrimination that has resulted in the underrepresentation of certain minorities, such as blacks. In India, Muslims and Christians were part of the privileged ruling class during Mughal and British rule. In addition, the Muslims already have a permanent 25 percent reservation of land, wealth, and opportunities in the form of Pakistan and Bangladesh (these nations were formed of 25 percent of the original British-ruled Indian land mass). Hence it is hard to justify preferences for Christians and Muslims in India. It can be argued that having been the community discriminated against in the past by alien rulers, perhaps the majority Hindus need some type of affirmative action protection in India.

The Hindu caste system consists of the upper caste (in traditional terms, people belonging to priestly and warrior professions), the lower caste (business and farmer professions), the scheduled caste (no profession, but serve the upper and lower castes), and the scheduled tribal (people making a living in the forests). Traditionally, a person born to a caste has to remain in that caste. In the order of privilege, the upper caste occupies the top stop, followed by the lower caste, and finally the scheduled caste and tribal.

Sections of lower-caste Hindus and what are called scheduled caste and scheduled tribes have some form of affirmative action programs to aid their development. But even with much help, they do not stand a chance against Article 30–driven apartheid practices, as seen in Kerala. However, the upper-caste Hindus are fully exposed to religious apartheid practices—and for all practical purposes, they are not covered by affirmative action programs in India. Due to these practices, it has now become very difficult for upper-caste students to get admission into good colleges or get governmental jobs upon graduation.

The United States Commission on International Religious Freedom (USCIRF) was created in response to the International Religious Freedom Act of 1998 to monitor the status of freedom of thought, conscience, and religion or belief abroad, as defined in the Universal Declaration of Human Rights and related international instruments, and to offer independent policy recommendations to the president, the secretary of state, and the Congress.[178] The commission produces annual reports covering practices that violate religious freedom around the world. In these annual reports, the religious apartheid practices in India are not mentioned at all. However, violence involving minorities such as Muslims is covered, but without the overall context of the Islamic conquest underway in South Asia.

I brought the issue of religious apartheid practices in India and the process of Islamic conquest of South Asia to the attention of both the USCIRF and the US state department but with unsatisfactory results. There is considerable disbelief on the part of these federal agencies that the Hindu majority, constituting 80 percent of the Indian population and being a powerful part of the political process, can't protect its own interests or that it could be marginalized. In a series of e-mail exchanges with me, USCIRF commissioner Preeta Bansal, although not speaking officially on behalf of the commission, claimed, even after receiving extensive amounts of data, including the spending patterns for revenues from Hindu temples: "[T]here is no evidence of general political system dysfunction that you have cited or evidence of the inability of the Hindu majority in India to protect its interests."[179] Furthermore, according to the commissioner:

> [E]ven if there remain many shortcomings in the practice of Indian democracy, those concerns are likely better addressed by other bodies. The charge of the Commission is to focus on the most systematic and egregious violations of religious freedom around the world—usually focusing on killings, torture, and the like—committed by or with the acquiescence of state actors. Not all acts of societal discrimination even if directed to a religious minority (much less to a population comprising an approximate 85% majority) will elicit public action or response of the Commission.[180]

Can a Hindu parent expect his/her sons and daughters, even if they are well qualified, to receive a college education in the Indian state of Kerala? Realistically, they stand a much lower chance, unless they convert to Islam or Christianity. There is no question that decimation of Hinduism is likely in Kerala; it's only a matter of time. Ironically, it is due to the discriminatory policies enacted by a secular and democratic state. Given the current trends, minority population percentages are expected to increase in the coming decades, further amplifying the devastating impact of religious apartheid in India.

There is a scientific basis to expect the worst for the future of Hinduism in India as long as religious discrimination practices sanctioned by Article 30 of the Indian constitution remain and an equivalent of the American Civil Rights Act of 1964 is missing. In a 1971 publication titled *Dynamic Models of* Segregation,[181] Nobel Prize–winning economist Thomas Schelling showed that small prejudice-induced racial preference leads to total segregation.[182] Translated to the discussion here, Article 30, along with the control of a disproportional number of educational institutions (over 40,000), can be seen as generating a discrimination-induced religious preference in favor of proselytizing Christianity in India.[183] In the long run, this preference would mean conversion of Hindus to Christianity—and eventually, Hinduism's decimation in India. As suggested by Schelling's theory, once the cycle of conversion-discrimination starts, it has a self-sustaining momentum. This is why early intervention to stop Article 30–induced discrimination of the majority is a must.

The northeast Indian states of Nagaland and Mizoram had less than a 1 percent Christian population (and the rest were either Hindus or Buddhists) at the beginning of the past century. However, by the 1991 census year, the Christian populations in these two states had increased to almost 90 percent.[184] The key factors behind the transformation were that the population consisted of mostly uneducated tribal caste and the missionaries were the pioneers in establishing and controlling most of the educational institutions—and they were free to discriminate in favor of Christians. Christianization of India as a whole has not occurred at this fast pace because the Hindu population in the rest of India has always consisted of an educated component. Still, the implication of Schelling's theory does not bode well long term for the Hindus in the rest of India.

In their response to these apartheid practices, the likes of the USCIRF, Commissioner Bansal, or the officials of the US State Department have shown an inability to process new emerging trends and adjust policy recommendations accordingly. We know from the experience of the 9/11 attacks that problems are best resolved at the initial stage; by letting them grow, they evolve into unmanageable ones. And it is the egregious ones that are usually the most entrenched—and as a result, the most difficult to address—be it Pakistan's treatment of its minorities or Saudi Arabia's religious intolerance.

In the name of maintaining social harmony and due to Muslims' sensitiveness, Indian media has taken a politically defensive stand on political Islam. Unfortunately, this has led to an unprepared nation standing as the world's worst victim of prolonged domestic terrorism (besides Iraq).[185] But Indian Muslim communities suffer from no such inhibitions; political sermons are the norm in Indian mosques and *madrassas*, as are inflammatory accusations against the Hindu majority and the government. The newspapers, including the ones published in Urdu (an Arabic script–based South Asian language mostly spoken by the south Asian Muslims)[186] have also played a significant role in promoting the views of regressive clergies.[187]

Although there has been considerable wealth creation in India during recent years, thanks to burgeoning software industries and call-center positions, the poor in most Indian villages and towns have not seen a share of this wealth. This is in part due to escalating expenses related to battling political Islam–inspired terrorism and subsidizing the Muslim-majority Kashmir; these expenses take up a considerable portion of India's scarce resources. Local governments, and even private and public corporations, are also saddled with extra security-related expenses. Indeed, India is racking up huge budget deficits—the combined 2005 state and federal budget deficit was running at 9 percent of the gross domestic product (GDP).[188] In comparison, China had a budget deficit of less than 1 percent for the year 2005.[189]

In the Indian government's estimation, at least $150 billion is needed over the next ten years to develop India's inadequate infrastructure.[190] Nonetheless, soon after coming to power in November 2004, Prime Minister Manmohan Singh announced a $5.3 billion four-year development and reconstruction package for Kashmir.[191] To put this in perspective, India's annual defense budget in 2004 dollars was about $17.5 billion.[192] The Muslim-controlled Kashmir government and legislature, with a track record of sympathy for political Islam, has a history of not using development money wisely. Also, these grants to Kashmir come at the expense of the rest of India, where most non-Muslims live. People in the rest of India, who pay most of India's taxes, need investments to improve the infrastructure for job creation.

While the Indian population has increased by about 200 million in the last twenty years, the official percentage of the population who live below poverty line has dropped only from about 33 percent to about 26 percent.[193] Even this incremental progress may be going away. Since the summer of 2008, for the first time in many years, India has been hit with a high inflation rate of about 7 percent. The inflation is not just confined to food, transportation, and fuel prices alone. There is a genuine pressure on wages, and the shortage of skilled labor has pushed up wage costs significantly. Deficiency in governance, credible fiscal policy, basic educational standards, agricultural productivity, and infrastructure are all dimming its growth prospects, in an increasingly competitive globalized economy.[194]

The effects of globalization and the penetration of television into the Indian heartland, exposing the material-richness of Western capitalism, have left the poor in India dissatisfied with their status. Maoist or naxal ideologies have stepped in to provide an alternate vision. Perhaps only a handful truly understand that the Maoist vision focuses not on creating new wealth, but on distributing what limited wealth there is through the use of force. This naxal insurgency situation developing in India is similar to the ongoing one in neighboring Nepal. But Nepal, unlike India, has very little ability to create wealth on its own, because it lacks an educated population and infrastructure.

In the past, India has put down local insurgencies, such as the one in Punjab by Sikh groups. Although the Sikhs are among the most prosperous communities in India, encouragement given to extremist religious elements in the community by the Congress Party in order to garner votes and meddling by Pakistan's intelligence led to separatism and insurgency. Once the Sikh extremists became politically powerful, they began to demand autonomy with implicit demands of a separate Sikh nation called Khalistan,[195] because they realized that in a secular democratic India they couldn't impose their regressive religious practices on the Sikh community—and keep the community under their control.

Maoist insurgency comes at a time when political Islam is asserting itself and Kashmir Muslim insurgency continues to bleed India. Maoists' modus operandi appears to be the use of its armed members to attack and destroy institutions of governing—such as police stations and courts. On the political side, the Maoists are looking to influence their ideological twins—the mainstream communist parties in India. According to a recent report, the Maoist insurgency has spread all over India and covers an area where 17 percent of the population lives.[196] In the words of Prime Minister Singh, from a speech delivered in April 2006: "[This insurgency is] the single biggest internal security challenge ever faced by our country."[197] The Indian government may be finally gearing up to militarily confront Maoists and their leadership. But the root causes that have created and sustained the Maoist insurgency are poverty and

vast swaths of India. This insurgency cannot be addressed the rampant political Islamic movement within its borders economic bleeding that results from Muslim-sponsored ter- erential treatments Muslims receive.

s, societies, or groups that were either directly or indirectly adrid, or London attacks may have backed off directly tar- lt of greater Western preparedness and the threat of retalia- ng and vulnerable India, there are no such inhibitions. A grim assessment of India's status comes from its own intelligence officials, quoted in

Newsinsight.net in March 2006: "Post-9/11, this [terrorism] shifted to the UK, and now, it is in India. India has suddenly become a most-favored destination for terrorist groups." With radical Islamists infiltrating the country and its institutions and the implications of this infiltration worsening, an intelligence officer further admits: "'First, we are not like the United States or [the] UK, we do not even know the full dimension of the penetration so as to be able to understand it and counter it,' said a security officer. 'But if we do not take countermeasures now, full safeguards, then we are going to have our own 9/11. We simply cannot prevent it.'"[198]

But due to political Islam's siege of its democracy, it seems unlikely that India will undertake effective countermeasures. The majority community in Indian society had been enslaved, first by Muslim invaders and later by British colonizers, for over six hundred years. Such a population doesn't nurture leadership, but instead prefers to avoid confrontation. Such a defensive posture indicates that India doesn't know how to protect its own interests.

It was only in the 1980s that India as a nation started competing successfully in just one area: software engineering. This competence has yet to permeate to other areas, including politics and governing. Manmohan Singh, a unelected technocrat now posted at the most important job of prime minister by his elected party leader, Sonia Gandhi, is known for his lack of worldview in matters of foreign policy and security matters. His former foreign minister, Natwar Singh, remarked in 2006, "I have worked with him (Manmohan Singh) for 40 years.... He knew nothing of foreign affairs."[199] Under the leadership of Singh and Gandhi, India is increasingly caving in to political Islam, even while other victim nations are strengthening their laws and their resolve to fight this enemy. By Singh's own admission, terrorism is India's most dangerous threat.[200] Arguably, Singh may be India's greatest weak link. A well-respected public affairs magazine says: "Manmohan Singh is not a politician. He has no political instinct. He has no memory of the wounds inflicted on this country, though he presumably witnessed [the 1947] Partition as a boy. He has no political constituency."[201]

In addition to making internal policy decisions that have led to enhancing the jihadist siege of India, Prime Minister Singh may be embarking on inadvertently enhancing the Pakistani thrust into India, by making borders between the two nations soft in an attempt to solve the Kashmir "dispute."[202] The Indian political leadership has yet to understand that any accords with the political leaders in Pakistan (even if they are made in good faith) are irrelevant to the de facto expansionist power in Pakistan—namely, political Islam.

The Indian army has thus far stopped people from Pakistan, with its high population growth rate, from coming to India in search of employment and opportunities—a country whose language, dress, and food they share. But non-Muslim Indians have no interest in looking for work or other opportunities in an Islamic Pakistan. The Indian government's efforts to soften the borders is sure to lead to a one-way transfer of Muslims into India (as with India's other Islamic neighbor, Bangladesh), along with jihadists from Pakistan.[203] This is certain to speed up the ongoing political Islamic conquest of India and the destruction it brings.

Congress Party president Sonia Gandhi's lack of experience, other than being a homemaker, and lack of education credentials, including a college degree, are also turning out to be a big handicap for a nation threatened by jihadists. The inability to talk about policy issues beyond the limits of a prepared text—which Manmohan Singh and Sonia Gandhi share—is disappointing for a democracy (although not surprising). Due to these leaders' inexperience on strategic issues, including matters related to Islam or Muslims, it appears that Muslim leaders who serve as aides or those who serve in the cabinet have taken the lead in formulating policies. It must be kept in mind that the Muslim leadership in India reflects the Bin Laden–loving, fundamentalist-oriented Muslim community. Even in cases of obvious Islamist violence, Congress Party Muslim leaders have worked to deflect the focus of government attention away from the roots of terror within their community.[204] Not surprisingly, every long-term decision taken by the Singh and Gandhi regime on Muslim-related issues has gone on to advance the cause of jihad.[205]

In my view, the nature and the extent of accommodation of jihadist interests by the Singh-Gandhi regime has been unprecedented. Hence, one has to wonder if the jihadist interests in India have an influential and inside access to the top Congress Party leadership. My worst fears came true. An article published in a prominent Indian Muslim journal in 2004 outlines the contribution of Ahmed Patel, a Muslim politician and political secretary to Sonia Gandhi. This position is the most important one as a political advisor to an inexperienced Gandhi.

> [Ahmed] Patel is a true sympathizer of Muslims and he does whatever he can for the betterment and welfare of his community. If he was not such a person, he would not have pressed for the promotion of education of Muslims and demanded the setting up of a [Sachar] commission to review the condition of minorities' educational institutions.[206]

In India, although policy decisions are made by the Congress Party–led United Progressive Alliance (UPA) cabinet, Gandhi and her staff play a major role in defining them and having them implemented.

In a startling revelation, *CNN-IBN* has in its possession 98 letters of historic significance that show how there was a dual power centre in the UPA [ruling United Progressive Alliance] regime. In response to an RTI [Right-To-Information] application
filed by *CNN-IBN*, the Prime Minister's Office revealed how in the first four years of
the UPA rule, Sonia Gandhi wrote and forwarded 98 letters to the Prime Minister
and in 90 percent of the cases, her requests were immediately acted upon.[207]

The Sachar Committee, identified previously as a major step forward in the
jihadist siege of India, was perhaps set up at the behest of Ahmed Patel. Arguably,
Ahmed Patel can be seen to occupy the most powerful decision-making position in
India vis-à-vis Islam/Muslim-related issues.

An overall literacy rate of only about 60 percent has given India a truly representative democracy, one that elects lawmakers and leaders who are not particularly
able.[208] Unfortunately yet increasingly, criminals are becoming career politicians in
India. For instance, in the state of Karnataka, 91 out of 104 candidates had criminal
records—many of them for violent acts—yet they stood for the state assembly, and
the same is true for 8 out of 12 of those who ran for the national assembly.[209]
According to a May 2007 report in the *Wall Street Journal*, about 25 percent of the
535 elected members of the Indian parliament have pending criminal cases.[210]

For Indian democracy to break out of the political Islamic siege and to set the
stage for an effective national response, the nonchalant Hindu majority, constituting
80 percent of the population, must be mobilized. The notion that caste divisions of
the Hindu majority are an obstacle to their mobilization is misplaced. For instance, in
the nearby country of Sri Lanka, irrespective of the caste origins, Hindus were mobilized against what was portrayed as Singhalese majority injustices. The success of the
political Islamic strategy lies in characterizing itself as a victim even as it, arguably, victimizes India. All of this proves that creating the perception of injustice or grievance,
whether the harm is real or invented, is among the best ways of mobilizing a population. A campaign based on political Islamic "injustices" not only has the potential to
mobilize the Hindu majority population, but it should also put Islamists on the defensive by discrediting their propaganda. The escalation of political Islam-inspired terror
against Hindus, the related cost to India's security, as well as land loss to Muslims, and
various preferences given to Muslims are legitimate grievances that the majority
Hindus should share.

Back-to-back bomb blasts in Bangaluru, Ahmedabad, and Surat, along with the
detection and diffusion of scores of other bombs elsewhere in July 2008 and the subsequent bombings in the Indian capital of New Delhi in September 2008, may have

signaled the next stage of jihad—from siege to attack, with conquest as the eventual goal.[211] Bangaluru was probably chosen due to its prominence as the emerging technology capital of India;[212] the city of Surat in Gujarat is the center for India's diamond business, and Ahmedabad is the capital of the Indian state of Gujarat—the engine driving India's economic growth and whose population is most resistant to jihad.[213] If the strategic goal was to destroy India's economy and to destabilize the nation, no other targets could be better chosen.

These serial blasts are not just terrorism but are part of the larger religious war (jihad) imposed on unbelievers, as evidenced by the manifesto sent minutes before one of the serial blasts.[214] This manifesto can be seen as a well-articulated call to arms. It warned of the impending blasts to note that Hindu blood is "the cheapest of all mankind" and contained Koranic justifications for killing unbelievers. Not surprisingly, the manifesto also called on the Hindu majority in India to embrace Islam in order to avoid further attacks. Students of the taxpayer-funded New Delhi–based Jamia Millia Islamia University were implicated in some of these bombings. In a move reflective of the political Islamic influence on educated Indian Muslims, the management of Jamia, backed by the predominantly Muslim faculty, immediately announced their intention to use the university funds to "defend" the suspected terrorists.[215] This is unprecedented for any educational institution let alone a taxpayer-funded one in India. However, public outcry forced the Islamists to use alternate sources of funding. Jamia's jihadist inclinations were going to get noticed and nurtured. Indeed, in 2006, the Saudis granted Jamia $30 million—easily the largest amount they have given to any Indian university.[216]

During this period, the simmering religion-based tensions exploded in the form of Hindu-Muslim clashes and rioting in the northern and central cities of Dhule, Thane, Malegaon, and in the northeastern Indian state Assam. In the Thane riots a top elected official pleaded helplessness, by saying, "What can one achieve by registering a complaint when a [Muslim] mob of 20,000 people attack policemen?"[217] It is hard to see how such a large mob could be mobilized without the involvement of mosques and clerics. These blasts and even the large-scale rioting show an exceptional level of organizational ability, logistical support in both men and material, and more important, confirm a dedicated following of extremist ideology among the Indian Muslim population. Notable was the leading role played in the blasts by suspected activists of SIMI.[218]

The ruling regime led by Prime Minister Singh did little to dispel the notion that it is subservient to a jihadist agenda. Terrorism went missing in the agenda set for the top-level National Integration Council meeting convened in the aftermath of the devastating serial bomb blasts in India. Chief Minister Narendra Modi of Gujarat, representing the opposition Bharatiya Janata Party (BJP), noted in his address at the meeting:

> I am shocked to find that the issue of terrorism didn't find any mention in the agenda, though it has direct bearing on the national integration. The Government is playing [Muslim] voting bloc politics. It doesn't want to mention terrorism....A stringent law is required not only to punish the perpetrators of terrorism, but also to prevent our educated being drawn into terrorist ideology."[219]

The investigations into the serial blasts were being stymied, with Muslim leaders managing to successfully transform the investigations into a trial of the entire Muslim community in India.[220] Indian columnist Swapan Dasgupta observed that "there is an organized attempt to coerce a confused [Indian] Government into abandoning the war on terror with the threat of withdrawal of political support by an entire [Muslim] religious community."[221] True to their role as the generals of political Islam and jihad, mostly Deoband-educated Indian Muslim clerics were at the forefront of mobilizing their community against cooperating with the government, and to undercut the various measures taken to discourage terrorism and to bring the perpetrators to justice.[222] Voicing mistrust of the nation's judicial system, the clerics also demanded a separate criminal trial system for the nation's Muslims.[223] Because the regimes in power are not seen as capable of securing the Hindu majority, the majority backlash may have started in the form of suspected Hindu involvement in blasts that killed some Muslims in the central Indian city of Malegaon.[224] Still, instead of focusing on tackling the escalating jihadist attacks, the Congress Party–led government did by now what was expected—it put resources and energy into neutralizing not just the Hindu groups who may be involved in retaliatory terror but also those involved in mobilizing the majority community to defend the nation from jihad.[225]

Toward the end of November 2008, the economic hub of Mumbai was attacked again, this time not by homegrown Muslim extremists, but by about ten trained terrorists who arrived from Pakistan by sea. Reports have identified the gunmen as belonging to Pakistan-based Lashkar-e-Taiba (LeT), which is linked to the Pakistani military through its intelligence agency (the ISI is staffed on a rotational basis by the serving officers of Pakistan's armed forces).[226] The Lashkar is also funded by Saudi Arabia.[227] An Israeli terrorism expert notes that "Saudi Arabia has contributed very much to what Lashkar-e-Taiba looks like, how it thinks, its motivation, ideology, and funding."[228] Given the army motto of "faith, piety, and jihad in the path of Allah," it shouldn't be surprising that Pakistan's military would use the terrorists to do its bidding.[229] Also, the Pakistani handlers of the terrorists who attacked Mumbai apparently told them to recite the following translated Urdu poem excerpts on jihad in order to keep focus on the "task" at hand!

> Jihad will continue till the Day of Judgment—and will not stop
> Jihad is the path and order of God
> Jihad has cut off evil from this earth
> Jihad alone gives voice
> Jihad will make false God become naked
> Avoiding jihad has made us slaves
> Enemies of Jihad will sink and will be dishonored[230]

Armed with sophisticated weapons, the gunmen simultaneously hit about ten landmarks with military precision and held hundreds of hostages in luxury hotels and in a guesthouse belonging to India's tiny Jewish population. The Mumbai police chief has claimed that Pakistani gunmen were assisted by many locals.[231] It took the Indian government more than sixty hours to lift the siege by killing or capturing the gunmen who made the city stand still. These attacks increased tensions between India and Pakistan—and further eroded the Indian public's confidence in the ruling Manmohan-Gandhi regime.

During the siege, the gunmen not only used Koranic injunctions to justify their terror, but they also propagandized the well-known "grievance" tactic of Indian Muslims who see themselves at the mercy of the "Hindu" Indian state. The terrorists also called on the Indian government "to return stolen Muslim lands."[232] The government under Prime Minister Singh did little to counter the jihadist propaganda directed at the restive Indian Muslim population. These attacks led to the massacre of 160 people, leaving several hundred more injured. The list of those selectively killed also included twenty-five foreigners. In addition, these attacks may well produce not only short-term but potentially long-term adverse effects on the Indian economy. The extensive coverage of this mayhem rekindled the international community's fear of terror and served to awaken the world to India's vulnerability to Islamic terror.

Many Western multinational corporations banned their employees from traveling to India until further notice. Analysts have claimed that these attacks were designed to disrupt the ever-so-gradual thawing of relations between India and Pakistan brought about by American diplomatic efforts behind the scenes. But these analysts are overlooking the fact that the planning for these attacks, including the scouting of locations and training of terrorists, had been under way for about a year.[233] The Pakistani government's commitment to undermine India's development has also been ignored. The former Indian ambassador to Pakistan, Gopalaswami Parthasarathy, has written that Pakistan's former president, Musharraf, told him around the year 2000 that if India does not make a "fair" deal on Kashmir (meaning one favorable to Pakistan), his government would destabilize India to the extent that it would not economically march too far ahead of Pakistan.[234]

India claims to possess evidence linking the Pakistani intelligence agency's involvement in these attacks.[235] Not only was Pakistan seen as not being adequately responsive to the roots of the Mumbai attack pointing in its direction,[236] it was amassing troops at the Indian border against possible Indian retaliatory strikes or to launch military strikes on a weakened India at an opportune time.[237] It took the threat of aid cutoff on the part of the determined United States to nudge the cash-strapped Pakistan to even admit that the attack and the perpetrators originated from its soil.[238]

A *Time* magazine article titled "India's Muslims in Crisis" by Aryn Baker, Jyothi Thottam, and Ershad Mahmud, published in the aftermath of the Mumbai massacre, tried to address the roots of terror.[239] A Muslim-centric view was projected, while ignoring that of the non-Muslim victims under the Muslim rule.

> [M]any south Asian Muslims insist Islam is the one and only force that can bring the [Indian] subcontinent together and return it to pre-eminence as a single whole. "We [Muslims] were the legal rulers of India, and in 1857 the British took that away from us," says Tarik Jan, a gentle-mannered scholar at Islamabad's Institute of Policy Studies. "In 1947 they should have given that [India] back to the Muslims." Jan is no militant, but he pines for the golden era of the Mughal period in the 1700s and has a fervent desire to see India, Pakistan and Bangladesh reunited under Islamic rule.
>
> That sense of injustice is at the root of Muslim identity today. It has permeated every aspect of society and forms the basis of rising Islamic radicalism on the subcontinent. "People are hungry for justice," says Ahmed Rashid, a Pakistani journalist and author of the new book *Descent into Chaos*. "It is perceived to be the fundamental promise of the Koran."[240]

Note the stamp of approval given by the *Time* journalists to the documented brutal Muslim rule by calling it the "golden era." Note also that the sense of Muslim injustice, after all, seems to derive from the frustration of not being able to subjugate and rule the largely non-Muslim India. These journalists have also failed to note that when the British left India in 1947, the population of the pre-partitioned subcontinent included only about 25 percent Muslims (see earlier pages in this section)—thus the idea of handing over India to the Muslims is hardly justified!

The nation with the most ideological leverage over Pakistan and Pakistan-based groups such as LeT is Saudi Arabia. The Mumbai attacks may have provided an opportunity to twist the Saudi hands to make it reign in Pakistan. I explored these ideas in a letter published in the *Washington Times* on December 6, 2008:

> The jihadist group behind the Mumbai massacre is Pakistan-based Lashkar-e-Taiba. Considerable funding for Lashkar comes from Saudi-government-linked "charities," and its logistical support comes from the government of Pakistan through its armed forces....
>
> How come we are unable to identify a single Muslim version of former Serbian President Slobodan Milosevic in either Saudi Arabia or Pakistan despite their association with a long-standing pattern of crimes against humanity conducted against non-Muslims in extended areas? It is unfortunate that the State Department's Office of War Crimes Issues, led by Ambassador Clint Williamson, seems to have ignored a mountain of evidence and not looked into these issues critically thus far.
>
> Putting these states on the dock may be one good way to mobilize the international community to neutralize the threat emanating from them.[241]

Many Muslim ministers in Singh's cabinet were busily undermining the nation already devastated by Islamic terrorists. The minister of minority affairs, Abdul Rahman Antulay, contrary to the official government position, suggested that people other than Islamic terrorists sent from Pakistan could have killed the Mumbai antiterrorism chief and his subordinates. He was also hinting that Hindu extremists were behind this killing.[242] The minister of state for external affairs, E. Ahmed, representing India at the United Nations in the aftermath of the Mumbai attacks, failed to mention the Jewish guesthouse (Nariman House) in his speech, despite its significance as the prime target of the attacks.[243] He has a longer history. In 2006, Ahmed went out of his way to avoid meeting the then American president George W. Bush on his state visit to India, but he made himself readily available when the Saudi king Abdullah had visited India a few months earlier. Ahmed also called for snapping India's ties with Israel (although India is dependent on Israel for military hardware used to repel Islamic terrorists) when the Jewish state attacked to neutralize Hamas's terrorist infrastructure in the Gaza Strip.[244] However, he conveniently didn't call for snapping India's ties with Pakistan in the aftermath of the Mumbai massacre. These examples give a strong indication of the political Islamist infiltration and siege of the beleaguered government itself.

Brahma Chellaney, a professor of strategic studies at the India-based Center for Policy Research, explains how policy decisions on national security are taken at the highest levels of the Indian government: "Had India's leaders not ignored institution-alized policymaking in favor of an ad hoc, personality-driven approach, not repeated the very mistakes of their predecessors, and not insisted on learning on the job, the ter-rorism problem would not have become so acute. In the manner a fish rots from the head down, the rot in India is at the leadership level." And he further adds: "[j]ust the way Pakistan goes through the motions of cracking down on its terror groups, New Delhi responds to each terrorist strike in a perfunctory or mechanical way, without commitment or resolve. And just as Pakistan has a track record of easing up on its terror groups when the spotlight is off, India's leaders go back to business as usual no sooner than a terrorist attack has begun to fade from public attention."[245] Indian defense analyst Bharat Verma has given an interesting perspective on the collapse of Indian security machinery:

> Pakistan's superior psychological warfare machinery further tied down [in the after-math of the Mumbai massacre] the already overstretched Indian security forces in knots. Airports and railway stations are the new fortresses that are heavily guarded. Next will be Metro stations or shopping malls. The list is endless. This is what the enemy wants—tire and dull the edges of the security forces of India by making them run hither and thither. This remains the single important reason why intelli-gence and police machinery of the Union and the states have collapsed. Perpetual red alerts, 24x7 for the past three decades have reduced them to dysfunctional enti-ties with no declared objectives to achieve.[246]

Jihadists have shown only a hint of what they are capable of in India. In my opinion, these attacks mark the beginning of an all-out effort to destabilize India, sim-ilar to the Direct Action Day in 1946 that led to a partitioning of India in the name of Islam.[247] With political leadership, its opposition, and the vast Hindu community caught totally unaware, a shell-shocked India is facing the most serious threat to its existence. I have noted this distinct possibility elsewhere: "At this rate, India is staring at the inevitability of mini Kashmir-like insurgencies based in its many Muslim com-munities. This could kill the Indian economy and make India highly destabilized.... India is going to have a hard time countering the Islamic challenge on its own."[248]

Predictably, the aftermath of the Mumbai massacre found policy reviews on the terrorist threat in India by established American think tanks; remarkable was the near-uniform inability of the specialists to project the extent of Islamic terrorism in India well before it became a *fait accompli.* The gaps in their comprehension reflected in the following critical missing link in their policy recommendations: to enforce any meaningful policies to battle terror, India must break out of the Islamist siege of its democracy, and for that, its majority community first needs to be mobilized.[249]

India with a weakened economy will also see an increasingly assertive and expanding naxal or Maoist influence, which should act to further destabilize the nation. In the wake of such instability, over the course of time, it is very likely that the epicenter of terror and political Islam would extend from Afghanistan-Pakistan through India and connect with Bangladesh. The successful political Islamic siege of India has important lessons for the rest of the civilized world and their non-Muslim (unbeliever) populations. It also shows the critical role played by Pakistan and Saudi Arabia in passionately sponsoring jihad.

JIHAD BUILDUP

The phenomena of multifront jihad-based conquest so many non-Muslim nations are now subjected to is a vision plotted and executed by external sponsors and internal nodes of political Islam—Muslim religious institutions. The first stage of this conquest involves jihad buildup during which resident Muslim populations are indoctrinated to shun mainstream social ideas, to hate non-Muslims, and to embrace increasingly medieval Arab customs in the name of Islam. Once the Muslim population becomes receptive, clerics issue *fatwas*—such as demanding that Muslims follow repressive *sharia* laws (Islamic religious law, see chapter 2) or stop serving *infidel* customers who use alcohol. These steps and the resulting narrow, highly conservative, fundamentalist outlook gradually alienate resident Muslims from the general populace as they fall behind in every measure of human development. Conveniently, the blame for Muslim backwardness (or lack of progress) is pinned on the non-Muslim majority in general or the state in particular—and this becomes grounds for "grievance" or claims of "injustice," and evolves into a movement for asserting Muslim "minority rights" or even in some cases, "self-determination" or "independence."

At the middle stage of this jihad buildup extremists come to represent Muslims in the political process. The emerging Muslim movement led by extremists evolves with demand to impose *sharia* selectively on Muslims. The previous section on India illuminates for us how Islamists are using the political process to subvert democracy. The implementation of medieval customs in the form of *sharia* ensures high Muslim birthrates, the comprehensive institutionalized repression of Muslim communities by extremists, which violates the community's human rights, and more important, diversion of their energies into a never-ending fight with nearby non-Muslims in order to impose Islam on them and ultimately to conquer the land for Islam.

Also, most notable is the role played by mainstream mosques in the process. At the initial stage of a jihad buildup, mosques appear innocuous, religious, and soft. As the jihad builds up (through the efforts of the mosque leadership), mosques increasingly take on a hard-line and political stance, appearing far less religious. In addition, they become the centers of the jihadist movement, including command and control centers of Muslim insurgencies.

By analyzing data from India and its surroundings, we now understand how the next phase of this jihad buildup is carried out: the nation under attack is sucked or pressured into spending its resources first unfairly to subsidize, then to allot a disproportionate share of opportunities to its Muslim population, and finally into efforts at controlling escalating Muslim-based violence or insurgencies. The support for the jihad buildup, and the eventual insurgencies, in material and in men, come from Muslim-majority nations with strong political Islamic movements.

In the meantime, the Muslim-minority population increases by leaps and bounds. Eventually, non-Muslims in this weakened region will be either expelled from areas with large Muslim concentrations or they will leave as a result of hostile conditions. This results in an expansion of Islamic frontiers or in outright conquest.

Singapore is a small developed nation in Southeast Asia with a sizable Muslim population. It is flanked by a giant neighbor in the form of Islamic Malaysia. Singapore has taken some innovative approaches to preempt extremism—that is, by denying Muslim extremists the opportunity to embark on a jihad buildup. Terrorism analyst Rohan Gunaratna of Singapore explains:

> Jihadist support activities (such as propaganda or recruitment) enable operational activity (such as surveillance or attack). By detecting and disrupting these components, the power of support and operational activities can be reduced to manageable levels. Of the support activities, countering jihadist propaganda requires knowledge of its content. This is largely the domain of the Muslim clerics, scholars and intellectuals. We need to mobilize them, support them, and work with them. This is what we have accomplished in Singapore.[250]

In my view, these efforts, while undoubtedly yielding impressive results in the short term, need to be augmented by better long-term strategies that undercut political Islam. The strategies tried at Singapore do little to address the reality that, at the fundamental level, Islamic ideology is overwhelmingly predisposed toward jihad (see chapter 2, "Conquest by Design")—and with the Muslim birthrate significantly higher (again, driven by political Islam's de-emphasis on community building as opposed to jihad building) than that of non-Muslims in Singapore, the current policies become unsustainable in the long term.

The government of Singapore is trying to address the higher birthrate of Muslims by preferentially attracting and helping to resettle people of Chinese ethnicity. Note that a higher population percentage of Muslims would mean a larger share of political power in a democracy. However, for any nation, especially a compact one such as Singapore, this immigration option is at best a temporary measure. Unfortunately, Singapore's heavy reliance on an increasingly Islamist Malaysia for critical resources, including water, is a big constraint in its ability to take on political Islam. Not just Singapore, but any non-Muslim-majority nation with a sizable Muslim population couldn't run away from the reality that a growing Muslim population with extremist tendencies can be a serious existential threat.

Analysis and data presented thus far show a critical need for ideological and political preemption in order to neutralize the ongoing jihad buildup in both non-Muslim and Muslim-majority nations. The need to use warfare to neutralize violent jihadist groups is not discounted. However, a broad-based counteroffensive must be designed to break the back of the worldwide political Islamic movement. Some ideas toward achieving these goals in the context of human rights and religious freedom are presented in the next chapter.

NOTES

1. *Muhammad and the Unbelievers: A Political Life* (Nashville, TN: Center for the Study of Political Islam, 2006), pp. 164–65; Andrew Bostom, *The Legacy of Islamic Anti-semitism: From Sacred Texts to Solemn History* (Amherst, NY: Prometheus Books, 2008).

2. "USA MSA Removes, Does Not Repudiate Genocidal Hadith," August 22, 2008, http://jihadwatch.org/archives/2008/08/022315print.html (accessed November 9, 2008).

3. "The Legacy of Islamic Anti-semitism," *Frontpage Magazine*, June 13, 2008, http://www.frontpagemag.com/Articles/Printable.aspx?GUID=E5D686EA-1936-4819-AA23-DAA71F27D767 (accessed July 20, 2008).

4. Efraim Karsh, *Islamic Imperialism: A History* (New Haven, CT: Yale University Press, 2006), p. 13.

5. Michael Kinsley, "It's Not Apartheid: Carter Adds to the List of Mideast Misjudgments," *Washington Post*, December 12, 2006, http://www.washingtonpost.com/wp-dyn/content/article/2006/12/11/AR2006121101225.html (accessed May 1, 2007).

6. Andrew Bostom, "Apocalyptic Muslim Jew-hatred," *American Thinker*, July 17, 2006, http://www.americanthinker.com/2006/07/apocalyptic_muslim_jewhatred.html (accessed October 20, 2008); Daniel Goldhagen, "A Manifesto for Murder," *Los Angeles Times*, February 5, 2006, http://articles.latimes.com/2006/feb/05/opinion/op-goldhagen5 (accessed October 20, 2008).

7. "Israeli Arabs 'Funding Hamas,'" *BBC*, May 13, 2003, http://news.bbc.co.uk/1/hi/world/middle_east/3023517.stm (accessed July 20, 2008); David Hornick, "Israel's Growing Internal Threat," *Frontpage Magazine*, July 23, 2008, http://www.frontpagemag.com/Articles/Read.aspx?GUID=16D5BAA0-40E3-4E29-BA9E-94588BBC9FB8 (accessed July 25, 2008).

8. "Arab Citizens of Israel," *Wikipedia*, http://en.wikipedia.org/wiki/Arab_citizens_of_Israel (accessed July 22, 2008).

9. Brigitte Gabriel, *Because They Hate: A Survivor of Islamic Terror Warns America* (New York: St. Martin's Press, 2006), pp. 16–17.

10. "The World Factbook—Netherlands," *CIA*, https://www.cia.gov/cia/publications/factbook/geos/nl.html (accessed March 2, 2007); Bruce Bawer, *While Europe Slept: How Radical Islam Is Destroying the West from Within* (New York: Doubleday, 2006), pp. 32–33.

11. Ibid.

12. Bawer, *While Europe Slept.*

13. Ibid., p. 236.

14. Daniel Pipes, "More Survey Research from a British Islamist Hell," *Danielpipes.org*, July 26, 2005, http://www.danielpipes.org/blog/483 (accessed March 2, 2007).

15. Daniel Allott, "Islam and Violence," *Washington Times*, December 4, 2006, http://www.washtimes.com/op-ed/20061203-100623-9818r.htm (accessed March 2, 2007).

16. Mark Steyn, "Who Will Raise the Siege of Paris?" *Washington Times*, November 7, 2005, http://www.washingtontimes.com/commentary/20051106-102157-9880r.htm (accessed May 2, 2007).

17. Graeme Wilson, "Young, British Muslims 'Getting More Radical,'" *Telegraph*, March 1, 2007, http://www.telegraph.co.uk/news/main.jhtml?xml=/news/2007/01/29/nmuslims29.xml (accessed March 2, 2007).

18. Bob Simon, "Killing in the Name of Islam Is a Cancer," *CBSNEWS.com*, March 27, 2005, http://www.cbsnews.com/stories/2007/03/23/60minutes/main2602308_page2.shtml (accessed May 2, 2007).

19. Hasan Suroor, "A Question of Identity," *Hindu*, August 17, 2004, http://www.hindu.com/2004/08/17/stories/2004081701341000.htm (accessed May 2, 2007).

20. Wilson, "Young, British Muslims 'Getting More Radical.'"

21. Eshan Masood, "British Muslims," *Britishcouncil.org*, 2006, http://www.british council.org/spain-society-british-muslims-media-guide.pdf (accessed November 14, 2008).

22. Amit Roy, "7/7 Report Links Bombers to Pak," *Telegraph*, May 11, 2006, http://www.telegraphindia.com/1060512/asp/foreign/story_6214208.asp (accessed May 2, 2007).

23. Bawer, *While Europe Slept*, p. 30.

24. Ibid., pp. 41–42.

25. Paul Belien, "Islamization of Antwerp," *Washington Times*, March 14, 2007, http://www.washingtontimes.com/op-ed/20070313-090315-9588r.htm (accessed March 22, 2007).

26. Rashmee Lall, "Islam Body to Guide UK Govt," *Times of India*, July 19, 2008, http://timesofindia.indiatimes.com/World/Islam_body_to_guide_UK_govt/article show/3251847.cms (accessed July 20, 2008).

27. Abul Taher, "Revealed: UK's First Official Sharia Courts," *Times Online*, September 14, 2008, http://www.timesonline.co.uk/tol/news/uk/crime/article4749183.ece (accessed September 27, 2008).

28. "Combating Sharia with Islamic Tools," *Frontpage Magazine*, November 20, 2007, http://frontpagemag.com/Articles/Read.aspx?GUID=D81A5112-A188-4290-87E9 -1050B7C28DB0 (accessed July 20, 2008).

29. "Sharia: Islam's Warden," *Frontpage Magazine*, April 2, 2008, http://www.front pagemag.com/articles/Read.aspx?GUID=8AD3D2F1-FD2C-4E78-B233-2F97FCF97B94 (accessed September 28, 2008).

30. Moorthy Muthuswamy, "Why the EU Does Not Want Turkey," *Washington Times*, December 18, 2002.

31. Paul Belien, "In Bed with Islamists," *Washington Times*, April 11, 2007, http://www.washingtontimes.com/op-ed/20070410-100624-4394r.htm (accessed April 27, 2007).

32. Koenraad Elst, *Negationism in India: Concealing the Record of Islam* (New Delhi: Voice of India, 1992), http://koenraadelst.bharatvani.org/books/negaind/index.htm (accessed March 10, 2007); Kishori Lal, *The Legacy of Muslim Rule in India* (New Delhi: Voice of India, 1992).

33. Kishori Lal, "Chapter 3: Muslims Invade India," in *The Legacy of Muslim Rule in India* (New Delhi: Voice of India, 1992).

34. R. Ohri, "The Other Side of Sufism," *Organiser*, April 27, 2008, http://www .organiser.org/dynamic/modules.php?name=Content&pa=showpage&pid=234&page=38 (accessed July 20, 2008).

35. Andrew Bostom, "Sufi Jihad?" *American Thinker*, May 15, 2005, http://www .americanthinker.com/2005/05/sufi_jihad.html (accessed July 20, 2008).

36. "Guru Gobind Singh," *Wikipedia*, http://en.wikipedia.org/wiki/Guru_Gobind _Singh (accessed November 19, 2008).

37. Balbir Punj, "Islamists Block Social Reform," *Pioneer*, October 31, 2008, http://www.dailypioneer.com/131270/Islamists-block-social-reform.html (accessed October 31, 2008).

38. Balbir Punj, "Hindu-Muslim Dishonesty," *Organiser*, May 22, 2006, http://www.organiser.org/dynamic/modules.php?name=Content&pa=showpage&pid=79&page=9 (accessed March 2, 2007).

39. Anjum Altaf, "View: Democracy—What Mr Jinnah Said," *Daily Times*, November 28, 2004, http://www.dailytimes.com.pk/default.asp?page=story_28-11-2004_pg3_2 (accessed July 24, 2008).

40. Ibid.

41. "Lahore Resolution," *Wikipedia*, http://en.wikipedia.org/wiki/Lahore_Resolution (accessed July 25, 2008).

42. "Direct Action Day," *Wikipedia*, http://en.wikipedia.org/wiki/Direct_Action_Day (accessed July 25, 2008).

43. K. Phanda, "Balkanizing India," *Pioneer*, April 14, 2006.

44. "Indian Muslim Nationalism," *Wikipedia*, http://en.wikipedia.org/wiki/Indian_Muslim_nationalism (accessed March 8, 2007).

45. S. Bhattacharyya, *Genocide in East Pakistan/Bangladesh* (Houston: A. Ghosh, 1987), preface.

46. Aakar Patel, "Jinnah after August 11, 1947," *News*, September 28, 2008, http://thenews.jang.com.pk/daily_detail.asp?id=138344 (accessed September 28, 2008).

47. N. Sridhar, "Ethnic Cleansing in Pakistan during Partition: A Preliminary Statistical Analysis," *Bharat Rakshak Monitor*, September/October 2003, http://www.bharat-rakshak.com/MONITOR/ISSUE6-2/sridhar.html (accessed July 2, 2008).

48. "Hindus in Bangladesh, Pakistan and Kashmir: A Survey of Human Rights," *Hindu American Foundation*, 2004, http://www.hinduamericanfoundation.org/HHR2004.pdf (accessed March 2, 2007).

49. "The World Factbook—Pakistan," *CIA*, 2006, https://www.cia.gov/cia/publications/factbook/geos/pk.html (accessed March 2, 2007).

50. "Muslim Population Growth in India," *Wikipedia*, http://en.wikipedia.org/wiki/Muslim_population_growth_in_India (accessed March 5, 2007).

51. "Assessment for Hindus in Bangladesh," *CIDCM*, http://www.cidcm.umd.edu/mar/assessment.asp?groupId=77102 (accessed December 29, 2008).

52. "Vested Property Act (Bangladesh)," *Wikipedia*, http://en.wikipedia.org/wiki/Vested_Property_Act_(Bangladesh) (accessed July 12, 2008).

53. "Hindus Lost 26 Lakh Acres of Land from 1965 to 2006 Says Study," *Organiser*, July 20, 2008, http://www.organiser.org/dynamic/modules.php?name=Content&pa=showpage&pid=246&page=10 (accessed July 20, 2008).

54. Richard Benkin, "No Outrage Over Ethnic Cleansing of Hindus," *Analyst-*

network.com, October 16, 2008, http://www.analyst-network.com/article.php?art_id=2500 (October 18, 2008).

55. Sachi Dastidar, *Empire's Last Casualty: Indian Subcontinent's Vanishing Hindu and Other Minorities* (India: Firma KLM, 2008).

56. K. Krishnakumar, "A Silent Genocide Is Taking Place in Bangladesh," *Rediff.com*, November 21, 2006, http://www.rediff.com/news/2006/nov/21rights.htm (accessed May 1, 2007).

57. Jehangir Pocha, "India Erecting a Barrier along Bangladesh Border," *Boston Globe*, May 30, 2004, http://www.boston.com/news/world/articles/2004/05/30/india_erecting _a_barrier_along_bangladesh_border (accessed March 2, 2007).

58. "Muslim Population Growth in India."

59. "Hindus in Bangladesh, Pakistan and Kashmir."

60. Subramanian Swamy, "A Strategy to Combat Terrorism in India," *Organiser*, October 8, 2006, http://www.organiser.org/dynamic/modules.php?name=Content&pa =showpage&pid=151&page=25 (accessed May 2, 2007); also from a note published by the author.

61. From the pages of Pakistani English language dailies (1999–2000).

62. "Musharraf for Developing Knowledge-Based Economy," *Daily Times*, November 19, 2006, http://www.dailytimes.com.pk/default.asp?page=2006\11\19\story_19-11-2006 _pg13_1 (accessed April 4, 2007).

63. "Education in Post-independence India: Some Milestones," http://www .education.nic.in/sector.asp#milestoneFrom (accessed March 2, 2007).

64. Paul Watson, "In Pakistan's Public Schools, Jihad Still Part of Lesson Plan," *Los Angeles Times*, August 18, 2005, http://articles.latimes.com/2005/aug/18/world/fg-schools18 (accessed July 20, 2008).

65. Praveen Swami, "Understanding Pakistan's Response to Mumbai," *Hindu*, January 26, 2009, http://www.hindu.com/2009/01/26/stories/2009012650570800.htm (accessed January 28, 2009).

66. Pervez Hoodbhoy, "The Saudi-isation of Pakistan," *Newsline.com*, January 2009, http://www.newsline.com.pk/NewsJan2009/cover2jan2009.htm (accessed February 1, 2009).

67. Farhan Bokhari, James Lamont, and Daniel Dombey, "Pakistani Army's Ties to Islamists Under Scrutiny," *Financial Times*, December 12, 2008, http://www.ft.com/ cms/s/0/6032d200-c84d-11dd-b86f-000077b07658.html (accessed December 30, 2008).

68. ANJ, "ISI Plans 'Islamic Republic of Pakistan' by 2020 in India," *Economic Times*, January 6, 2009, http://economictimes.indiatimes.com/News/PoliticsNation/ISI_plans _Islamic_Republic_of_Pakistan_by_2020_in_India/articleshow/3943044.cms (accessed January 6, 2009).

69. B. Raman, "India & Pakistan: Can Mindsets & Perceptions Change?" *SAAG*,

December 10, 2006, http://www.southasianalysis.org/papers21/paper2057.html (accessed March 2, 2007).

70. Maloy Dhar, *Fulcrum of Evil: ISI, CIA, Al Qaeda Nexus* (New Delhi: Manas, 2006).

71. Ibid., pp. 216–37.

72. "LeT Terrorists Kill 22 Hindus in Kashmir," *Times of India*, May 1, 2006, http://timesofindia.indiatimes.com/articleshow/1511180.cms (accessed March 2, 2007).

73. Qudssia Akhlaque, "Dialogue to Start Next Month: Joint Statement on Musharraf-Vajpayee Meeting," *Dawn*, January 7, 2004, http://www.dawn.com/2004/01/07/top1.Htm (accessed February 2007).

74. "No Pakistani to Be Handed Over to India," *Dawn*, January 13, 2002, http://www.dawn.com/2004/01/07/top1.htm (accessed March 2, 2007).

75. Jagmohan, *My Frozen Turbulence in Kashmir* (New Delhi: Allied, 2002), p. 180.

76. "Kashmir Region," *Wikipedia*, http://en.wikipedia.org/wiki/Kashmir (accessed March 5, 2007).

77. Sunil Fotedar, Subodh Atal, and Lalit Koul, "Living Under the Shadow of Article 370," *Kashmir Herald*, January 1, 2002, http://kashmirherald.com/featuredarticle/article370.html (accessed April 23, 2007).

78. "Hindus in Bangladesh, Pakistan and Kashmir."

79. Aditi Bhaduri, "Erased from Memory: Kashmir's Forgotten," *Kashmir Herald*, November 9, 2008, http://www.kashmirherald.com/main.php?t=OP&st=D&no=288 (accessed November 10, 2008).

80. "LeT Terrorists Kill 22 Hindus in Kashmir."

81. Arvind Lavakare, "The Woes of Jammu and Ladakh," *Rediff.com*, July 17, 2002, http://www.rediff.com/news/2002/jul/17arvind.htm (accessed April 3, 2007).

82. Rajeev Srinivasan, "India, the Kashmiri Colony," *Rediff.com*, November 9, 2002, http://www.rediff.com/news/2002/nov/09rajeev.htm (accessed May 2, 2007).

83. "The World Factbook—India," *CIA*, 2007, https://www.cia.gov/library/publications/the-world-factbook/geos/in.html (accessed November 8, 2008).

84. "The World Factbook—China," *CIA*, 2007, https://www.cia.gov/library/publications/the-world-factbook/geos/ch.html (accessed November 8, 2008).

85. Aasha Khosa, "PDP Works Hand in Glove with Terrorists: Ex-Governor," *Rediff.com*, July 14, 2008, http://www.rediff.com/news/2008/jul/14inter1.htm (accessed July 20, 2008).

86. PTI, "Central Aid for J&K Slain Militants' Kin, Says NGO," *Rediff.com*, http://www.rediff.com/news/2008/jul/30jk.htm (accessed July 30, 2008).

87. Press Trust of India (hereafter PTI), Mukhtar Ahmad, "J&K Assembly Passes Shariat Bill," *Rediff.com*, February 9, 2007, http://www.rediff.com/news/2007/feb/09mukhtar.htm (accessed March 8, 2007).

88. "Amarnath," *Wikipedia*, http://en.wikipedia.org/wiki/Amarnath (accessed July 8, 2008).

89. Khosa, "PDP Works Hand in Glove with Terrorists."

90. Prafull Goradia, "Waxing the Crescent," *Pioneer*, July 4, 2008, http://www.dailypioneer.com/archives2/default12.asp?main_variable=oped&file_name=opd2%2Etxt&counter_img=2&phy_path_it=D%3A%5CWebSites%5CDailyPioneer%5Carchives2%5Cjul408 (accessed July 20, 2008).

91. PTI, "Amarnath Land Row: VHP to Observe All-India Bandh on July 3," July 1, 2008, http://timesofindia.indiatimes.com/India/File_VHP_to_observe_all-India_bandh_on_July_3/articleshow/3185376.cms (accessed July 20, 2008).

92. Subodh Ghildiyal, "We Are Pakistanis, Says Syed Geelani," *Times of India*, August 19, 2008, http://timesofindia.indiatimes.com/We_are_Pakistanis_says_Geelani/articleshow/3378137.cms (September 1, 2008).

93. "Full Text of the Amarnath Accord," *Rediff.com*, August 31, 2008, http://www.rediff.com/news/2008/aug/31amar2.htm (accessed September 1, 2008).

94. Vicky Nanjappa, "How to Tackle Economic Terrorism?" *Rediff.com*, September 30, 2007, http://ia.rediff.com/news/2007/sep/30vicky.htm (accessed October 8, 2007).

95. Vicky Nanjappa, "How Fake Currency and Terror Are Related," *Rediff.com*, August 13, 2008, http://www.rediff.com/news/2008/aug/13beng.htm (accessed August 14, 2008).

96. Praveen Swami, "A Bend in the Road," *Outlook India*, March 18, 2008, http://www.outlookindia.com/fullprint.asp?choice=1&fodname=20080318&fname=simi&sid=1 (accessed July 20, 2008).

97. Dhar, *Fulcrum of Evil*, p. 185.

98. PTI, "ISI's Friday Sermons in Dubai," *Rediff.com*, October 3, 2003, http://in.rediff.com/news/2003/oct/08blasts.htm (accessed January 24, 2009).

99. "Syed Ahmed Khan," *Wikipedia*, http://en.wikipedia.org/wiki/Syed_Ahmed_Khan (accessed July 22, 2008).

100. Ramashray Upadhyay, "Anti-terrorism Conference Dar-ul-Uloom Deoband—A Failed Exercise?" *SAAG*, March 27, 2008, http://www.southasiaanalysis.org/%5Cpapers27%5Cpaper2646.html (accessed July 20, 2008).

101. Swami, "A Bend in the Road."

102. Animesh Roul, "Student Islamic Movement of India: A Profile," *Jamestown Foundation*, April 6, 2006, http://www.jamestown.org/terrorism/news/article.php?articleid=2369953 (accessed July 20, 2008).

103. Ramashray Upadhyay, "SIMI and Its Alarming Growth," *SAAG*, April 22, 2008, http://www.southasiaanalysis.org/%5Cpapers27%5Cpaper2676.html (accessed July 20, 2008).

104. Upadhyay, "Anti-terrorism Conference Dar-ul-Uloom Deoband—A Failed Exercise?"

105. TNN, "Deoband First: A Fatwa against Terror," *Economic Times*, June 1, 2008, http://economictimes.indiatimes.com/News/PoliticsNation/Deoband_first_A_fatwa _against_terror/rssarticleshow/3089426.cms (accessed July 20, 2008).

106. Mohammed Siddique, "Don't Link Terror to Religion, say Clerics," *Rediff.com*, November 8, 2008, http://www.rediff.com/news/2008/nov/08dont-link-terror-to-religion -say-islamic-clerics.htm (accessed November 15, 2008).

107. Aakar Patel, "Where Indian Muslims Have Gone Wrong?" *Mid-Day*, September 5, 2004, http://ww1.mid-day.com/news/city/2004/september/91708.htm (accessed March 2, 2007).

108. Ramashray Upadhyay, "Islamic Institutions in India—Protracted Movement for Separate Muslim Identity?" *SAAG*, February 6, 2003, http://www.southasiaanalysis.org/ papers6/paper599.html (accessed March 2, 2007).

109. Associated Press, "Bush: India a Jobs Opportunity, Not an Obstacle," *MSNBC .com*, March 3, 2006, http://www.msnbc.msn.com/id/11650277 (accessed May 2, 2007).

110. PTI, "Two Terrorists Killed in J&K Belong to Kerala," *Rediff.com*, October 25, 2008, http://www.rediff.com/news/2008/oct/25kerala.htm (accessed October 5, 2008).

111. PTI, "800 Terror Cells Unearthed in India," *Rediff.com*, August 12, 2008, http://www.rediff.com/news/2008/aug/12terror.htm (accessed August 18, 2008).

112. Damien McElroy, "Mumbai Attacks: How Indian-Born Islamic Militants Are Trained in Pakistan," *Telegraph*, December 15, 2008, http://www.telegraph.co.uk/ news/worldnews/asia/india/3741868/Mumbai-attacks-How-Indian-born-Islamic-mili- tants-are-trained-in-Pakistan.html (accessed December 30, 2008).

113. Fareed Zakaria, *The Future of Freedom: Illiberal Democracy at Home and Abroad* (New York: Norton, 2003), p. 145.

114. Fareed Zakaria, "India Rising," *Newsweek*, March 2, 2006, http://www .msnbc.msn.com/id/11564364/site/newsweek (accessed March 2, 2007).

115. Suman Mozumder, "India Occupying Kashmir, Says Newsweek's Zakaria," *Rediff.com*, June 25, 2001, http://www.rediff.com/us/2001/jun/25us6.htm (accessed March 22, 2007).

116. Surinder Oberoi, "Ethnic Separatism and Insurgency in Kashmir," *Asia Pacific Center for Security Studies*, Spring 2004, http://www.apcss.org/Publications/Edited%20 Volumes/ReligiousRadicalism/PagesfromReligiousRadicalismandSecurityinSouthAsia ch8.pdf (accessed July 25, 2008).

117. Moorthy Muthuswamy, "Pakistan and Militant Islam," *Washington Times*, Sep- tember 25, 2004.

118. Fareed Zakaria, "Vengeance of the Victors," *Newsweek*, January 8, 2007, http:// www.msnbc.msn.com/id/16409404/site/newsweek (accessed March 2, 2007).

119. "Konkani Muslims," *Wikipedia*, http://en.wikipedia.org/wiki/Konkani_Muslims (accessed July 8, 2008).

120. Moorthy Muthuswamy, "American Policy Advice in South Asia: Fatal Flaws," *SAAG*, June 2, 2004, http://www.southasiaanalysis.org/%5Cpapers10%5Cpaper914.html (accessed July 20, 2008).

121. Ashutosh Varshney, *Ethnic Conflict and Civic Life: Hindus and Muslims in India* (New Haven, CT: Yale University Press, 2002).

122. Tarun Vijay, "A Secular Protocol," *Times of India*, October 11, 2008, http://times ofindia.indiatimes.com/Opinion/Columnists/Tarun_Vijay/The_Right_View/A_secular _protocol/articleshow/3584631.cms (accessed October 14, 2008).

123. K. Anurag, "61 Killed in Serial Blasts across Assam," *Rediff.com*, October 30, 2008, http://www.rediff.com/news/2008/oct/30blasts.htm (accessed November 3, 2008).

124. PTI, "ISI Fomenting Trouble in India's North-East: US Intelligence," *Rediff.com*, April 23, 2006, http://www.rediff.com/news/2007/apr/23isi.htm (accessed March 2, 2007).

125. Moorthy Muthuswamy, "New Ideas for a New War," *Sulekha*, April 2, 2003, http://news.sulekha.com/newsanalysisdisplay.aspx?cid=2651 (accessed March 2, 2007).

126. Commentary, "Terrorists & Politicians," *Newsinsight.net*, March 9, 2006, http://www.newsinsight.net/archivedebates/nat2.asp?recno=1349&ctg=politics (accessed March 2, 2007).

127. Manjari Mishra, "Produce Babies, Get Reward," *Times of India*, January 23, 2007, http://timesofindia.indiatimes.com/articleshow/1386975.cms (accessed April 20, 2007).

128. C. Issac, "For Hindus in Kerala It's Now or Never," *Organiser*, October 23, 2004, http://www.hvk.org/articles/1104/25.html (accessed April 5, 2007).

129. PTI, "Bukhari Meets PM, Demands Economic Package, Reservation," April 18, 2006, http://www.outlookindia.com/pti_news.asp?id=378727 (accessed March 2, 2007).

130. "Shahi Imam 'Absolves' LeT, Blames RSS for Mumbai Blasts," July 18, 2006, http://news.webindia123.com/news/articles/India/20060718/394446.html.

131. "Muslim Population Growth in India."

132. Warner MacKenzie, "Understanding Taqiyya—Islamic Principle of Lying for the Sake of Allah," *Islam Watch*, April 30, 2007, http://www.islam-watch.org/Warner/Taqiyya-Islamic-Principle-Lying-for-Allah.htm (accessed July 20, 2008).

133. Omar Khalidi, *Khaki and the Ethnic Violence in India* (Gurgaon, India: Three Essays Collective, 2003).

134. Balbir Punj, "The Two-Regiment Theory," *Outlook India*, March 20, 2006.

135. Omar Khalidi, *Muslims in Indian Economy* (Gurgaon, India: Three Essays Collective, 2006).

136. O. Gupta, "Hindu Youth Reduced to Second-Class Status," *Organiser*, March 25, 2007, http://www.Organiser.org/dynamic/modules.php?name=Content&pa=showpage &pid=176&page=3 (accessed April 20, 2007); "Census India 2001," http://www.census india.net/results/2001census_data_index.html (accessed May 2, 2007).

137. "New Survey Busts Sachar Panel Report," *IBNlive.com*, April 6, 2007, http://

www.ibnlive.com/news/new-survey-busts-sachar-panel-report/top/37856-3.html (accessed May 2, 2007).

138. "Major Indian Voices Back Self-Determination for JK," *Kashmir Observer*, September 10, 2008, http://www.kashmirobserver.com/index.php?id=1121:major-indian -voices-advocate-self-determination-for-kashmir-&option=com_content&catid=50:local news &Itemid=81 (accessed September 13, 2008).

139. Sunil Jain, "Sachar Report: Myth and Reality," *Rediff.com*, December 11, 2006, http://www.rediff.com/news/2006/dec/11sachar.htm?zcc=rl (accessed May 1, 2007).

140. Gupta, "Hindu Youth Reduced to Second-Class Citizens."

141. Peter Wonacott, "Lawless Legislators Thwart Social Progress in India," *Wall Street Journal*, May 4, 2007.

142. Mridu Bhandari, "In Booming India, Hunger Kills 6,000 Kids Daily," *IBNLive*, March 29, 2008, http://www.ibnlive.com/news/in-booming-india-hunger-kills-6000-kids -daily/62220-17.html (accessed July 20, 2008).

143. "Interim Budget Gives Boost to AI Holding Company," *PTI*, February 16, 2009, http://www.rediff.com/money/2009/feb/16interim-budget-gives-boost-to-ai-holding -company.htm (accessed February 16, 2009).

144. B. Raman, "National Security: My Jaipur Musings," *SAAG*, February 6, 2007, http:// www.southasiaanalysis.Org/%5Cpapers22%5Cpaper2123.html (accessed March 2, 2007).

145. PTI, "Sachar Report to be Implemented in Full: Minister," *Rediff.com*, December 28, 2006, http://www.rediff.com/news/2006/dec/28sachar.htm?zcc=rl (accessed March 2, 2007).

146. Subodh Ghildiyal, "Muslim Recruitment Up in Central Forces," *Times of India*, October 12, 2007, http://timesofindia.indiatimes.com/Muslim_recruitment_up_in _central_forces/articleshow/2450770.cms (accessed October 20, 2007).

147. Zia Haq, "Jumps in Jobs for Minorities," *Hindustan Times*, December 24, 2008, http://www.hindustantimes.com/StoryPage/StoryPage.aspx?sectionName=Cricket&id =02aa7935-ad63-4848-a5e7-039a70092adb&&Headline=Jump+in+jobs+for+minorities (accessed December 30, 2008).

148. O. Gupta, "O Hindu Parents! O Students! Wake Up, Wake Up," *Organiser*, February 1, 2009, http://www.organiser.org/dynamic/modules.php?name=Content&pa=show page&pid=275&page=12 (accessed January 30, 2009).

149. "Now 'Marginalization of Muslims' in NCERT Textbook," May 28, 2008, http:// www.expressindia.com/latest-news/Now-Marginalisation-of-Muslims-in-NCERT -textbook/ 315760/ (accessed July 20, 2008).

150. Mohammed Siddique, "'The MIM Has Been Given Rs 5,000 Crore,'" *Rediff.com*, July 20, 2008, http://www.rediff.com/news/2008/jul/20inter1.htm (accessed November 15, 2008).

151. "2002 Gujarat Violence," *Wikipedia*, http://en.wikipedia.org/wiki/2002_Gujarat _violence (accessed March 5, 2007).

152. Commentary, "Terrorists & Politicians."

153. Balbir Punj, "Realpolitik: In Defence of the Rashtriya Suraksha Yatra," *Organiser*, April 2, 2006, http://www.organiser.org/dynamic/modules.php?name=Content&pa=show page&pid=124&page=7 (accessed May 2, 2007).

154. Ibid.

155. Ibid.

156. Ibid.

157. PTI, "Muslims Must Have First Claim on Resources,'" *Indian Express*, December 9, 2006, http://www.expressindia.com/fullstory.php?newsid=77972 (accessed March 2, 2007).

158. "First Look: Sonia Gandhi's Urdu Letter to UP Muslims," *Rediff.com*, April 20, 2007, http://www.rediff.com/news/2007/apr/20uppoll6.htm (accessed July 20, 2008); "Congress Communal Campaign," *Organiser*, April 29, 2007, http://www.organiser.org/dynamic/modules.php?name=Content&pa=showpage&pid=181&page=7 (accessed April 30, 2007).

159. The Hindu literacy percentage in India is similar to the national average; accessed from *CIA World Factbook* in 2007.

160. Anjali Patel, "Revenues from Temples Diverted for Haj Subsidy and Madarasas in Karnataka," *IVarta.com*, October 29, 2003, http://www.ivarta.com/columns/OL_031029 .htm (accessed July 20, 2008).

161. "India Census 2001—State-wise Religious Demography," December 26, 2006, http://www.crusadewatch.org/index.php?option=com_content&task=view&id=580&Item id=27 (accessed July 20, 2008); "India Census 2001—State-Wise Religious Demography," http://www.censusindia.gov.in/Census_Data_2001/Census_data_finder/C_Series/ Population_by_religious_communities.htm (accessed January 5, 2009).

162. "New Survey Busts Sachar Panel Report."

163. Varun Shivhare, "Minority Rights: The Judicial Approach," *Legalservicesindia.com*, http://www.legalservicesindia.com/articles/judi.htm (accessed July 20, 2008).

164. "India Census 2001—State-wise Religious Demography."

165. Moorthy Muthuswamy, "Religious Apartheid in India and American Policy Response," *IVarta.com*, July 4, 2005, http://www.ivarta.com/columns/OL_050704.htm (accessed July 20, 2008).

166. Ibid.

167. The author extracted these statistics from the college Web site in June 2008.

168. Muthuswamy, "Religious Apartheid in India and American Policy Response."

169. "India Census 2001—State-wise Religious Demography."

170. "Jamia Hamdard Gets Minority Institution Status," *Hindu*, February 7, 2004, http://www.hinduonnet.com/2004/02/07/stories/2004020711760300.htm (accessed July 20, 2008).

171. Sonia Sarkar, "St. Stephen's to Have 50% Christian Quota," *NDTV.com*, June 9,

2008, http://www.ndtv.com/convergence/ndtv/story.aspx?id=NEWEN20080052488 (accessed July 10, 2008).

172. Issac, "For Hindus in Kerala It's Now or Never."

173. PTI, "VHP Criticised LDF's Muslim Appeasement Policy," *Outlook India*, July 31, 2008, http://www.outlookindia.com/pti_news.asp?id=594383 (accessed August 2, 2008).

174. "Universal Declaration of Human Rights," UN Charter, December 10, 1948, http://www.un.org/Overview/rights.html (accessed May 2, 2007).

175. Hari Kumar, "Faiths Clash, Displacing Thousands in East India," *New York Times*, August 28, 2008, http://www.nytimes.com/2008/08/29/world/asia/29india.html (accessed September 12, 2008).

176. "Religion and Apartheid," *US Library of Congress*, http://countrystudies .us/south-africa/53.htm (accessed October 26, 2008).

177. "The Civil Rights Act of 1964 and the Equal Employment Opportunity Commission," http://www.archives.gov/education/lessons/civil-rights-act (accessed July 20, 2008).

178. USCIRF, "What Is the U.S. Commission on International Religious Freedom?" http://www.uscirf.gov/index.php?option=com_content&task=view&id=337&Itemid=44#1 (accessed July 20, 2008).

179. Preeta Bansal, e-mail message to author, June 15, 2008.

180. Ibid.

181. Thomas Schelling, "Dynamic Models of Segregation," *Journal of Mathematical Sociolgy* 1 (1971): 143–86.

182. "Thomas Schelling," *Wikipedia*, http://en.wikipedia.org/wiki/Thomas_Schelling (accessed September 12, 2008).

183. Kumar, "Faiths Clash, Displacing Thousands in East India."

184. "Christian Conversions and Terrorism in North East India," *Christianaggression.org*, March 10, 2006, http://www.christianaggression.org/item_display.php?type =ARTICLES&id=1141970933 (accessed September 12, 2008).

185. Somini Sengupta, "Terrorist Attacks Unsettling India," *New York Times*, July 29, 2008, http://www.nytimes.com/2008/07/29/world/asia/29india.html (accessed November 10, 2008).

186. "Urdu," *Wikipedia*, http://en.wikipedia.org/wiki/Urdu (accessed November 10, 2008).

187. Upadhyay, "Anti-terrorism Conference Dar-ul-Uloom Deoband—A Failed Exercise?"

188. Andy Mukherjee, "India's Fiscal Advance, Sadly, Is an Illusion," *International Herald Tribune*, June 3, 2005, http://www.iht.com/articles/2005/06/02/bloomberg/ sxmuk.php (accessed March 2, 2007).

189. "Economic Survey of China 2005," *OECD.org*, September 16, 2005, http:// www.oecd.org/document/31/0,3343,en_2649_34595_35343711_1_1_1_1,00.html (accessed November 10, 2008).

190. Harish Khare, "Manmohan Seeks $150 Billion U.S. Investment," *Hindu*, Sep-

tember 23, 2004, http://www.hindu.com/2004/09/23/stories/2004092308921101.htm (accessed May 1, 2007).

191. Sultan Shahin, "Manmohan's Kashmir Dreams," *Asia Times*, November 14, 2004, http://www.atimes.com/atimes/South_Asia/FK19Df02.html (accessed May 2, 2007).

192. George Iype, "Why Chidambaram Hiked Defense Outlay," *Rediff.com*, July 9, 2004, http://ia.rediff.com/news/2004/jul/09spec1.htm (accessed May 1, 2007).

193. Sumit Ganguly, "India Watch," *Commentary*, April 2008, http://www.commentary magazine.com/viewarticle.cfm/india-watch-11284?search=1 (accessed July 10, 2008).

194. S. Narayan, "Not a Rosy Picture Anymore," *Livemint.com*, June 22, 2008, http://www.livemint.com/2008/06/22222811/Not-a-rosy-picture-anymore.html (accessed July 20, 2008).

195. "Jarnail Singh Bhindranwale," *Wikipedia*, http://en.wikipedia.org/wiki/Jarnail_Singh_Bhindranwale (accessed November 11, 2008).

196. Swapan Dasgupta, "Asia's Other Maoist Threat," *Daily Times*, April 25, 2006, http://www.dailytimes.com.pk/default.asp?page=2006%5C04%5C25%5Cstory_25-4-2006_pg4_22 (accessed March 2, 2007).

197. PTI, "Naxalism Single Biggest Internal Security Challenge: PM," *Rediff.com*, April 13, 2006, http://www.rediff.com/news/2006/apr/13naxal.htm (accessed March 2, 2007).

198. Commentary, "Terrorists & Politicians."

199. "Natwar's Tirade: Steps Up Attack on PM," *Central Chronicle*, August 10, 2006, http://www.centralchronicle.com/20060810/1008001.htm (accessed March 2, 2007).

200. Ramesh Kandula, "Terrorism Most Dangerous Threat, Says Manmohan," *Tribune*, October 26, 2006, http://www.tribuneindia.com/2006/20061027/main1.htm (accessed May 1, 2007).

201. "Seal His Lips," *Newinsight.net*, April 7, 2007, http://www.newsinsight.net/archivedebates/nat2.asp?recno=1560 (accessed April 20, 2007).

202. "10 Questions: What about Pakistan?" *Stimson.org*, March 2, 2007, http://www.stimson.org/pub.cfm?id=401 (accessed May 2, 2007).

203. Moorthy Muthuswamy, "Talks with Pakistan: Overcoming Prithiviraj Syndrome," *SAAG*, January 23, 2004, http://www.southasiaanalysis.org/papers10/paper901.html (accessed March 2, 2007).

204. "Congress Minority Cell Wants Encounter Doubts Cleared," *Economic Times*, October 17, 2008, http://economictimes.indiatimes.com/News/PoliticsNation/Cong_minority_cell_wants_encounter_doubts_cleared/articleshow/3606000.cms (accessed November 9, 2008).

205. Punj, "Realpolitik: In Defense of the Rashtriya Suraksha Yatra."

206. "Ahmed Patel: UPA Govt. Is Sincere," *Milli Gazette*, September 1–15, 2004, http://www.milligazette.com/Archives/2004/01-15Sep04-Print-Edition/011509200458.htm (accessed August 30, 2008).

207. Diptosh Majumdar, "Whose UPA? 98 Letters Show Sonia's the Boss," *CNN-IBN*, August 3, 2008, http://www.ibnlive.com/news/whose-upa-98-letters-show-sonias-the-boss/70334-3.html?xml (accessed August 30, 2008).

208. "Demographics of India," *Wikipedia*, http://en.wikipedia.org/wiki/Demographics_of_India (accessed March 8, 2007).

209. "Could These Candidates Be Lawmakers?" *Indiatogether.com*, May 2004, http://www.indiatogether.org/2004/may/gov-karpolls.htm (accessed March 2, 2007).

210. Wonacott, "Lawless Legislators Thwart Social Progress in India."

211. "2008 Delhi Bombings," *Wikipedia*, http://en.wikipedia.org/wiki/2008_Delhi_bombings (accessed September 16, 2008).

212. "2008 Bangaluru Serial Blasts," *Wikipedia*, http://en.wikipedia.org/wiki/2008_Bangalore_bombing (accessed July 27, 2008).

213. "2008 Ahmedabad Bombings," *Wikipedia*, http://en.wikipedia.org/wiki/2008_Ahmedabad_serial_blasts (accessed July 28, 2008).

214. "The Rise of Jihad," *Islamicterrorism.wordpress.com*, August 7, 2008, http://islamicterrorism.wordpress.com/2008/08/07/full-text-of-indian-mujahideen-14-pages-email-on-terror-attacks/ (accessed November 15, 2008).

215. "Jamia University to Defend Students Held on Terror Charges," *Rediff.com*, September 23, 2008, http://www.rediff.com/news/2008/sep/23delblast2.htm (accessed October 11, 2008).

216. "Saudi King Donates USD 30 m to Jamia Millia Islamia," June 2, 2006, http://www.zeenews.com/Nation/2006-06-02/299497news.html (accessed January 21, 2009).

217. Yogesh Naik, "Many Cops Would've Died Had SRPF Not Opened Fire: Bhujbal," *Times of India*, October 1, 2008, http://timesofindia.indiatimes.com/Mumbai/Many_cops_wouldve_died_had_SRPF_not_opened_fire_Bhujbal_/articleshow/3547102.cms (accessed October 16, 2008).

218. "2008 Delhi Bombings."

219. "BJP CMs Take on UPA, Want Strict Terror Laws," *IBNLive.com*, October 13, 2008, http://www.ibnlive.com/news/bjp-cms-take-on-upa-want-strict-terror-laws/75721-3.html (accessed October 14, 2008).

220. Ramashray Upadhyay, "Restive Muslims—Impact on Internal Security?" *SAAG*, October 27, 2008, http://www.southasiaanalysis.org/papers29/paper2897.html (accessed October 27, 2007).

221. Swapan Dasgupta, "Treason Can't Be Made Respectable," *Pioneer*, October 19, 2008, http://www.dailypioneer.com/128749/Treason-can't-be-made-respectable.html (accessed October 19, 2008).

222. "Ulema Blind to National Interest," *Pioneer*, January 31, 2009, http://www.dailypioneer.com/153358/Contempt-for-the-truth.html (accessed January 31, 2009).

223. "Muslims Now Want to Be Tried Under Separate Law," *Pioneer*, January 30, 2009,

http://www.dailypioneer.com/153236/Muslims-now-want-to-be-tried-under-separate-law.html (accessed February 1, 2009).

224. "Ex-armymen Face Probe in Malegaon Case," *IBNLive.com*, October 25, 2008, http://ibnlive.in.com/news/malegaon-blasts-exarmymen-under-scanner/76721-3.html (accessed October 25, 2008).

225. "Insidious Investigations," *News Today*, November 15, 2008, http://news todaynet.com/newsindex.php?id=12309%20&%20section=13 (accessed November 15, 2008).

226. "Inter-Services Intelligence," *Wikipedia*, http://en.wikipedia.org/wiki/Inter-Services_Intelligence (accessed January 8, 2009).

227. "Lashkar-e-Taiba," *Satp.org*, http://www.satp.org/satporgtp/countries/india/states/jandk/terrorist_outfits/lashkar_e_toiba.htm (accessed December 4, 2008).

228. Jonathan Fighel, "The Saudi Connection to the Mumbai Massacres: Strategic Implications for Israel," *Jerusalem Center for Public Affairs*, February 12, 2009, http://www.jcpa.org/JCPA/Templates/ShowPage.asp?DRIT=1&DBID=1&LNGID=1&TMID=111&FID=442&PID=0&IID=2854&TTL=The_Saudi_Connection_to_the_Mumbai_Massacres:_Strategic_Implications_for_Israel (accessed February 15, 2009).

229. Bokhari, "Pakistani Army's Ties to Islamists Under Scrutiny."

230. Vicky Nanjappa, "An Urdu Poem Keeps Terrorists Going," *Rediff.com*, December 15, 2008, http://www.rediff.com/news/2008/dec/15mumterror-urdu-poem-keeps-terrorists-going.htm (accessed December 30, 2008).

231. Sheela Bhatt, "14–16 Indians Involved in 26/11 Attack, Says Mumbai Police," *Rediff.com*, February 12, 2008, http://www.rediff.com/news/2009/feb/12mumterror-26-11-had-local-help-mumbai-police.htm (accessed February 12, 2009).

232. Don Feder, "Were There Muslims in Mumbai?" *GrassTopsUSA.com*, December 4, 2008, http://www.frontpagemag.com/Articles/Read.aspx?GUID=284B7E05-7736-42E8-9351-E3FA3984AE98 (accessed December 6, 2008).

233. Manish Pachouly, Presley Thomas, and Haider Naqvi, "26/11 Planning Started a Year Ago, and We Had the Evidence," *Hindustan Times*, December 5, 2008, http://www.hindustantimes.com/StoryPage/FullcoverageStoryPage.aspx?id=ecd15cbe-5d40-4af4 ssed December 5, 2008).

Parthasarathy, from a published opinion in an Indian newspaper d 2007.

ndia Has Proof of ISI Hand in Mumbai Attacks," *Hindustan Times*, http://www.hindustantimes.com/StoryPage/FullcoverageStory 8fcb-452b-b424-0baffb3e47a2 (accessed December 5, 2008).

ainst Terrorism Not Enough, Says US," *IANS*, December 20, 2008, ws/paks-fight-against-terrorism-not-enough-says-us/80997-2.html 2008).

237. Razaul Laskar, "India Denies Troop Build-up along Border with Pak," *PTI*, December 27, 2008, http://www.rediff.com/news/2008/dec/27mumterror-india-denies-troop-build-up-along-border.htm (accessed December 30, 2008).

238. Indrani Bagchi, "Mumbai Attack: US, Western Pressure Worked," *Times of India*, February 13, 2008, http://timesofindia.indiatimes.com/India/Mumbai_attack_US_western_pressure_worked/articleshow/msid-4120445,curpg-1.cms (accessed February 12, 2009).

239. Aryn Baker, "India's Muslims in Crisis," *Time*, November 27, 2008, http://www.time.com/time/world/article/0,8599,1862650-2,00.html (accessed December 5, 2008).

240. Ibid.

241. Moorthy Muthuswamy, "Muslim War Criminals," *Washington Times*, December 6, 2008.

242. "Furor in Parliament over Antulay's Remarks," *Rediff.com*, December 18, 2008, http://www.rediff.com/news/2008/dec/18mumterror-furore-in-parliament-over-antulay-remarks.htm?zcc=rl (accessed December 30, 2008).

243. "Ahmed Says Sorry for Omitting Nariman House," *Sify.com*, December 17, 2008, http://sify.com/news/fullstory.php?id=14820493 (accessed December 30, 2008); Somendra Sharma, "Nariman House, Not Taj, Was the Prime Target on 26/11," *Daily News & Analysis*, January 5, 2009, http://www.dnaindia.com/report.asp?newsid=1218869&pageid=0 (accessed January 6, 2009).

244. Prafull Goradia, "Roots of Extremism Lie in India," *Pioneer*, January 21, 2009, http://www.dailypioneer.com/151282/Roots-of-extremism-lie-in-India.html (accessed January 21, 2009).

245. Brahma Chellaney, "Words Are All we Have," *Hindustan Times*, December 30, 2008, http://www.hindustantimes.com/StoryPage/StoryPage.aspx?id=4b9d0a27-ecb4-4c9b-8bd9-fc2f3720fdc0 (accessed January 1, 2009).

246. Bharat Verma, "Take the War to the Enemy," *Rediff.com*, December 22, 2008, http://www.rediff.com/news/2008/dec/22mumterror-take-the-war-to-the-enemy.htm (accessed December 30, 2008).

247. "Direct Action Day."

248. "India's Standoff with Jihad," *Frontpage Magazine*, March 28, 2008, http://frontpagemag.com/Articles/Read.aspx?GUID=B870EAA8-DC54-462B-8857-3AB88E021202 (accessed July 20, 2008).

249. Lisa Curtis, "After Mumbai: Time to Strengthen U.S.–India Counterterrorism Cooperation," *Heritage Foundation Backgrounder #2217*, December 9, 2008, http://www.heritage.org/Research/AsiaandthePacific/bg2217.cfm (accessed January 18, 2009); Angel Rabasa et al., "The Lessons of Mumbai," *RAND Occasional Papers #249*, January 16, 2009, http://www.rand.org/pubs/occasional_papers/2009/RAND_OP249.pdf (accessed January 18, 2009).

250. "Al Qaeda's Central Leadership," *Frontpage Magazine*, June 20, 2008, http://www.frontpagemag.com/Articles/Read.aspx?GUID=D5C28389-B48B-4189-B993-AB61D1B689C6 (accessed July 20, 2008).

Chapter Four

WINNING THE NEW COLD WAR

I t would be valuable to summarize the previous chapters in an effort to prepare the ground to discuss specific ideas on winning the new cold war against political Islam.

State sponsorship of political Islam and jihad (chapters 1 and 3):

- The terror war is primarily a consequence of the previous and continuing policies of nations that constitute the axis of jihad. Saudi Arabia, Pakistan, and Iran may be seen as constituting the axis; these are nations at the forefront of spreading political Islam and sponsoring worldwide jihad for Islamic conquest.
- Political Islam is primarily a tool for Arab expansion and conquest.
- Al Qaeda, the Taliban, or Hezbollah are either symptoms of the policies pursued or proxies of this axis.
- The resurgence of political Islam is mostly due to Saudi funding of Muslim institutions and distribution of literature around the world that promotes an Islam that emphasizes literal emphasis of the doctrines—the Wahhabi interpretation of Islam.
- Under pressure from America, Saudi Arabia has scaled down jihad directed at American interests. But it has not done so against countries such as India or Israel.
- Using charities, Saudi Arabia continues to sponsor the Talibanizing of Muslim-majority nations such as Bangladesh and of Muslim communities

around the world. In other words, Saudi Arabia is still pursuing jihad buildup throughout the world.

- In nations where political Islam is dominant, jihad building—not nation building—is the aspiration of the country.
- Within the past sixty years, in every Muslim-majority area of South Asia, without exception, upon achieving power Muslims have set about expelling most non-Muslims to nearby non-Muslim areas. This data unequivocally proves that a growing Muslim population can be an existential threat to the local non-Muslims.
- By focusing on the symptoms and on Iraq, and by failing to develop a strategy to fundamentally change or neutralize the axis of jihad nations, America has wasted valuable time and resources in the war on terror.

The origin and modalities of political Islam (chapter 2):

- The Islamic trilogy—consisting of the Koran, the Hadith, and the Sira, is considered to constitute the complete way of life for Muslims.
- Statistically, political Islam dominates the trilogy; this makes political Islam mainstream and its outlook remarkably similar across continents. Political Islam determines both the politics of internal governing of Muslims and the way Muslims should relate to unbelievers or non-Muslims.
- Inner political Islam has kept Muslims from progressing and being open to new ideas.
- External political Islam commands Muslims to wage a religious war (jihad) until the entire world is Islamized. Through its emphasis on jihad, political Islam converts Muslim civilians into warriors—literally a state within the state. This political Islamic goal of conquest grossly violates unbelievers' inalienable right to exist and to do so unmolested.
- Statistical analysis of the Islamic trilogy shows that it is the theology or the ideology of Islam that is driving political Islam's inability to coexist with unbelievers.
- Prominent Islamic theologians and scholars, ever since the birth of Islam, have emphasized the duty to wage jihad on unbelievers. This emphasis is by no means a minority view.
- Jihad is a multifront struggle, with warfare or terrorism constituting just one component. The rules of jihad are that there are almost no rules; only unbelievers are expected to adhere to the Geneva Conventions.

- Political Islam is propagated by mainstream Islamic institutions and by mainstream clerics. Radical Islam is one component of political Islam. Political Islam establishes bases for radicals among the Muslim populace and gets ordinary Muslims to sponsor radicals, extremists, and jihadists.
- The killings and wanton destruction of the property of unbelievers are part of a systematic effort toward achieving conquest of non-Muslim lands. This is a primary vision of political Islam, and these actions constitute crimes against humanity.
- Political Islam vastly exaggerates historical Muslim accomplishments in order to instill a sense of Muslim superiority, and deliberately and often falsely depicts non-Muslims as the root cause of Muslim deprivation and shortcomings, also called "grievances" or "injustices," to divert Muslim anger and to justify waging jihad.
- The origins of Islamic scriptures, which are used to justify the killing of unbelievers, deserve considerable scrutiny. Scientific analysis utilizing information in Islam's own trilogy suggests that these scriptures are likely neither to be complete nor accurately reproduced from "God's revelations."

INTERNATIONAL ORDER DISTURBED

The esteem in which religions are held by nations and societies is such that when a threat builds in God's name, nations tend to be blindsided. Even now, the parties most affected at the hands of political Islam—Europe and the nations of America, Israel, Europe, India, Russia, the Philippines, and Thailand—are all struggling to come up with an effective policy framework without resorting to an indiscriminate retaliation against Muslims generally. Political Islam has profoundly affected the international order. It is going to take a serious effort to restore that order.

The primary purpose of a religion is to define a code of conduct for its adherents to function within the framework of a society. Hence, a religion must be capable of preaching tolerance and allowing of its adherents to acquire new knowledge, compete, and create wealth in order to survive and grow. Under normal circumstances, any religion not following these requirements will lose out to other religions or other ways of life such as agnosticism or atheism. This is the law of nature and may be seen as the basis for trusting an established religion.

The inherited oil wealth in many Islamic countries—especially in Saudi Arabia, the birthplace of Islam and the place from which political Islam is directed though Wahhabism—has changed these requirements. This unearned wealth meant that the old rules of a "good religion" no longer apply. When this vast reservoir of money was mixed with the idea of Islamic conquest, as emphasized in the trilogy and consistently interpreted by Islamic scholars in subsequent centuries as a duty of Muslims, it resulted in jihad to convert the entire world to Islam. It is no stretch to say that oil wealth has empowered political Islam and has resulted in the war on terror.

For hundreds of millions of Muslims, most, if not all, of the important knowledge they require can be found in the Islamic trilogy. This interpretation has several consequences: Muslims are less likely to be open to sources of modern knowledge, and the clergy, due to their command of the Islamic trilogy, are the only people qualified to interpret it and hence to guide Muslims. Especially since the cleric does not consider progress to be among the desired objectives, Muslims, for the most part, have not progressed. Progress requires figuring out new ways of doing things and seeking out new knowledge. But such an approach contradicts the presumption that the trilogy is the dominant source of all important knowledge; this makes it unacceptable to most Muslim clerics. This has made Islamic civilization extraordinarily nonperforming. The evidence is there for all to see, in the form of a lack of scientific, manufacturing, and artistic outputs (for instance, Egypt produces just 375 new books a year as compared to 4,000 from Israel, which is one-tenth of its population).[1] Since according to most clerics there is no new important knowledge to be acquired, they channel the energy and attention of Muslim masses into worldwide jihad—the unfinished chapter of *infidel* conquest started by Islam's founder, Muhammad.

Except for oil—an inherited wealth—contemporary Islamic civilization, for the most part, has become incapable of creating new wealth on its own. With a rapidly growing population that is sustained by modern medicine and relatively easy availability of food due to technology, Islamic civilization is becoming increasingly poorer. The Human Development Index (HDI), published each year by the United Nations, is a comparative measure of life expectancy, literacy, education, and standards of living. Of the 32 countries rated "High" in 2006, not one was a Muslim-majority country. However, of the 30 countries rated "Low," 16 were Muslim countries.[2] This is despite oil wealth.

There is a tendency to underestimate jihadists and their sponsoring nations. Indeed, nations such as Saudi Arabia or Pakistan are governed poorly and their scientific and technological know-how are limited. But most of this came as a result of focusing on Islamic history and, in particular, on conquest through jihad.[3] However, considerable creativity, conceptualization, and idea development has gone into *infidel* conquest, as it has for centuries (see chapters 2 and 3).

Even with this historical passion for conquest, poorly organized Muslim communities were not able to translate their vision into reality until, as the best-selling American author Lawrence Right explains in his book *The Looming Tower: Al Qaeda and the Road to 9/11*, America inadvertently helped them set up a framework to create and sustain an armed jihad, starting in the early 1980s.[4] This American involvement, while it can be seen as a strategic success in driving out a declining Soviet Union from Afghanistan, may have set the stage for a strategic assault on Western civilization, Israel, and India by Islamists. With the Islamic trilogy as the undisputed common ideological source of inspiration or platform, Muslim groups in many parts of the world have started thinking and acting along very similar lines. Now we understand why Muslim populations, who otherwise seem disorganized, come together for the cause of jihad.

Indeed, the sophistication with which a multifront jihad is waged on unsuspecting nations is nothing short of phenomenal. This endeavor is sustained by the ongoing jihadist activities of Muslim organizations and the day-to-day emphasis of jihad in sermons from the mosques. It shouldn't be a surprise that the number one activity of Muslims when acting as a community appears to be toward the cause of jihad.

Some Western leaders have now begun to realize how jihadists think on a long-term basis, and more important, in stages of advancement related to Islamic conquest. The former chief justice of the Israeli Supreme Court, Moshe Landau, commented in 2000:

> I believe that we face adversaries who are much cleverer than we are, adversaries who know that they have to proceed in stages. As far as they are concerned, things are entirely clear—they don't want us here, but in the meantime, they are prepared to make do with whatever they can get at each stage that moves them closer to their ultimate objective.[5]

We saw how even without oil wealth, in modern times, political Islam has marginalized non-Muslims in South Asia (see chapter 3, "Siege of India"). Increasingly, Muslim civilians are being indoctrinated to become foot soldiers for jihad, and Muslim communities have been influenced to act in a support role and as recruitment bases. We now understand who does that; it is mainstream mosques and their clerics who play the dominant and most influential role behind political Islam. This is enhanced by the resources coming from many oil-rich nations, notably Saudi Arabia and Iran.

America's policy response, in recent times, has become too predictable and has operated within the confines of very restrictive rules of engagement. The exhausting American involvement in Iraq has weakened the US military and has exposed the limits of its power. The Bush administration, the regime behind the Iraq occupation policy, stood discredited and found itself short on political capital. The Islamist enemy knows the parameters within which a weakened America now responds to threats. Still, the Islamist enemy does not obey any rules when it comes to dealing with America. Jihadists claim, being part of or associated with much weaker nations, that they can't afford to play by international rules, which they claim were set by America. In other words, jihadists dictate the terms on which the terror war is conducted. This is among the primary reasons why America is making little headway in a very expensive and asymmetric war.

By 2008 the direct and indirect costs of the war on terror added up to at least a trillion dollars.[6] This enormously high figure is likely due to the initial shock and cost to the US economy of the 9/11 attacks. However, operationally, as Lawrence Lindsay, the former White House budget director, points out, the war is expected to cost about 2 percent of the GDP, which, in today's dollars, is about $160 billion per year. According to the Congressional Joint Economic Committee, the estimated cost of engagement in Iraq and Afghanistan for the years 2003 through 2017 is around $3.5 trillion dollars, compared to the estimated GDP output for those fifteen years of $300 trillion.[7]

These are not backbreaking expenses. However, the amount spent on the war on terror is a big chunk of America's budget deficit. For instance, the budget deficit for the fiscal year 2004 was about $476 billion.[8] Putting a price tag of about $200 billion, in both direct and indirect costs, on the overall war on terror, this broad-based war cost about 40 percent of the deficit itself—by no means a small amount. There are other disturbing financial trends. Steep losses occurred by the real estate and financial industries and the ensuing massive bailouts have led to a ballooning of the budget deficit and declining stock markets. The onset of what appears to be an extended recession is likely to result in a significant revision of the GDP projections noted previously.

With the rest of the world closing the gap with the United States in technology and innovation, the money could be better spent—to better educate future generations of Americans and improve its infrastructure. This deficit financing by borrowing is being passed on to the future generations.

Political Islam's resurgence, and its adverse impact even in secular democracies, has raised inconvenient questions about what a religion is, as opposed to a political or imperialistic ideology masquerading as a religion. The statistical analysis of the Islamic trilogy (see chapter 2, "Conquest by Design") throws a new perspective onto this question. In this context, there is also a question of what is meant by religious freedom as defined in the Universal Declaration of Human Rights and adopted and proclaimed by United Nations General Assembly resolution 217 A (III) of December 10, 1948.[9]

Saudi-funded or -trained imams have propagated political and terror-sponsoring Wahhabi Islam all over the world, including in American prisons, on the grounds of religious freedom (odd, since the Saudi state doesn't even allow the Bible to be brought onto its soil). It is unlikely that those who drafted the Universal Declaration of Human Rights foresaw religion becoming a destabilizing force on an international scale. Classifying any version of political Islam, including Wahhabi ideology, strictly as religion, especially after the 9/11 attacks, should be considered unwise. Yet federal institutions such as the State Department's Bureau of Democracy, Human Rights, and Labor and the United States Commission on International Religious Freedom may be doing just that. The congressional mandate issued to these federal entities to view religious freedom in the context of the obviously outdated Universal Declaration of Humans Rights needs to be revisited.

Jihadists understand that if Islamic doctrines are put under the microscope of a scientific analysis, they would find themselves in a hopeless situation (see chapter 2, "Science to the Rescue"). Hence, as American activist Janet Levy points out efforts are now underway to effectively eviscerate the Universal Declaration of Human Rights:

> [I]n March of 2008, the fifty-seven Muslim states that make up the Organization of Islamic Conference (OIC) struck a blow against free speech by successfully forcing through the United Nation's Human Rights Council (UNHRC) an amendment to a resolution on Freedom of Expression. The amendment, requiring extensive changes to the Universal Declaration of Human Rights, officially characterizes as abuse and an act of religious discrimination any criticism of Islam. It also calls for the UN Special Rapporteur on Freedom of Expression to report any individuals and news media issuing negative comments about Islam.
>
> In June, this limitation on free speech was further underscored when representatives of two non-governmental organizations sought to address stonings, honor killings and female genital mutilation sanctioned under *sharia* law. As part of the effort to mute criticism of Islam, the Egyptian UNHRC delegate demanded that the speakers be silenced, proclaiming, "Islam will not be crucified in this Council."
>
> Thus, banned from UNHRC sessions is criticism of *sharia* laws that oppress women, condemn homosexuals, and threaten converts and non-Muslims. Also banned are statements against Islamic law-sanctioned child marriage, honor killings, the hanging of homosexuals, and the murder of apostates.[10]

REFORM OF ISLAM AND ITS INSTITUTIONS

At a discussion with the *Washington Post* editorial board in December 2006, Secretary of State Condoleezza Rice talked of the struggle inside Islam to define the role for politics and religion. She was of the opinion that this struggle is between extremism and moderation. Here we take a closer look at the secretary's presumptions.

There is a claim that about 1 percent of the Muslim community consists of extremists and about 10 percent are said to approve of Bin Laden.[11] This data brings up the following questions: Where do the majority of Muslims stand? Is there any strong moderate component within Islam?

Even if most Muslims identify with political Islam's goals, only some can be in the position of full-time activists, like many extremists are. Most have more pressing needs, such as feeding their families. Given this reality, most Muslims have to look for easier ways by which they can contribute to the strengthening of political Islam. This includes monetary contributions to jihadist organizations and mosques and, of course, electing or supporting Muslim community leaders who are extremists or extremist sympathizers. Indeed, we find this to be the case in most Muslim communities across the world. Conclusion: Muslim communities are themselves under the spell of political Islam, with moderation almost nonexistent at the community level.

The above conclusion is diametrically opposed to the observation of Secretary Rice noted earlier. This book asserts that with political Islam dominating the scene, the struggle inside Islam is among different shades of extremism. This distinction is important in making policy initiatives.

Under what conditions do religions reform? Historically, and for good reasons, religious institutions—not individuals (such as moderate Muslims)—carry out reforms. For reform to take place, the following condition must exist: schools of alternate or moderate religious thought must flourish in an institutionalized way. Such a condition must involve tolerance for alternate views, and the doctrine itself should be amenable to reform. The Islamic doctrine, defined through the trilogy, is dominated by a political component and a violently hostile view of unbelievers (see chapter 2, "Conquest by Design"). How can this political component be deemphasized in order for reform to take place? Here is another damning but legitimate possibility: if Islam is designed for conquest, why should it be amenable for reform?

This raises the question of what a moderate form of Islam might look like. A moderate form of Islam would view Saudi Arabian Wahhabi Islam as the antithesis of moderation—as a fascist ideology. Here is the crux of the problem: most prominent

Sunni mosques around the world have been generously funded by Saudi Wahhabis or by Iranian ayatollahs on the Shiite side. A moderate mosque not only has to find its own funding but also go against the Muslim "mainstream."

With Wahhabism yet to be singled out before 2001, even in America, where the Muslim population is well educated, one would be hard-pressed to find moderate mosques. An April 2001 survey by the Council on American-Islamic Relations found 69 percent of Muslims in America saying it is "absolutely fundamental" or "very important" to have Salafi (similar to Wahhabi) teachings at their mosques (67 percent of respondents also expressed agreement with the statement "America is an immoral, corrupt society").[12] There was another poll conducted in Detroit area mosques in 2003. In this poll, 81 percent of the respondents endorsed the application of the medieval *sharia* in Muslim-majority lands.[13]

These statistics are an indication of political Islam's influence on Muslims. Based upon these statistics, it would be reasonable to conclude that roughly 65 percent of American Muslims identified with political Islam over the American system of liberty and tolerance.

American scholar Robert Spencer astutely observes on the lack of moderation among American Muslims: "[W]hen Muslims in America get angrier at me for discussing how other Muslims are using Islam to justify and spread an expansionist, totalitarian, and discriminatory ideology, than they do against those Muslims, it does not inspire confidence. In fact, it should make every non-Muslim who witnesses it wonder at their misplaced priorities, and at just how insincere are their protestations of moderation."[14]

A revealing statistic from the world's largest democracy—about 90 percent of the surveyed Mumbai Muslims preferring *sharia* "law" over secular civil code—was discussed in the previous chapter (see chapter 3, "Siege of India").[15] It shows an overwhelming majority of Indian Muslims, in a secular democratic nation with a non-Muslim majority, identifying with the extremist views of political Islam.

For Muslim scholars, brought up under the influence of exaggerated claims of glory of Islamic civilization, it is difficult to admit that Islam needs reform or that it may be fundamentally not amenable for reform (given its conquest-oriented dominance, as outlined in chapter 2). *Newsweek* commentator Fareed Zakaria writes: "The key is not religious reform, but political and economic reform. The entire emphasis on a transformation of Islam is misplaced."[16] Best-selling American Muslim author Reza Aslan claims that Islamic reformation is taking place at the individual level when Muslims seek out to study and interpret Islamic scriptures by themselves.[17]

The example of how India and Pakistan—sharing similar culture, language, and food habits but differing on religion—went their divergent ways (see chapters 1 and 3) shows that the emphasis on religious reform is perhaps more important than other reforms. Saudi money was not even in the pipeline when Pakistan began its descent into jihad, which occurred immediately after it was partitioned from British India in 1947.

People with Muslim background such as Zakaria, unlike many outsiders, have grossly misunderstood how political Islam has acted in overbearing ways using constitutional methods to ensure that meaningful political reforms do not take place.

When the world's first modern Islamic state was created in the form of Pakistan in 1947, the Objectives Resolution was passed that rested sovereignty with Allah or God.[18] This is unlike Western democracies or India where sovereignty rested with the people. Whenever a military regime overthrew a democratically elected government in Pakistan, the military dictators always proclaimed that they were chosen by God to rule over Pakistan since the sovereignty lies with him.[19]

Even American-supervised Iraqi and Afghan constitutions have some form of Islamic supremacy instilled in them. The Iraqi constitution specifically states: "Islam is the national religion and a basic foundation for the country's laws."[20] In Afghanistan, no law can be enacted that may contradict the beliefs and provisions of Islam (this is also a requirement of its neighbor Pakistan's constitution).[21] Also, when Afghan courts lack constitutional provisons, they may use the more Islamic theology–based *hanafi* jurisprudence, a form of *sharia*.[22] When the most important document of a nation, its constitution, becomes subservient to a thought process developed over a thousand years ago, it is hard to achieve what one customarily defines as progress or reform of a society.

Reza Aslan has overlooked the reality that Islamic scriptures themselves can be overwhelmingly seen as promoting puritanism and bigotry (see chapter 2). Hence, even as many Muslims bypass clerics to read the doctrines themselves, the ongoing reformation of Islam may not necessarily lead to (moderate) reform of Islam! Besides, historically, with every religion, reformation is always accompanied by the loosening of the grip that religious heads and their institutions hold over the masses. But in Islam in the last thirty-plus years, clerical control seems to have only gone up, with funding and books for mosques coming from Wahhabi-intensive Saudi Arabia. This is accompanied by other indicators of consolidation of political Islam: the spreading of *sharia* courts, from Saudi Arabia to Iran, Pakistan, Sudan, India, Nigeria, Somalia, and even in England. It is important to note that al Qaeda is a movement and that this movement has a widespread ideological following in the Muslim world. All of this data is telling us an inconvenient truth: increasingly, regressive forces are taking over Islam—this is no reform!

This reality is not lost on some scholars. In an op-ed titled "A More Islamic Islam" in the *Washington Post* in early 2007, American journalist Geneive Abdo points out:

> The self-proclaimed secularists represent only a small minority of Muslims. The views among religious Muslims from CAIR (Council on American-Islamic Relations) more closely reflect the views of the majority, not only in the United States but worldwide (CAIR denounced any notion of a reformation as another attempt by the West to impose its history and philosophy on the Islamic world).
>
> Consider the facts: Islamic revivalism has spread across the globe in the past 30 years, from the Middle East to parts of Africa. In Egypt, it is hard to find a woman on the street who does not wear a headscarf. Islamic political groups and movements are on the rise—from Hezbollah in Lebanon, to Hamas in the Gaza Strip and West Bank, to the Muslim Brotherhood in Egypt. Even in the United States, more and more American Muslims, particularly the young, are embracing Islam and religious symbolism in ways that their more secular, immigrant parents did not.
>
> Similarly, the political future of the Arab world is likely to consist of Islamic parties that are far less tolerant of what has historically been the U.S. foreign policy agenda in the region and that domestically are far more committed to implementing *sharia* law in varying degrees.
>
> In Europe and the United States, where Muslims have maximum exposure to Western culture, they are increasingly embracing Islamic values. In Britain, a growing number of Muslims advocate creating a court system based upon Islamic principles.
>
> What all this means is that Western hopes for full integration by Muslims in the West are unlikely to be realized, and that the future of the Islamic world will be much more Islamic than Western.[23]

The imposition of *sharia* law, more than any other, serves to place Muslim populations firmly in the control of extremists and to channel their energies into a never-ending warfare with unbelievers for the purpose of Islamic conquest (see chapter 3, "Jihad Buildup"). *Sharia* laws not only reflect the customs of medieval Islamic tribes but are also contradictory. In an interview, Canadian Muslim activist Hasan Mahmud makes the following observation:

> There are six thousand plus laws in *Shafii sharia*, a similar number in *Hanafi sharia*, about fifteen hundred in three volumes of Codified Islamic Law. But the Koran has only five or arguably seven social laws. The hadiths give us another few dozens, that's it. Then where do the thousands of other laws came from? Surely from non-divine sources. Now, if you drop a drop of milk in a pond can you call it a pond of milk?

Actually *sharia* laws were derived from at least eleven sources; of those ten are human and worldly sources.... The presence of at least five major sets of *sharia* laws conclusively proves they are not divine.... Many *sharia* laws are not only different from each other but are also contradictory.[24]

There are other indications that the attention of Muslim masses is directed toward the conquest of unbelievers through the formation of a supranational Islamic caliphate and the institution of *sharia* to keep them under the control of the clerics. Scholar Andrew Bostom notes:

[T]he preponderance of contemporary mainstream Muslims from Morocco to Indonesia apparently share with their murderous, jihad terror waging co-religionists from al Qaeda the goal (if not necessarily supporting the gruesome means) of re-establishing an Islamic Caliphate. Polling data just released (April 24, 2007) in a rigorously conducted face-to-face University of Maryland/WorldPublicOpinion.org interview survey of 4384 Muslims conducted between December 9, 2006, and February 15, 2007, 1000 Moroccans, 1000 Egyptians, 1243 Pakistanis, and 1141 Indonesians—reveal that 65.2% of those interviewed—almost 2/3, hardly a "fringe minority"—desired this outcome (i.e., "To unify all Islamic countries into a single Islamic state or Caliphate"), including 49% of "moderate" Indonesian Muslims. The internal validity of these data about the present longing for a Caliphate is strongly suggested by a concordant result: 65.5% of this Muslim sample approved the proposition "To require a strict application of *sharia* law in every Islamic country."[25]

As the homegrown jihadists increasingly turn their attention toward Saudi Arabia itself, Saudis, too, are now getting a taste of their own medicine. Saudi authorities are trying to use the top Wahhabi leadership in the kingdom to dissuade its youth from armed jihad. "The aggression against Muslims and the occupation of their lands," emphasizes grand mufti of Mecca al-Sheikh, "cannot justify attacks and violence: obeying the dictates of the Koran without fomenting hatred and division is a basic principle of Islam, in accord with the precepts sanctioned by the prophet Muhammad."[26]

The primary (manufactured or exaggerated) grievance of jihadists is "oppression" of Muslims and the "occupation of their lands" by unbelievers. In this context, the above statement by the cleric only encourages this grievance. Also, as discussed in chapter 2, several dictates in the Koran can be seen to foment hatred and division, and the grand cleric's broad statement does little to undercut the doctrine that drives Muslims into violence.

Saudi attempts to reform school texts that hatefully speak of non-Muslims in the context of Islamic doctrines came to naught due to the overwhelming anti-unbeliever content of the doctrines themselves and their interpretation by all of the authoritative schools of jurisprudence that command unbeliever subjugation (see chapter 2, "Conquest by Design").[27]

Madrassas are known as Muslim religious schools. The students who study there for a number of years usually graduate to become clerics. A typical course of study involves the memorization of the Koran as well as courses in the Hadith, the Arabic language, and Muslim history.[28] In addition, lacking a strong component of a modern education, these institutions are destined to produce graduates who only reinforce regressiveness within Islamic populations—and not lead reform of Muslim communities.

Not knowing Arabic (the original language in which the Koran was written) is a big hurdle for non-Arab Muslims who want to understand the Koran. Even for those who know Arabic, the complexity of the Koran, considered "exceedingly poetic and difficult to grasp," is such that mastering it is considered difficult.[29] These are among the main reasons the *madrassa*-educated clerics continue to play a prominent role in Muslim communities.

Even the door on the process of *ijtihad*, that of arriving at a decision on a point of Islamic law through the study of the Koran and Sunnah (which represents, broadly, the sayings and deeds of Muhammad), is considered closed. The last such scholar of *ijtihad* lived over nine hundred years ago, and since then independent study of the Koran and Sunnah has been discouraged—that is, authoritative reinterpretation of Islamic scriptures from a moderate angle is ruled out.

Even if *ijtihad* is possible, as discussed by American scholar Bill Warner below, when the doctrine itself is dominated by violent politics of its founder, its credible moderate interpretation is not feasible. He notes that about 61 percent of the Koran consists of anti-unbeliever material and that removing this material destroys the Koran. He states: "[T]he Koran cannot be reformed; or if it is reformed, it is no longer the Koran. . . . And there is no mechanism for reform. There is no body or group that could vote or agree on any change. . . . There is no way to control it. It has no center."[30]

One can ask an interesting question of how mainstream Islamic institutions respond in the modern era if a Muslim group or a sect interprets jihad in a much more defensive way. The Ahmadiyya Muslim sect was founded in 1889 (see chapter 2, "Islam in Modern Age"). It has a very small following in South Asia and among the transplanted people in Western nations. Interestingly, Ahmadiyyas view jihad as a tool that "can only be used to protect against extreme religious persecution."[31] However, the mainstream Islamic schools of thought such as orthodox Sunnis see the members of this sect as heretics due to the Ahmadiyya practices that are seen as inconsistent with Islamic doctrines. For instance, *not* defensive jihad, but offensive jihad—geared toward conquest of unbelievers—can be seen as the dominant call for jihad in Islamic doctrine (see chapter 1, "Resurgent Political Islam"). Besides, it is an open question whether this hounded sect would continue to view armed jihad as a defensive tool if it were to increase in number and gain controls of power in a nation. The fact that this sect can at best be described as a fringe Muslim group with little influence over mainstream Islam should be seen as confirming the difficult task of moderating Islam.

RIGHT TO EXIST

The inability of Muslim populations influenced by political Islam to coexist raises deep risk-management issues regarding the survival of unbelievers. Political Islam, regardless of where it is practiced, follows one set of texts—the Islamic trilogy—and this is the reason for the remarkable similarity in practice among Muslims across continents. Also, as was discussed previously, the lack of any reputed Muslim religious institution that offers alternate and moderate versions of Islam is notable, but not surprising, given the dominant political nature of the trilogy (see chapter 2, "Conquest by Design"). Political Islam is self-perpetuated by high birthrates within Muslim populations, even in nations where Muslims are a minority. Hence, it is no stretch to conclude the following: non-Muslims have no future as the resident Muslim population grows to reach majority status (see the data on South Asia in the previous chapter).

Along with the rise in the Muslim population, instabilities originating from this population will also escalate well before a Muslim majority is reached. This has no parallel with any other religion. This is what distinguishes Islam from other religions. An effective policy response should not only address the terror threats of the immediate future but should also address the much more serious strategic issue, the unbelievers' right to exist in the long run and to preemptively put forth policy measures to ensure their secure existence—a premier human rights issue.

Even if mainstream Islamic institutions in non-Muslim-majority nations appear to practice moderation in certain ways, given political Islam's track record, there is every reason to believe that these institutions will resort to more open and aggressive jihad once their power base increases.

Here is a situation described in British mosques, reported in *Dispatches* in 2006, with Saudis again playing the primary role in sponsoring jihad abroad:

A *Dispatches* reporter attends mosques run by organizations whose public faces are presented as moderate and finds (Muslim) preachers condemning integration into British society, condemning democracy and praising the Taliban for killing British soldiers....

Dispatches has investigated a number of mosques run by high-profile national organizations that claim to be dedicated to moderation and dialogue with other faiths. But an undercover reporter joined worshippers to find a message of religious bigotry and extremism being preached. He captures chilling sermons in which Saudi-trained preachers proclaim the supremacy of Islam, preach hatred for non-Muslims and for Muslims who do not follow their extreme beliefs and predict a coming jihad. "An army of Muslims will arise," announces one preacher. Another preacher said British Muslims must "dismantle" British democracy. They must "live like a state within a state" until they are "strong enough to take over." The investigation reveals that the influence of Saudi Arabian Islam, Wahhabism, extends beyond the walls of some mosques to influential organizations that advise the British government on inter-community relations and prevention of terrorism. The investigation reveals Saudi Arabian universities are recruiting young Western Muslims to train them in their extreme theology, then sending them back to the West to spread the word. And the *Dispatches* reporter discovers that British Muslims can ask for *fatwas*, religious rulings, direct from the top religious leader in Saudi Arabia, the Grand Mufti.[32]

In his book *Battling Terrorism: Legal Perspectives on the Use of Force and the War on Terror*, Australian political scientist Jackson Nyamuya Maogoto examines the legitimate use of force in counteracting state-sponsored terrorism. After examining the issues in the context of International Chief Justice rulings and UN resolutions, he points out: "The prohibition on the use of force has been traditionally balanced against the 'inherent' right to self-defense as contained in the UN charter," and on the evolution of retaliatory defense he notes, "It will be submitted that the UN charter regime on the use of force [on the states sponsoring terror] is visibly engaged in the process of change, especially in light of the September 11, 2001, attacks."[33] Conclusion: a victim nation of terror is left to decide how best it can retaliate against the unconventional terror war imposed in the name of Islam.

Consider the fictional scenario of aliens visiting Earth. If the evidence gradually develops that the alien intends to exterminate humans, this alien-human conflict becomes a death fight. Without either driving out the aliens or destroying them, humans have no future. In such a situation, if time is not on their side, humans have to hit back swiftly and decisively. A human retaliation may lead to the destruction of the entire alien civilization, including alien noncombatants.

A proportionate response to acts of jihad has proven to be ineffective and very costly. Instead of reducing the threat, it has emboldened political Islam and increased its power base among its adherents. When an enemy is proven in its intent to annihilate us, the ethics of warfare allow a response designed to comprehensively remove the enemy's ability to exterminate us. This should naturally mean that such a response cannot be proportionate, because a proportionate response largely leaves the enemy's diabolic capabilities intact. The needed disproportionate response at times may lead to high civilian casualties, as political Islam has set up base among indoctrinated and largely sympathetic Muslim civilian populations.

As discussed before, reform of Islam appears unlikely in the near future. As part of a robust risk-management policy and in line with civic responsibility, the time may have come to ask whether non-Muslim states should initiate policy measures that will break the back of political Islam, so that their Muslim residents are liberated to pursue alternate faiths or ways of life. This liberation can be seen as enabling religious freedom for a community repressed by a political ideology.

THINK POLITICAL ISLAM

By now, it must be clear that the unbelievers are at war with a political Islamic movement, not just with radical Islam. This necessary paradigm shift must be understood going forward. This approach still doesn't call for war on most Muslims. After all, Muslim civilians, too, are victims of political Islam. Political Islam's basis is in the trilogy and is identified with mainstream mosques and Muslim religious schools. In most Muslim-majority nations, political Islam determines the dynamics of the nation's outlook toward itself and outsiders. As a rule, this outlook is destabilizing and is geared toward conquest of unbelievers through jihad.

As we now know fully well, Americans as a whole, both liberals and conservatives, have not understood the new political Islamic enemy. On the right, former president George W. Bush's consistent emphasis of Islam as a "religion of peace" in the early part of his presidency couldn't have been helpful to the war on terror and neither it can be justified (see chapter 2, "Conquest by Design"), although he did stop using this phrase in his second term and began to use the phrases "Islamic fascism" and "Islamic fascists" more frequently.[34]

Peter Wehner, deputy assistant to former president Bush and director of the White House Office of Strategic Initiatives, showed a limited understanding of the ideological underpinnings of conquest in Islam and the passion it generates in its adherents to commit terror. He stated in January 2007 that the United States was involved in a struggle against "a global network of extremists who are driven by a twisted version of Islam."[35]

A nonbinding advisory given to the US State Department, the Department of Homeland Security (DHS), and the National Counter Terrorism Center advises appropriate terminology:

> Never use the terms "jihadist" or "mujahedeen" in conversation to describe the terrorists.... Calling our enemies "jihadis" and their movement a global "jihad" unintentionally legitimizes their actions.
>
> Use the terms "violent extremist" or "terrorist." Both are widely understood terms that define our enemies appropriately and simultaneously deny them any level of legitimacy.
>
> On the other hand, avoid ill-defined and offensive terminology: We are communicating with, not confronting, our audiences. Don't insult or confuse them with pejorative terms such as "Islamo-fascism," which are considered offensive by many Muslims.[36]

Scholar Robert Spencer articulates the pitfalls associated with the new lexicons:

> The problem here, in short, is that many Muslims believe that jihad essentially means holy war, and refusing to talk about it will not make it go away.... In reality, jihadists routinely claim "moral and religious legitimacy," and that has to be confronted, not ignored.... Instead, it [the new lexicon] is being dogmatically forced upon State and DHS officials, which will only have the effect of making them hesitant to study the nature of the jihadist appeal within the Islamic world.[37]

Mercifully there was an alternate school of thought within the US government. A report released later, titled "Freedom of Speech in Jihad Analysis: Debunking the Myth of Offensive Words," by unnamed Pentagon writers charged with "challenging conventional thinking," noted that "the fact is our enemies cite the source of Islam as the foundation for their global jihad.... We are left with the responsibility of portraying our enemies in an honest and accurate fashion."[38]

Even the study and understanding of Islam in the context of jihad has become difficult in certain American institutions. Hasham Islam, a top Muslim outreach aide to Deputy Secretary of Defense Gordon England, who was described by American terrorism expert Steven Emerson as "an Islamist with a pro-Muslim brotherhood bent," has been known to have brought groups to the Pentagon who have been unindicted coconspirators of an Islamic charity's trial.[39] Maj. Stephen Coughlin, described as "the most knowledgeable person in the US government on Islamic law," was let go because Hasham Islam wanted Coughlin to soften the hard-to-refute relationship between Islamic law and Islamist jihad doctrine, and Coughlin declined.[40]

Organizations with an Islamic extremist bent have been allowed to train military and law enforcement personnel. In one situation, Muslim chaplains for the US military were recruited, trained, and credentialed by a system funded by the Saudis. In another, FBI personnel were given "sensitivity training" by an Islamic organization unindicted as a coconspirator in an Islamic charity case.[41] Terrorism expert Steven Emerson's 2006 book, *Jihad Incorporated: A Guide to Militant Islam in the US*, gives an in-depth view of political Islamist penetration in America.[42]

The nature of the war itself, which has seen groups or actors that are unofficially patronized by states with global reach and influence but that obey no rules of engagement, has created tricky policy options. A clarification is in order here: although al Qaeda was not officially patronized by states such as Saudi Arabia or Pakistan, there have been reports of it receiving assistance from sympathetic government officials (for instance, through Pakistan's ISI) and nongovernmental organizations linked to these governments (see chapter 1, "Axis of Jihad and the New Cold War"). What this shows is the power and influence of political Islam, in defiance of policies set up by top national leaders. In his book *Frontline Pakistan: The Struggle with Militant Islam*, Pakistani journalist Zahid Hussein mentions that the former Pakistani president, Gen. Pervez Musharraf, was in an impossible position due to jihadist penetration of Pakistan's army and intelligence.[43] His successor, Asif Ali Zardari, too inherits a nation immersed in political Islamic culture. Hence, relying on governments in Islamic nations such as Pakistan or Saudi Arabia where political Islam is the overriding power is no way to win the war.

The June 2008 suicide attack near the Danish embassy in Pakistan that killed six people (it was claimed as retaliation for publishing cartoons of Islam's founder, Muhammad, in Denmark) exemplifies the above view and more. Instead of reining down on jihadists who tried to deny freedom of speech and exhibit violent intolerance, the Pakistani government was planning to ask the European Union (EU) to amend laws (i.e., make more restrictions) on the freedom of expression. There was even an element of intimidation on the part of the elected Pakistani government in "advising" the EU—"the [official] delegation [sent to Europe] would also tell the EU that if such acts against Islam are not controlled, more attacks on the EU diplomatic missions abroad could not be ruled out."[44]

Ahmed Rashid, a noted Pakistani author and journalist, mentioned the dilemma faced by leaders such as Musharraf as rulers of nations dominated by political Islam: "In the rapidly unfolding crisis in Pakistan, no matter what happens to President Pervez Musharraf—whether he survives politically or not—he is a lame duck. He is unable to rein in Talibanizing in Pakistan or to guide the country toward a more democratic future."[45]

With regard to political Islam, America faces three types of enemies: quasi-independent groups such as al Qaeda, openly antagonistic ones such as Iran, and superficial allies such as Pakistan or Saudi Arabia. America is still powerful enough to deal with the first kind, but given the damage done to the American military and due to the lack of political capital, the United States will find it hard to confront Iran militarily all by itself. A weakened America has little leverage in dealing with Pakistan or Saudi Arabia. Increasingly emboldened, it is a return to old habits for these nations in their sponsoring of worldwide jihad. However, by going after the theological and ideological foundations of political Islam, America can weaken the entire movement.

In this new cold war, the enemy builds up military strength in a non-Muslim state through indoctrination, infiltration from Islamic lands, and increasing the population growth of Muslim minorities under political Islamic control. The next step involves laying siege to the nation, and, finally, putting into place a Muslim insurgency. Such a multifront strategy drains the resources of the host country as the power of jihad escalates. Political Islam's siege of India shows us how this type of internal jihad is carried out (see chapter 3, "Siege of India"). The victimized nation faces poverty, expulsions of non-Muslims from Muslim-majority areas through fear and intimidation, and eventually the shrinkage and destruction of the host region.

Through indoctrination, political Islam prepares Muslim populations to impose a war of attrition on unsuspecting unbelievers. The Geneva Convention did not foresee this kind of warfare. Fundamentally, the success of the war on terror comes down to the willingness of nations to adapt to the strategies of political Islam.

The political Islamic movement's power structure is commanded by clerics, and their violent domineering influence has thus far prevented its trilogy of holy works from being put under a rational microscope. This is in sharp contrast with other world religions, which have gone through their own reformations that have forced introspection by the faithful and have evolved with the times.

The simplicity and strength of political Islam lies in its claims of associating all important information and a complete way of life with the trilogy of Islamic holy works. This simplicity means there can now be well-defined ideological and physical targets associated with political Islam. Seen in a different context, this simplicity can also be construed as political Islam's greatest weakness.

The core ideological strength of Western societies is their understanding of nature—called science—and the commonsense views that derive from it. The essence of the West's ideology is the reality of the modern world in which we live, while political Islam's ideology is ritualistic and relies on a rigid authoritarianism that is incapable of standing up to scrutiny (see chapter 2, "Science to the Rescue"). I differ from popular Canadian columnist Mark Steyn's view that "Islamism is militarily weak but ideologically confident. The West is militarily strong but ideologically insecure."[46]

Progress is gained by manipulating nature to achieve important human ends. It uses tools of science and engineering to solve problems and creates technological processes. The largely non-Muslim Chinese and the non-Christian Hindus in India are achieving progress by embracing this modern ideological vision, which was first developed in the West. For instance, common sense tells us that the technology existing at the time of Islam's founder, Muhammad, was not good enough to reproduce accurately what he was said to have received in the form of "God's revelations." It is this modern science–based rational and critical vision that is capable of discrediting the doctrinaire regressive approach of political Islam (see chapter 2, "Science to the Rescue"). But to execute this strategy as part of a policy response, Western societies must graduate from being politically correct to being politically smart.

With the war on terror dominating the federal government's bureaucracy, it should be immensely useful to make it mandatory for all federal employees to undertake a short course on political Islam. Even some of the US State Department's policies appear to be inadvertently aiding political Islam, at the expense of its victims. For instance, the State Department's inability to sufficiently acknowledge political Islam's role in keeping Palestinians repressed and channeling their energies into jihad directed at Israel and its viewing of the Hindu-Muslim conflict in India without the larger context of the jihad under way in South Asia are some of the examples.[47] Hence, without this mandatory course, even federal executives could get stuck in outdated views and inadvertently undermine the war effort.

A leader of a Muslim-majority nation or a community could be opposed to radical Islam but is unlikely to take a firm stand against political Islam, because political Islam represents the mainstream. Radical Islam could be kept in check through policies such as regulating what is being said in influential mosques and by denying radical parties from contesting elections, as is the case in Hosni Mubarak's Egypt or as was the case in Saddam Hussein's Iraq. But political Islam, mostly left untouched by these countermeasures, will continue to destabilize a nation through the preaching of the Islamic trilogy, whose contents and thrust discourage wealth creation and encourage conflict with unbelievers (see chapter 2), eventually putting it in a no-win situation. In other words, political Islam is the fertile environment that creates and sustains Muslim radicals, extremists, and jihadists. Since political Islam is based on and is the consequence of the Islamic doctrines themselves, neutralizing or weakening political Islam requires downgrading the importance Muslims attach to the Islamic trilogy.

The American policy of working with "moderates" within the Saudi leadership, or with heads of state such as former president Musharraf in Pakistan, has not led to the weakening of political Islam in these nations. These relationships may have led to a reduction of jihadist efforts directed at the West for the time being. But Pakistan and Saudi Arabia have continued direct jihad at Israel, India, and others. With political Islam as their guiding influence, these societies have changed little since 2001. The educational reforms carried out in these nations, at the behest of America, do almost nothing to discredit political Islam, because this requires, as mentioned in the previous paragraph, pointed questioning of Islam's doctrines and scriptures at the theological level—a very explosive proposition for the ruling class. Under the current circumstances, as well as in the near future, no Muslim leader can be expected to do this without being considered a heretic, an apostate, and a traitor to Islam. Therefore, only an outside non-Muslim power or powers with ideological, military, technological, and economic clout can do the job.

A great deal of resources and much effort has gone into the so-called public diplomacy aimed at reducing "Muslim Street's" anger toward America. This has involved taking Muslim students to World Cup soccer games in Germany, hosting training seminars for Arab journalists, or former undersecretary of state Karen Hughes talking to Muslim women around the world.[48] Unfortunately, none of these initiatives drive a much-needed wedge between political Islam (the instigator behind the street's anger) and its followers.

Al-Hurra is a US-financed Arab-speaking television network—a propaganda tool in the cold war against terrorism. Despite spending over $350 million since 2003, it has not succeeded all that well in attracting Arab viewers. In a Zogby public opinion poll of six Arab countries released in March 2008, about 54 percent said that they watched Al-Jazeera and 9 percent said Al-Arabiya for international news, while only 2 percent said that they had watched Al-Hurra. Interestingly, the Al-Hurra executives were quoted as saying that "[the purpose of Al-Hurra is] to offer a credible alternative news source." While the executives have clearly understated their objectives, the thrust of their program, which is designed to promote democracy and give positive impressions of America, has been considered "boring" by the Arab viewers.[49]

In my view Al-Jazeera's popularity has been primarily due to its ability to sensationalize jihad-related news and to provide the opportunity for jihadists to air their views. This is consistent with the reality that, as populations heavily influenced by political Islam, jihad is the primary passion of Arab populations. Hence if Al-Hurra were to launch propaganda discrediting political Islam and jihad (that could include a discussion of statistics of the trilogy, see chapter 2), it would become controversial and likely compel many in the Arab world to tune in. Also, such an approach would be consistent with a very successful form of propaganda that America and its allies used against Soviet-based communism—that of discrediting the communist ideology through wheels such as Radio Free Europe.

America and western Europe have had considerable success and experience as nonoccupying powers when they discredited and eventually defeated the Soviet-sponsored communist movement, thereby winning the Cold War. First, Soviet communism failed to bring progress to the people it ruled. The Soviet communist system simply could not generate enough wealth to make its people happy and to keep up with the United States on arms spending. But what made it collapse was when the United States demonstrated to the people of the Eastern Bloc why their system did not work and showed them alternatives that did: namely, the democracy, liberty, and free markets embodied in America and in most Western nations. In the end, it is this realization—not Western occupation—that led to the revolutions from within former Soviet satellites.

As discussed in chapter 1, "The Democracy Angle," American occupation succeeded in both Germany and Japan because their strongest institutions were weakened and discredited by defeat. However, when America entered Iraq and vanquished Saddam's Baathists, it inadvertently created an opening for the leading opposing power—political Islam—to flourish. In Afghanistan, radical Islam was considerably weakened when the Taliban and al Qaeda were defeated by America and its allies. However, political Islam in Afghanistan, the leading opposition power behind radical Islam, was left intact. The radical and militant forces of Islam were initially crushed, but the basic Muslim beliefs that supported these forces were not undermined. As an occupying power in need of local cooperation, America could in no way afford to totally discredit political Islam, since it is represented in mainstream Muslim religious institutions. The conclusion follows that, as an occupying power and a former adversary, America is not well positioned to liberate Iraq or Afghanistan from political Islam.

America's best chance of weakening political Islam and achieving true liberation in these areas, as it did with the former Soviet Union–based communist movement, is to function as a nonoccupying power.

In the end, it was the cultural superiority that won the old cold war for the Western world vis-à-vis the former Soviet Union, by giving access and means of influencing the Soviets and their satellites. After all, the residents of the Soviet bloc were overwhelmingly aping the Western culture, unlike the other way around. This is also true of Western civilization vis-à-vis the Saudi- and Iranian-led Islamic bloc.

During the Cold War, the communist movement was largely seen as a front for advancing the imperialist ambitions of the former Soviet Union. Today the political Islamic movement can rightly be seen as a front for Saudi Arabian conquest. This angle opens up the possibility of liberating followers of political Islam by putting policy initiatives—along the lines discussed here—in place.

FINANCING JIHAD

An in-depth article in the *Washington Post* has pointed out that by relying on the low-cost operations of the local cells and on their ability to execute criminal scams, al Qaeda has managed to bypass the financial dragnet set up by the United States and Europe. This article quotes a former counterterrorism official in Europe, noting: "I think there is a realization that they [stricter antiterrorism financing laws] are not that effective."[50] However, the financing of jihad buildup, the precursor to terror, is possibly less difficult to deal with. In chapter 1, "The Axis of Jihad and the New Cold War," we briefly discussed the role of Saudi-based charities and others in funding jihadist groups. While funding for jihad buildup comes from many Islamic nations, by most accounts, Saudi Arabia remains the dominant contributor. The US Treasury undersecretary, Stuart Levey, told the American Israel Public Affairs Committee (AIPAC) back in March 2005:

> For too long, wealthy donors and multinational charities in Saudi Arabia were underwriting terrorism of all kinds, without any meaningful controls.... We impatiently await the creation of a commission to monitor the charitable sector, and continue to insist that this commission regulate all Saudi charities, without exception of such groups as the Muslim World League and the International Islamic Relief Organization, or "IIRO." Also, in addition to the export of terrorist funds, we are extremely concerned about the export of terrorist ideologies. These teachings are as indispensable to terrorists as money, and possibly even more dangerous. We must

do all we can to ensure that extremist, violent ideologies are not disseminated under the cover of religious organizations, charities, or schools.[51]

Finally, in June 2008, the US Treasury Department designated the Saudi charity Al Haramain Islamic foundation as "having provided financial and material support to al Qaeda, as well as a wide range of designated terrorists and terrorist organizations."[52] Interestingly, this charity operated out of the Saudi embassy in many nations.[53] It is seen as a Saudi state-sponsored, funded, and run organization. However, other major government-linked Saudi charities such as the Muslim World League (MWL) or World Assembly of Muslim Youth (WAMY) have been left unchallenged. For instance, Rabita Trust, a Pakistan-based subsidiary of MWL is said to have played an indispensable role in the founding of al Qaeda and WAMY has been implicated in terror sponsorship in many parts of the world.[54]

Now more diverse sources of funds for jihad are developing. In recent years *Sharia*-Complaint Finance (SCF) banking has been rapidly gaining ground both in Islamic states and in the Western world in order to facilitate their Muslim residents' and resource-rich Muslim investors' desire to undergo "interest free" Islamic banking (considered a requirement for *sharia* compliance).

The reason for basing this banking system on *sharia*, was to show Muslims that Islam offers a complete system of guidance for life, and for a more insidious reason: to perpetuate the practice of *sharia*, to drive Muslim residents away from mainstream financial institutions into the hands of jihadists, and to fund jihadist causes in a more institutionalized way. Once this Islamic banking is instituted, SCF can become an avenue for collecting the 2.5 percent or more of their income that Muslims are expected to donate for religious causes each year. With fundamentalist-inclined Muslims typically running these *sharia* banking operations, there exists considerable scope for using these funds to promote jihad. This may already be happening in some nations.[55]

This banking may be fundamentally flawed, because it aims to prohibit interest (*riba*) and risk (*gharar*), both of which are rejected by the Koran. As a middleman and financial resource, traditional banks have to use both risk and interest in order to be financially sustainable. *Sharia* banking, by supposedly not doing either, has to undertake various gimmicks in order to stay afloat. In doing so, a *sharia* financial institution becomes a less efficient operation, while trying to function as a bank.[56] Scholar Alex Alexiev claims:

> There is plenty of evidence that the largest SCF banks also get involved in the financial support of extremism and terrorism.... They get away with that on a regular

basis. These include Islamic banks such as Al Rajhi Bank, the Dallah al-Baraqa group and the Prince Al-Faysal banking conglomerate. These banks are owned respectively by Suleiman Abdul Aziz al-Rajhi, Saleh Kamel and Prince Faysal al-Saud. All three of these individuals are extremely rich and highly influential members of the Saudi establishment, as well as being Wahhabi zealots and key promoters of *sharia* finance. Generally, the large SCF institutions provided funds to terrorist and extremist groups through various Islamic "charities" and cutouts that served to conceal the origin of the funds. A favorite vehicle was, for example, the International Islamic Relief Organization (IIRO), which is actually a department of the Muslim World League (MWL). Here is how the system works. The banks donate money to IIRO or a similar cutout, which "invest" in organizations like Bank Al-Taqwa or BMI [Bait ul Mal al Islami] that, in turn, steer the funds to terrorist groups.[57]

In what should be seen as a major reversal in fighting jihad funding and implementation of the medieval *sharia*, the United States Treasury Department under the outgoing George W. Bush administration decided to further legitimize *sharia* finance by conducting an "Islamic Finance 101" seminar.[58]

NODES OF SOCIAL NETWORK

The Australian military analyst David Kilcullen has pointed out in an essay the importance of a social network in spawning insurgencies (armed jihad is a form of insurgency).[59] Here we will explore these ideas further. The entities that hold a network (or a political movement) together and allow it to grow are known as nodes. In the context of political Islam or jihad, these nodes are typically mosques, *madrassas*, Muslim organizations, associations, or any platform that brings Muslims together as a community to work on a political Islamic agenda.

The onset of violent jihad in Muslim-majority southern Thailand shows how these nodes can create and sustain a violent jihadist outlook among the Muslim populace. This is usually the first step in which there is no identifiable leadership other than the mosque and clerics. We can note this "leaderless jihad" in an analysis of the Indian security analyst Raman:

[In southern Thailand] targeted attacks with small arms and ammunition on individuals with extreme cruelty, multiple explosions with minimum casualties, and attacks on places considered anti-Islam, such as places of entertainment, continue to be reported almost every day. The individuals targeted are not only Buddhists, but also public servants, including Muslims, viewed as collaborators of the government. … Unidentifiable jihadi forces orchestrated by an invisible command and control have been keeping the security forces at bay. … The jihadi leaders are neither visible nor audible. [There are] no recorded messages, no statements, no intercepts, no human intelligence derived either from sources or during the interrogation of arrested suspects. There are hardly any arrests—not even accidental.[60]

As the jihad buildup intensifies, mainstream mosques become the core nodes. By now Muslim communities are under the full control of political Islam and are indoctrinated toward jihad. The former governor of Kashmir, Jagmohan, describes in his book the role played by mosques in Kashmir:

> Besides subverting almost all the organs of the state power structure, establishing complete control over the local press, and setting in motion a vast propaganda machine of their own, the subversives used mosques extensively for rearing, nursing and fanning their activities. … From the mosques, fitted with numerous powerful loudspeakers, came the exhortations, slogans, declarations, announcements and programs. … The religious functions held in the mosques were fully exploited and the masses indoctrinated in the name of Islam and freedom. In the event of death of any "freedom fighter," special funeral prayers were held in big mosques and the occasion was used to make inflammatory speeches to whip up mass hysteria.[61]

Wealth creation is one very good measure of the extent of organization of communities and nations. It takes people working together in an organized manner to create wealth. The generally low human development index of Muslim nations can be seen as a reflection of Muslim communities' general disorganization.[62] Yet the effective jihad waged by Muslim groups the world over is undoubtedly due to their ability to organize under the leadership of the local mosques and the clergy. The fact that there is just one well-defined entity that brings Muslims together to wage jihad can also be a sign of weakness. This major weakness must be exploited. The nodes can be weakened. Nodes get their ideological standing from theology; their financial and logistical sponsorship is predominantly from the axis of jihad nations.

In fact, there is no way of building up jihad without the involvement of the mosques; it takes a religious institution to serve as a base for a religious war. That mosques act as the nerve centers of a religious war shouldn't be surprising; they were "the general headquarters of the time of Muslim armies."[63] In the section "Conquest by Design" in chapter 2, we said that "61 percent of the Koran speaks ill of unbelievers versus, at best, 2.6 percent of the Koran speaks well of humanity.... Fully 19 percent of the Koran calls for the violent conquest and subjugation of unbelievers. From the position of power and strength the Medina Koran speaks even more insistently on the violent conquest and subjugation of unbelievers." Hence, even if a mosque appears outwardly moderate in a non-Muslim nation, by preaching the trilogy dominated by political Islam, it is still stealthily building up jihad in the local Muslim community.

The enemy nodes of the social network, which were off-limits previously due to a lack of knowing the enemy and restrictive rules of engagement, are now ready for ideological, political, military, economic, and social assault on the basis of right of pre-emption. This means that policy measures can be taken at the nodal level without directly discriminating against individual Muslims. In this chapter, ideas are presented on how to discredit the standing of the nodes, shutting them down if need be, and going after the backer nations of these nodes. This way of waging war works to America's and other victim nations' advantage and exploits the enemy's vulnerabilities. This book envisions the use of force, but only sparingly, and in a devastating and focused manner.

The first priority is to address the issue of American military deployment in Iraq and Afghanistan.

DIRECTION CHANGE

There are now signs that the security situation in Iraq may finally be improving for the better. However, in Afghanistan the security situation has actually worsened. The improving security scenario in Iraq may offer the United States a phased withdrawal option with the tentative date for the complete redeployment of the last of its troops set for 2011. This option will allow for the transfer of some troops to Afghanistan.[64]

Among the questions are whether these shifts are tactical or long term and whether they are strategic in nature. In the case of a phased American withdrawal from Iraq, meddling by Iraqi neighbors and the deep-rooted Shia-Sunni rivalry may yet scuttle the recovery process and plunge Iraq into chaos. The Shia-Sunni rivalry is the most dangerous one; it has the potential to fracture the Iraqi police and army and significantly reduce the gains America has made in building up Iraq's security in recent years. Setting the above possibilities aside, we can now understand these shifts in the context of Islam's dynamics in Iraq.

As discussed in chapter 1, "Resurgent Political Islam," the worsening of the security situation in Iraq soon after the 2003 American invasion may itself be due to clerics and mosques playing the role of spoilers.[65] Aided by the sense of insecurity and defeat, people were flocking to the mosques to find religious solace. As a result, in 2003, immediately after the liberation of Iraq by US-led forces, and in 2004 and 2005, many of the Iraqi mosques were overflowing. With Saddam Hussein out of power, this situation in Iraqi allowed religious factions to step in to fill the power vacuum. But by the summer of 2008, mosques in Baghdad and elsewhere were seeing much smaller crowds. Along with these thinning crowds in mosques was a reduction in the overall level of violence in Baghdad and elsewhere.[66] I discuss later in this section reasons for increasing the unpopularity of Iraqi clerics and what it means for a pullout of American troops stationed in Iraq.

There were also reports of al Qaeda leaving Iraq for trouble spots such as Sudan, Somalia, and Afghanistan, partly because of an indifferent public and partly because of effective military operations by allied and Iraqi forces.[67] The United States successfully set up and funded the so-called Awakening Council Movement led by many non-fundamentalist Sunni Iraqi leaders in order to drive out al Qaeda from Sunni strongholds in Iraq.[68] According to Bob Woodward of the *Washington Post*, the successful impact of "groundbreaking new covert techniques enabled US military and intelligence officials to locate, target, and kill insurgent leaders and key individuals in extremist groups such as al Qaeda in Iraq."[69]

Among the challenges faced by both the Iraqi regime and the United States is how the Sunni militia set up by the United States is going to be integrated into the security forces. Only a small fraction of the militia members are expected to be absorbed into the Iraqi army. If the discarded members become disgruntled due to the lack of employment or the lack of power of being no longer a member of the militia, it may open up an avenue for al Qaeda's renewal in Iraq.

In the summer of 2008, the Mahdi militia army of the major Shia religious leader Muktada al-Sadr too saw its fortunes sink rapidly in its stronghold, of the Sadr City, aided in no small part by its use of extortion and violence. Iraq's US-backed Maliki government took advantage of the situation by sending Iraqi army units to take over many of al-Sadr's former strongholds.[70]

A revealing article published in the *New York Times* describes the evolving situation in Iraq:

> In two months of interviews with 40 young people in five Iraqi cities, a pattern of disenchantment emerged, in which young Iraqis, both poor and middle class, blamed clerics for the violence and the restrictions that have narrowed their lives. . . .

Professors reported difficulty in recruiting graduate students for religion classes. Attendance at weekly prayers appears to be down, even in areas where the violence has largely subsided, according to worshipers and imams in Baghdad and Falluja.... In a nod to those changing tastes, political parties are dropping overt references to religion.... Of the 900 juvenile detainees in American custody in November [2005], fewer than 10 percent claimed to be fighting a holy war, according to the American military. About one-third of adults said they were.[71]

Interviews conducted across Iraq for the *New York Times* article showed people's disenchantment with political Islam and dissociation from terrorism:

"The young people, they think that [violence committed in its name] is Islam," he [interviewee] said. "So Islam is a failure, not only in the students' minds, but also in the community."..."Before, parents warned their sons not to smoke or drink," said Muhammad Ali al-Jumaili, a Falluja father with a 20-year-old son. "Now all their energy is concentrated on not letting them be involved with terrorism."..."Now I hate Islam," she [an interviewee] said, sitting in her family's unadorned living room in central Baghdad. "Al Qaeda and the Mahdi Army are spreading hatred. People are being killed for nothing."[72]

The disenchantment with political Islam had been possible in Iraq because the secular regime of Saddam Hussein never allowed any Muslim institution or cleric, be it Sunni or Shia, to rise to prominence there. This is unlike most other Muslim nations. In almost every other Islamic country, whether they be elected, autocratic, or monarchic, the ruling regimes have sought to associate themselves with theocracy either to gain support or to legitimize themselves. But decades of Saddam's secular rule left political Islam and Muslim clerics as unlikely leaders in the minds of Iraqis and their role readily questioned when the going got tough.

This analysis sheds insight on how to weaken political Islam. But this change in trend in Iraq shouldn't be confused with marginalizing political Islam completely—the latter being a necessary requirement for functional democracy to take root in Iraq. The same *New York Times* article also notes, "A tremendous piety still predominates in the private lives of young Iraqis, and religious leaders, despite the increased skepticism, still wield tremendous power."[73]

Increasing troop strengths in Iraq as part of a "surge" put forward by former president George W. Bush in January 2007,[74] in my view, took advantage of the changing mind-set of the Iraqis. This mind-set change, as noted earlier, is due to disenchantment with political Islam—translated to mean lessened influence of clerics and mosques, and in turn, led to a reduced recruitment of Iraqis for terror attacks and a weakened insurgency. It is unlikely that this surge, by itself or in combination with other groundbreaking tactics, including the efficient liquidation of insurgency leadership (developed by the then American commander in Iraq Gen. David Petraeus, Gen. Raymond Odierno, and others), led to the shift toward Iraqi political and military autonomy discussed at the beginning of this section. After all, informed observers have been talking about increasing troop levels to more than 300,000 in order to stabilize Iraq.[75] Even with the additional 30,000 troops that the surge increase injected, the total number of American troops in Iraq was increased to only about 170,000 in the summer of 2008.

Even a weakened political Islam is still capable of driving a wedge between America and the Iraqis—and will likely keep the fires of insurgency burning. In what may be a disturbing sign of things to come, a cleric named Nadhim Khalil has become the new local strongman in the Sunni region of Thuluyah in central Iraq.[76] Since the United States doesn't appear to have any long-term plan (as previously noted) to marginalize political Islam in Iraq completely, America's ability to fully stabilize and transform Iraq will remain limited.

Hence the question of whether America needs to cut its losses and get out of both Iraq and Afghanistan as soon as possible is an appropriate one to ask. As is pointed out in the excerpts below, America is not ready for the kind of rules of engagement that it would take to stabilize Iraq or even Afghanistan in the short term.

As America military scholar Edward Luttwak points out in a decisive analysis, titled "Dead End: Counterinsurgency Warfare as Military Malpractice:"

> All its best methods, all its clever tactics, all the treasure and blood that the United States has been willing to expend, cannot overcome the crippling ambivalence of occupiers who refuse to govern, and their principled and inevitable refusal to out-terrorize the insurgents, the necessary and sufficient condition of a tranquil occupation.[77]

If "out-terrorizing" is what it takes to stabilize Iraq, America will have to enact a Saddam Hussein–type crackdown in Iraq—and that's an unlikely proposition. Even then, these steps would do little to neutralize political Islam and therefore not aid in reaching the stated US ultimate goal: a functional democracy in Iraq.

The Iraq Study Group, also known as the Baker-Hamilton Commission, was a ten-person bipartisan panel appointed in 2006 by the United States Congress. It was charged with assessing the situation in Iraq and the US-led Iraq War and making policy recommendations. This study group has also reached the conclusion that

America should pull out of Iraq.[78] But several knowledgeable observers have voiced reservations about many of the group's recommendations. For instance, its suggestion that America work with Iran and Syria to stabilize Iraq may be a nonstarter, owing to strategic and important ideological divergences both nations have with the United States globally and in Iraq. Likewise, the suggestion of increasing the number of American advisors for the Iraqi army while withdrawing a significant proportion of American troops would mean these advisors would be left with little protection. Based upon the backgrounds of the people comprising the study group, there is little to suggest that the group understands how political Islam operates. This fundamentally limits the group's utility and the value of its recommendations.

American defense analyst Carl Conetta points out the evolution of anti-Americanism in Iraq:

> Most disturbing, support among Iraqis for attacks on coalition forces registered at 61 percent in the September 2006 poll—up from 47 percent in January 2006. Among Shia, support for attacks is 62 percent; among Sunnis, 92 percent. A September 2006 poll for the Defense Department found somewhat lower levels of support for the attacks, but still quite disturbing: 75 percent of Sunnis supported them—up from 14 percent in 2003. An October 2006 poll by the British Ministry of Defense found similar results. And a January 2005 poll by Zogby International found that 53 percent of Sunnis supported attacks on U.S. troops at that time.... Generally speaking, Iraqi sentiments regarding the U.S. presence have grown steadily more negative since the summer of 2003... [with] 79 percent of Iraqis saying that the United States is having a negative influence on the situation in Iraq, and with just 14 percent saying that it is having a positive influence.[79]

Being under the influence of political Islam means at least a dislike if not a downright hatred of America. The exception would be the Kurds of northern Iraq; a bare majority of them, due to strategic compulsions that make them vary of Sunnis and Shiites, have embraced a pro-American stance. Even if some American forces are kept in friendly Iraqi Kurdish areas to protect Kurds from Turkey (which sees this area as a stronghold base for the Kurdish separatists in its Kurd-majority areas), it may not come as a surprise if the governing Islamic party in Turkey encourages Iraqi Sunnis, Shiites, or even al Qaeda to go after American troops in order to clear the way for Turkey's incursion into Kurdish areas of northern Iraq. Another reason for Turkey's interest in the Iraqi Kurdish region is the presence of large deposits of fossil fuels.

This book takes the view that American reluctance to leave Iraq is partly due to a lack of comprehensive policy on how to successfully execute the war on terror. Bush administration officials have claimed that by fighting al Qaeda in Iraq, they have prevented it from going elsewhere—including America—to fight the unbelievers. Even that reason may no longer be valid with the news that al Qaeda fighters are moving away from Iraq (presumably due to lack of public sympathy) and into Afghanistan and other trouble spots. An American establishment that identifies political Islam and its sponsors recognizes the axis of jihad as the real enemy and knows how to deal with them may be willing to expedite a quick redeployment from Iraq.

There exists the potential for continued Sunni-Shia conflict, as the United States begins a phased withdrawal from Iraq. Among the issues is the question of how this conflict will shape the dynamics of the struggle within Iraq and beyond, as well as its impact on the broader war on terror itself. Already there are reports of private Saudis funneling cash to Sunni Iraqi insurgents.[80] According to news reports, Saudis told Vice President Cheney in late 2006 of their intention to come to the aid of Sunnis in Iraq.[81] Iran is already seen to be siding with the Shiite majority there, with considerable resources and energy from Saudi Arabia and Iran getting pulled into any renewed Shia-Sunni conflict, if it erupts there.[82] Otherwise, it's likely that these resources would have gone into jihad directed at unbelievers. This may not be a bad thing; so long as the Muslim groups are fighting one another, they will be less inclined to terrorize the West and others.

The first order of priority is to make the best out of the strategic necessity of leaving Iraq. American military engagement in Iraq is a huge endeavor, involving well over 100,000 troops. Supplying and sustaining this military deployment has been taxing even for a resourceful nation like America. In order to supply the main divisions in and around Baghdad, the lines of communication traverse about four hundred miles of hostile, insurgent-infested territory to and from Kuwait. Our extended stay has drained American troops both emotionally and psychologically. The sights of welcoming Iraqis and nation building have fast given away to a hostile Iraqi public and a full-fledged insurgency. With casualty figures now exceeding 4,000 dead and many times more injured, the American military is hurting. This war has also resulted in a horrendous death toll among Iraqis, with the number exceeding 100,000.[83]

Starved of cash due to a very expensive war, the American military hasn't been able to replenish its hardware adequately. New purchases are either put on hold or drastically scaled down. The Pentagon's own reports have questioned its ability to simultaneously deploy a large contingent of US armed forces in other hot spots while America is still engaged militarily in Iraq. Gen. Barry McCaffrey, a retired US Army four-star general, told *Time* magazine in January 2005, "The Army's wheels are going to come off in the next 24 months.... We are now in a period of considerable strategic peril."[84] A redeployment of the American military away from battle zones in Iraq should lead to a much-needed healing and an opportunity for rebuilding the American war machine.

The situation is turning for the worse in Afghanistan. But with jihadist recruitment unlikely to taper down in Pakistan or in Afghanistan, America and its allies find themselves in a no-win situation. Pakistanis attempted to wash their hands of the Taliban infiltration from tribal North Waziristan, claiming that they have little control over this region despite repeated supposed attempts to assert such control through political and military means. Pakistan cut a "peace" deal with a Taliban advisory council in 2005 and again in 2008.[85] Since then, in violation of these agreements, Taliban infiltration into Afghanistan has increased several fold, making American attempts to stabilize Afghanistan untenable. Also, this deal has backfired on Pakistan; it has given Taliban–al Qaeda forces time to regroup and attack the local Pakistani forces with renewed vigor.

Political and popular compulsions in nations with strong political Islamic movements such as the one in Pakistan tend to identify with extremists, as extremists are the foot soldiers of political Islam. This is true of the newly elected coalition government in Pakistan that had initially taken a soft line toward extremist groups, including the Taliban. The new regime initially tried to scale down Pakistani cooperation with the United States, including the effort to hunt down Bin Laden.[86] However, the cosmopolitan elite who rule the establishment in Pakistan do not wish to see the Taliban in their backyard. With the Pakistani Taliban pressing down on the northwestern city of Peshawar, the new Pakistani regime took another U-turn and decided to work with the United States to weaken the Taliban–Al Qaeda hold on the northwest frontier of Pakistan (adjacent to Afghanistan). Still, it is useful to note the evolution of the Pakistani approach to dealing with extremism. In my view, Pakistan will side with the United States only to the extent that the Taliban is made no longer a threat to itself— and once the Taliban is seen as containable, Pakistan will resort to the old habit of using extremists to hedge against the West in Afghanistan and in the East against its archrival India.

In 2008, as noted earlier, the newly elected Pakistani regime signed another "peace" deal with the Taliban. American author and analyst Daveed Gartenstein-Ross and American freelance military analyst Bill Roggio offered these observations in the *Weekly Standard:*

It is not surprising then that Pakistan's new government launched a round of negotiations with the country's Islamic extremists. What was unexpected, though, was the
scale of the negotiations. Talks have been opened and agreements entered with virtually every militant outfit in the country. But the government has done nothing to
answer the problem of the past accords and is again accepting promises that it has
no means of enforcing.... This strategy of accelerated appeasement only empowers
groups with a history of violence who are devoted to undermining Pakistan's sovereignty. In addition to creating breathing space for extremists (since it is the militants
who determine when an agreement is broken), the accords allow a greater flow of
recruits to the training camps and further violence. At best, the politicians are
shunting the problems down the road—and these problems will be larger by the
time Pakistan is forced to confront them.[87]

There are other reasons for Pakistan to take the "peace" route. For a nation in
which political Islam is the de facto power, Pakistan's military and paramilitary units
find themselves reluctant to engage al Qaeda and Taliban fighters even within their
own territory.[88] How the Pakistani public sees the United States—vis-à-vis its archen-
emies, al Qaeda and the Taliban—is revealed in this May–June 2008 poll:

Fifty-eight percent of Pakistanis favor negotiating with Taliban militants rather than
fighting them.... The poll found 50 percent of respondents wanted talks with Al
Qaeda, and 19 percent wanted the government to fight the local Taliban. Only 8
percent blamed Al Qaeda and 4 percent the Pakistani Taliban for violence in the
county... [while] 52 percent hold their United States allies in the war on terror most
responsible for violence in the country.[89]

The result of a survey in which 79 percent of the Pakistanis polled agree with
seeking to "require Islamic countries to impose a strict application of *sharia*" appears
to indicate that the vast majority of Pakistanis are not moderates. In this survey only
those living in urban areas were polled. Had the rural Pakistanis been polled, the percentage would likely have been overwhelming.[90]

According to a June 2008 Rand Corporation report, the US think tank found that
"Pakistani intelligence agents and paramilitary forces have helped train Taliban insurgents and have given them information about American troop movements in
Afghanistan."[91] This shouldn't be surprising at all given the way Pakistanis view the
Taliban vis-à-vis America and the fact that most Pakistanis cannot be construed as
moderates. In July 2008, the Bush administration finally decided to confront Pakistan,
"[w]ith new information about ties between the country's powerful spy service and

militants operating in Pakistan's tribal areas."[92] The Afghan government also lashed out at Pakistan by accusing its intelligence service and army of sponsoring the Taliban and calling its security forces the "world's biggest producers of terrorism and extremism."[93] India joined the bandwagon by pointing a finger at the Pakistani role in the suicide bombing near the Indian embassy in Kabul. This bombing has called into question its construction efforts there.[94] An additional complication has arrived in the form of the mullah regime in Tehran taking on the new role of sponsoring the Taliban—by giving the Afghan insurgents shelter, arms, and money.[95]

Economic realities and an unwillingness to give up expansionist ambitions may have forced Pakistan's establishment to use the Taliban or al Qaeda to extract billions in assistance from the West. A retired Pakistani official was quoted in a *New York Times* article, "The reason the Pakistani security services support the Taliban, he said, is for money: after the 9/11 attacks, the Pakistani military concluded that keeping the Taliban alive was the surest way to win billions of dollars in aid that Pakistan needed to survive. The military's complicated relationship with the Taliban is part of what the official called the Pakistani military's 'strategic games.'"[96] Pakistan's actions continued to remind America that it held many cards. In November 2008, it cut off the main supply route through the Khyber Pass for NATO troops in Afghanistan citing Taliban and al Qaeda attacks. This supply line runs from the Pakistani port city of Karachi to the Afghan capital Kabul—and transports 70 percent of the oil, clothes, and food needed for the troops in Afghanistan.[97] This was followed by the torching, in the eastern Pakistani city of Peshawar, of about 150 trucks carrying supplies to the US and NATO forces in Afghanistan.[98]

American journalist and terrorism analyst Peter Bergen urges that "there should be a military, diplomatic, and reconstruction 'surge' to Afghanistan, a country where such efforts have a fighting chance of real success."[99] Bergen probably didn't expect the tide to turn in Iraq. Few others did as well. Having now understood why it did, one has to conclude that the prerequisite for stabilizing Afghanistan is the weakening of political Islam there (and in Pakistan), and that is unlikely for some time to come. There appears to be no evidence that the clerics have become unpopular in Afghanistan. As a society that has traditionally held clerics in high esteem, increasing violence there will more likely be associated with the presence of alien Western powers (as polls in neighboring Pakistan have indicated) than seen as being due to clerics—and by extension political Islam. Besides, the United States policy in Afghanistan vis-à-vis political Islam has been one of inadvertently empowering it—by building mosques and *madrassas*, in addition to constructing schools and infrastructure.[100]

The heroin trade now said to account for about 50 percent of the Afghan economy and aiding the funding of the Taliban is not helping matters.[101] Adding to the mix is the overall literacy rate in Afghanistan of only 28 percent—among the world's worst (in comparison, Iraq has an overall literacy rate of about 78 percent).[102] While the United States could enroll the still-powerful Sunni tribal chiefs against al Qaeda in Iraq, due to the Taliban–Al Qaeda decimation of the tribal leaders, it is unlikely that a similar approach would work in northwest Pakistan.[103]

Exhausted by its efforts in Iraq, the American public and its military are not ready for another deadly and prolonged fight with a nuclear-armed adversary. Still, the United States began stepping up unilateral air strikes by unmanned aircraft inside Pakistan by March 2008.[104] According to US officials, these unmanned strikes in Pakistan were "aimed at disrupting Al Qaeda's ability to attack the West.... The strikes in Pakistan's tribal areas have disrupted Al Qaeda and the Taliban's operations, but will not dislodge the groups from power in the region."[105] But by the summer of 2008, the United States was increasingly left with the unpleasant choice of whether or not to send its military into Pakistan to neutralize the Taliban and al Qaeda. But such an intervention is certain to destabilize Pakistan further. Previously, former president Musharraf was seen as someone who didn't want to give up on the Taliban, due to the possibility of using it later as a strategic leverage against India—Pakistan's archenemy. With pressure from the Taliban mounting within Pakistan and Musharraf finally out of power, the Pakistani military started fighting back under its new army chief, Gen. Ashfaq Kiyani.[106]

By October 2008, both Britain's ambassador in Afghanistan and its senior most military commander there felt that the war on the Taliban could not be won.[107] A concerned Saudi Arabia fearing an expanding Iranian influence in Afghanistan and an America limited by its options in Afghanistan and Pakistan saw their interests temporarily converging in Afghanistan. These nations were reported to be working together to use the Saudi influence on the Taliban and Pakistan to bring the Taliban into the Afghan government as a way toward ending the Taliban insurgency and to expedite the withdrawal of allied troops from Afghanistan.[108] If the Taliban were to be back in power in Afghanistan, it is hard not see it as a strategic failure for the West in the region.

All of this points to the reality that the United States has no other alternative but to take on the political Islamic movement as a nonoccupying power and use strategies similar to the ones used to successfully discredit the old Soviet-based communist ideology.

An American pullout from Iraq and Afghanistan could lead to the following: Iraq becoming a Shia or al Qaeda terror base; intense conflict between Shiites and Sunnis emerging there, and the Taliban and al Qaeda coming back to power in Afghanistan. Given the Shia-Sunni-Kurd fault lines in Iraq and the natural skepticism toward clerics among the populace, turning it into a powerful terror base for al Qaeda or a radical Shia group wouldn't be easy. A long drawn-out and intensifying conflict between Sunnis and Shiites in Iraq will eventually destabilize the region. But that is likely going to take several years. In the case of Afghanistan, Western powers simply wouldn't allow Pakistan and Saudi Arabia to repeat the level of sponsorship they gave to terror entities there before 2001.

Like it did recently in Somalia and now in using unmanned aircraft in the regions of Pakistan bordering Afghanistan, the American military can be utilized without occupation to disrupt and destroy jihadist groups. Such steps should discourage jihadist groups from using weak nations or sympathetic ones as staging posts for jihad directed at America and its allies, while alternate strategies to confront political Islam and the axis of jihad nations are developed. It is understandable for America to work with the Saudis to curtail the Iranian influence in Lebanon, but it must refrain from the temptation of aligning with quasi-independent Sunni extremists to contain Iran.

First and the foremost the responsibility of America is toward its citizens and allies who are victimized by political Islam. Short-term hardships brought to Iraqis or Afghans in the event of an American pullout, while regrettable, are not entirely the fault of the United States. Indeed, it can be argued that sectarian warfare in Iraq and the Taliban infiltration from sanctuaries in Pakistan have their roots in political Islam. By redirecting the war on terror and by breaking the back of the political Islamic movement worldwide, America can bring about the best gift for all—the gift of long-term peace, development, and stability.

GRIEVANCE BUILDUP

Anger and hatred are mechanisms that get humans to come together to fight an enemy even at the cost of personal suffering. High priests of Islam know this only too well. While the theological underpinnings of political Islam are used to justify terrorism directed at unbelievers, various Islamic "causes" or "grievances," often exaggerated or unjustified, have been created by Islamists to rally Muslim masses around the world. They range from pan-Islamic issues, such as the Israel-Palestinian conflict (due to the involvement of Jews and Muhammad's descendents, the Arabs, this conflict has a pan-Islamic flavor to it), to regional ones, such as the Kashmir conflict. Invariably, unbeliever nations are always portrayed as being at fault. The list of grievances also includes bread-and-butter issues such as poverty and unemployment of Muslims. In Muslim-majority nations the blame for poverty is squarely placed on the regime if a non-Islamist regime is running the show (as is the case in Egypt) or on Western nations if the mullahs are running the show (as is the case in Iran). In non-Muslim nations, it is always the non-Muslim majority and the regime in power that is to be blamed. Invariably, we see world over that mosques form the exclusive platform of this grievance buildup.

This blame game is thus brought to a personal level and mixed with pan-Islamic causes. And it can lead to a buildup of anger and hatred against local and global "oppressors." In the course of time, these grievances take on a political overtone and eventually morph into a fight for "injustice" or jihad (see chapter 3, "Jihad Buildup"). However, because mosques and clerics form the core of the social network around which Muslim communities function, Muslim communities are easily pulled into jihad. Saudi funding of mosques around the world can be seen as an investment in the nodes of a social network aimed at arming it with ideology and resources in order to build up grievances that will help to mobilize Muslims for jihad.

The 9/11 attacks on America and what is yet to come are an outcome of the grievance buildup of Muslim masses worldwide. Specific acts such as the 9/11 attacks were not predictable, but the die was cast when the Muslim grievance buildup was allowed to go on for decades, uncontested.

It is not necessary for a population to be particularly religious or belong just to one religion to identify with a cause and to embrace violence as a means of getting back at its perceived enemies. Although the Tamil Tigers in Sri Lanka get their recruits mostly from the secular Hindu community, there is also a strong Tamil Christian component. In this case, Tamils had long felt that the majority Singhalese discriminated against them by taking away employment and other opportunities unfairly and giving their language second-class treatment. In other words, personalizing the grievance led to community mobilizing.

Political Islam, particularly through the axis of jihad, has caused immense physical and material suffering to nations, communities, and individuals around the world. This constitutes a grievance. For instance, Americans have their own grievances against Saudi Arabia and Pakistan, which were the primary sponsors of the entities (such as al Qaeda or the Afghan Taliban) who were responsible for the 9/11 attacks. Indians have their own; so do the Israelis and countless other nations.

The key toward mobilizing victimized non-Muslim populations is to develop a personal sense of grievance toward Saudi Arabia and other Islamic states that sponsor terror. Millions have seen their wealth shrink due to instabilities created by the 9/11 attacks; the cost of borrowing has increased at the individual level due to the budget deficits, which have been hastened by financing expensive war on terror; infrastructure and research and development are not funded adequately due to the high cost of fighting terror, and the result is a less competitive America. Millions of people in impoverished India are seeing their future evaporate due to the extensive terrorism-induced economic and social costs caused by Pakistan, Saudi Arabia, and many other Islamic nations. It is no exaggeration to say that Saudi Arabia and other jihad sponsors have hit the pocketbooks of hundreds of millions of non-Muslims, thus compromising their future.

A global effort to mobilize nations, in my view, has to be based on building up a feeling of grievance in the minds of their citizens. Without this buildup, political leaderships will not be able to generate a strong and sustained base of support to act. I will discuss more in subsequent sections how Western nations and others can act to take advantage of such a grievance buildup. From this point of view, among the desired booklets one could create for this purpose: *Unbeliever Grievance List: Saudi Sponsorship of Unbeliever Atrocities.* There is a precedent: among the most important mobilizing documents produced in American history is Thomas Jefferson's and Colonel John Dickinson's *Declaration of the Causes and Necessity for Taking up Arms against the British.*[109] This document was produced a year before the Declaration of Independence in 1976.

In chapters 1 and 3 of our discussion, there is an extensive outline of terror attacks and political Islam's siege of India. This data clearly portray the acts in the name of political Islam and the nations at the forefront of jihad sponsorship: Pakistan and Saudi Arabia. This is the kind of data that America needs to mobilize opinion worldwide—data that could include examples from a non-Christian, non-white, and largely impoverished nation that has been extensively victimized, its civilians killed, and its Muslim citizens brainwashed to sponsor terror, all in the name of jihad.

But what can such a buildup of grievance in non-Muslim populations lead to? As best-selling American author and mathematician Nassim Taleb observes in his book *The Black Swan: The Impact of the Highly Improbable,* "History does not crawl, it jumps." He mentions how certain precipitous, rare, and unpredictable events changed the course of history or societies.[110] These rare trend-changing events, described as "Black Swans" in his book, appear in complex fields where a multitude of factors can play a role—such as in economy or sociology. In other words, in Taleb's view, history or societies don't change in predictable and small incremental steps. There is always this pattern: Certain unpredictable events affect a significant percentage of a population leading to evolution of a society in some new direction. An unexpected massive defeat and disgrace at the hands of Allied forces convinced most Germans to change the way they viewed fellow Europeans. The nuclear strikes on Hiroshima and Nagasaki, combined with major reverses on the battlefield, played a major role in convincing the Japanese that their war was not winnable.

While the trend-changing events themselves may be unpredictable, it should be understood that these events are an indirect consequence of a society's buildup toward broadly achieving certain goals. For instance, the events in the above quoted examples were a consequence of the Allies' determined effort to defeat their enemies in World War II. The 9/11 attacks, while not predictable, were a consequence of a jihad buildup mainly sponsored by Saudi Arabia that went on for decades.

Here I differ with Taleb's contention that only Black Swan–like events can change the course of history. I categorize the approach of changing the course of history through small incremental steps as an "Incremental Strategy." Here are a few examples. One could argue that winning the cold war and the installation of a form of democracy in Russia was not due to any single event but a series of small events spread over decades and their cumulative consequences. These events arose from the former Soviet Union's own policy decisions and those by its adversaries, namely, the Western powers, who successfully managed to discredit the Soviet ideological foundation and articulate an alternate ideology based upon liberty and capitalism. Just to add one more: the modern technological age may be characterized by a multitude of inventions ranging from the development of quantum mechanics to the invention of semiconductor technology to building the first computers. Here again, these (unexpected) sequence of inventions and discoveries were a result of a society's buildup of institutionalized creation of knowledge.

The 9/11 attacks on America abruptly changed the focus of the American security establishment. It was the most devastating and daring attack on American soil. At the heart of this book and in policymaking circles in the United States and elsewhere in the Western establishment is this question: What approach is suited to changing the mind-set of Muslim populations away from identifying and sponsoring (violent and socially oppressive) jihad?

Although it appears that America and its allies are using the Incremental Strategy approach now, in reality, their efforts lack a crucial ingredient needed to become successful: namely, the need to discredit the ideology or theology that drives political Islam. In reviewing the conflict with the Soviet Union, Westerners had no qualms about offering an ideological counteroffensive to Soviet communism. While I certainly advocate using this missing ingredient to create a more robust Incremental Strategy against the new enemy, this approach alone is unlikely to be sufficient to win the new cold war with political Islam.

Among the primary reasons for the internal collapse of Soviet communism was its inability to help generate wealth and the resulting dissatisfaction it generated among its own people. However, in jihad-sponsoring states such as Saudi Arabia or Iran, oil-based revenues continue to keep their economies financially afloat and shield weaknesses of the political Islam–based system from being exposed. This scenario is likely to persist for the foreseeable future due to a strong demand for oil, despite the oncoming of a global recession. Having a nuclear capability has convinced the Pakistani elite in its political Islam–dominated nation that they can pursue jihad without being taken to task—and extract generous handouts using the threat of nuclear and terror assets. America needs both: the long-term Incremental Strategy and the short-term Black Swan–like events to win this new cold war.

Unlike the previous cold war in which both sides had the ability to annihilate one another and the Western world, yet behaved as rational entities, aided in no small part by the fear of mutually assured destruction, the new cold war with political Islam might end abruptly. The new threat is irrational and nonnegotiable (due to the leadership of medieval and retrogressive clerics), and more important, is likely to lack a strategic nuclear counterpunch.

America needs to help build up the grievance offensive in the minds of non-Muslim populations in jihad-victim nations toward creating trend-changing events in the axis of jihad nations. These events should send an unequivocal message that jihad is a losing proposition at both the individual and the community levels. A robust Incremental Strategy is needed in any event to make the trend-changes long-lasting.

The strong political Islamic movements in nations such as Saudi Arabia, Iran, or Pakistan will likely continue to push these nations to the brink in their escalating confrontations with their non-Muslim neighbors by funding the jihad enterprise. Countries such as Israel and India are not only faced with fast-growing Muslim populations but are also seeing this resident population increasingly act as foot soldiers of the axis of jihad nations. Running out of options and unable to counter the devastating consequence of an escalating jihad (that could cumulatively be equivalent to the impact of strategic nuclear strikes) by both internal and external proxies of the axis of jihad, these victim states might end up exercising their strategic nuclear option as a last resort in order to avoid being overrun by jihadists. Discussed in detail in the section titled

"Scope for Nuclear Retaliation," this strategic retaliation possibility might constitute a Black Swan that could abruptly persuade jihad-sponsoring populations in the axis states to take a U-turn vis-à-vis their support for jihad.

GETTING EDUCATED MUSLIMS TO LISTEN

The most effective political Islamists, including jihadists, are invariably educated Muslims. This should surprise no one. It takes modern knowledge to operate effectively in the Western world; a college degree is a good way of obtaining this knowledge. Educated Muslims play a key role in producing material for public consumption and translating the aspiration of clerical leadership into reality. They even help al Qaeda compete successfully in the propaganda war with the United States. This is exemplified in this article by *Washington Post* reporter Craig Whitlock (before some of these Web sites were put out of business through a consorted effort by suspected Western intelligence agencies):[111]

Every three or four days, on average, a new video or audio from one of Al Qaeda's commanders is released online by as-Sahab (an Al Qaeda media network), the terrorist network's in-house propaganda studio. Even as its masters dodge a global manhunt, as-Sahab produces documentary-quality films, iPod files and cellphone videos....

Analysts said that as-Sahab is outfitted with some of the best technology available. Editors and producers use ultralight Sony Vaio laptops and top-end video cameras. Files are protected using PGP, or Pretty Good Privacy, a virtually unbreakable form of encryption software that is also used by intelligence agencies around the world.... Al-Fajr (another Al Qaeda media network) is heavily decentralized, with its webmasters generally unaware of one another's true identities for security reasons, intelligence analysts said. It also has separate "brigades" devoted to hacking, multimedia, cyber security and distribution....

The network receives propaganda material from individual terrorist groups and then posts it online. Each release is announced on popular Islamist Web forums, where thousands of members are encouraged to copy the videos and redistribute them on other sites.... The Web forums are password-protected and highly regulated. In certain sections, only high-ranking moderators have the authority to post material—such as bulletins announcing a new bin Laden video. As a result, Al-Fajr and others can quickly spot fake material, ensuring that the propaganda maintains a high level of reliability and consistency, analysts said.[112]

Mainstream media in Muslim-majority nations and mosques around the world spew out anti-American and anti-Israeli political literature and often give one-sided, exaggerated, or even falsified analyses. This indoctrination appears to have influenced most educated Muslims, if surveys are to be believed. However, many other educated Muslims involved in terror attacks abroad also read or listen to mainstream media. Without this reading, they couldn't function effectively in non-Muslim societies. Unfortunately, a lack of well-developed critical analysis of Islamic doctrines and Muslim claims of "grievance" in the Western media has been a significant setback to our efforts in the war on terror. This has meant that the one-sided indoctrination carried out on educated Muslims by political Islamists for decades has been left unchallenged. The need to empower educated Muslims to confront Islamists is underscored in this piece by Indian reporter Sushant Sareen regarding Islamist efforts to take over Pakistan:

> Clearly, the Islamists are winning the ideological debate on the role of Islam in Pakistan. The liberal, and moderate, sections of Pakistani society are unable to present any convincing argument against the Islamists. Partly because of this, and partly as a result of the persecution complex that Muslims around the world have developed, Pakistani society is getting more and more Islamized and radicalized.[113]

In my view, the inability of moderates to present a convincing argument against the Islamist view is due to the extremist nature and thrust of the Islamic doctrines themselves (see chapter 2, "Conquest by Design"). The end result of this failure is increasing recruitment of educated Muslims by Islamic terrorist groups. Indeed, a report from Pakistan notes that "[t]he profile of those joining the militant group Laskhar-e-Taiba is changing to include more young, educated men, some of whom even hold advanced degrees."[114]

The first group of educated Muslims may have been more jihad prone due to this mostly one-sided indoctrination. But the second need not be so. Saudis and Muslims from other Muslim nations coming for higher education studies in Western nations would benefit from the local media and the government propaganda machinery willing to discredit the theological roots of political Islam. These Muslims must be confronted with the reality that information taken down from leaves, stones, or people's memory, and written down almost one hundred years later couldn't be accurate or complete enough to be called God's words. This profound reality, which is not likely to be raised in a Muslim-majority nation due to death threats from political Islam, should appeal successfully to the common sense of the educated Muslim elite. Also worth pointing out is the statistical analysis of the Islamic trilogy and, specifically, the extent of their anti-unbeliever content and the lack of goodness toward humanity (see chapter 2, "Conquest by Design"). Such "liberated" Muslims, who should form the elite of Islamic nations, will likely work to discredit political Islam upon return to their homelands, to set off a revolution from within. Admittedly this approach would take decades to make an impact. But it is still a must as part of a multipronged approach to the war on terror.

Indeed, Hirsi Ali, a well-known author and former Muslim, reinforces these ideas in a 2008 book review: "The problem, however, is not too much reason but too little." She further adds: "I see [Western leaders] squandering a great and vital opportunity to compete with radical Muslims for the minds of Muslims, especially those within their borders."[115]

The strategy outlined here is about empowering educated Muslims to successfully confront local political Islamic movements. Without the support of educated Muslims, many clerics and mosques would lack prestige and credibility—and consequently, the ability to sponsor jihad effectively. Another way of seeing this is to view the Muslim clerics as the source of jihad inspiration but educated Muslims as the ones who transform jihad into reality. The more the educated Muslims see the irrational nature of Islam and jihadist claims, the less likely they will further the jihadist cause.

It is illustrative to study how a critical section of a community or an organization may be influenced in order to initiate a revolution from within. Among the reasons that the white elite in South Africa gave up power to the black majority was that whites from Europe and America confronted them (in people-to-people interactions when they encountered each other during travels) and told them that it was immoral for them to keep native blacks illegally away from power. Unable to muster a convincing response, the white South Africans found themselves looked down upon and feared being ostracized by their fellow whites abroad. Increasingly, these South African whites put pressure on their leadership to give up power to blacks.

Visitors from the former Soviet Union and its satellites always found themselves in a no-win situation in standing up for their ideology and the economic performance of their nations in front of Western liberty and capitalism. In the long run, the ideology and the system collapsed from within as they ran out of believers.

The executive and legislative branches of the United States should work to rectify the existing situation of meaningless political correctness by calling for a critical look at the theology behind political Islam; its overwhelming anti-unbeliever content, inconsistencies, evident incompleteness, and lack of authenticity should be pointed out (see chapter 2). Political Islamic theology, seen by many Islamists as its greatest strength, is its greatness weakness when seen through the lens of science-derived rational common sense. This may be the most important long-term strategy in neutralizing political Islam—discrediting political Islamic theology and by extension the teachings of its clerics and its mosques, which make up the nodes of the social network responsible for spawning jihad.

DEALING WITH SAUDI ARABIA AND PAKISTAN

Along with Shiite Iran, Saudi Arabia is the dominant ideological and funding source for nodes of the social network spawning jihad. Spending well over $85 to 90 billion since the mid-1970s through its governmental and nongovernmental organizations, as well as countless billions more through private Saudi donors, it is no exaggeration to say that the resurgence of political Islam in the past few decades has been mostly due to Saudi funding and proselytizing activities in favor of Wahhabism.[116] American scholar and terrorism analyst Alex Alexiev calls this "the largest worldwide propaganda campaign ever mounted" in the history of the world.[117] Saudi Arabia is dedicated to empire building of a different kind: It is using time-tested old-style Islamic conquest to create and expand regions of Saudi influence. Unlike the former Soviet Union, it has done so in the name of God and has enhanced an inherited ideology called political Islam. This Saudi empire building has caused immense suffering to people around the world, including Muslims themselves. Sermons in Saudi-funded mosques have kept millions of Muslims around the world from embracing modern education and being part of a larger society or community of nations. What is notable is the nature of the funding: it's geared toward a jihad buildup (see chapter 3, "Jihad Buildup").

Data exposing the extremist claim of "Islam as the solution to everything" and the role played by Saudi Arabia in advancing its interests at the expense of Muslims in far off places (for the cause of jihad) are abundant. This is one area in which Western nations must take the lead as part of the all-important ideological warfare. They can't just leave it up to some handful of individuals.

In Algeria, the government is beginning to understand the folly of Arabization or Islamization of its precollege education system. Extensive religious teaching has left children unfocused in school—and ill prepared for employment. A telling comment comes from an Algerian advisor to the ministry of education: "We would never have imagined Algeria could one day be faced with violence that would come from Islam."[118] The role played by Saudi-originated Wahhabism also stands out: "The strictest form of Islam, Wahhabism from Saudi Arabia, has become the gold standard for the young."[119] Furthermore, according to a *New York Times* article:

> The schools were one center of that [Islamization] drive. French was banned as the language of education, replaced by Arabic. Islamic law and the study of the Koran were required, and math and science were shortchanged....Algeria's young men leave school because there is no longer any connection between education and employment, school officials said. The schools raise them to be religious, but do not teach them skills needed to get a job....More than 500,000 students drop out each year, officials said—and only about 20 percent of students make it into high school. Only about half make it from high school into a university. A vast majority of dropouts are young men, who see no link between work and school.[120]

The long-term policy approach should be one of developing a grievance against Saudi Arabia as the root cause of Muslim suffering. British Muslims are many times more likely to be unemployed or put in prison, and perform poorly in schools, compared to their non-Muslim compatriots.[121] Pakistan has become synonymous with terror in Britain. British prime minister Gordon Brown remarked in Pakistan in December 2008 that "[t]hree quarters of the most serious plots investigated by the British authorities have links to Al-Qaeda in Pakistan."[122] For instance, propaganda directed at young British Muslims should be toward portraying Islamic ideology, Saudi Arabia, and Pakistan as the root cause of their inability to succeed in British society (see chapter 3, "The European Survival Threat").

The Western propaganda along these lines should reach those who count in the long run: the educated Muslims. In particular, the nodal power centers of political Islam, the mainstream mosques, need to be exposed as doing the bidding for the Saudis, indirectly ensuring the Saudi control of communities. Many nations in the Middle East and in Africa have lost their religions, languages, and cultures after Islamic conquest that either originated in or was inspired by Saudi Arabia. The Saudi oil wealth has ensured further consolidation of this conquest and the use of these nations and their people for further conquest of *infidel* lands to extend the Saudi sphere of influence. In a nutshell, Saudi Arabia has destroyed the future of hundreds of millions of Muslims around the world. Indeed, it could be argued that Saudi Arabia—not America or Israel—is the real enemy of Muslim nations and Muslim communities.

Being a recipient of free wealth in the form of oil, the Saudis could afford to practice a regressive form of political Islam, relying on imported skilled and unskilled labor. The dependence on foreign labor is due to its education system that is excessively focused on Islam at the expense of subjects that would have better prepared Saudi students for a professional career. The majority of skilled laborers in Saudi Arabia are still foreigners. This is a reflection that this nation offers no future even for its own people, apart from a shrinking share of oil revenue brought by high population growth rates. This is by design—and perhaps the only way the ruling combo of the royals and clerics in Saudi Arabia can keep their hold on power and massive wealth.

America's complex relation with the Saudis dates back to the early 1900s. From an ideological perspective, this relationship has always been one-sided. American democracy and its various church groups have no access to Saudi Arabia, while the country kept a large contingent of religious propagators in its embassy and consulates in America, at least until 2001. The statistics on the American Muslim outlook discussed earlier showed significant Saudi contribution to the growth of political Islam in America through mosques, organizations, civic groups, and the like.[123]

The Saudi ambassador's regrettable extraordinary access to sitting and past American presidents is an indication of how little we know about the dynamics of political Islam—the de facto power in Saudi Arabia and an archenemy of America. It seems that the Saudis have known very well which buttons to push in the White House in order to get their jihadist agenda across, even at the expense of America's close allies, such as Israel. In July 2001, a particular Israeli crackdown on Palestinians appeared harsh in Saudi eyes. Through Ambassador Bandar, the Saudis cautioned former president George W. Bush: "The Crown Prince will not communicate in any form, type or shape with you, and Saudi Arabia will make all its political, economic, and security decisions based upon how it sees its own interests in the region without taking into account American interests anymore." Swiftly, the former president wrote back to pledge for the first time: "The Palestinian people have a right to self-determination and to live peacefully and securely in their own state, in their homeland, just as Israelis have the right to live peacefully and safely in their own state."[124]

The continued sponsorship of terror by America's purported "allies," Saudi Arabia and Pakistan, gives an inevitable impression of America being considered a "useful idiot" by these two nations. The Saudis have played the victim card skillfully on behalf of the Palestinians. Playing the victim while victimizing unbeliever nations in ways that have included the largest genocide of non-Muslims of the past sixty years in then East Pakistan (see chapter 1, "Axis of Jihad and the New Cold War"), Pakistan has manipulated America to the tune of billions of dollars in aid and in deadly armaments, without any real benchmark results to show for it. According to American analyst specializing in Asia Selig Harrison, since 2001 Pakistan has milked America to the tune of $27.5 billion, including direct funding and debt write-offs.[125] After Iraq, Pakistan has received the most aid from America. Agreeing to massively aid and arm a still jihad-sponsoring Pakistan with advanced offensive American weaponry must be reassuring to the Pakistani religious and military elite that terrorism really does pay![126] Regetttably, the eight billion dollars or so worth of advanced American military hardware given to Pakistan as part of this aid may have emboldened it to escalate terror directed at India without the fear of Indian military retribution.

Indeed, the new president of Pakistan, Ali Zardari, suggested that Pakistan be given $100 billion in order that it does not become a failed state "with its stockpile of as many as 200 nuclear warheads, [that] could be toppled by Al Qaeda and its allies"![127]

Some terrorism experts have called for more Western investments in Pakistan in order to ensure that its economy continues to grow.[128] However, the Pakistani army motto of "faith, piety, and holy war in the path of Allah" is an important reflection of the influence of political Islam in Pakistan.[129] In my view, with political Islam being the de facto power in Pakistan, it is unlikely that money meant for development will be put to good use, other than being substantially channeled to redirect jihad elsewhere (against India, for instance).[130] Hence, the above suggestion, if implemented, will surely further empower Pakistan and make it far more formidable as a terror sponsor. Indeed, the Biden-Lugar bipartisan plan for a ten-year, $15 billion nonmilitary commitment by the United States may do just that.[131] Specifically, there is virtually no discussion of how political Islam (not just radical Islam) within Pakistan will be weakened or neutralized.[132] Similar weaknesses are present in the framework published recently by American political scientist Barnett Rubin and Pakistani author Ahmed Rashid, titled "Ending Chaos in Afghanistan and Pakistan," in *Foreign Affairs*.[133]

Some of the most educated and wealthy people in Pakistan are backers of jihad—from its nuclear scientists and businessmen to the top officials of its intelligence (ISI). For intance, in a 2008 interview, the director general of the ISI, Ahmed Pasha, defended the Taliban's embrace of jihad: "They [the Taliban] believe that jihad is their obligation. Isn't that freedom of opinion?"[134] Commitment to Islamism has reached the highest level of Pakistan's government. A gathering of religious leaders presided over by the then president of Pakistan, Rafiq Tarar, ruled that any Muslim who changes his religion must be put to death and his property confiscated.[135]

We know from our collective experience of a thousand years of human history that rewarding criminal behavior as the dominant response almost never reforms a criminal. Here I caution against either arming or building up Pakistan in any way at this time and suggest policies that specifically weaken political Islam within Pakistan as part of an integral approach to the war on terror. In the section "Building Up India as a Counterforce to the Axis of Jihad" a discussion is presented on how the United States can leverage India to deal with Pakistan.

The new democrat-controlled Congress tried but failed to take a meaningful second look at America's relations with Pakistan and Saudi Arabia. In proposed legislation, three countries had been singled out regarding the need to show accountability with regard to terror sponsorship: Pakistan, Afghanistan, and Saudi Arabia. The provisions of this new regulation form part of the Implementation of 9/11 Commission Recommendations Act of 2007, which was aimed at revamping the US national security and foreign policy apparatus to address challenges post-9/11.[136]

The earlier indictment of Saudi Arabia came in the form of the Saudi Arabia Accountability Act of 2005, which was introduced by Senator Arlen Specter of Pennsylvania. This act was intended to "halt Saudi support for institutions that fund, train, incite, encourage, or in any other way aid and abet terrorism, and to secure full Saudi cooperation in the investigation of terrorist incidents, and for other purposes."[137] This act never saw the light of day because it failed to muster enough support in the Senate, as some senatorial critics of the Saudis considered the act too weak, while others were fearful of the Islamic reaction.[138]

Lawsuits directed at Saudi Arabia may be a promising avenue worth mentioning. The law firm of Cozen O'Connor has filed a lawsuit on behalf of American and global insurance companies alleging:

> Senior Saudi officials and members of the royal family or their representatives served as executives or board members of the suspect charities when they were financing Al Qaeda operations. Overall, the Saudi government substantially controlled and financed the charities, the lawsuit alleges.
>
> The charities laundered millions of dollars, some from the Saudi government, into Al Qaeda and other terrorist groups and provided weapons, false travel, and employment documents, and safe houses.
>
> Regional offices of the charities employed, in senior positions, Al Qaeda operatives who helped coordinate support for terror cells.[139]

In a ruling, a US district court judge removed the Saudi government and members of the royal family as defendants. Among the reasons why the Saudi government and the royals seem to have been let off is because there is an apparent lack of direct evidence linking them with the al Qaeda plot to attack the United States. The Cozen law firm has appealed this decision. However, a judge has declared that there is enough evidence to proceed against several Islamist charities, banks, and alleged terrorism financiers named in the lawsuit.

Emboldened by the lack of accountability, Saudi and Pakistani jihad sponsorship continued for decades and finally led to the 9/11 attacks on America. Yet America's policy response to the dastardly 9/11 attacks has been one of accommodating and appeasing nations such as Saudi Arabia and Pakistan. Needless to say, such an approach is fundamentally flawed, although one may argue that the lack of policy options led to making the deal with the "devils."

America continues to benefit tactically through an alliance with a "friendly" monarchy in Saudi Arabia. This includes, for instance, getting Saudi help to limit Iranian influence in the region. But on the larger strategic front America and the monarchy have opposing worldviews. America, for its own prosperity and security, wants to spread development, capitalism, and democracy around the world, while Saudi Arabia wants a subservient world through Islamic conquest. In this clash of worldviews America is losing the war on terror. The ruling elite in Saudi Arabia that consists of the monarchy and the Wahhabi clergy can keep their powerbase, prestige, and wealth only by maintaining political Islam's influence within the nation. But political Islam is an inherently destabilizing force, repressing the Saudi population and sponsoring jihad worldwide through its immense oil-derived wealth. With time and resources no longer on its side, America is now forced to look at its larger strategic goals vis-à-vis Saudi Arabia.

As part of a winning war strategy, the enemy must be put on the defensive; we must turn the tables on nations such as Saudi Arabia and Pakistan by pointing out their policies of exporting political Islam, and we must expose their bloody record of jihad directed at non-Muslims and hold them accountable.

Like it did with the Soviet Union, America has no choice but to launch a propaganda campaign aimed at discrediting and isolating Saudi Arabia. With over 15 percent of America's oil imports coming from this adversary, it is not an easy decision to make. Indeed, our allies are even more dependent on the Saudi oil. But the time may have come to try some innovative ideas designed to overcome our long-exploited oil weakness. In my view, the talk of reducing oil dependence as opposed to holding Saudis accountable is a defeatist attitude. This is not to say that oil dependence shouldn't be reduced—which is a long-term issue, easier said than done. But America is a long-standing victim of Saudi-funded terrorism—and there is no running away from that.

The indecisive measures that have been taken until now will only make the terror war more difficult to manage in the near future. The cost of what is yet to come if Saudi Arabia is not effectively confronted may surpass the cost of a temporary or short-term disturbance to the flow of oil from the Middle East. In subsequent sections, we will consider more nonmilitary and military options regarding Saudi Arabia.

DEALING WITH IRAN

America may have to launch military strikes in order to take out the Iranian nuclear infrastructure, or at least slow down its nuclear program. However, in a *Washington Post* op-ed piece, American political scientists Vali Nasr and Ray Takeyh articulate that the "United States would do better to shelve its containment strategy and embark on a policy of unconditional dialogue and sanctions relief."[140] In my view, such a policy would only embolden and empower political Islam—both its power base and the ruling clique through the clergy. What these authors suggest could lead to an Iran that is far more powerful and still adversarial to Western interests.

Ex–CIA director James Woolsey rejects the Baker-Hamilton Iraq Study Group's proposal that advocates engaging Iran and Syria "constructively." He says that this would "legitimize their regimes, embolden them and their terrorist cohorts, buy time for Iran's nuclear weapons program, and create the illusion of useful effort and thus discourage more effective steps." He also suggests that America hit the Iranian leadership with travel and financial sanctions, and seek to bring charges against President Mahmoud Ahmadinejad in an international tribunal for "violation of the Genocide Convention in calling publicly for the destruction of Israel."[141]

A number of US courts have already passed judgments against Iran and its leaders for their involvement in terrorism directed at Americans.[142] American investigative reporter Kenneth Timmerman advocates that "we should enforce the huge number of judgments against top regime leaders in courts around the world for their terrorist attacks."[143]

It was thought that the 2007 National Intelligence Estimate (NIE) report may have reduced the possibility of a near-term US-led military strike on Iran to degrade its nuclear capability.[144] However, in July 2008 talks with the United States and its allies Iran rebuffed their efforts to freeze the Iranian uranium enrichment program.[145] This enrichment program is a must for a nuclear bomb-making capability. The legal basis for clamping down on the Iranian program through the demands that Iran should "verifiably disband its uranium-enrichment program, thus jettisoning all possibility of developing an atomic bomb" is derived from UN Security Council Resolutions.[146] The legitimacy of the resolutions themselves were derived from Iranian noncompliance with the Non-Proliferation Treaty (NPT) and its International Atomic Energy Agency (IAEA) safeguards agreement (both of which Iran is a signatory to, unlike India, Pakistan, and North Korea, which have tested nuclear bombs, and Israel, which has not).

With its mullah regime still in power in Tehran, the Iranian capital, it is hard to see how military strikes can be avoided in the short term. In the event of military strikes, the responsibility for the resulting damage must be pinned on the ruling mullahs and political Islam. It could be stated that had Iran practiced *Bhai* (pre-Islamic) faith, it might not have become a pariah and a dysfunctional nation. In particular, an anti-Arab campaign may single out those with black turbans, signifying their claims of lineage to Islam's Arab founder, Muhammad. This may even include Hassan Nasrallah, the chief of the radical group Hezbollah, an Iranian proxy. With the Taliban almost universally seen as a despicable group of religious fanatics in Iran, an opportunity has arisen to use the issue of the ruling mullah regime's sponsorship of the Taliban to discredit the standing of these clerics among the populace.[147]

In the meantime, the United States should continue the policy of aiding states or groups targeted by Iran-sponsored proxies: be it Fatah, targeted by Hamas, or the beleaguered Lebanese government, under pressure from Hezbollah. The United States should also continue targeting Iranian agents—who are working to destabilize Iraq—inside Iraq.

The Bush administration's pledge to provide $75 million in democratic and humanitarian assistance to Iranians and others involved in toppling the mullah regime in Tehran in the hope of replacing it with a West-friendly regime is an example of just how little we know about what makes the ruling mullahs tick (the mullahs derive legitimacy as high priests of political Islam).[148] In my view—not just in Iran—any talk of democracy or human rights is irrelevant in any Islamic nation where a movement based upon political Islam (an antithesis of democracy and human rights) or a mullah regime is the overriding power.

In the long run, a different policy direction vis-à-vis Iran may be advisable. American journalist Roya Hakakian, writing in the *Wall Street Journal*, points out interesting statistics released by Tehran's office of cultural affairs, "showing a dramatic drop in the number of Iranians who pray daily." There is also the growing popularity of pre-Islamic festivals such as *Nowrooz*—a traditional, pre-Islamic Iranian New Year Celebration.[149]

Mainstream education in Shiite Iran was made far more modern and inclusive than the one in Sunni-majority Saudi Arabia, due to the realization even among ayatollahs that a strong Iran requires a more modern education. This has made a segment of the Iranian population, especially the educated class, open to new knowledge and new ideas. This decision by the mullahs has an inadvertent consequence: the educated in Iran, disenchanted with the overly religious ruling elite, develop a yearning for a secular and modern leadership.[150]

The data outlined in the previous two paragraphs indicate the weakening grip of political Islam in Iran. The educated Iranian population may be ready to embrace the view of the clerics as enforcers of Arab imperialist political Islam on Iranians, preventing Iran and its people from developing and reaching their potential (see the section "Dealing with Saudi Arabia and Pakistan"). Decreasing oil revenues, in addition to economic sanctions, could put pressure on the ruling clergy in Iran to make concessions. However, it is only by weakening political Islam within Iran that the United States and its allies can hope to neutralize the Iranian nuclear or terror threat.

NEUTRALIZE THE POWER BASE OF POLITICAL ISLAM

As a primary target of political Islam, America needs to take the lead in moving beyond an ineffective focus on radical Islam and concentrate on the power structures that sustain and promote political Islam and jihad. As has been emphasized here, political Islam must first be neutralized simply to win the war on terror, let alone for democracy to take root or for a civilized order to be established.

Before identifying the power structures of political Islam, we need to identify certain flaws that are even more fundamental. In chapter 2, "Conquest by Design," I discussed the thrust of Islamic doctrines utilizing a statistical analysis. To set the stage for further discussion here, let me quote the conclusions:

> Now, utilizing this new statistical analysis we can assert that Islam's (doctrinal) outlook toward unbelievers is definitely *not* one of peace (61 percent of the Koran speaks ill of unbelievers versus, at best, 2.6 percent of the Koran speaks well of humanity).[151] I have estimated from Bill Warner's figures listed in this section that fully 19 percent of the Koran calls for violent conquest and subjugation of unbelievers. From the position of power and strength the Medina Koran speaks even more insistently on the violent conquest and subjugation of unbelievers.
>
> More important, the above statistical analysis forms the basis not just for con-

testing, but even for comprehensively discrediting the often quoted description of Islam as a "religion of peace." In fact, an appropriate and statistically acceptable characterization is that Islamic doctrines overwhelmingly preach dislike, hatred, and conquest of unbelievers and that this material constitutes the majority of the content in the Koran and the Sira.... When this anti-unbeliever-rich Islamic doctrine is preached through mainstream mosques, one could justifiably claim that neither the mosques nor the people who deliver the sermons there or those who listen to them are likely to have a moderate outlook toward unbelievers.... What is notable is the irrational and absurd nature of the overwhelming hostility to unbelievers in Islamic scriptures. They do not appear to give the possibility for Muslims to coexist with non-Muslims, to learn, and to trade with them.

Conclusion: The real culprit behind Islamic terrorism is the Islamic doctrine. Therefore, power structures of political Islam, or political Islam–influenced religious institutions, are taken here to mean any Muslim religious institution or organization that stocks, distributes, or propagates the Islamic trilogy of the Koran, Hadith, and Sira or any material derived from it.

Without the involvement of mainstream mosques, there is no way of disseminating the largely intolerant theology to the masses. In fact, as it was discussed in the section "Jihad Buildup" (see chapter 3), mosques are the power structures that are involved in all of the stages of a jihad buildup, where terrorism is a manifestation of one of the more advanced stages of this process. Terrorism by members of a Muslim community is a symptom that considerable jihad buildup has already taken place in the community. Clearly, any meaningful policy approach has to address the roots of terrorism at the earliest stage.

If mosques are ideologically geared to drive Muslims to extremism, why was it that in Indonesia, fifty years ago, Muslims were much more moderate than they are apparently now? Putting it another way, what has been so different about Islam in Indonesia? For centuries Indonesia was ruled by indigenous kings—not by some Arab or Persian transplants (as was the case in South Asia). Also, there was hardly any large-scale Muslim migration from the Middle East to Indonesia (again, unlike South Asia). Indonesia was mostly Islamized by Sufi Muslim preachers—not through conquest and subjugation. Hence, the underlying Hindu/Buddhist culture and traditions thrived for a long time, despite Islam. Finally, the Koran is famous for its complexity— and in the orthodox view, needs to be read in original Arabic, an alien language for most Indonesians. My answer to the original question of why Indonesians have now become less moderate is, they listen to and discuss Islamic theology much more now than they did fifty years ago. This assertion is empirically supported. During the past almost thirty years, with funds from the Middle East pouring in to build gleaming and better-funded mosques, the theology gets preached from a far more credible platform and, apparently, is finding more listeners.[152]

As emphasized in our discussion, the increase in Islamic extremism seen all over the world coincides with the increase in funding for propagating Islamic theology. We can see consistently that more exposure to Islamic theology leads to more extremism—exactly the kind of correlation expected, based upon the statistics we've discussed. This data analysis doesn't support President Obama's assertion given in the first interview of his presidency, that "[w]e cannot paint with a broad brush a faith [Islam] as a consequence of the violence that is done in that faith's name."[153]

One could argue that some scriptures belonging to other faiths also urge violent attacks against people of alternate faiths. How could America or any other non-Muslim nation be justified and not be seen as biased in going only after political Islam–influenced religious institutions, as opposed to, say, Hindu, Buddhist, or Christian religious institutions? In our discussion throughout, including the contemporary outlook and behavior of Muslim populations, overwhelming statistical evidence points to the reality that Muslim populations do not believe in coexisting with unbelievers and strive for conquest and subjugation of them (see chapter 3, "Many a Face of Jihad")—just as the way Islamic doctrines intend them to be. This is unlike any other major religion—be it Christianity, Hinduism, Buddhism, Judaism, or Sikhism.

The jihadists, otherwise known as activists of political Islam, are radicalized by Muslim clerics in mainstream mosques (Islamic scholars are also considered clerics due to their knowledge of the Islamic trilogy). Hence, it is appropriate to consider Muslim clerics as the leaders of the political Islamic movement. The institutions clerics head, be they mosques, seminaries, or *madrassas*, are power structures or nodes of political Islam. Clerical association with and propagation of scriptures in the trilogy (see chapter 2) that instigate unprovoked violence against the non-Muslim citizens of the United States imply a requirement to purposefully and materially support hostilities against the United States (as an *enemy entity*). Also, there could be grounds for viewing these portions of the Islamic trilogy and their consequent track record around the world as constituting politically motivated hate crimes.[154]

As the birthplace of Islam, the location of its holy sights, and a nation that uses Islamic scriptures in place of a constitution, Saudi Arabia's outlook can be seen to manifest the core outlook of Islam itself. Powerful clerics are behind the Saudi decision not to allow any temple, church, or synagogue in the kingdom, although there is a very substantial unbeliever population there. Yet these clerics are also behind the Saudi effort to build mosques around the world, including in non-Muslim-majority nations. This lack of reciprocity, along with the arguments outlined above, strongly suggests that mosques' primary role is one of advancing a political Islamic agenda.

All Nazi Party institutions were shut down in Germany in the aftermath of the Second World War (because the Nazi ideology was deemed dangerous). There were some "good" Nazis staffing some institutions; of course, these institutions too were shut down—for the reason that they too represented Nazism. There is also a recent example of the United States trying to undermine what was perceived as an enemy ideology. In 1954, the Communist Control Act outlawed the Communist Party of the United States and criminalized membership in, or support for, the party.[155] The current outlook and laws in the Western world are such that it is unlikely that mosques in Western nations will be shut down in the near future, although it is fairly obvious by now that if this step is *not* taken it is not possible to address the alienation of Muslim residents, political Islam's repression of Muslims, the subversion of the political process and democracy by Muslim leaders, and even homegrown Muslim terrorism. Since shutting down mosques is not even an option, I am not going to discuss whether such a step might violate liberty or not.

It appears that Western governments, at least for now, are willing to apply law only when a specific mosque can be proven to be associated with the breaking of the law, such as through acts of terrorism by its members and the mosque administration. In such a scenario, my suggestion is that politicians and law enforcement officials should at least publicize the point of how the underlying theology laid the foundation for making terrorists out of mosque goers. At the very least, this message will make many other mosque goers take an alternate view of the impact of Islamic theology.

Historian Serge Trifkovic has been a proponent of a model to restrict Islamic activism similar to the McCarran Internal Security Act of 1950. This act "is a United States federal law that required the registration of communist organizations with the United States Attorney General and established the Subversive Activities Control Board to investigate persons suspected of engaging in subversive activities or otherwise promoting the establishment of a 'totalitarian dictatorship,' fascist or communist. Members of these groups could not become citizens, and in some cases, were prevented from entering or leaving the country. Citizen-members could be denaturalized in five years."[156] Trifkovic's model, articulated in his book *Defeating Jihad: How the War on Terrorism Can Be Won—in Spite of Ourselves,* includes Islamist activism as the grounds for the exclusion or deportation of any alien, regardless of status or ties, as "prejudicial to the public interest and injurious to national security." It also calls for mandatory registration of Islamic centers and their individual members with the attorney general, thereby subjecting them to the same legal limitations and security supervisions that apply to violence-prone cults and to "hate groups."[157]

However, during its time the McCarran Act was seen even by President Truman as "the greatest danger to freedom of speech, press, and assembly since the Alien and Sedition Laws of 1798." Sections of the McCarran Act were gradually ruled unconstitutional by the US Supreme Court.[158] Under the current climate, it appears that any measure that affects individual liberty, either of US citizens or even aliens, is unlikely to find majority support among the American public or the Western judiciaries.[159]

AID ALLIES

The nations defined as allies in this section are those where political Islam is not the de facto power but those that are threatened by it. For want of space, only a few critical allies are discussed in this section. From this point of view, even Turkey is considered an ally even though it is predominantly a Sunni-Muslim-majority nation. Israel and France, representative of Europe with large radical Muslim populations, are also included in this list.

The strategy just outlined in the previous section, all by itself, may not be effective in non-Muslim nations where the Muslim population is a sizable percentage of the total population, has a high birthrate, and where political Islam is entrenched among Muslims. The nations facing this demographic threat from political Islam may not have time on their side. These nations may require certain extraconstitutional measures to tackle the mushrooming political Islamic threat.

As was discussed in the previous chapter, Europe is under a serious threat from political Islam. Some of the steps enacted by European nations in response to Islamic radicalism, such as the requirement to preach in the indigenous language in local mosques, the *burqa* (a dress that completely covers a Muslim woman's body) ban in France, or restrictions on immigration, are too little and too late. These steps do little to significantly weaken political Islam and to help assimilate Muslims into the mainstream.

Of all the European nations, France faces the gravest challenge by far, with about one in four newborns now being born to Muslim immigrants—an indication of the magnitude of the potential threat. The data and analysis presented in the section titled

"Siege of India," in chapter 3, tells us that the Muslim threat in France is more than theoretical. When a civilization faces annihilation from an enemy political ideology masquerading as a religion, innovative solutions must be found.

Under these circumstances, an overarching human rights principle could be invoked—that is, the right of indigenous civilizations to exist as entities in their respective homelands. This means sending those of the threatening alien civilization who reside in ethnic ghettos back to their native lands voluntarily or by creating unfavorable conditions through the use of force. Clearly, there is no incentive for Muslims in French ghettos whose ancestors were originally from Algeria to go back to their homeland, given the massive economic disparity between France and Algeria and due to the benefits they get from a generous French welfare system. The Muslim ghettos in France also have a substantial percentage of people from Algeria's neighbor, Morocco. What is proposed in the next paragraph is also applicable for the ghetto Muslims of Moroccan origin.

The French, in my view, have to take extraconstitutional measures to discriminate (justified by the overarching human rights principle outlined previously) against those in the ghettos by cutting off their welfare benefits and give financial incentives for Algeria to take these Muslims back. If Algeria refuses, France would have to wage war on Algeria in order to occupy its land and then ship these French residents of Algerian origin back to Algeria. Algeria's refusal to take these people back can be justifiably seen as its tacit support for overrunning France with radical Muslims of Algerian origin. Clearly, this is a very "messy" solution. Backed by data in our discussion and elsewhere, I can assert that those who do not wish to acknowledge the big picture and the need for far-reaching solutions, but instead try some easy or unproven way out are bound to lose their civilization to Islam, lock, stock, and barrel.

What shouldn't be lost sight of is that political Islam appears to be commanding most of the French Muslims in the ghettos and is waging a demographic war that is already showing signs of escalating into a full-fledged jihad (see chapter 3, "The European Survival Threat"). What is proposed here, if executed, is bound to create hardship for the displaced Muslim population and its descendents. But this population is not entirely blameless, having deliberately refused to assimilate not only in the sense that they choose not to integrate into their new society but also that they encourage isolation and emphasize their differences with those of the host country and become a genocidal threat to the generous host nation.

Israel, too, faces a similar challenge, with the native Arab Muslim population fast outpacing Jews in its rate of growth. Being a small nation both in population and in area, Israel faces significant jihadist threats from adjacent Muslim-majority Palestinian territories of the West Bank and Gaza Strip.

The lack of recognition of Israel and threats to annihilate it come not just from Arab Muslim nations but also from Iran and mosques in faraway Indonesia—nations that do not even share boundaries with the Jewish state. Indeed, the inability to accept Israel or the existence of Jews in the Middle East is deeply rooted in the trilogy, reaching all the way back to Islam's founder, Muhammad.[160]

The fact that political Islam is really, first and foremost, a front for Arab expansion and conquest (even at the expense of non-Arab Muslims), and how unfairly Israel is singled out, is exemplified in several ways. Here is one. In the Darfur region of Sudan, Arab tribes were in the process of conquering land belonging to black African Muslims and others. At a March 2007 meeting of the newly formed UN Human Rights Council, according to a report in the *New York Times*:

> [The] Organization of the Islamic Conference, an association of 57 states promoting Muslim solidarity, have dashed those [less politicized behavior] hopes by voting as a bloc to stymie Western efforts to direct serious attention to situations like the killings, rapes and pillage in the Darfur region of Sudan, which the United Nations has declared the world's worst humanitarian crisis. Most notably, as happened with the [UN Human Rights C]ommission, the council has focused its condemnation almost exclusively on Israel. It has passed eight resolutions against Israel, and the Islamic group is planning four more for the current session. The council has cited no other country for human rights violations.[161]

American historian and scholar on Islam Daniel Pipes makes an eloquent point regarding Israel's enemies: "One does not, in fact, make peace with one's enemy; one makes peace with one's former enemy."[162] For the purposes of our discussion, the enemy in this case is the political Islamic movement, with Hamas or even Fatah among its many manifestations or influenced entities. As long as political Islam is a power broker in the Middle East, any attempts to settle the Israeli-Palestinian conflict appear to be doomed.

Blaming Israelis for deficiencies created by political Islam that rules them, while calling itself a victim, is part of the Palestinian strategy of waging jihad and passing the buck. Arguably, the Arab-Israeli conflict can be seen as a religious war on an *infidel* nation and an attempt at conquest of the Jewish land. For humanitarian considerations and for strategic reasons, American policy must be geared toward securing a permanent Jewish state in the Middle East, with the acknowledgment that Arabs in Israel, the West Bank, and the Gaza Strip could be absorbed into the nearby Arab states. This formula once again ensures the right of civilizations to exist. As part of an ideological offensive, America could encourage nations such as France or Israel toward these types of human rights–based innovative solutions.

Turkey, which has a vast Muslim majority, has strong secular traditions—a remnant of Kemal Ataturk's legacy. This tradition is under serious threat. The ruling Islamic party (the Justice and Development Party) has been systematically promoting Islamism through various means. For instance, this party's support for the establishment of religious schools has meant that political Islam is increasingly taught to Turkey's children. This results in the gradual Islamization of the country. Already, there are signs of the creeping Islamization of Turkish society, such as the increasing clamor for wearing the headscarf to universities and Turkey's newfound public quarrel with Israel over the Jewish state's military offensive in the Gaza Strip. Looking at it from a different perspective, political Islam is using the ballot box to obtain power and is gradually consolidating its position by promoting all-too-familiar religious "values."

A concerned military leadership and segments of the public in Turkey are making a last-ditch effort to save themselves and their nation from political Islam. In April 2007, Ankara and Istanbul saw huge demonstrations by secularists against the ruling Islamic party and government. In my view, both Europe and Washington should do better than to follow a hands-off policy of letting the "democracy take its course."

An interesting development under way in Turkey is the pro-growth policies of the ruling Islamic party. Since this regime came to power in 2002, the nation has averaged 6.5 percent economic growth, compared to the average growth of 2.5 percent in the previous six years under a secular regime.[163] In my view, the Islamic party took advantage of the strong secular "values" of the civic society (thanks to decades of rule by secular regimes) and married them with pro-growth policies to achieve impressive growth. However, in due course, owing to the increasing Islamization carried out by the ruling regime, the strong secular values will be gradually eroded, thereby putting a damper on economic growth. For instance, it was noted in the section on Europe in chapter 3, how the second-generation Muslims there have fallen behind in every measure of development due to increasing exposure to "Islamic values." As it has been noted in many discussions, the Islamist outlook encourages jihad building, not wealth creation.

Despite wealth creation, the developing situation in Turkey should be seen as a political Islamic siege of Turkey and its secular democracy, undoubtedly aided by long-term Saudi funding for political Islamic causes there. This situation should be seen as an opportunity both to assist the secularists in Turkey and to drive a wedge between political Islam and the Turks. A propaganda drive could be formulated along the lines that the encroaching of political Islam in Turkey might be seen as a Saudi effort to bring Turkey under its wing, slowly and systematically impose an Arabian tribal way of life, and compromise the future of millions of Turks.

JIHAD AS A CRIME AGAINST HUMANITY

Nations represent people and their interests. It is therefore not surprising for them to behave like humans. The hallmark of a secure and functional society is a robust criminal justice system; the hallmark of a functional international order is an international justice system that works. These are among the reasons that the Geneva Convention was established.

When violent jihad involves terrorism—which it almost always does—these acts fall under the category of war crimes. As we saw in chapter 1, "Taliban or Al Qaeda Were Proxies," many nonstate terror sponsors, such as al Qaeda, thrive either through state sponsorship or because states turn a blind eye when their residents sponsor them. When these crimes are planned or committed in a systematic fashion and on a large scale, they may be prosecuted under crimes against humanity as defined by the Geneva Convention.

The largest genocide of the past six years was conducted by Pakistan against Hindus in what was then East Pakistan and against Bengali Muslims, which it considered Hindu influenced.[164] Yet it escaped punishment, and that may have influenced its evolution into one of the world's preeminent terror states.

In the present convention, genocide means any of the following acts committed with the intent to destroy, in whole or in part, a national, ethnic, racial, or religious group:

- Killing members of the group
- Causing serious bodily or mental harm to members of the group
- Deliberately inflicting on the group conditions of life calculated to bring about its physical destruction in whole or in part
- Imposing measures intended to prevent births within the group
- Forcibly transferring children of the group to another group[165]

A complete listing of all breaches is beyond the scope of this book. Only a few of them are listed here to inform readers that acts of jihad may be prosecuted under the convention. Articles 3 and 4 of the Geneva Convention deal with acts constituting war crimes.[166] There is also an internal component, possibly applicable to crimes conducted by homegrown jihadists. Grave Breaches—International (of the four Geneva Conventions of August 12, 1949) include the following:

- Willful killing
- Extensive destruction and appropriation of property, not justified by military necessity and carried out unlawfully and wantonly
- Taking of hostages

Other Serious Violations (of laws and customs applicable in international armed conflict):

- Intentionally directing attacks against the civilian population as such or against individual civilians not taking direct part in hostilities
- Intentionally directing attacks against civilian objects, that is, objects which are not military objectives

Some progress has been made in passing judgment against the state sponsorship of genocide. In a 15–1 landmark decision, the sixteen-member International Court of Justice, on February 26, 2007, ruled for the first time that states can be held responsible for genocide (till now, only individuals have been held responsible). But this judgment may have exposed the limitation of the international justice system, which went by the letter rather than the spirit of the international conventions. This means that as long as states did not keep a documented trail of their intent, their actions may be able to escape conviction.[167]

Serbian strongman Slobodan Milosevic and his associates were tried for crimes against humanity, ironically, conducted mostly against Kosovar Muslims. While many deserving Muslim Milosevics are yet to be identified, Sudan's president, Omar Hasan al-Bashir, was deservedly indicted by the International Criminal Court on charges of genocide, crimes against humanity, and war crimes committed during the past five years of bloodshed in the Darfur region of his country.[168]

Clearly, not only individuals but also many Islamic states have been involved in armed jihad. While an offensive jihad could be arguably categorized as a war crime, certain other types of armed jihad may constitute crimes against humanity. An analysis and publicizing of jihad as a crime against humanity should strengthen the legal and moral standing of America and its allies in their long battle with political Islam. It also creates a new and powerful way of putting pressure on state sponsors of jihad. This could become an effective mobilizing tool, by creating a sense of grievance in the minds of jihad victims against jihad-sponsoring nations and their local collaborators.

In the last sixty years, non-Muslims have been systematically and violently driven out of many Muslim-majority areas. This has happened due to state sponsorship. However, there is hardly any discussion in the media about these crimes or their implications.

To take one example, Pakistan has a long history of conducting jihad against *infidels* (see chapter 1, "Axis of Jihad and the New Cold War," and chapter 3, "Siege of India"). An apparent admission of Pakistan's sponsorship of jihad in Kashmir came in a 2006 lecture at the South Asia Program of the School of Advanced International Studies of Johns Hopkins University by the then Pakistan ambassador to the United States, Mahmud Ali Durrani: "Jihad, insurgency or whatever you want to call it in Kashmir... yes, Pakistan may have helped the jihad at some time, but it was not started by us."[169]

Specifically, there is a dire need to investigate whether the axis of jihadist nations—most notably the primary axis nation or the anchor state of the political Islamic movement, Saudi Arabia—have been involved in jihad-related crimes that could be categorized as crimes against humanity.

Centuries ago "offensive" or "expansionist" armed jihad was used to conquer land and people for Islam. It is interesting to note the view of a retired *sharia* judge of Pakistan's Supreme Court, Taqi Usmani (also the deputy chairman of the influential Islamic Fiqh Council of the Organization of Islamic Conference (OIC)):

> "Even in those days... aggressive jihads were waged... because it was truly commendable for establishing the grandeur of the religion of Allah."... He [Taqi Usmani] argues that Muslims should live peacefully in countries such as Britain, where they have the freedom to practise Islam, only until they gain enough power to engage in battle.... His views explode the myth that the creed of offensive, expansionist jihad represents a distortion of traditional Islamic thinking.[170]

Now, with an international criminal justice system in place, and also because many Muslim nations no longer have the military might to impose an expansionist jihad on unbeliever nations, the concept of "defensive" armed jihad has been invoked to justify arming and funding Muslim insurgencies in many non-Muslim-majority nations.

As part of the grand vision of the so-called defensive jihad, Saudi charities and others have worked to deliberately drive a wedge between the Muslim minorities and the non-Muslim majorities in many nations; new mosques were established and hateful material distributed and preached. These measures, as well as funds for mobilizing the faithful and indoctrinating the necessity of waging armed jihad, have given Muslim populations the sense of empowerment, ideology, logistics, and motivation needed to mobilize and to finally wage armed jihad. In Muslim-majority nations such as Pakistan, the above process has created a steady stream of recruits for global jihad. In other words, worldwide Islamic terror is the likely result of a grand vision of Saudi Arabia and other jihadist nations.

In a court case in Canada, Arafat El-Asahi, the Canadian director of both the International Islamic Relief Organization (IIRO) and the Muslim World League (MWL), declared in sworn testimony: "The Muslim World League, which is the mother of IIRO, is a fully government funded organization. In other words, I work for the Government of Saudi Arabia."[171]

For instance, a former al Qaeda fighter named Ali Ahmed Ali Hamad has accused the Saudi state and its charities of knowingly funding terrorism. His account of al Qaeda associations in the Balkans went largely uncontested during the UN war crimes trial on Bosnia, where he was a prosecution witness.

> He contends that the Saudi High Commission, an agency of the Saudi government, and other Islamist charities supported Al Qaeda–led units that committed atrocities. Mujahaddin units, he said, recruited fighters, prepared for battle, and financed their operations in the Balkans.
>
> He said the Saudi High Commission had poured tens of millions of dollars into mujaheddin units led by Al Qaeda operatives who fought with Osama bin Laden in Afghanistan. Money intended for humanitarian relief bought weapons and other military supplies.
>
> The charities also provided false identification, employment papers, diplomatic plates, and vehicles that permitted Islamist fighters to enter the country and pass easily through military checkpoints, Hamad said.
>
> Several charity offices, including those of the Saudi High Commission, were led by former mujahaddin or Al Qaeda members, at least one of whom trained with Hamad in an Al Qaeda camp in Afghanistan, he said.
>
> Like other Al Qaeda fighters, Hamad said, he was an employee of the Saudi High Commission for a time and traveled through the war zone in commission vehicles with diplomatic plates.[172]

Having financed and provided logistics for the charities, the Saudi government itself provided material for indoctrination and to prepare local Muslim minorities to wage jihad on their non-Muslim compatriots. Before adverse publicity compelled the Saudis to remove the following statement, the Islamic Affairs Department of the Saudi embassy in Washington defined the motive for jihad:

> The Muslims are required to raise the banner of jihad in order to make the Word of Allah supreme in this world, to remove all forms of injustice and oppression, and to defend the Muslims. If Muslims do not take up the sword, the evil tyrants of this earth will be able to continue oppressing the weak and [the] helpless....[173]

Here is a sample of the official Saudi school material for both internal and external consumption:

> In these verses is a call for jihad, which is the pinnacle of Islam. In (jihad) is life for the body; thus it is one of the most important causes of outward life. Only through force and victory over the enemies is there security and repose. Within martyrdom in the path of God (exalted and glorified is He) is a type of noble life-force that is not diminished by fear or poverty (*Tafsir*, Arabic/Sharia, 68).[174]

Now let's review the specific case of the Kashmir jihad. Pakistan and Saudi Arabia have pursued this jihad aggressively, while exposing their hand because they seem to think that they are dealing from a position of the "moral high ground" and because India is seen as a weak state.

"Self-determination" for "oppressed" or "alienated" Muslims in Kashmir is among the most popular causes (of "defensive" jihad) in the Muslim world. It is supported not just by religious leaders in nations such as Pakistan or Saudi Arabia but also by the regimes in power, including the reigning King Abdullah of Saudi Arabia.[175] Funding for building mosques and indoctrinating Muslim populations was funneled through Saudi charities linked to the ruling regime. While supporting Muslim self-determination in the Indian part of Kashmir (so that the Muslims would vote to join Pakistan and take the land with them to Islamic Pakistan), nothing is said about non-Muslim ethnic cleansing in the Pakistani part of Kashmir or in Pakistan itself (see chapter 2, "Siege of India").

Just as India found itself absorbing non-Muslims driven out of the Pakistani part of Kashmir and from the rest of Pakistan, Pakistan could simply absorb the Muslim population in the Indian part of Kashmir (without annexing the land), if these people feel so alienated—and that would be considered an equitable arrangement. But clearly that is not the case here; the invoked principle has been: What is mine is exclusively mine and what is yours is also mine! In other words, this is an offensive jihad aimed at extending Islamic boundaries at the expense of non-Muslims by imposing a no-holds-barred warfare on the state controlling Kashmir: India.

Below are more details of the jihad buildup in India aided by Saudi Arabia (and assisted by Pakistan). Also notice the role played by other Muslim nations in advancing jihad.

- Funds for Muslim insurgents, including the Kashmir Muslim insurgency and al Qaeda, were funneled through charity organizations closely linked with the Saudi regime.[176] A Muslim World League communiqué in 2000 called for "all assistance to the people of Kashmir, and support [for] its steadfast struggle."[177] Since a major part of this "struggle" is armed insurgency, this call for materials and support of the struggle can be taken to mean supplying funds, arms, and ammunition for an armed insurgency. According to the Indian government, "90 percent of the funding [for Kashmir militants] is from other countries and Islamic organizations like the [Saudi-funded] WAMY."[178]
- A cursory review of over thirty years of the MWL's publication, the *Muslim World League Journal*, indicates that it has consistently ignored the expulsions of more than three hundred thousand non-Muslim Kashmiris as well as Kashmir Muslim complicity in this cleansing act; also ignored are Kashmiri Muslims' religious apartheid practices on non-Muslim Kashmiris (see chapter 3, "Siege of India").[179]
- The key first step toward building up jihad is the construction of new mosques. Starting in 1980, scores of new mosques were constructed. Since the 1990s, a very large number of new mosques were constructed in Kashmir, many with Saudi assistance.[180]
- With a helping hand from the authorities in Saudi Arabia, Pakistan, Egypt, Libya, and Sudan, about $700 million was raised to further the growth of Islam and Islamic institutions and religious places in India. As part of this plan, new mosques and *madrassas* were to be constructed outside of Kashmir.[181]
- Indian security agencies have detailed how Saudi Arabia acts as a meeting point of Indian- and Pakistani-backed terrorists who plot their strikes in Indian Kashmir and elsewhere. Indian security officials have been unhappy with the Saudi efforts in monitoring sizable amounts of funding that are transferred to India, a big portion of which is suspected to be routed to fundamentalist institutions.[182]

- Saudi-funded mosques in Kashmir were at the forefront of jihadist efforts against non-Muslims in Kashmir that led to more than three hundred thousand of them being driven out of Kashmir, while many others were murdered and raped.[183]
- Saudi Arabia is also indirectly sponsoring jihad against India, "subsidizing Pakistan's terrorism training infrastructure and ISI terrorist operations by a whole host of Islamic fundamentalist terrorist outfits against India."[184] In addition to trying to "liberate" Kashmir from India, these outfits are working to create additional "homelands" for Muslims in India.[185]
- In January 2006, India approached the Saudis to sign an extradition treaty covering terrorism. Indians balked at the Saudi demand that India agree to incorporate "freedom struggles" as a justification for acts of violence.[186]
- India banned its largest domestic Muslim terrorist organization, the Student Islamic Movement of India (SIMI). "[Its] spectacular growth after 1982 lay in the support it gained from Islamists in west Asia, notably the Kuwait-based World Association of Muslim Youth and the Saudi Arabia–funded International Islamic Federation of Student Organizations."[187]
- Terror has expanding into India. An ex-activist of SIMI claimed that "funds are available for the asking for LeT [a Pakistan-based Islamic terrorist outfit] not only from Pakistan, but also from Wahhabi fundamentalists in Saudi Arabia and the UAE [United Arab Emirates]."[188] According to the Indian national security advisor, M. K. Narayanan, there are at least eight hundred known terror cells operating in Muslim communities all over India with "external support."[189]
- A report associated with an investigation of the September 2008 New Delhi serial blasts noted that "although the police did not divulge the name of the country, . . . Intelligence Bureau (IB) sources say the money could have come from Saudi Arabia. In the past also, they point out, funds for terrorist activities have come from that country. For instance, Rizwan Daware, an LeT/SIMI operative, had allegedly transferred Rs 24 lakh from Riyadh to fund the Mumbai train blasts of July 2006."[190]

All of the available evidence appears to show Saudi Arabia's (and other nations', including Pakistan's) desire, intent, and willingness to execute an offensive jihad on the whole of India—not just restricted to Kashmir—using bogus excuses that have either been exaggerated or invented. Even the so-called alienation of Indian Muslims is to a great extent overblown by Saudi charities in an effort to use Indian Muslims as foot soldiers to purposefully extend the Islamic sphere of influence. The apparent Saudi policy of an offensive jihad is sanctioned by the Koran and the Sunnah, which appear to act as its pseudo-constitution (Saudi Arabia doesn't have a constitution). These scriptures have widely quoted verses that urge believers to conquer and subjugate unbelievers through violence.[191]

Battling terrorism has placed an increasing burden on an impoverished India. Nearly six thousand children die every day in India due to malnourishment brought about by poverty.[192] Even sub-Saharan African states are no worse than India when it comes to malnourishment of their children. Serial blasts by suspected Islamists, in major Indian technology and economy hubs such as Bangaluru, Ahmedabad, and New Delhi, and commando-style massacres in Mumbai are poised to drive capital and investment out of India, drive millions more Indians into poverty, and make it easier for jihadists to destroy India from within.[193]

As discussed in the section titled "Siege of India," terror is just one of the means of waging a jihad designed to marginalize a non-Muslim majority in order to achieve Islamic conquest and the subjugation of unbelievers. This deliberate, long-term, and large-scale execution of terrorist plans is poised to devastate and kill tens, if not hundreds, of millions of Indians and take away the future of many more in the coming decades. It's hard not to view this as genocide. I suspect that in the jihadist calculation, without weakening India by destroying its economy through acts of terror, India couldn't be made to submit. Hence, Islamists view the killing of millions of innocent Indians as an unavoidable price to pay for the greater cause of Islamic conquest.

In my view, if Pakistan, Saudi Arabia, or some other nation can be shown beyond a reasonable doubt to have been involved in the indoctrination of the local Muslim community from which the terrorist act originated, India should launch a propaganda campaign portraying both Pakistan and Saudi Arabia (and possibly others) as conductors of crimes against humanity directed at the Indian state and its people. India should also demand considerable compensation, probably running into hundreds of billions of dollars, from the Saudis and require their leading clerics to deemphasize Islamic doctrine and to tell Indian Muslims to desist from attacking the state and the majority community in India.

I am under no illusion that such demands are going to be met. The reality is, not just India, even the United States has only very limited leverage against Saudi Arabia. Besides, oil imports from Saudi Arabia make India very dependent on the kingdom. This bleak situation brings up the option of utilizing India's strategic assets to defend itself. This is taken up in a later section, titled "Scope for Nuclear Retaliation."

One may note how thoughtfully the Saudis are framing and carrying out jihad abroad. In reality, the Muslim "freedom struggle" in South Asia, which Saudi Arabia has sponsored, has become a front for marginalizing non-Muslims. This raises credibility questions when Saudis claim support for similar "freedom struggles" in other parts of the world, including its support for Palestinians in the Israel-Palestinian conflict. This gives credence to the alternate view that the Saudis are using the freedom struggle bogey as a cover to drive Jews out from their ancient land—the unfinished chapter of the trilogy—through a jihad conducted by their Palestinian proxies. This may show the extent of the commitment that Saudi Arabia has toward the use of crimes conducted against humanity to secure its ends in violation of international and local laws.

The examples I have cited show a great potential that lies in pursuing this angle of political Islam as it relates to terrorism and its sponsors. Terrorism is not an end in itself but a means of achieving the political aim of conquest. The point is, there is a manner in which jihad-sponsoring nations could take corrective measures for their past misdeeds, and there is room for taking responsibility. These options need to be further explored in order to build up leverage against these sponsors of political and jihadist Islam.

As part of this approach, America needs to help victim nations who have suffered at the hands of the axis of jihad develop and prosecute local lawsuits seeking severe damages for the acts of terror. The victim nations include, besides America, Israel, India, the Philippines, Lebanon, Thailand, England, France, Russia, and many others. Indeed, multiple lawsuits directed at jihad-sponsoring nations, including suits originating in developing countries, demonstrate a consolidation of victims against jihad, which is the first step toward a more unified response. These suits are an important step, but the unity of nations' willingness to stand up to jihadist sympathizers is even more important.

Associating Saudi Arabia and other nations with genocide and other crimes against humanity gives us an unprecedented new ability to regulate their funding for "religious causes" in the West and to even retroactively shut down any religious institution built with their funding. Successful lawsuits containing compelling evidence could potentially be used as a basis for taking more extreme steps such as the seizure of oil assets or even land to satisfy the claims.

INDIA AS A COUNTERFORCE TO THE AXIS OF JIHAD

While obeying no rules, state sponsors of political Islamic terror, through their proxies, have successfully managed to impose an asymmetric war on America and its Western allies, including Israel. Asymmetric war in this context is understood to mean that the weaker parties—the Islamic states and their proxies, unlike the United States and its allies—are using unconventional means (such as terrorizing an enemy's civilians or using irregulars to fight the war) of waging war and are not adhering to the Geneva Conventions. When an enemy imposes an asymmetric warfare, it becomes not only difficult to fight it tactically, but it is also very expensive to counter. Faced with Islamist enemies sponsored by civilian populations, at times, Israeli armed response on Islamic terrorists embedded in sympathetic populations has created unfortunate civilian casualties. Jihadist nations have exploited these casualties to create a guilt complex to restrain America's policy toward terror. Time and again, western Europeans who are mired in socialism that stifles innovation, including how to respond to political Islam and with few or no expendable youngsters due to low birthrates, have not shown the stomach for a fight. Diverging interests, ranging from the 56-bloc Organization of the Islamic Conference that openly sides with jihadists to the differing views of permanent members such as Russia and China, have made the UN Security Council ineffective. With two ongoing military conflicts and an economic crisis to manage, America is no longer capable of containing the entrenched and expansionist political Islamic forces on its own.

As a nation of laws and due to its international status as a superpower, America's ability to respond to this "dirty war" will likely remain constrained (and therefore indecisive) as long as jihadists restrict themselves to a war of "thousand cuts" (taken to mean inflicting thousands of small wounds on a powerful enemy), as opposed to nuclear strikes directed at American or other Western interests. But not all victim states of Islamic terror are obligated to respond with restraint.

Data and analysis presented in the sections titled "Axis of Jihad and the New Cold War" (see chapter 1) and "Siege of India" (see chapter 3) make it unequivocally clear that non-Muslim Indians, specifically majority *infidel* Hindus, are in a fight to the death with Islamic forces. Understandably, non-Muslims are terrified of political Islam in South Asia. As a matter of basic survival, India's relatively weak government is compelled to engage in a "dirty war" with Islamists. In other words, political Islamic thuggery may well find its match in India, if Washington can help to script this. In a nutshell, this is about leveraging the collective will of 850 million cornered Indians to take the war to the jihadists and their sponsoring states. As I discussed in chapter 3, "Siege of India," American scholars' limited understanding of the dynamics of Islam in South Asia has led so far to a very meager American backing of India's fight with political Islam.

If America could help deliver a fatal blow to the former Soviet Union by backing Muslim nations against the Soviet occupation of Afghanistan, why not back cornered Indians and other nations to fight political Islam and its international sponsors? Unlike a resurgent political Islamic movement, which turned its guns on its former benefactor, America, an India strongly backed by the West in its war with political Islam is no threat to the Western civilization because it shares with the West a secular and democratic mode of governing.

In terms of population, location, and size, India matches the extended global network of Muslim populations that are influenced by political Islam. I have mentioned that when a nonwhite, non-Christian developing nation such as India claims to have been victimized at the hands of Islamic nations, it is bound to create ideological difficulties for Islamists who have made the traditional Muslim grievance the bedrock upon which to build their jihad campaign. Inserting India and Indians into a prominent role in the war on terror and publicizing Indian suffering at the hands of political Islam should have another benefit: the Left in both Europe and America may take a second look at their sympathy for what they believe to be misunderstood Islam.

The strategic importance of successfully repulsing political Islam in India is enormous. It could put a full stop to the geopolitical goal of bringing radicals together, from Indonesia to Algeria, on a contiguous landmass. Since conquest is the primary passion of the axis of jihad and their followers, this will be an immense blow. An integral part of this project would be the neutralizing of the influence of the Deoband Islamic seminary in India. This seminary has long been behind the political Islamic movement and jihad in South Asia and Afghanistan (home to about a third of the world's Muslim population).[194] An India working to successfully neutralize the expansionist efforts of political Islam within its own borders can do more. Sharing languages and culture with Pakistan and Bangladesh, India could help to liberate these nations by projecting alternate faiths or more productive ways of life. The hugely popular Hindi films made in India can be used to deprogram Muslims in India, Pakistan, Afghanistan, and Bangladesh away from political Islam and can help to mobilize unbelievers against the Islamist threat. While these ideas may seem far-fetched now, policy decisions should be geared toward rapidly building up India in order to create a new future.

India has significant land claims over Pakistan, land that is owed because of non-

Muslim expulsions to India.[195] This is not a classical border dispute; these land claims are about reversing the effect of Islamic conquest of *infidel* land. The three of the six rivers Pakistan depends upon originate from the Himalayan mountain range and flow through India before entering Pakistan. It has been pointed out that India could use these three rivers—Sutlej, Ravi, and Beas—and their tributaries as a strategic leverage against Pakistan.[196] India could have substantial compensation claims against Saudi Arabia for sponsoring extensive jihadist actions within Indian territories. Hence, India may be justified in hitting back and helping to achieve a decisive shift in the war on terror.

I have suggested a rapid buildup of India as a counterforce to political Islam and its sponsors. In the event of an oil embargo against India by the supporters of political Islam, as part of an integral strategy, America and other nations of the world must be able to step in to fulfill India's limited needs. A side point to be noted is that in a geopolitical and strategic sense an India that is increasingly destabilized by Islamic forces will be unlikely to counterbalance China in the region—a point to ponder as the face of Asia changes with the increasing economic and military presence of China.

There is much work to be done, with India currently suffering under a dysfunctional democracy that is being overrun by Islamists (see chapter 3, "Siege of India"). But that can be changed by providing Western backing of Indian nationalists and by realizing that Indian democracy will not overcome this losing trend on its own. By indoctrinating Indian Muslims, political Islam and its sponsoring nations such as Pakistan and Saudi Arabia have turned many of them against the Indian state. The national government in New Delhi, the regional governments, and even non-Muslim Indians are made to feel that they are occupiers in the Muslim-majority regions and towns of India. This is bad news, because the dysfunctional Indian democracy is facing an uphill task, as American scholar Stefan Halper writes in the *Washington Times*: "Since World War II, with hardly any exceptions, insurgencies have succeeded against occupying democratic powers."[197]

The conventional contemporary wisdom is that India is rising (thanks to building quality technical and professional higher educational institutions in 1950s and 1960s, recent wealth creation has become feasible) despite its otherwise poorly run government.[198] Not surprisingly, in areas where governance is essential—such as providing security—India's democracy has failed to perform. This should not be a surprise anymore (see chapter 1, "Democracy through Wealth Creation"). Democracy as a mode of governing in developing nations has been a failure, almost without exception.

The above conclusion calls for the declaration of emergency by a visionary Indian regime that might include a prominent role for its armed forces in order to neutralize political Islam. However, there is always the question of whether such a regime would misrule India. Culturally, religiously, and in terms of nation building, Indians are much closer to East Asians than to Middle Easterners or Africans. Like East Asians, Indian immigrants in Western countries have done very well, unlike the immigrants of Middle Eastern or African origin or even immigrants from the Muslim-majority regions of Pakistan or Bangladesh. Many of the East Asian nations had authoritarian governments that ensured stability while focusing on development but still did not misrule the nations (see chapter 1, "Democracy through Wealth Creation"). India, too, may be best suited for a similar style of governing. This is certainly a worthwhile option compared to the certain dissolution of the India state and the impending large-scale killing and subjugation of its citizens in the hands of political Islam.

As discussed in the previous chapter, political Islam is making rapid strides in India because the Hindu majority is disunited and politically divided. An India destabilized by Pakistan and Saudi Arabia (as well as by China, possibly, and now Iran, too, may be entering the fray) needs counterbalancing forces in the form of aiding Western nations. Helping India is helping to empower a West-friendly Hindu majority to mobilize and take on a very active political Islamic movement. This also involves aiding Hindu organizations and promoting able and strong leaders such as Narendra Modi of the Bharathya Janata Party (BJP), who have the wherewithal to take on political Islam. India's polls have shown Modi to be the most admired chief minister in India.[199] Beating the widely prevalent anti-incumbency trends in national politics, Modi managed to get reelected as the chief minister in the western Indian state of Gujarat.

Those who back the weak and ineffectual Congress Party in India are backing those who promote political Islam, either inadvertently or otherwise, which are among the parties (unlike the BJP) that Indian intelligence indirectly claims to have been infiltrated by jihadists.[200]

My December 2006 letter to the *Washington Times* articulates the need for a new US policy response concerning India:

JIHADIST THREAT IN INDIA

The timely editorial welcoming the formal signing of U.S.-Indian nuclear ties is notable for its foresightedness ("U.S.-India Nuclear Ties," yesterday). However, jihadists and their sponsors have voiced displeasure over the emerging close ties between the two nations. This deserves close attention.

Pakistan and the usual suspects from [the] Middle East have made a passionate

30-plus-year effort to indoctrinate, establish and fund terror cells in Indian Muslim communities. This investment toward Islamic conquest of *infidels* is finally paying off. In the beginning of 2007, according to the Indian home minister the nations' nuclear installations are on an Islamic terror hit list along with oil refineries. Prime Minister Manmohan Singh's regime, elected through a voting bloc controlled by jihadists, has been more than accommodating toward them. This regime even has rescinded an anti-terror law and has made India's ability to defeat radical Islam difficult. A disorganized and divided Hindu majority has been taken advantage of by united jihadists.

In the long run, if the United States wants an effective ally in India and wants democracy to succeed there, it must side with Hindu-majority organizations and help them undermine Indian jihadists. Otherwise, the trend in intensifying Islamic terrorism and its siege of Indian democracy shows that the promise of U.S.-Indian ties likely will go unfulfilled and jihadists will destroy another critical democratic ally in South Asia.[201]

The extent of jihadization of the Indian Muslim community can be grasped by this jaw-dropping statistic: eight hundred terrorist cells are said to be operating in India with external support.[202] In my view, the Bush administration's push to have the nuclear accord signed with India is an indication of an American establishment not knowing what the critical issues concerning India are. Under this agreement, India proposes to build many nuclear reactors with Western help.[203] India's existing nuclear installations are known to be vulnerable to terrorist attacks, and under the current trends, in fifteen years, the proposed new nuclear reactors may not even be safely operable, even if they could be built.

The matter of priority should be to build up India rapidly so it can take on the jihadist threat; without that, in my view, India will be destabilized by Islamic forces irrecoverably and we will lose the opportunity to leverage 850 million Indians for a win-win situation in the war on terror and beyond. While noting that a concerted international effort is needed in the war on terror, I am skeptical about the overall effectiveness of such broad-based and diverse effort. That is why I would like to emphasize the need to back a major power such as India to take the war to the political Islamic movement, as an increasingly desperate India is left with no other soft option. Among the major blunders of Hitler's regime during the Second World War was not just starting to fight with so many nations, but the end came more quickly when it ordered the invasion of a massive and resourceful Russia—and had many of its powerful army divisions destroyed there. The political Islamic movement led by the likes of Saudi Arabia and Pakistan may have reasons for their sense of theological invincibility. However, in strategic terms, by going after a nuclear-armed major power such as India recklessly, they may have created an opening for a blowback response from India they might be least prepared for. Therefore, in my view, the strategic challenge for the West in the coming years is how effectively they can leverage India to decisively crush political Islam's sponsors.

SCOPE FOR NUCLEAR RETALIATION

A nuclear device smuggled through American ports could be among the likely ways a nuclear attack might be carried out on American soil. The Department of Homeland Security has been aware of this possibility and is looking into setting up a massive system of radiation detectors in many American ports.[204] However, the annual trillion dollars of complex trade that the United State would not wish to disrupt with nervous measures, nuclear proliferation initiated by Pakistan, and possible loose nukes from the former Soviet Union are likely to keep American ports vulnerable for many years to come.

The physics and technology of making a nuclear bomb is well known to many countries. A nation determined to build an infrastructure that is geared toward achieving the nuclear threshold may just get there—ask Pakistan, North Korea, or possibly even Iran—a few years down the road. The United States and its allies may be successful in slowing the Iranian momentum toward the bomb, but we are unlikely to stop it completely without a full-scale invasion. Thanks to its likely funding of the Pakistani nuclear program, Saudi Arabia may already have nukes.[205] This has created tricky policy options in Washington and in European capitals. It is not just the Islamists; even non-Islamist nationalist Iranians want the bomb. But having the nuclear trigger within the ready grasp of the likes of a volatile, Islamist, and rhetorical Ahmadinejad is a cause of serious concern. Israel should feel particularly threatened, with Ahmadinejad virulently threatening its existence. Many Sunni Arab states are also getting restless about the Iranian nuclear thrust and have started clamoring for nuclear energy, which is a step toward achieving nuclear bomb-making capability.[206]

The fact that the primary jihad-sponsoring nations either have nukes or are close to achieving the threshold is truly a nightmare come true. Pakistan's acquiring of nuclear weapons and spreading nuclear technology was intended to further an "ideological" cause, taken to mean jihad; this was admitted by none other than the disgraced Pakistani nuclear scientist Qadeer Khan himself.[207] The other architect of Pakistan's nuclear weapons program, Sultan Bashiruddin Mahmood, declared that Pakistan's bombs were "the property of a whole *ummah* [worldwide Muslim community]," so that some Muslim nations or groups could use them on *infidels* to bring about "the end of days" and lead the way for Islam to be the supreme religious force in the world.[208] The transfer of Pakistani nuclear technology to North Korea (in exchange for missile technology), including the shipment of centrifuges, couldn't have occurred without the support of Pakistan's military under Pervez Musharraf, as Khan himself has alleged.[209] No doubt, some jihadists see the distribution of nukes among Muslim nations as desirable, both for waging jihad and for attacking America with nukes at an opportune time. It comes as no surprise that a report in 2008 stated that the supposedly defunct Khan smuggling network had been in possession of an advanced nuclear warhead design—a design and instructions to build compact nuclear bombs deliverable through a ballistic missile. This technological leap is now seen as enhancing the nuclear strike delivery capabilities of Islamic nations.[210]

Even Arab nations may not see a nuclear-armed Israel as a threat to their existence. The reason is simple: Israel does not believe in a conquest-oriented ideology similar to political Islam like its Arab neighbors do. Thus, the long-term solution to the Muslim nuclear threat remains a consorted effort to discredit the ideological basis of political Islam itself (see chapter 2).

Former secretary of defense William Perry, former assistant secretary of defense Ashton Carter, and former director of the Lawrence Livermore National Laboratory Michael May have explored the scenario of the aftermath of nuclear strikes on American soil:

> The United States government, probably convened somewhere outside Washington by the day after [nuclear strikes], would be urgently trying to trace the source of the bombs. No doubt, the trail would lead back to some government—Russia, Pakistan, North Korea or other countries with nuclear arsenals or advanced nuclear power programs—because even the most sophisticated terrorist groups cannot make plutonium or enrich their own uranium; they would need to get their weapons or fissile [nuclear bomb] materials from a government.... The temptation would be to retaliate against that government. But that state might not even be aware that its bombs were stolen or sold, let alone have deliberately provided them to terrorists. Retaliating against Russia or Pakistan would therefore be counterproductive. Their cooperation would be needed to find out who got the bombs and how many there were, and to put an end to the campaign of nuclear terrorism.[211]

In the scenario of the day after any nuclear strike on its soil, the United States' establishment and its shell-shocked population would find themselves far more vulnerable and primed for subsequent nuclear strikes—a critical point missed by the above analysts. The current nuclear doctrine announced in 2002 with regard to weapons of mass destruction (WMD) strikes on the United States is based upon "strong declaratory policy" to discourage anyone from using nukes or other WMD on the United States. It also "requires an enhanced ability to determine the source of an attack quickly and effectively." Furthermore, the document says, "The United States will continue to make clear that it reserves the right to respond with overwhelming force—including through resort to all of our options [that includes retaliatory nuclear strikes]—to the use of [WMD] against the United States, our forces abroad, and friends and allies."[212] While the 2002 doctrine called for retaliation only on the state actors who may have enabled the use of WMDs, the latest revision, announced in 2008, expands it a bit further and says, "those states, organizations, or individuals who might enable or facilitate terrorists in obtaining or using weapons of mass destruction."[213]

Analyzing nuclear material left over after the blast to look for "signatures" and determining the origin of the nuclear bomb-making material has become increasingly feasible.[214] But on the downside, this approach is not only time consuming, but is unreliable in a world in which nuclear technology has proliferated. This may be one of the weaknesses of the stated American doctrine of WMD retaliation, and it makes the whole policy of WMD retaliation rather uncertain. In addition, in the aftermath of an attack, the United States would likely be perceived as a weak and vulnerable nation and likely have reduced means to wage an expensive war of attrition with the existing existential threat: the political Islamic movement. The surprising omission in this language is the exclusion of the states that have played a long and systematic role in jihad buildup (directed against America and its allies) in the communities from which WMD attacks originate.

Jihadists are also developing arguments to justify nuclear attacks on America. A refined effort from a legal standpoint has been advanced by Saudi jihadist Nasir Bin Hamad al-Fahd in a 2003 document called *A Treatise on the Law on the Use of Weapons of Mass Destruction against Unbelievers*. This jihadist asserts that under the conditions of Muslim military inferiority, methods of warfare that violate laws of jihad can be used. "If the unbelievers can be repelled" only by using weapons of mass destruction, then "their use is permissible, even if you kill them without exception." He softened his proposals by saying that Muslims fighting jihad may not inflict disproportionately more harm on the enemy than the enemy inflicted on them. "Some brothers have added up the number of Muslims killed directly or indirectly by [American] weapons and come up with a figure of nearly 10 million." This total would authorize the use of WMD to kill about 10 million Americans.[215]

Some jihadists may prefer extensive bleeding of certain *infidel* nations through terror or through other forms of jihad, rather than resorting to nuclear strikes. Under what conditions can America, Israel, or India, the primary targets of political Islam, strike back preemptively with strategic nuclear weapons? Before even thinking about devising a policy along these lines, we must be prepared. Enemy nations, such as those of the axis of jihad, need to be identified; our list of grievances needs to be publicized; and the theological roots of political Islam need to be discredited. It is estimated here, based upon the overall cost of the war on terror, that Saudi Arabia owes America upwards of a trillion dollars in damages for either directly or indirectly sponsoring terrorism against its interests and its citizens.[216] The victim list can be further expanded to include Israel, India, Russia, and many others, who may be owed from several tens of billions to several hundreds of billions of dollars in damages.

In determining preemptive measures, what needs to be factored in also is the extent of damage yet to occur through jihad in the years and decades ahead. With the largest petroleum reserves anywhere in the world expected to last several decades and with no viable fuel alternative yet to be found, the Saudis will continue to have the wealth needed to sponsor jihad. There should be plenty of jihadists emanating from Saudi Arabia, due to its growing population—an estimated four children born on average to every Saudi woman.[217] The extent of the clerical grip on its society will likely ensure that Saudis do not get a well-rounded and modern education, which will also serve to maintain jihad and its sponsorship among the desired professions. A classified American intelligence report, taken from a Saudi intelligence survey in mid-October 2002 of educated Saudis between the ages of twenty-five and forty-one, concluded that 95 percent of them supported Bin Laden's cause.[218] As pointed out by American scholar and terrorism analyst Walid Phares, the recent statistic of only 15 percent of the Saudis polled supporting Bin Laden is probably due to the unpopular strikes mounted within the kingdom by al Qaeda—and do not necessarily reflect reduced support for jihad in the Wahhabi-dominated nation.[219] Pakistan, with a similarly high population growth rate, an outlook toward jihad, and a long track record of genocide against unbelievers, will be more than happy to be Saudi Arabia's favorite outsourced nation for jihad. Indeed, violent jihad is deeply and overwhelmingly enshrined in these societies. With these national attitudes, having America "friendly" rulers is largely irrelevant. The reality is that these countries have continued to sponsor jihad.

The conventional military advantage Israel has enjoyed over its Arab neighbors is shrinking. The surprisingly tough Hezbollah resistance to Israel's defensive thrust into southern Lebanon in 2006 points to the near impossibility of conventionally defeating the armed Muslim groups embedded in civilian areas while keeping Muslim civilian casualties to a minimum. Israel will find it difficult to justify very large casualty figures among the Lebanese Muslim population, even as that population sponsors terror against Israel. Now comes the news of Hamas's military buildup in the Gaza Strip—dangerously similar to Hezbollah's in southern Lebanon—by constructing tunnels and underground bunkers and smuggling in ground-to-air missiles and military-grade explosives.[220] Toward the end of 2008 Israel launched strikes to decapitate Hamas's leadership and to degrade its ability to conduct terror and launch rockets into Israel.[221] With a virulently anti-Israel Iran now seen belligerently marching toward achieving nuclear bomb capability, the overall security scenario is testing Israel's ambiguous nuclear doctrine.[222]

In the section titled "Getting Educated Muslims to listen," I wrote about an ideological offensive directed at educated Muslims. I noted that "admittedly this approach would take decades to make an impact." The reality is that soft options (such as the one mentioned in the previous line) to deal with genocidal jihad take time. It might take years or maybe even decades before we know their effectiveness. But *not* all nations have time. I would like to discuss the emerging terrorism scenario in India, because there might be some scope for using nuclear retaliation as a lawful and legitimate response to genocidal jihad. Besides, unlike America or even Israel, India is one of the rapidly deteriorating theaters of jihad. This might force Indian hands to act sooner than one might think.

There is a distinct possibility that if the jihadist nuclear weapons explode anywhere, they would do so in India. Pakistani newspapers have already mentioned the possibility of smuggling a device into India as a means of delivering it there.[223] India does have a retaliatory policy that might involve using its own nukes if it were to be subjected to WMD strikes.[224]

However, unlike the case of any other country, jihadists do have conventional means of achieving mass killings in India. While frequent terrorist attacks kill and maim scores of Indians, systematic destruction of the Indian economy would have a far more lethal impact. As we stated earlier, it is estimated that nearly six thousand Indian children die every day due to malnutrition brought about by poverty.[225] As we discussed in the section "Siege of India" (see chapter 3), the economic bleeding of India at the hands of jihadists is undoubtedly contributing to the death of these innocent children. The thrust and nature of escalating jihad in India is such that within the next few years, as its Muslim jihadist problem grows, India will likely see many of its strategic assets—such as oil refineries or nuclear installations—placed in jeopardy by local jihadists who are set up and funded by Saudi Arabia, Pakistan, and many other Islamic states. If this happens, India's war on terror may have reached a point of no return. The cumulative effects of such terror strikes and what is yet to come could be the equivalent to multiple nuclear strikes both in terms of lives lost and material devastation. In Kashmir and in the rest of India, jihadist efforts have already cost close to a hundred thousand lives and about half a million unbelievers have been driven off their land. In the years and decades ahead, if this jihad is not stopped, it is reasonable to conclude that millions will likely die or be displaced and hundreds of millions more of India's *infidel* children will be malnourished, which will eventually lead to an Islamic conquest of the land of India and its people. Indeed, it is hard *not* to view this as genocide. This kind of an act of genocide is of a slow form, likely taking several decades to conduct (less likely to be noticed, as a result), unlike the classic one in the Darfur region of Africa, which is measured in years.

How should India react as this gruesome genocide likely emerges in the near future? I think that there exists enough documentation (see "Jihad as a Crime against Humanity") that might implicate Pakistani and Saudi involvement, including the long-term indoctrination of Indian Muslims geared toward armed jihad against their own state. I also believe that the Indian government has shared much more comprehensive data implicating both Pakistan and Saudi Arabia with their American and other Western counterparts. In my view, India needs to take a calibrated and escalating response to the acts of genocidal jihad. It could proceed along these lines. India should:

- publicize the documentation to prove beyond a reasonable doubt that Pakistan and Saudi Arabia have been involved in the indoctrination of the local Muslim community from which the terrorist acts originated.
- use this documentation to bring crimes against humanity charges against these nations at the International Criminal Court.
- demand compensation from these nations.
- demand that Saudi Arabia, Pakistan, or other jihad-sponsoring nations require their leading clerics to tell Indian Muslims to deemphasize Islamic doctrine and to instruct Indian Muslims to stop further armed jihad.

If the acts of terror by indoctrinated Indian Muslims continue and if the international justice system is unresponsive or unwilling to act and if Pakistan and Saudi Arabia continue their belligerent ways, or if Saudi Arabia uses the threat of stopping its oil exports to India to silence it, India can elevate its response to the next level.

With a nuclear-armed Pakistan or the likely nuclear-armed Saudi Arabia, a conventional Indian military response is unlikely to be effectual. But we *do* know historically what does work; if the extent of the retaliation on a jihad-sponsoring nation is devastating enough that it affects most of that nation's population significantly, then these devastating retaliations might constitute, in the words of Nassim Taleb's book, the "Black Swan"—the unexpected and devastating event that compel jihad-sponsoring populations that are part of the political Islamic movement to make a U-turn vis-à-vis terror support (see "Grievance Buildup").[226]

Every state, including India, has the right under international law to act preemptively when facing a long pattern of genocidal assault. The 1996 Advisory Opinion of the International Court of Justice even extends such authority to the preemptive use of strategic weapons in certain existential circumstances.[227] Under the conditions of genocidal jihad, India could inform Saudi Arabia and Pakistan that if these nations do not follow through on the earlier demands of compensation, the issuance of edicts by their religious leaders to stop armed jihad in India, and not take the relevant Koranic revelations seriously, it will resort to preemptive strategic strikes on Saudi Arabia and Pakistan.

If this ultimatum were to be given, it is hard to predict what would be the response of Saudi Arabia, Pakistan, or the community of nations, including the United States. Yet it is in the interest of all civilized nations to raise the stakes—to force jihad-sponsoring states to stop the present policies that are leading to the slow extermination of unbeliever civilizations in certain parts of the world or risk the devastation of their "believer" population centers. The point can't be overemphasized; we can no longer afford to rely only on soft or long-term options. The issue is not just the beleaguered nations such as India. By allowing the problem of political Islam to fester, countries such as the United States or Israel risk having their population centers nuked by political Islam–inspired nations, groups, or individuals. With the ideology behind the error intact and the nuclear genie out of the bottle, the magnitude of the risk is only expected to increase in the subsequent years. It's a moot point whether or not "Islamists" or mullahs are in power in Pakistan, especially when its most powerful institution—its army's—motto is "holy war in the path of Allah."[228] In December 2008, the members of the Commission on the Prevention of Weapons of Mass Destruction Proliferation and Terrorism made themselves clear in Washington on the dangers of Pakistan's nuclear weapon technology going awry.[229] From the Indian point of view, the Rubicon could have been crossed; India might be forced to choose between a slow extermination at the hands of jihadists or using its nuclear weapon stockpile to defend itself.

Due to the unique position of Saudi Arabia in Islamic theology, its role in financing jihad, and its prestige in the eyes of jihadists, neutralizing its sponsorship of jihad one way or another would probably be the most decisive step toward breaking the back of political Islam. And finally, Pakistan's bluff could also be called.

While the tactical or strategic use of nuclear weapons in warfare should be discouraged, their use in certain existential circumstances warrants a careful study. Among the major factors that discourage their usage is their perceived long-term adverse medical impact on human populations. However, other than the short-term devastating consequences of blast heat associated with a nuclear strike, the long-term medical impact may be limited. In fact, studies of surviving populations in Hiroshima and Nagasaki, exposed to nuclear strikes during the Second World War, have shown the bombings to be without significant long-term or genetic effects.[230] Even if the devastatingly far more powerful "hydrogen bombs" were to be used, their long-term medical impact may be similar, because these bombs' radioactive content is relatively comparable to that of the "fission" type bombs used in Japan. Hence, for all practical purposes, a nuclear strike is equivalent to the synergy of thousands of conventional bombs exploding at the same time and at the same point. This argument is provided to indicate that in certain existential circumstances it might be prudent to use strategic nuclear weapons.

POPE'S DILEMMA

As a leader of the world's dominant religion, Christianity, the pope should be concerned. He also lives in the heart of Europe—a focused area of political Islamic attention and potential assault. Pope Benedict's reference to a fourteenth-century Byzantine emperor's remark about Islam imposing itself fostered angry responses and demonstrations around the Muslim world.[231] In his November 2006 visit to Turkey, he tried to mend fences and establish a dialogue with Muslim clerics, specifically on the need for reciprocity on the part of Muslim nations to allow the establishment of religious institutions for non-Muslims in Muslim lands. The pope correctly reminded them of the scores of mosques that are being constructed in western Europe.

But the pope was dealing from a situation of weakness; Muslim nations are under no compulsion to be reciprocal, and he is dealing with political Islam, a conquest-driven entity. The core strategy of political Islam is to keep an iron grip on what it has conquered already while reaching out for more. The reason for the lack of reciprocity is articulated by well-known Indian Islamist Zakir Naik:

In some Islamic countries propagation of other religions is prohibited. Even con-struction of any place of worship is also prohibited. So, many non-Muslims ask: when we allow Muslims to preach and build their mosques in our countries, then why are they [non-Muslims] not allowed to do so in these Muslim countries? ... As far as matters of religion are concerned we [Muslims] know for sure that only Islam is a True religion in the eye of God. In [the] Koran it is mentioned that God will never accept any religion other than Islam. As far as building of Churches or Tem-ples is concerned, how can we allow this when their religion is wrong and when their worshipping is wrong? Thus we will not allow such wrong things in our Islamic country. In religious matters only we know for sure that we Muslims are right—they [non-Muslims] are not sure. Thus in our Islamic country we can't allow preaching other religions because we know for sure that only Islam is the right religion. How-ever, if a non-Muslim likes to practice his religion in [an] Islamic country, then he can do so inside his home—but he can't propagate his religion. Non-Muslims are no doubt experts in science and technology. They [non-Muslims] are not sure about religious Truths. Thus we are trying to get them to the right path of Islam. Therefore we propagate our religion to the non-Muslims.[232]

The pope may have initiated this dialogue for political reasons, by pointing out the duplicitous nature of political Islam's dealings with unbelievers. Nonetheless, there may be a downside to this: by talking with insincere Muslim clerics, the pope may be unnec-essarily giving them credibility, both to the Muslim world and to non-Muslims. The above articulation by an Indian Islamist is a typical one, showing the futility of the pope's "dialogue." This outlook by Islamists underlines the need to discredit the ideological foundations of political Islam (see chapter 2, "Science to the Rescue").

It is relevant to note here the views of the nearest Muslim equivalent to a pope, the grand imam of Egypt's Al-Azhar University, Muhammed Tantawi—again funda-mentally showing the inability to coexist, let alone reciprocate:

[The] Koran describes the Jews with their own particular degenerate characteristics, i.e., killing the prophets of Allah [Koran 2:61/ 3:112], corrupting His words by putting them in the wrong places, consuming the people's wealth frivolously, refusal to distance themselves from the evil they do, and other ugly characteristics caused by their deep-rooted lasciviousness.... [O]nly a minority of the Jews keep their word. ... [A]ll Jews are not the same. The good ones become Muslims [Koran 3:113], the bad ones do not.[233]

In another speech, Tantawi even goes on to advocate violence against Israeli citizens, deriving the violent legitimacy from Islamic scriptures:

"The great Imam of Al-Azhar Sheikh Muhammad Sayyed Tantawi, demanded that the Palestinian people, of all factions, intensify the martyrdom operations [i.e., suicide attacks] against the Zionist [Jewish] enemy, and described the martyrdom operations as the highest form of Jihad operations. He says that the young people executing them have sold Allah the most precious thing of all.... [Tantawi] emphasized that every martyrdom operation against any Israeli, including children, women, and teenagers, is a legitimate act according to [Islamic] religious law, and an Islamic commandment, until the people of Palestine regain their land and cause the cruel Israeli aggression to retreat."[234]

Some of the arguments presented in chapter 2, "Science to the Rescue," also cast a shadow on the theological underpinnings of the pope's own faith. Arguably, under this scenario, a pope may not want to be part of an ideological counteroffensive directed at political Islam. In fact, to save his own base, he could undermine such an effort. Here is the biggest irony: the faiths most threatened by political Islam may be opposed to the most effective way of dealing with it.

ALTERNATE ANALYSIS

In an article titled "Political Islam: Image and Reality," Indian American political scientist Muhammad Ayoob gives an entirely different view of political Islam.

[A]t first glance, Islam has a distinct record that inextricably links the religious to the political, that it is possible to politicize Islam much more easily than other religions. On closer scrutiny, however, it is clear that even in this respect there is nothing unique about Islam.[235]

It is true that all religions have a political component. Ayoob goes on to write about the political deeds of all contemporary religions. But he failed to address the extent of internal and external political content (including the dominant conquest content) in Islamic doctrine and the track record of Muslims vis-à-vis unbelievers historically, and in contemporary times, and their inability and/or unwillingness to coexist with unbelievers (see chapters 2 and 3). American scholar Bill Warner's statistical analysis discussed in earlier chapters shows an overwhelming political composition of the doctrine and a special focus on the conquest of unbelievers that continues today.[236] This has no parallels with any other contemporary widely practiced religion. Unlike most other religions, Islam's founder's unique position as a military commander explains why the use of force is the preferred method of achieving political objectives.

Ayoob then goes on to ask and answer the question of why Islam is singled out:

> Why is Islam singled out in the West as uniquely supportive of the mixing of religion and politics? The answer is relatively simple. Most other religio-political movements either emanate from Western societies or, like the Hindu manifestation of politicized religion, do not challenge Western hegemony, but seek rather to accommodate themselves to it. However, Islamists stubbornly refuse to accept the current distribution of power.

Pioneered by the West, the modern era is defined by industrialization, followed by institutional knowledge development. It has produced public education, science and technology, industrial and agricultural revolutions, and capitalism and commerce. This has led to tremendous wealth creation that has benefited communities and given them liberty. Nations such as India have inherently understood that by following Western countries they can bring about development in their own land. Ayoob has failed to realize that by taking a confrontational stance against the West, Muslim societies, as shown by all developmental indicators, have shortchanged themselves.[237]

Ayoob takes an easy route to identifying the root cause of political Islam, which he claims to be a modern phenomenon:

> It is the Muslims' collective memory of subjugation and the current perception of weakness in relation to the West that provides the common denominator among the many divergent manifestations of political Islam.

As discussed extensively here, the reality is different. Islamic conquest of the past centuries is a political act. Political Islam has been responsible for decimating non-Muslims from *all* Muslim-majority regions of South Asia in the modern era. This phenomenon is repeated in other parts of the developing world, including in parts of

Thailand. Muslim grievances have to be discovered and appreciated in order to advance the "common denominator" of political Islam—the conquest and subjugation of unbelievers.

In a 2005 article titled "Deterring Terrorism: It Can Be Done," political scientists Robert Trager and Dessislava Zagorcheva argued the case for deterring terrorism by making a case study of the apparently effective Philippine and American governments' approach to dealing with the Moro Islamic Liberation Front.[238] This Muslim separatist group has been waging a bloody insurgency since the 1980s. Religious preachers called the Sufis from Muslim-ruled India as well as traders from India and Arabia are said to have brought Islam to the Southeast Asian nations of Malaysia and Indonesia in the eleventh century. From there, starting in the fourteenth century, Islam was brought to the Philippines. Muslims constitute about 5 percent of the Philippine population and are predominantly located on islands in the southern part of the country.[239]

Through repression and by emphasizing a medieval Arabic way of life, political Islam has created poverty and influenced Muslims in the Philippines to embrace jihad. Aided by America, the deterrence strategy against Muslim insurgency has involved artificially increasing economic opportunities for the Muslims in the region. This approach of addressing the symptoms without adequately addressing the root cause is hardly sustainable in the long run.[240] Based upon the data and arguments provided in chapters 2 and 3, political Islam offers little or no positive vision—and drives Muslims toward conflict with others. More important, it also creates conditions for Muslims to have large families, such that Muslims far surpass the growth rate of people of other denominations. All of this inherently creates an unstable situation. In some Muslim nations, repression, a form of deterrence, has been used to keep political Islam at bay. In Turkey, Mustafa Kemal Ataturk repressed political Islam; in Iraq, it was Saddam Hussein. But once a power vacuum was created in these nations, political Islam was able to be revived. Indeed, with the advent of democracy in Turkey and the removal of Saddam, political Islam is making a comeback. Conclusion: either containment or deterrence of radical Islam, while it can be effective in the short term, is not effective in the long term.

Psychiatrist Marc Sageman argues in his book *Understanding Terror Networks* that we are facing something closer to a cult network than an organized global enemy.[241] From David Ignatius's op-ed in the *Washington Post* we see these observations:

> Like many cults through history, the Muslim terrorists thrive by channeling and perverting the idealism of young people. As a forensic psychiatrist, he [Sageman] analyzed data on about 400 jihadists. He found that they weren't poor, desperate

sociopaths but restless young men who found identity by joining the terrorist underground. Ninety percent came from intact families; 63 percent had gone to college; 75 percent were professionals or semi-professionals; 73 percent were married.

What transformed these young Sunni Muslim men was the fellowship of the jihad and the militant role models they found in people such as Osama Bin Laden. The terrorist training camps in Afghanistan were a kind of elite finishing school— Sageman likened it to getting into Harvard. The Sept. 11 hijackers weren't psychotic killers; none of the 19 had criminal records. In terms of their psychological profiles, says Sageman, they were as healthy as the general population.

The implication of Sageman's analysis is that the Sunni jihadism of al Qaeda and its spin-off groups is a generational phenomenon. Unless new grievances spawn new recruits, it will gradually ebb over time. In other words, this is a fire that will gradually burn itself out unless we keep pumping in more oxygen.[242]

In my view, as discussed in previous chapters, the so-called grievances are mostly either self-inflicted or are even invented to spawn new jihadist recruits. In other words, we are not the ones pumping more oxygen. In fact, the grievance strategy—contrary to what Sageman articulates—is at the core of the political Islamic movement to channel Muslim energy toward the conquest of unbelievers.

In a *Washington Post* op-ed titled "Bin Laden, The Left and Me," which was a response to criticism of his book,[243] conservative best-selling author Dinesh D'Souza declares the American Left to be partly responsible for the Muslim rage:

> I also argue [in my book, *The Enemy at Home: The Cultural Left and Its Responsibility for 9/11*] that the policies that U.S. "progressives" promote around the world—including abortion rights, contraception for teenagers and gay rights—are viewed as an assault on traditional values by many cultures, and have contributed to the blowback of Islamic rage.
>
> The thrust of the radical Muslim critique of America is that Islam is under attack from the global forces of atheism and immorality—and that the United States is leading that attack.[244]

The moral high ground D'Souza gives Islamists can hardly be justified. Nations such as Saudi Arabia, Pakistan, or Egypt that have a large political Islamic base have some of the highest levels of corruption anywhere in the world. As has been argued in our discussion, radicals had to discover and market often-unjustified "grievances" (such as blaming the West for self-induced poverty) against the United States in order to justify using terror. The trilogy from which extremists derive their inspiration and governance commands conquest of unbelievers; for that, unbeliever nations had to be attacked. If Muslim extremists had an alternate positive vision other than this "rage," one could take D'Souza's analysis seriously. In fact, radical Muslims do not offer a positive vision, and this makes peace with them impossible to achieve. Having been born and reared in India, D'Souza should have known better—that there is an Islamic conquest under way in South Asia. This offensive conquest devalues his acknowledgement of the radical claim that "Islam is under attack."

In his 2006 book, *Overblown: How Politicians and the Terrorism Industry Inflate National Security Threats, and Why We Believe Them*, political scientist John Mueller articulates the view that the terror threat arising from Islamists is overblown.[245] He examines how hypervigilance regarding terrorism is threatening liberties, the economy, and lives. Mueller calls for the creation of policy that reduces fear and the cost of overreaction.

Mueller makes the mistake of not realizing that Islamic terrorism is a consequence of the ongoing conquest of land and people for political Islam. He likewise fails to recognize that terrorism is its one manifestation. Contrary to his central thesis that the political goals of terrorist movements can't succeed, we noted in the section "Siege of India" that within the past sixty years, entire lands have been captured systematically and almost exclusively for Islam and Muslims. This process is still ongoing because of state sponsorship of these movements, notably by Saudi Arabia, Iran, Pakistan, and others. Also, due to high Muslim population growth and to the vast majority of Muslim populations being under political Islamic control, the terror war will only escalate in the coming years. It is no longer a containable problem. What this means is that America and its allies must respond now decisively by roping jihad victim states such as India to neutralize political Islam and its sponsors, which are at the root of the terror and mayhem.

REORIENT AMERICA

America stands today as probably the most powerful nation ever to exist on earth. It has pulled the rest of the world along to unprecedented levels of civilizational progress. Yet, it is also a caring nation, with both the government and the public generously funding schools and hospitals and giving food for the needy in the developing world.

But America is also on a path of paying a high price both socially and economically due to the extraordinary and escalating security-related expenses imposed by the terror war, with no end in sight. These burdens are accentuated by the precipitous drop in capital markets—and the American government is potentially saddled with at least a trillion dollars of short-term budget deficit as it works to alleviate the credit crunch.

Among the take-home messages of American scholar Amy Chua's analysis about the decline of past hyperpowers (states that were militarily and economically far more powerful than any others of the era) is that they were all—as a rule—tolerant toward minority cultures and religions, open to infusion of new ideas, and harnessed the human capital of their subjects regardless of their background.[246] Yet these hyperpowers were also ruthless toward civilizations that never accepted their terms of coexistence. Not surprisingly, these characteristics are shared by the current hyperpower of our times, the United States of America, except for one thing: the inability of America to be ruthless toward the political Islamic movement that clearly doesn't accept not just America's terms, but internationally accepted terms of coexistence.

Just because certain widely believed notions, including the one that Earth is flat, have been around for thousands of years did not necessarily make them real. The fact that this notion has been much discredited by science-based reasoning is particularly relevant for our discussion. The point can't be overstated: we need to be open to the possibility that Islam was primarily designed to be a political ideology of conquest.

That a minority in a Muslim population appears to be spiritual without identifying with jihadism shouldn't be a surprise, because a portion of the Islamic doctrine is spiritual (see chapter 2, "Conquest by Design"). However, this is not necessarily the criterion for considering Islam to be a religion, like any other. Indeed, as most available data indicate, and as discussed in preceding sections, every authoritative school of interpreting Islamic scriptures, history, the outlook, and deeds of most followers of Islam invariably points credence to the following alternate view: that Islam is a political ideology designed to extend its founder Muhammad's power base during his times and that of his extended tribes of Arabs, and to conquer non-Arab Muslims beyond his time.

Since the dominant focus of jihad is the conquest of land and people for Islam, identifying with Muslims who "fight" for their "rights" in a non-Muslim nation is one form of jihadism. As discussed here, such fights are part and parcel of the process called the Islamic conquest.

The less a Muslim population is immersed in Islamic doctrine, the more it appears to be inclined away from jihadism. For instance, in Indonesia where the Muslim outlook was considerably influenced by local Hindu philosophies, the population had been less inclined toward jihadism. With funds from the Middle East pouring in to build gleaming and better-funded mosques, the theology gets preached from a far more credible platform and apparently has less difficulty in finding believers.

Hence, the trend in Muslim outlook in Indonesia is toward increasingly identifying with extremism.

Indeed, the potent Muslim terrorists are the educated ones who increasingly identify with Islamic doctrines. Even those educated Muslims who had otherwise received secular education find themselves taking up jihad through their exposure to Islamic doctrines in orthodox religious institutions such as the Quran Foundation in the central Indian city of Pune.[247] A proposal by Indian intelligence agencies advises Indian companies to "initiate steps to have an in-house set-up to keep tabs on 'suspicious and changed behavior' among their employees, in particular, on 'abnormally religious' staff," in order to identify new and emerging jihadists.[248] Extremists better schooled in theology are winning arguments and are increasingly taking over the control of mosques in Europe. Again, the reason is readily understood: as noted in chapter 2, "Conquest by Design," the Islamic theology itself is predominantly hostile to unbelievers. It is in fact more likely for a Muslim to be hostile to unbelievers, the more he/she identifies with Islamic scriptures.

Putting it another way, with external politics focused on jihad and internal politics discouraging wealth creation, Islam's character vis-à-vis that of unbelievers is conquest-oriented—and not one of coexistence. Indeed, an enduring, successful, and uncontested political ideology finds it advantageous to invoke Almighty God, albeit in a token way. What makes Islam stand out is its adherents' inability to coexist, unlike that of any other religion (see chapters 2 and 3)—which, in my view, is the defining characteristic of a religious pretender. In other words, the conquest model of Islam—not the religion model of Islam—fits the data better.[249]

Andrew McCarthy, a former American prosecutor of jihadists, notes: "It is an unrelenting fact that Islamic doctrine is the catalyst for the cataracts of Islamic terror raining down on the globe."[250] The Dutch politician and member of its parliament Geert Wilders makes an astute observation consistent with what is portrayed here: "Sure, there are a lot of moderate Muslims. But a moderate Islam is nonexistent," and adds further, "Let no one fool you about Islam being a religion. Sure, it has a god, and a here-after, and 72 virgins. But in its essence Islam is a political ideology."[251]

Almost eight years after the 9/11 attacks on America, it is hard to comprehend that the nature and roots of the Islamic threat are still unclear to its analysts and policymakers. Identifying with flawed preconceived notions of Islam has been symptomatic of the entire US establishment. Starting at the very top, here is former president Bush: "Our enemy doesn't follow the great traditions of Islam. They have hijacked a great religion.... [Islam] is a faith that brings comfort to people. It inspires them to lead lives based on honesty, justice, and compassion."[252] The analysis—subject to data and statistics—outlined here suggests that Muslim populations strongly driven by Islamic doctrines find "mutual interest and mutual respect" vis-à-vis Western civilization rather elusive. Hence, without exposure to the relevant data, the Unites States is in continued danger of pursuing flawed policies. Then new American president Barack Obama's declaration in his inauguration is one such an example—"[t]o the Muslim world, we seek a new way forward, based on mutual interest and mutual respect."[253]

After ideology-based Nazi Germany and imperial Japan were defeated by America and its allies, as the dominant occupying power, America led the effort to ensure that constitutionally enshrined ideological supremacy wouldn't be allowed to happen again in these nations. Unfortunately, as the leading occupying power in both Iraq and Afghanistan, America allowed the new constitutions to uphold the supremacy of Islamic ideology.[254]

What could be the reason for America's inability to recognize this ideological threat? While Europe is under the grip of what Bruce Bawer calls "self-destructive passivity, its softness toward tyranny, its reflexive inclination to appease," America's strong identification with faith likely made it vulnerable to the new threat that projects itself as a religion.[255]

In my view, the deceptive nature of the Islamic threat, which shows a soft and a religious side when it is weak or during the jihad buildup stage (see chapter 3, "Jihad Buildup") and its claims of victimization, has thus far prevented it from being appropriately identified. However, the kind of data analysis presented in our discussion, that of Muslim interaction with weaker civilizations, such as the Hindus in South Asia and Bill Warner's significant statistical analysis of the Islamic trilogy published in 2007 and 2008, could play a critical role in exposing the threat's real nature.[256]

When a political ideology makes a token invocation of God for the purpose of conquest and has proven its genocidal intent across continents, it can no longer be seen as a conventional religion or faith. Some of the arguments used to question the religious foundations of Islam—such as authenticity, accuracy, or completeness of scriptures—can also pose difficulties for other faiths, including the majority religion in America. Still, the American establishment must adapt to the new enemy by using tactics that in the past would have been considered unthinkable. It is a useful reminder that the religious outlook could undermine a hyperpower. Amy Chua also points out that as the hyperpower of its times, the great Roman Empire declined when it embraced Christianity and became intolerant toward its subjects in far-flung regions that were practicing different faiths.[257]

If America decides it can't afford to be critical of the religious basis of Islam because this could indirectly undermine its powerful church, such an America may be rightly seen as no longer capable of making necessary adjustments to win the war on terror. Such an American outlook may be undercutting the most important component of a potentially successful strategy toward winning the war on terrorism: the ability to comprehensively discredit the theological or ideological foundations of Islam and to see Islamic religious institutions for what they are: nodes of a social network that spawns jihad.

History is replete with failed or declining civilizations that, for religious or philosophical reasons, refused to embrace a potential winning strategy. In our case, that strategy is confronting the theological roots of Islam with science-based reasoning. A surging China, which is potentially the next superpower and which is relatively free of the cost of the war on terror, and not particularly religious, may be best positioned to exploit the spoils. While many Western nations might be loath to admit it, China has been one of the most successful nations in keeping a lid on political Islam, despite a significant and concentrated population of Muslims in its western region. The short-sighted may call it religious repression, but the informed would realize it as a policy of repressing a repressive political ideology. Tolerating the intolerance, as we do in the West, is not something to write home about.

A survey released by Rasmussen Reports in April 2005 found that most Americans—63 percent—believe the Bible is literally true and is the Word of God, with just 24 percent thinking otherwise.[258] This literal interpretation is not backed by science. But a June 2008 Pew Research Center poll showed 27 percent of the above 63 percent felt that the scriptures shouldn't be interpreted literally.[259]

Still, these statistics expose some weakness in American society's approach to new knowledge and ideas. It also shows a deficiency in the American appreciation of scientific knowledge in building modern civilizations. Such a civilization doesn't attract sufficient number of its bright students to specialize in science or engineering.

As part of the American strategy for attracting and keeping the best in America, a certain percentage of graduate enrollments in science or engineering are expected to be of foreign origin. But the data stating that at least 30 percent of graduate students in American science or engineering graduate programs are of foreign origin (the average is much more in physics—43 percent) may lead one to conclude that the underlying strong religious outlook reflected in the Rasmussen Report is having a negative impact on American youth.[260]

The present popularity of books questioning the origins of religious doctrines from a scientific point of view and discussing their inconsistencies, the June 2008 Pew poll where more Americans were willing to discount the literal interpretation of scriptures, and an America that is increasingly diverse in religion and ethnicity may be an indication of an American public trying to break open the long-standing taboo against discussing religions critically.[261] When educated individuals, acting in the name of God, smash loaded airliners into skyscrapers, these questions become inevitable.[262]

A shift toward a better public appreciation of science will also help develop a nuanced outlook toward faith or religion. In this era, maintaining real wealth, national confidence, and overall security comes down to creating and owning intellectual property in the form of patents. A 2005 bipartisan study by economists Rob Shapiro and Kevin Hasset estimates that US intellectual property is worth between $5 trillion and $5.5 trillion, equivalent to about 45 percent of the GDP.[263] After peaking in the 1960s, the American share of worldwide industrial patents has reduced to about 52 percent.[264] Although globalization can be seen as contributing to this reduction, this trend also points to the need for America to remain competitive through education, training, and infrastructure investments. Even as the Internet opens up America to achieve the next level of progress, the grip of theology can be a retarding force.

All of this contrasts with China or even India, where the younger generation has realized lucrative career paths by embracing science and engineering. And the majorities in these countries are not dominated by an outlook that puts emphasis on book(s) of "God's revelations" to help guide them. In an era of an increasingly information-based world, this could be a significant advantage over a theology-influenced America; the emphasis on religious information that was essentially designed for different times and conditions ultimately restricts the ability to perform in the modern world.

America was able to out-compete and bankrupt the communist former Soviet Union because, unlike America or even China, the Soviet Union never focused on wealth creation for its citizens. However, past history is no guarantee for predicting the future. The European elite, who saw themselves as the leading civilization in the early twentieth century, were surprised to find that the America they had underestimated surged past them in every way during the latter part of the last century. We now understand why. America embraced capitalism (which encourages wealth creation), while Europeans got stuck in socialism (which is good in distributing existing wealth but not in creating new wealth). It is conceivable that this new century will likely favor those civilizations that, in addition to capitalism, embrace science and engineering. An Israel led by capitalism and education-embracing secular Jews with high levels of economic growth may be an example of such a civilization.

A number of scholars, including Robert Spencer, have identified Western civilization as a "Judeo-Christian civilization"—a civilization defined by Judeo-Christian "values."[265] One such value is the principle that individual freedom is a prerequisite for virtue. I certainly accept the idea that certain attributes of these values, including the one pertaining to liberty, have likely contributed to the emergence of Western civilization. However, these values and the way they are interpreted continue to evolve, especially shaped by science and technology that create the parameters for the world in which we live. After all, even the very concept of liberty and how it has been applied has evolved over centuries. Even in America, in the past century, blacks or women didn't enjoy the same degree of liberty to which white males were entitled.

Hence, in this work I dispense with the notion that embracing more Judeo-Christian values will somehow lead to a victory over the Islamic threat. Just like building a dam on a challenging river doesn't require reaffirmation of Judeo-Christian values, neutralizing the Islamic threat needs to be faced quite simply as a problem to be solved.

Preconceived notions, such as democracy as the antidote for terror (see chapter 1 "The Democracy Angle"), have been an expensive lesson learnt for the American Right in the form of the debacle in Iraq. Now with the new Democratic president, Barrack Obama, in power, the American Left is beginning to articulate its own version of the democracy "vision." Will Marshall, president of the Progressive Policy Institute writes in his *Wall Street Journal* opinion piece on how Islamic terrorism can be neutralized while focusing just on a model of economic development in Muslim nations: "[A] sweeping tariff-reduction initiative designed to spur Western trade and investment and integrate Muslim countries into the world trading system."[266] However as pointed out in the first chapter and in this chapter, entrenched and regressive ideologies retard developmental efforts; Western resources spent in Muslim nations will likely be used to finance jihad directed at unbelievers.

I suggest proven approaches to dealing with the threat. First, letting data—not some romantic notions of religion—define the enemy and then bringing out the excellent problem-solving skills of Western civilization. The objective interpretation of data can also be seen as an integral part of problem solving. After all, America has taken the ideas of problem solving and project management to new levels. Such an approach was responsible for the America-led victory over the Soviet-based communist movement during the old cold war era.

Fortunately, there are other signs of America adjusting to the enemy. One area involves shielding scholars from expensive libel suits brought by plausible financiers of terror. Author Rachel Ehrenfeld lost a libel case in the British High Court of Justice to a Saudi Businessman named Khalid bin Mahfouz concerning her book *Funding Evil: How Terrorism Is Financed—and How to Stop It.* In response to this and similar incidents, the New York State legislature passed a law in April 2008 to offer New York residents greater (retroactive) protection against libel judgments in nations whose laws are inconsistent with the freedom of speech granted by the US Constitution.[267] In addition, federal legislation called the Free Speech Protection Act of 2008 has been introduced by Congressman Peter King of New York. This act, if passed, also offers a deterrent value, by enabling US authors to sue foreign libel plaintiffs who obtained judgments against them and obtain treble damages if those foreign libel plaintiffs engage in intentional schemes to suppress First Amendment (Free Speech) rights.[268]

A proposal by the Justice Department calls for the FBI to investigate residents without any evidence of wrongdoing, relying instead on a terrorist profile that could single out a religious, racial, or ethnic group. With this directive, the profiling of Muslims could become a possibility.[269] It is very likely that these measures will face stiff constitutional challenges in the US courts. I would argue that unless these directives are followed up by a campaign that clearly connects Muslim behavior and justifiable profiling with fundamental deficiencies in Islam (i.e., putting the blame on the other side), it will only help create a sense of Muslim grievance and put America in a morally unsound position.

If America and its allies relentlessly identify Islam predominantly as a political ideology of conquest and discredit its theological foundations, only then can they break the Muslim passion for conquest and win this emerging new cold war. America can then free up its vast resources to invest in the future of its children and in other priorities. Such an America will also reinvigorate itself to take on the strategic, scientific, technological, and economic challenge posed by China and the rest.

EXECUTIVE SUMMARY

Based upon the analysis and discussion in this chapter, the following summary is presented for an easy review. It outlines major elements of the dos and don'ts of a policy response going forward. (The reader is also urged to read the summary given at the beginning of this chapter.)

- First and foremost, using a statistical analysis of Islamic doctrines, it can be unequivocally shown that Islam does not preach peace; it should be seen less as a religion and more as an ideology of conquest (61 percent of the Koran either talks ill of unbelievers or calls for their violent conquest and subjugation, but only 2.6 percent of it talks about the overall good of humanity).

- Accordingly, increased exposure to Islamic doctrine is seen to propel Muslim populations to embrace jihad and *sharia* fervently.
- Instead of focusing on bringing democracy to Muslim-majority nations, policies should be geared toward first weakening political Islam in these societies in an effort to create conditions that will help to win the war on terror.
- It is futile to talk about the reform of Islam or to hope for moderates to exercise power and influence in most Muslim societies; the political Islamic movement must first be weakened.
- *Sharia* is an important tool for facilitating jihad—by conforming Muslims to a medieval Arabic way of life and by channeling their resources toward it.
- Muslim religious institutions under the influence of political Islam act as the nodes of the social network that spawns jihad. With political Islam's power so concentrated, they are also political Islam's greatest weakness.
- Using science, we must question and discredit the theological foundations of political Islam in order to influence educated Muslims against the political Islamic movement, thereby weakening it.
- *Sharia* law should be portrayed correctly as representing medieval—human-made and often-contradictory—customs of certain Arabian tribes.
- Using the data of Islam-inspired atrocities, we must discredit the grievance basis that is used to mobilize Muslims.
- Troops should be either redeployed or withdrawn from untenable situations in Iraq and Afghanistan. As an occupying power, America's ability to weaken political Islam in these nations is limited.
- A long-term focus on al Qaeda, Hezbollah, Hamas, or the Taliban is a wrong way of responding to terror. Instead, the focus should be on the primary sponsors—the axis of jihad, consisting of Saudi Arabia, Iran, and Pakistan.
- Even leaders who are "friendly" to America in nations such as Pakistan or Saudi Arabia are prisoners of the entrenched and dominant forces of political Islam, and are largely irrelevant to the war on terror.
- Saudi Arabia plays a role similar to the former Soviet Union in this emerging new cold war against political Islam.
- It is important to discredit and distance Saudi Arabia and to create a sense of grievance regarding the Wahhabi nation in the eyes of Muslim communities around the world.

- We should portray the political Islamic movements based in Saudi Arabia, Pakistan, and the regime in Iran as waging genocidal terror warfare against both developing and advanced nations. This propaganda should be geared toward building up grievances against the axis of jihad nations in non-Muslim victim nations. Such a buildup should lead to anomalous events favorable to America and others.
- Emphasizing Iran's pre-Islamic way of life and secularism at the expense of the Arabian influence may be one way of eventually marginalizing ruling mullahs and getting them to give up the reins of power in a nation that is increasingly tired of them.
- We should rapidly help to build India as a counterforce to political Islamic movements based in Asia and leverage the 850 million cornered Indians to fight the war on terror.

NOTES

1. Fareed Zakaria, *The Future of Freedom: Illiberal Democracy at Home and Abroad* (New York: Norton, 2003), p. 135.

2. Richard Rahn, "Economic Liberty and Islam," *Washington Times*, March 5, 2007, http://www.washingtontimes.com/commentary/20070304-094010-8712r.htm (accessed May 2, 2007).

3. Steven Stalinsky, "Saudi Arabia's Education System," *FrontPage Magazine*, December 30, 2002, http://www.frontpagemag.com/Articles/ReadArticle.asp?ID=5243 (accessed July 20, 2008).

4. Lawrence Right, *The Looming Tower: Al Qaeda and the Road to 9/11* (New York: Knopf, 2006), p. 291.

5. Ari Shavit, "Judgment Day—Israel Facing Apocalypse," *Ha'aretz Magazine*, October 6, 2000, http://christianactionforisrael.org/isreport/septoct00/landau.html (accessed July 20, 2008).

6. Ted Barrett, Becky Brittain, and K. Fabian, "War Costs Could Total $1.6 Trillion by 2009, Panel Estimates," *CNN*, November 14, 2007, http://www.cnn.com/2007/POLITICS/11/13/hidden.war.costs/index.html (accessed July 20, 2008).

7. Marilyn Adamo and Joan Levinstein, "Then vs. Now," *Fortune*, February 4, 2008.

8. "Deficit," *Wikipedia*, http://en.wikipedia.org/wiki/Deficit (accessed July 8, 2008).

9. "Universal Declaration of Human Rights," *UN Charter*, December 10, 1948, http://www.un.org/Overview/rights.html (accessed May 2, 2007).

10. Janet Levy, "The Erosion of Free Speech," *FrontPage Magazine*, July 4, 2008,

http://frontpagemag.com/Articles/Read.aspx?GUID=1CAC2897-674D-44AB-ADF4 -BA77930F421E (accessed July 20, 2008).

11. Arnaud de Borchgrave, "Al Qaeda on the Ropes?" *Washington Times*, September 28, 2007, http://www.washingtontimes.com/article/20070928/COMMENTARY/10928 0001/1012/commentary (accessed October 15, 2007).

12. Sarah Downey, "A Safe Heaven," *Newsweek*, September 30, 2002, http://www .hvk.org/articles/1002/69.html (accessed March 2, 2007).

13. Daniel Pipes, "The Moderation of American Muslims," *FrontPage Magazine*, April 8, 2004, http://frontpagemag.com/Articles/Read.aspx?GUID=F9C71B00-156C-48EF- A3DC-A7E61162C89D (accessed April 5, 2008).

14. Robert Spencer, "SUNY-Stonybrook: Manufactured Outrage," *Jihad Watch*, October 27, 2008, http://www.jihadwatch.org/archives/023239.php (accessed October 28, 2008).

15. Aakar Patel, "Where Indian Muslims Have Gone Wrong?" *Mid-Day*, September 5, 2004, http://ww1.mid-day.com/news/city/2004/september/91708.htm (accessed March 2, 2007).

16. Zakaria, *The Future of Freedom*, p. 150.

17. Reza Aslan, *No God but God: The Origins, Evolution, and Future of Islam* (New York: Random House, 2005); Reza Aslan, "The War for Islam," *Boson Globe*, September 10, 2006, http://www.boston.com/news/globe/ideas/articles/2006/09/10/the_war_for _islam/ (accessed January 3, 2009).

18. "Objectives Resolution," *Wikipedia*, http://en.wikipedia.org/wiki/Objectives _Resolution (accessed July 8, 2008).

19. Kishan Bhatia, "Flawed Democracies," *IVarta.com*, June 27, 2008, http://www .blogs.ivarta.com/india-usa-blog-column126.htm (accessed July 20, 2008).

20. "Constitution of Iraq," *Wikipedia*, http://en.wikipedia.org/wiki/Constitution _of_Iraq (accessed July 8, 2008).

21. "Constitution of Pakistan," *Wikipedia*, http://en.wikipedia.org/wiki/Constitution _of_Pakistan (accessed July 8, 2008).

22. "Constitution of Afghanistan," *Wikipedia*, http://en.wikipedia.org/wiki/ Constitution_of_Afghanistan (accessed July 8, 2008).

23. Geneive Abdo, "A More Islamic Islam," *Washington Post*, March 17, 2007, http://www.washingtonpost.com/wp-dyn/content/article/2007/03/16/AR200703160 1941.html (accessed April 5, 2007).

24. "Combating Sharia with Islamic Tools," *FrontPage Magazine*, November 20, 2007, http://frontpagemag.com/Articles/Read.aspx?GUID=D81A5112-A188-4290-87E9- 1050B7C28DB0 (accessed July 20, 2008).

25. Andrew Bostom, "The Muslim Mainstream and the New Caliphate," *American Thinker*, April 27, 2007, http://www.americanthinker.com/2007/04/the_muslim _mainstream_and_the.html (accessed July 20, 2008).

26. "Saudi Muftis: Terrorists and Their Supporters Are Committing a 'Grave Sin,'" *AsiaNews.it*, July 5, 2008, http://www.asianews.it/index.php?l=en&art=12691&geo =1&size=A# (accessed July 20, 2008).

27. "2008 Update: Saudi Arabia's Curriculum of Intolerance," *Hudson Institute*, 2008, http://www.hudson.org/files/pdf_upload/textbooks_final_for_pdf.pdf (accessed July 20, 2008); "The Study of Political Islam," *FrontPage Magazine*, February 5, 2007, http://www.frontpagemag.com/Articles/ReadArticle.asp?ID=26769 (accessed May 2, 2007); Robert Spencer, "The American Muslim, Terrorism, and Islamic Supremism," *Jihad Watch*, October 6, 2008, http://www.jihadwatch.org/archives/022992.php (accessed October 6, 2008).

28. "Madrasah," *Wikipedia*, http://en.wikipedia.org/wiki/Madrasah (accessed November 12, 2008).

29. Ira Rifkin, "Complexities of the Koran Make Mastery a Challenge," *Washington Post*, January 17, 1998, http://www.iol.ie/~afifi/BICNews/Islam/islam30.htm (accessed November 12, 2008).

30. "A New Koran," *FrontPage Magazine*, April 18, 2008, http://frontpagemagazine .com/Articles/Read.aspx?GUID=A00F3895-42BB-4A7D-9FA5-4A19F3286EAD (accessed July 20, 2008).

31. "Ahmadiyya," *Wikipedia*, http://en.wikipedia.org/wiki/Ahmadiyya (accessed November 8, 2008).

32. "Undercover Mosque," *Dispatches*, January 15, 2007, http://www.channel4 .com/news/articles/dispatches/undercover+mosque/158390 (accessed May 2, 2007).

33. Jackson Maogoto, *Battling Terrorism: Legal Perspectives on the Use of Force and the War on Terror* (Hampshire, UK: Ashgate, 2005), p. 152.

34. Moorthy Muthuswamy, "Waffling on Islamic Ideology," *Washington Times*, December 8, 2002.

35. Peter Wehner, "The War against Global Jihadism," *RealClearPolitics.com*, January 8, 2007, http://www.realclearpolitics.com/articles/2007/01/the_nature_of_our_enemy .html (accessed July 20, 2008).

36. Matthew Lee, "White House Bars Loaded Labels from Words of War," *San Francisco Chronicle*, April 25, 2008, http://www.sfgate.com/cgi-bin/article.cgi?f=/c/a/2008/ 04/24/MNVJ10BAEJ.DTL (accessed July 20, 2008).

37. Robert Spencer, "'Jihadist' Booted from Government Lexicon," *Jihad Watch*, April 24, 2008, http://jihadwatch.org/archives/020777.php (accessed July 20, 2008).

38. Bill Gertz, "Military Report: Terms 'Jihad,' 'Islamist' Needed," *Washington Times*, October 20, 2008, http://washingtontimes.com/news/2008/oct/20/report-says-terms-jihad-islamist-needed/ (accessed October 20, 2008).

39. Steven Emerson, "Expert on Radical Islam Fired from Pentagon," *Fox News*, January 11, 2008, http://www.investigativeproject.org/article/584 (accessed July 20, 2008).

40. Bill Gertz, "Caughlin Backed," *Washington Times*, January 11, 2008, http://washingtontimes.com/news/2008/jan/11/inside-the-ring-99910007/ (accessed July 20, 2008).

41. Joshua Price, "Emerson Interview Part II," *Conservative Beacon*, September 27, 2007, http://www.investigativeproject.org/article/490 (accessed July 20, 2008).

42. Steven Emerson, *Jihad Incorporated: A Guide to Militant Islam in the US* (Amherst, NY: Prometheus Books, 2006).

43. Zahid Hussain, *Frontline Pakistan: The Struggle with Militant Islam* (New York: Columbia University Press, 2007).

44. Tahir Niaz, "Pakistan to Ask EU to Amend Laws on Freedom of Expression," *Daily Times*, June 8, 2008, http://www.dailytimes.com.pk/default.asp?page=2008%5C06%5C08%5Cstory_8-6-2008_pg7_14 (accessed July 20, 2008).

45. Ahmed Rashid, "Musharraf at the Exit," *Washington Post*, March 22, 2007, http://www.washingtonpost.com/wp-dyn/content/article/2007/03/21/AR2007032101786.html (accessed May 2, 2007).

46. Mark Steyn, *America Alone: The End of the World as We Know It* (Washington, DC: Regnery, 2006), p. 208.

47. Moorthy Muthuswamy, "Religious Apartheid in India and American Policy Response," *IVarta.com*, July 4, 2005, http://www.ivarta.com/columns/OL_050704.htm (accessed July 20, 2008).

48. Helene Cooper, "Unfriendly Views on U.S.-Backed Arabic TV," *New York Times*, May 17, 2007, http://www.nytimes.com/2007/05/17/washington/17hurra.html (accessed July 28, 2008).

49. Craig Whitlock, "U.S. Network Falters in Mideast Mission," *Washington Post*, June 23, 2008, http://www.washingtonpost.com/wp-dyn/content/article/2008/06/22/AR2008062201228.html (accessed July 20, 2008).

50. Craig Whitlock, "Al Qaeda Masters Terrorism on the Cheap," *Washington Post*, August 24, 2008, http://www.washingtonpost.com/wp-dyn/content/article/2008/08/23/AR2008082301962.html (August 25, 2008).

51. Victor Comras, "Treasury Designates Major Saudi Charity—Al Haramain—for Financing Terrorists," *Counterterrorismblog.org*, June 19, 2008, http://counterterrorismblog.org/2008/06/treasury_designates_major_saud.php (accessed July 20, 2008).

52. Ibid.

53. "Saudi 'Charities' and the War against America," *FrontPage Magazine*, July 16, 2008, http://frontpagemag.com/Articles/Read.aspx?GUID=B164102B-EAB6-4407-9263-D2C34C43D838 (accessed July 20, 2008).

54. Ibid.; Steven Emerson, "National Commission on Terrorist Attacks upon the United States: Third Public Hearing," *U.S. Govt. Press*, July 9, 2003, http://www.9-11commission.gov/hearings/hearing3/witness_emerson.htm (accessed March 2, 2007).

55. "Sharia Finance," *FrontPage Magazine*, April 15, 2008, http://www.frontpagemag

.com/Articles/Read.aspx?GUID=A228AF1E-A0E5-429A-9AA8-BF9CEEC8F366 (accessed July 20, 2008).

56. Ibid.

57. "The Threats of Sharia Finance," *FrontPage Magazine*, June 11, 2008, http://www.frontpagemag.com/Articles/Read.aspx?GUID=9876D480-1E6C-46EC-AA3C-851A46FBF9FF (accessed July 20, 2008).

58. Department of the Treasury, "Islamic Finance 101," November 6, 2008, http://www.saneworks.us/uploads/news/applications/7.pdf (accessed November 6, 2008).

59. David Kilcullen, "'Twenty-eight Articles': Fundamentals of Company-Level Counterinsurgency," *Military Review*, May 1, 2006, http://www.d-n-i.net/fcs/pdf/kilcullen_28_articles.pdf (accessed July 29, 2008).

60. B. Raman, "Waziristanization of Southern Thailand—International Terrorism Monitor," *SAAG*, February 22, 2007, http://www.southasiaanalysis.org/%5Cpapers 22%5Cpaper2148.html (accessed March 2, 2007).

61. Jagmohan, *My Frozen Turbulence in Kashmir* (New Delhi: Allied, 2002), p. 401.

62. Rahn, "Economic Liberty and Islam."

63. Aijazz Ahmed, "Pakistan's Wonderlands with Little Wonder," *Asia Times*, February 19, 2003, http://www.atimes.com/atimes/South_Asia/EB19Df02.html (accessed July 8, 2008).

64. Michael Smith, "British Government 'to Troops Out of Iraq by Mid-2009,'" *Sunday Times*, July 13, 2008, http://www.timesonline.co.uk/tol/news/politics/article 4322710.ece (accessed July 20, 2008); David Stout, "Iraq Seems on Verge of Deal on American Presence," *New York Times*, October 17, 2008, http://www.nytimes.com/2008/10/18/world/middleeast/17forcescnd.html (accessed October 18, 2008).

65. Edward Luttwak, "Dead End: Counterinsurgency Warfare as Military Malpractice," *Harper's*, March 5, 2007, http://www.harpers.org/archive/2007/02/0081384 (accessed March 15, 2007).

66. Sabrina Tavernise, "Violence Leaves Young Iraqis Doubting Clerics," *New York Times*, March 4, 2008, http://www.nytimes.com/2008/03/04/world/middleeast/04youth.html (accessed July 20, 2008).

67. Basil Adas, "Al-Qaida 'Leaving Iraq for Sudan, Somalia,'" *Gulfnews.com*, July 11, 2008, http://frontpagemag.com/Articles/Read.aspx?GUID=2E4B3901-F66A-47FA-A4F8-F231DFC59D24 (accessed July 20, 2008); Kristin Roberts, "Pentagon Chief in Afghanistan as Al Qaeda Regroups," Reuters, December 3, 2007, http://www.reuters.com/article/topNews/idUSN0328131520071203 (accessed July 20, 2008).

68. "Awakening Movements in Iraq," *Wikipedia*, http://en.wikipedia.org/wiki/Awakening_movements_in_Iraq (accessed July 8, 2008).

69. Steve Luxenberg, "U.S. Spied on Iraqi Leaders, Book Says," *Washington Post*, September 5, 2008, http://www.washingtonpost.com/wp-dyn/content/article/2008/09/04/AR2008090403160.html (accessed September 5, 2008).

70. Sabrina Tavernise, "Shiite Militia in Baghdad Sees Its Power Ebb," *New York Times*, July 27, 2008, http://www.nytimes.com/2008/07/27/world/middleeast/27 mahdi.html (accessed July 20, 2008).

71. Tavernise, "Violence Leaves Young Iraqis Doubting Clerics."

72. Ibid.

73. Ibid.

74. David Sanger, "Bush Adds Troops in Bid to Secure Iraq," *New York Times*, January 10, 2007, http://www.nytimes.com/2007/01/11/world/middleeast/11prexy.html (accessed March 23, 2007).

75. Paul Alexander, "The Generals Speak," *Rolling Stone*, November 3, 2004, http://www.rollingstone.com/politics/story/6593163/the_generals_speak/ (accessed July 20, 2008).

76. Anthony Shadid, "New Paths to Power Emerge in Iraq," *Washington Post*, January 13, 2009, http://www.washingtonpost.com/wp-dyn/content/article/2009/01/12/AR 2009011203295.html (accessed January 13, 2009).

77. Luttwak, "Dead End: Counterinsurgency Warfare as Military Malpractice."

78. "The Iraq Study Group Report," http://bakerinstitute.org/Pubs/iraqstudygroup _findings.pdf (accessed March 2, 2007).

79. Carl Conetta, "Resolving Iraq: Progress Depends on a Short Timeline for US Troop Withdrawal," Project on Defense Alternatives Briefing, Memo #40, January 18, 2007, http://www.comw.org/pda/0701bm40.html (accessed March 30, 2007).

80. AP, "Saudis Reportedly Funding Iraqi Sunni Insurgents," *USA Today*, December 8, 2006, http://www.usatoday.com/news/world/iraq/2006-12-08-saudis-sunnis_x.htm (accessed April 5, 2007).

81. Elise Labott, "Official: Saudis to Back Sunnis If U.S. Leaves Iraq," *CNN*, December 13, 2006, http://www.cnn.com/2006/WORLD/meast/12/13/saudi.sunnis/index.html (accessed January 22, 2007).

82. Sudarsan Raghavan, "Iran Said to Support Shiite Militias in Iraq," *Washington Post*, August 15, 2006, http://www.washingtonpost.com/wp-dyn/content/article/2006/08/ 14/AR2006081400477.html (accessed July 29, 2008).

83. "Casualties of the Iraq War," *Wikipedia*, http://en.wikipedia.org/wiki/Casualties _of_the_Iraq_War (accessed July 12, 2008).

84. Mark Thompson, "Where Are the New Recruits?" *Time*, January 10, 2005, http://www.time.com/time/magazine/article/0,9171,1015898,00.html (accessed March 2, 2007).

85. Pazir Gul, "Waziristan Accord Signed," *Dawn*, September 6, 2006, http://www.dawn.com/2006/09/06/top2.htm (accessed March 23, 2007); Dexter Filkins, "Right at the Edge," *New York Times*, September 5, 2008, http://www.nytimes.com/2008/09/07/ magazine/07pakistan-t.html?pagewanted=1&ref=magazine (accessed September 6, 2008).

86. Associated Press, "Pakistan: 'U.S. Can't Hunt bin Laden Here," *Newsmax.com*, July

14, 2008, http://www.newsmax.com/newsfront/pakistan_hunt_bin_laden/2008/07/14/112644.html (accessed July 20, 2008).

87. Daveed Gartenstein-Ross and Bill Roggio, "Descent into Appeasement," *Weekly Standard*, June 9, 2008, http://www.weeklystandard.com/Content/Public/Articles/000/000/015/169cxzga.asp (accessed July 20, 2008).

88. Arnaud de Borchgrave, "Afghanistan Quandary," *Washington Times*, July 17, 2008, http://www.washingtontimes.com/news/2008/jul/17/afghanistan-quandary/ (accessed July 20, 2008).

89. "Pakistanis Favor Talks with Militants: Poll," *Daily Times*, June 21, 2008, http://www.dailytimes.com.pk/default.asp?page=2008%5C06%5C21%5Cstory_21-6-2008_pg7_41 (accessed July 20, 2008).

90. "Muslims Believe US Seeks to Undermine Islam," *WorldPublicOpinion.org*, April 24, 2007, http://www.worldpublicopinion.org/pipa/articles/home_page/346.php?nid=%3E (accessed July 20, 2008).

91. Jason Straziuso, "US Think Tank: Pakistan Helped Taliban Insurgents," Associated Press, June 9, 2008, http://www.breitbart.com/article.php?id=2008-06-09_D916OJLG0&show_article=1&cat=breaking (accessed July 20, 2008).

92. Mark Mazzetti and Eric Schmitt, "C.I.A. Outlines Pakistan Links with Militants," *New York Times*, July 30, 2008, http://www.nytimes.com/2008/07/30/world/asia/30pstan.html (accessed July 30, 2008).

93. Fisnik Abrashi, "Afghanistan Accuses Pakistan of Supporting Taliban," Associated Press, July 14, 2008, http://news.yahoo.com/s/ap/20080714/ap_on_re_as/afghan_pakistan (accessed July 20, 2008).

94. "ISI Involved in Kabul Bombing on Indian Embassy: NSA," *Indian Express*, July 12, 2008, http://www.expressindia.com/latest-news/ISI-involved-in-Kabul-bombing-on-Indian-embassy-NSA/334809/ (accessed July 20, 2008).

95. Robin Right, "Iranian Unit to Be Labeled 'Terrorist,'" *Washington Post*, August 15, 2007, http://www.washingtonpost.com/wp-dyn/content/article/2007/08/14/AR2007081401662_pf.html (accessed September 2, 2007).

96. Filkins, "Right at the Edge."

97. Bruce Loudon, "Pakistan Shuts NATO Supply Line," *Australian*, November 17, 2008, http://www.theaustralian.news.com.au/story/0,25197,24660347-2703,00.html (accessed November 17, 2008).

98. Farhan Bokhari, James Lamont, and Daniel Dombey, "Pakistani Army's Ties to Islamists Under Scrutiny," *Financial Times*, December 12, 2008, http://www.ft.com/cms/s/0/6032d200-c84d-11dd-b86f-000077b07658.html (accessed December 30, 2008).

99. Peter Bergen, "Afghanistan Testimony before the House Committee on Foreign Affairs," *New American Foundation*, April 7, 2007, http://www.newamerica.net/publications/resources/2007/peter_bergens_afghanistan_testimony_before_the_house_committee_on_foreign_affairs (accessed April 28, 2007).

100. Ann Marlowe, "Madrassas Built with Your Money," *New York Post*, July 15, 2008, http://www.frontpagemag.com/Articles/Read.aspx?GUID=1310110E-0079-4549-871 E-CA8A5FFFD251 (accessed July 20, 2008).

101. Mark Mazzetti and Eric Schmitt, "U.S. Study Is Said to Warn of Crisis in Afghanistan," *New York Times*, October 9, 2008, http://www.nytimes.com/2008/10/09/ world/asia/09afghan.html (accessed October 9, 2008).

102. "The World Factbook—Afghanistan," CIA, 2008, https://www.cia.gov/library/ publications/the-world-factbook/geos/af.html (accessed January 11, 2009); "The World Factbook—Iraq," CIA, 2008, https://www.cia.gov/library/publications/the-world-fact-book/geos/iz.html (accessed January 11, 2009).

103. Filkins, "Right at the Edge."

104. Robin Wright and Joby Warrick, "U.S. Steps Up Unilateral Strikes in Pakistan," *Washington Post*, March 27, 2008, http://www.washingtonpost.com/wp-dyn/content/ article/2008/03/27/AR2008032700007.html (accessed July 20, 2008).

105. Bill Roggio, "US Targets Compound in North Waziristan," *Long War Journal*, November 14, 2008, http://www.longwarjournal.org/archives/2008/11/us_targets _compound.php (accessed November 14, 2008).

106. Stephen Brown, "Pakistan vs. the Taliban," *FrontPage Magazine*, September 4, 2008, http://www.frontpagemag.com/Articles/Read.aspx?GUID=F3F48A82-6B59-4D6A-9CA5-CBB008ACED34 (accessed September 4, 2008); Jane Perlez and Pir Shah, "Pakistan Mired in Brutal Battle to Oust Taliban," *New York Times*, November 10, 2008, http:// www.nytimes.com/2008/11/11/world/asia/11pstan.html (accessed November 14, 2008).

107. Christina Helmand, "War on Taliban Cannot Be Won, Says Army Chief," *Sunday Times*, October 5, 2008, http://www.timesonline.co.uk/tol/news/uk/article4882597.ece (accessed October 5, 2008).

108. M. Bhadrakumar, "US, Saudi Arabia Revive Taliban's Comeback," *Rediff.com*, October 7, 2008, http://www.rediff.com/news/2008/oct/07guest.htm (accessed October 7, 2008); Yochi Dreazen, Siobhan Gorman, and Jay Solomon, "US Mulls Talks with Taliban in Bid to Quell Afghan Unrest," *Wall Street Journal*, October 28, 2008.

109. "Declaration of the Causes and Necessity of Taking Up Arms," July 6, 1775, http://odur.let.rug.nl/~usa/D/1751-1775/war/causes.htm (accessed March 2, 2007).

110. Nassim Taleb, *The Black Swan: The Impact of the Highly Improbable* (New York: Random House, 2007), p. 10.

111. "Al Qaeda Websites 'Hit by Western Cyber Attacks,'" *Telegraph*, October 22, 2008, http://www.telegraph.co.uk/news/worldnews/asia/afghanistan/3237930/AlQaeda-websites-hit-by-Western-cyber-attacks.html (accessed October 22, 2008).

112. Craig Whitlock, "Al Qaeda's Growing Online Offensive," *Washington Post*, June 24, 2008, http://www.washingtonpost.com/wp-dyn/content/story/2008/06/23/ ST2008062302295.html (accessed July 20, 2008).

113. Sushant Sareen, "Islamists Taking Over Pakistan," *Pioneer*, January 8, 2008,

http://www.dailypioneer.com/archives2/default12.asp?main_variable=oped&file_name
=opd3%2Etxt&counter_img=3&phy_path_it=E%3A%5Cdailypioneer%5Carchives2%5
Cjan808 (accessed January 20, 2008).

114. Ayesha Akram, "Lashkar-e-Taiba Draws Well-Educated Youths," *Washington Times*, December 25, 2008, http://www.washingtontimes.com/news/2008/dec/25/lashkar-e-taiba-draws-well-educated-youths/ (accessed December 30, 2008).

115. Hirsi Ali, "Blind Faiths," *New York Times*, January 6, 2008, http://www.nytimes.com/2008/01/06/books/review/Ali-t.html (accessed March 5, 2008).

116. Rachel Ehrenfeld, "Saudi Dollars and Jihad," *FrontPage Magazine*, October 24, 2005, http://www.frontpagemag.com/Articles/ReadArticle.asp?ID=19938 (accessed March 2, 2007).

117. "Profile: World Muslim League," *History Commons*, http://www.historycommons.org/entity.jsp?entity=muslim_world_league (accessed July 20, 2008).

118. Michael Slackman, "In Algeria, a Tug of War for Young Minds," *New York Times*, June 13, 2008, http://www.nytimes.com/2008/06/23/world/africa/23algeria.html (accessed July 20, 2008).

119. Ibid.

120. Ibid.

121. Eshan Masood, "British Muslims," *Britishcouncil.org*, 2006, http://www.britishcouncil.org/spain-society-british-muslims-media-guide.pdf (accessed November 14, 2008).

122. Gaby Hinsliff, "Gordon Brown: 75% of UK Terror Plots Originate in Pakistan," *Guardian*, December 14, 2008, http://www.guardian.co.uk/world/2008/dec/14/mumbai-terror-attacks-india (accessed January 2, 2009).

123. Downey, "A Safe Heaven."

124. Bob Woodward, *State of Denial: Bush at War, Part III* (New York: Simon & Schuster, 2006), p. 76.

125. Selig Harrison, "Pressuring Pakistan to Curb the Taliban," *Boston Globe*, February 19, 2007, http://www.boston.com/news/globe/editorial_opinion/oped/articles/2007/02/19/pressuring_pakistan_to_curb_the_taliban/ (accessed March 20, 2007).

126. Filkins, "Right at the Edge"; Moorthy Muthuswamy, "Pakistan's 'Irrational Jihad Factory' a Threat to Global Stability," *Washington Times*, July 18, 2001.

127. "Zardari Expects the World to Come Up with $100bn," *Dawn*, October 5, 2008, http://www.dawn.com/2008/10/05/top2.htm (accessed October 5, 2008).

128. "The First Nuclear Terrorist Power," *FrontPage Magazine*, March 23, 2007, http://www.frontpagemag.com/Articles/ReadArticle.asp?ID=27517 (accessed July 20, 2008).

129. Bokhari, "Pakistani Army's Ties to Islamists Under Scrutiny."

130. David Rohde et al., "U.S. Officials See Waste in Billions Sent to Pakistan," *New York Times*, December 24, 2007, http://www.nytimes.com/2007/12/24/world/asia/24military.html (accessed July 20, 2008).

131. "Biden, Lugar Introduce Legislation on Tripling Pakistan Aid," *Associated Press of Pakistan*, July 15, 2008, http://www.app.com.pk/en_/index.php?option=com_content &task=view&id=45391&Itemid=2 (accessed August 14, 2008).

132. "The First Nuclear Terrorist Power."

133. Barnett Rubin and Ahmed Rashid, "Ending Chaos in Afghanistan and Pakistan," *Foreign Affairs*, November/December 2008.

134. Susanne Koelbl, "Terror Is Our Enemy, Not India," *Spiegel*, January 6, 2009, http://www.spiegel.de/international/world/0,1518,599724,00.html (accessed January 24, 2009).

135. Kunwar Idris, "The Brutalizing Laws," *Dawn*, August 3, 2008, http://www.dawn.com/2008/08/03/op.htm (accessed August 14, 2008).

136. "Implementation of 9/11 Commission Recommendations Act of 2007," *Americanprogress.org*, http://www.americanprogress.org/issues/2007/01/securing_america.html (accessed March 12, 2007).

137. Stephen Schwartz, "The Saudi Arabia Accountability Act of 2005," *Weekly Standard*, June 8, 2005, http://www.weeklystandard.com/Content/Public/Articles/000/000/005/703azlsf.asp (accessed March 2, 2007).

138. Stephen Schwartz, "The Senate Holds a Hearing on the Saudi Arabia Accountability Act," *Weekly Standard*, November 10, 2005, http://www.islamicpluralism.org/articles/2005a/05senatejudiciarycom.htm (accessed November 14, 2008).

139. Chris Mondics, "Pinning the Blame for 9/11," *Philadelphia Inquirer*, May 31, 2008, http://www.philly.com/philly/hp/news_update/20080531_Pinning_the_blame_for_terror.html (accessed July 20, 2008).

140. Vali Nasr and Ray Takeyh, "The Iran Option That Isn't on the Table," *Washington Post*, February 8, 2006, http://www.washingtonpost.com/wp-dyn/content/article/2007/02/07/AR2007020702136.html (accessed March 2, 2007).

141. Arnaud Borchgrave, "'Long War,' Not WW IV," *Washington Times*, February 28, 2007, http://www.washtimes.com/commentary/20070227-0847316067r.htm (accessed March 2, 2007).

142. Josh Gerstein, "Legal Judgments Soaring against Iran," *New York Sun*, April 3, 2006, http://www.nysun.com/national/legal-judgments-soaring-against-iran/30230/ (accessed November 14, 2008).

143. Borchgrave, "'Long War,' Not WW IV."

144. "Iran: Nuclear Intentions and Capabilities," National Intelligence Estimate, December 12, 2007, http://www.dni.gov/press_releases/20071203_release.pdf (accessed July 20, 2008).

145. Associated Press, "U.S., Allies Give Iran Ultimatum after Nuclear Talks Stall," *FOXNews.com*, July 19, 2008, http://www.foxnews.com/story/0,2933,386542,00.html (accessed July 20, 2008).

146. Amir Taheri, "A Dubious Mission," *New York Post*, July 22, 2008, http://

www.frontpagemag.com/Articles/Read.aspx?GUID=90E44A37-79BF-435D-B0F1-6823 92A1C633 (accessed July 22, 2008).

147. Right, "Iranian Unit to Be Labeled 'Terrorist.'"

148. Akbar Atri, "Solidarity with Iranian?" *Wall Street Journal*, October 15, 2007.

149. Roya Hakakian, "Persian … or Iranian?" *Wall Street Journal*, December 28, 2006.

150. Ilan Berman, "Detente with Tehran?" *Washington Times*, April 9, 2007, http://www.washingtontimes.com/op-ed/20070408-101851-9786r.htm (accessed April 20, 2007).

151. "A New Koran."

152. Robert Hardy, "Indonesia: The Shadow of Extremism," *BBC*, February 21, 2005, http://news.bbc.co.uk/1/hi/world/asia-pacific/4283357.stm (accessed November 15, 2008).

153. "Obama Al-Arabiya Interview: Full Text," January 26, 2009, http://www .huffingtonpost.com/2009/01/26/obama-al-arabiya-intervie_n_161127.html (accessed January 28, 2009).

154. "Hate Crime Laws," *Anti-defamation League*, http://www.adl.org/99hatecrime/ intro.asp (accessed May 2, 2007).

155. "Communist Control Act of 1954," *Wikipedia*, http://en.wikipedia.org/ wiki/Communist_Control_Act_of_1954 (accessed July 2, 2008).

156. "McCarran Internal Security Act," *Wikipedia*, http://en.wikipedia.org/wiki/ McCarran_Internal_Security_Act (accessed July 12, 2008).

157. Editorial Reviews of *Defeating Jihad: How the War on Terrorism Can Be Won— in Spite of Ourselves, Amazon,* http://www.amazon.com/Defeating-Jihad-Terrorism-Spite -Ourselves/dp/192865326X/ref=pd_bxgy_b_text_b (accessed July 12, 2008).

158. "McCarran Internal Security Act."

159. "Military Commissions Act of 2006," *Wikipedia*, http://en.wikipedia.org/ wiki/Military_Commissions_Act (accessed July 5, 2008).

160. Andrew Bostom, *The Legacy of Islamic Antisemitism: From Sacred Texts to Solemn History* (Amherst, NY: Prometheus Books, 2008).

161. Warren Hoge, "Dismay over New U.N. Human Rights Council," *New York Times,* March 11, 2007, http://www.nytimes.com/2007/03/11/world/11rights.html (accessed April 5, 2007).

162. Daniel Pipes, "Next Steps in Israeli-Palestinian Peace Process: Hearing of the Subcommittee on the Middle East and South Asia of the House Foreign Affairs Committee," *U.S. Govt. Press,* February 14, 2007, http://www.danielpipes.org/article/4322 (accessed March 2, 2007).

163. Andrew Higgins and Farnaz Fassihi, "Muslim Land Joins Rank of Tigers," *Wall Street Journal,* August 6, 2008.

164. Mashuqur Rahman, "The Demons of 1971," *Rediff.com,* January 4, 2007, http://www.rediff.com/news/2007/jan/04spec.htm (accessed March 2, 2007).

165. "Convention on Genocide," *Human Rights Web*, http://www.hrweb.org/legal/genocide.html (accessed July 25, 2008).

166. "International Crimes," http://www.internationalcrimes.com/war.htm (accessed May 2, 2007).

167. R. Hariharan, "War against Terror: ICJ Ruling on State's Role in Genocide," *SAAG*, March 11, 2007, http://www.southasiaanalysis.org/papers22/paper2163.html (accessed April 25, 2007).

168. Marlise Simons, Lydia Polgreen, and Jeffrey Gettleman, "Arrest Is Sought of Sudan Leader in Genocide Case," *New York Times*, July 15, 2008, http://www.nytimes.com/2008/07/15/world/africa/15sudan.html (accessed July 20, 2008).

169. Sridhar Krishnaswami, "Pak Admits Having Helped Insurgency in J&K," *Rediff.com*, October 6, 2006, http://www.rediff.com/news/2006/oct/06pak.htm (accessed May 1, 2007).

170. Andrew Norfolk, "Our Followers 'Must Live in Peace until Strong Enough to Wage Jihad,'" *Times*, September 8, 2007, http://www.timesonline.co.uk/tol/comment/faith/article2409833.ece (accessed July 20, 2008).

171. "Profile: World Muslim League."

172. Chris Mondics, "A Former Al Qaeda Fighter Accuses a Saudi Charity," *Philadelphia Inquirer*, May 31, 2008, http://www.philly.com/philly/hp/news_update/20080531_A_former_al Qaeda_fighter_accuses_a_Saudi_charity.html (accessed July 20, 2008).

173. Steven Stalinsky, "The 'Islamic Affairs Department' of the Saudi Embassy in Washington, D.C.," *MEMRI*, November 26, 2003, http://www.memri.org/bin/articles.cgi?Area=sr&ID=SR2303 (accessed July 20, 2008).

174. "USCIRF Confirms Material Inciting Violence, Intolerance Remains in Textbooks Used at Saudi Government's Islamic Saudi Academy," *USCIRF*, June 11, 2008, http://www.uscirf.gov/index.php?option=com_content&task=view&id=2206&Itemid=1 (accessed July 8, 2008).

175. "Statement by Prince Abdullah," *United Nations*, September 6, 2000, http://www.un.org/millennium/webcast/statements/saudi.htm (accessed July 8, 2008).

176. "Saudi 'Charities' and the War against America"; Bhabani Dikshit, "Free Flow of Funds Sustains Terrorism," *Daily Excelsior*, April 17, 2002, http://www.dailyexcelsior.com/02apr17/edit.htm#3 (accessed July 20, 2008).

177. "Communiqué of MWL Council's 36th Session," Embassy of Saudi Arabia, November 2, 2000, http://www.saudiembassy.net/2000News/Statements/StateDetail.asp?cIndex=370 (accessed July 22, 2008).

178. Emerson, "National Commission on Terrorist Attacks upon the United States: Third Public Hearing."

179. The author gratefully acknowledges material assistance from the law firm of Cozen O'Connor.

180. Surinder Oberoi, "Ethnic Separatism and Insurgency in Kashmir," *Asia Pacific Center for Security Studies*, Spring 2004, http://www.apcss.org/Publications/Edited %20Volumes/ReligiousRadicalism/PagesfromReligiousRadicalismandSecurityinSouth Asiach8.pdf (accessed July 25, 2008).

181. "Foreign Funds for New Mosques, Madrassas in J&K," *Daily Excelsior*, February 12, 2000, http://www.jammu-kashmir.com/archives/archives2000/kashmir20000212b .html (accessed July 8, 2008).

182. Siddarth Srivastava, "India and Saudi Arabia Move beyond Oil," *Asia Times Online*, January 28, 2006, http://www.atimes.com/atimes/South_Asia/HA28Df02.html (accessed July 20, 2008).

183. "Hindus in Bangladesh, Pakistan and Kashmir: A Survey of Human Rights," Hindu American Foundation, 2004, http://www.hinduamericanfoundation.org/HHR2004.pdf (accessed March 2, 2007).

184. Subhash Kapila, "South Asia's Conflict Generation and Its External Inputs," *SAAG*, November 22, 2004, http://www.southasiaanalysis.org/papers12/paper1170.html (accessed March 20, 2007).

185. B. Raman, "Bosnia and Hyderabad," *SAAG*, March 9, 2001, http://www.south asiaanalysis.org/papers4/paper306.html (accessed September 9, 2008).

186. Iftikar Gilani, "Saudi Arabia, India Fail to Sign Anti-terror Accord," *Daily Times*, January 27, 2006, http://www.dailytimes.com.pk/default.asp?page=2006%5C01%5C27%5 Cstory_27-1-2006_pg7_46 (accessed March 2, 2007).

187. Praveen Swami, "A Bend in the Road," *Outlook India*, March 18, 2008, http://www.outlookindia.com/fullprint.asp?choice=1&fodname=20080318&fname=simi& sid=1 (accessed July 20, 2008).

188. S. Balakrishnan, "Attacks Retaliation for Gujarat Riots?" *Times of India*, July 13, 2006, http://timesofindia.Indiatimes.com/articleshow/1742854.cms (accessed March 2, 2007).

189. Press Trust of India, "800 Terror Cells Unearthed in India," *Rediff.com*, August 12, 2008, http://www.rediff.com/news/2008/aug/12terror.htm (accessed August 18, 2008).

190. Abhishek Sharan, "Money Came from the Gulf, Claim Police," *Hindustan Times*, September 22, 2008, http://www.hindustantimes.com/StoryPage/FullcoverageStoryPage .aspx?sectionName=&id=f5f2b286-cf12-4705-91c8-b769b654d2ceTerrorStrikesDelhi _Special&&Headline=Money+came+from+the+Gulf%2c+claim+police (accessed September 22, 2008).

191. "The Study of Political Islam"; "Non-Muslims: Worse Than Animals," *FrontPage Magazine*, July 4, 2008, http://frontpagemag.com/Articles/Read.aspx?GUID=CBA566EA -A36C-470D-9DD6-88D752FA5A4B (accessed August 24, 2008).

192. Mridu Bhandari, "In Booming India, Hunger Kills 6,000 Kids Daily," *IBNLive*, March 29, 2008, http://www.ibnlive.com/news/in-booming-india-hunger-kills-6000-kids -daily/62220-17.html (accessed July 20, 2008).

193. "2008 Bangaluru Serial Blasts," *Wikipedia*, http://en.wikipedia.org/wiki/2008 _Bangalore_bombing (accessed July 27, 2008); "2008 Ahmedabad Bombings," *Wikipedia*, http://en.wikipedia.org/wiki/2008_Ahmedabad_serial_blasts (accessed July 28, 2008); "2008 Delhi Bombings," *Wikipedia*, http://en.wikipedia.org/wiki/2008_Delhi_bombings (accessed September 16, 2008); "2008 Mumbai Attacks," *Wikipedia*, http://en .wikipedia.org/wiki/26_November_2008_Mumbai_attacks (accessed January 5, 2009).

194. Ramashray Upadhyay, "Islamic Institutions in India—Protracted Movement for Separate Muslim Identity?" *SAAG*, February 6, 2003, http://www.southasiaanalysis.org/ papers6/paper599.html (accessed March 2, 2007); Ramashray Upadhyay,"Anti-terrorism Conference Dar-ul-Uloom Deoband—A Failed Exercise?" *SAAG*, March 27, 2008, http:// www.southasiaanalysis.org/%5Cpapers27%5Cpaper2646.html (accessed July 20, 2008).

195. Moorthy Muthuswamy, "New Ideas for a New War," *Sulekha*, April 2, 2003, http://news.sulekha.com/newsanalysisdisplay.aspx?cid=2651 (accessed March 2, 2007).

196. Virendra Parekh, "The Way Out: Do a 'Pakistan' to Pakistan," December 19, 2008, http://www.vijayvaani.com/FrmPublicDisplayArticle.aspx?id=295 (accessed December 30, 2008).

197. Stefan Halper, "Generals Dodge a Bullet on Iraq War," *Washington Times*, April 23, 2007, http://www.washingtontimes.com/commentary/20070422-110538-9555r.htm (accessed April 25, 2007).

198. Gurcharan Das, "The India Model," *Foreign Affairs*, July/August 2006.

199. Narendra Modi was rated either as the most admired or as the most able chief minister in India in at least two polls.

200. Commentary, "Terrorists & Politicians," *Newsinsight.net*, March 9, 2006, http:// www.newsinsight.net/archivedebates/nat2.asp?recno=1349&ctg=politics (accessed March 2, 2007).

201. Moorthy Muthuswamy, "Jihadist Threat in India," *Washington Times*, December 21, 2006.

202. Press Trust of India, "800 Terror Cells Unearthed in India."

203. Chidanand Rajgatta, "Bush Keeps His Word on Nuke Deal, Assures Fuel Supply and Reprocessing Rights," *Times of India*, October 9, 2008, http://timesofindia.india times.com/articleshow/3575312.cms (accessed October 19, 2008).

204. Pam Fessler, "DHS Seeks Radiation-Sensing Gear Despite Critics," *PBS*, April 17, 2007, http://www.npr.org/templates/story/story.php?storyId=9626755.

205. Arnaud de Borchgrave, "Pakistan, Saudi Arabia in Secret Nuke Pact," *Washington Times*, October 22, 2003, http://www.washtimes.com/world/20031021-112804-8451r.htm (accessed March 2, 2007).

206. William Broad, "Eye on Iran, Rivals Pursuing Nuclear Power," *New York Times*, April 15, 2007, http://www.nytimes.com/2007/04/15/world/middleeast/15sunnis.html (accessed April 20, 2007).

207. Akaki Dvali, "Will Saudi Arabia Acquire Nuclear Weapons?" *Monterey Institute of*

International Studies, March 2004, http://www.nti.org/e_research/e3_40a.html (accessed March 2, 2007).

208. David Sanger, "Obama's Worst Pakistan Nightmare," *New York Times*, January 8, 2009, http://www.nytimes.com/2009/01/11/magazine/11pakistan-t.html (accessed January 10, 2009).

209. Munir Ahmad, "Pakistani Scientist Accuses Military," Associated Press, July 5, 2008, http://www.sfgate.com/cgi-bin/article.cgi?f=/c/a/2008/07/05/MN1H11K73C.DTL (accessed July 20, 2008).

210. Joby Warrwick, "Smugglers Had Design for Advanced Warhead," *Washington Post*, June 15, 2008, http://www.washingtonpost.com/wp-dyn/content/article/2008/06/14/AR2008061402032.html (accessed July 16, 2008).

211. William Perry, Ashton Carter, and Michael May, "After the Bomb," *New York Times*, June 12, 2008, http://www.nytimes.com/2007/06/12/opinion/12carter.html (accessed July 20, 2008).

212. Bryan Bender, "White House Threatens Nuclear Retaliation to Attacks on U.S.," *Government Executive*, December 11, 2002, http://www.govexec.com/dailyfed/1202/121102gsn1.htm (accessed November 15, 2008).

213. Elbridge Colby, "The New Deterrence," *Weekly Standard*, April 10, 2008, http://www.weeklystandard.com/Content/Public/Articles/000/000/014/959tnykn.asp?pg=1 (accessed November 15, 2008).

214. James Zumwalt, "Nuke Forensics: No 'Cold Cases,'" *Washington Times*, March 8, 2007, http://www.Washtimes.com/commentary/20070307-091631-2252r.htm (accessed May 2, 2007).

215. Noah Feldman, "Weighing the Threat of an Islamic A-Bomb," *International Herald Tribune*, October 28–29, 2006.

216. Barrett, Brittain, and Fabian, "War Costs Could Total $1.6 Trillion by 2009, Panel Estimates."

217. "The World Factbook—Saudi Arabia," CIA, https://www.cia.gov/cia/publications/factbook/geos/sa.html (accessed March 2, 2007).

218. Elaine Sciolino, "Our Saudi Allies," *New York Times*, January 27, 2002, http://www.sullivan-county.com/identity/saudi_support.htm (accessed July 28, 2008).

219. "Poll: Most Saudis Oppose Al Qaeda," *CNN*, December 17, 2007, http://www.cnn.com/2007/WORLD/meast/12/17/saudi.poll/index.html (accessed January 8, 2008); Walid Phares, "How to Measure Al Qaeda's Defeat," *American Thinker*, June 4, 2008, http://www.americanthinker.com/2008/06/how_to_measure_al_qaedas_defea.htm (accessed July 20, 2008).

220. Steven Erlanger, "Israel Warns of Hamas Military Buildup in Gaza," *New York Times*, April 1, 2007, http://www.nytimes.com/2007/04/01/world/middleeast/01gaza.html (accessed July 20, 2008).

221. Steven Erlanger and Sabrina Tavernise, "Israeli Officials Say Hamas Damaged but Not Destroyed," *New York Times*, January 13, 2009, http://www.nytimes.com/2009/01/14/world/middleeast/14mideast.html (accessed January 13, 2009).

222. "Nuclear Weapons and Israel," *Wikipedia*, http://en.wikipedia.org/wiki/Nuclear_weapons_and_Israel (accessed November 15, 2008).

223. This was noted in a Pakistani English-language daily between the years 1998 and 2004.

224. "Pakistanis See New Aggression in Indian Nuclear Doctrine," *Agence France-Presse*, January 24, 2003, http://www.dailytimes.com.pk/default.asp?page=story_24-1-2003_pg7_39 (accessed November 15, 2008).

225. Bhandari, "In Booming India, Hunger Kills 6,000 Kids Daily."

226. Taleb, *The Black Swan*.

227. Louis Beres and Isaac Ben-Israel, "The Limits of Deterrence," *Washington Times*, November 21, 2007, http://www.washingtontimes.com/apps/pbcs.dll/article?AID=/20071121/EDITORIAL/111210011 (accessed December 2, 2007).

228. Bokhari, "Pakistani Army's Ties to Islamists Under Scrutiny."

229. Sanger, "Obama's Worst Pakistan Nightmare."

230. K. Parthasarathy, "Health Effects at Hiroshima, Nagasaki," *Hindu*, September 6, 2001, http://www.hindu.com/thehindu/2001/09/06/stories/08060003.htm (accessed March 2, 2007).

231. Charles Krauthammer, "Tolerance: A Two-Way Street," *Washington Post*, September 22, 2006, http://www.washingtonpost.com/wp-dyn/content/article/2006/09/21/AR2006092101513.html (accessed May 1, 2007).

232. "Thus Spake Dr. Zakir Naik," *Google.groups*, http://groups.google.to/group/soc.culture.pakistan/msg/431f6988e7683ee5 (accessed May 2, 2007).

233. Andrew Bostom, "A Study in Contrasts," *National Review*, April 23, 2008, http://article.nationalreview.com/print/?q=MGNjNGU4OGE2OWVjMDQ1NDY3NmM1OGRlNGI4ZDBjMmY= (accessed September 22, 2008).

234. "Leading Egyptian Government Cleric Calls For: 'Martyrdom Attacks That Strike Horror into the Hearts of the Enemies of Allah,'" *MEMRI*, April 7, 2002, http://www.memri.org/bin/articles.cgi?Area=sd&ID=SP36302 (accessed January 17, 2009).

235. Muhammad Ayoob, "Political Islam: Image and Reality," *World Policy Journal*, Fall 2004, http://worldpolicy.org/journal/articles/wpj04-3/ayoob.htm (accessed July 15, 2008).

236. "The Study of Political Islam."

237. Rahn, "Economic Liberty and Islam."

238. Dessislava Zagorcheva and Robert Trager, "Deterring Terrorism: It Can be Done," *International Security* 30, no. 3 (2005/2006): 87–123.

239. "Islam in the Philippines," *Wikipedia*, http://en.wikipedia.org/wiki/Islam_in_the_Philippines (accessed November 16, 2008).

240. Jonathan Adams, "In Basilan, Philippines, a US Counterterrorism Model Frays," *Christian Science Monitor*, December 11, 2008, http://www.csmonitor.com/2008/1211/p04s04-wosc.html (accessed December 30, 2008).

241. Marc Sageman, *Understanding Terror Networks* (Philadelphia: University of Pennsylvania Press, 2004).

242. David Ignatius, "Young Anger Foments Jihad," *Washington Post*, September 6, 2006, http://www.washingtonpost.com/wp-dyn/content/article/2006/09/12/AR2006091201298.html (accessed April 5, 2007).

243. Dinesh D'Souza, *The Enemy at Home: The Cultural Left and Its Responsibility for 9/11* (New York: Doubleday, 2007).

244. Dinesh D'Souza, "Bin Laden, the Left and Me," *Washington Post*, January 28, 2007, http://www.washingtonpost.com/wp-dyn/content/article/2007/01/26/AR2007012601624.html (accessed March 2, 2007).

245. John Mueller, *Overblown: How Politicians and the Terrorism Industry Inflate National Security Threats, and Why We Believe Them* (New York: Free Press, 2006).

246. Amy Chua, *Day of Empire: How Hyperpowers Rise to Global Dominance—and Why They Fall* (New York: Doubleday, 2007).

247. "Mansoor Peerbhoy: An Unlikely Jihadi, He Shows No Remorse," *Times of India*, October 7, 2008, http://timesofindia.indiatimes.com/Mansoor_Peerbhoy_An_unlikely_jihadi_he_shows_no_remorse/articleshow/3567756.cms (accessed October 12, 2008).

248. Vikram Sharma, "IT Cos to Keep Tabs on Techies," *Express Buzz*, October 8, 2008, http://www.expressbuzz.com/edition/story.aspx?Title=IT+cos+to+keep+tabs+on+techies&artid=tJitjVcLSbc=&SectionID=b7ziAYMenjw=&MainSectionID=b7ziAYMenjw=&SectionName=BUzPVSKuYv7MFxnS0yZ7ng==&SEO=IT,+multinational,+companies (accessed October 12, 2008).

249. Moorthy Muthuswamy, "Conquest Model of Islamic Terrorism," *FrontPage Magazine*, March 20, 2008, http://frontpagemag.com/Articles/Read.aspx?GUID=85447CC0-5BC0-4B50-BD31-7718A136D661 (accessed July 20, 2008).

250. Andrew McCarthy, "The Jihad in Plain Sight," *Hudson Institute*, June 4, 2008, http://www.hudson.org/files/pdf_upload/2008_Bradley_Symposium_McCarthy_Essay.pdf (accessed July 20, 2008).

251. Geert Wilders, "America as the Last Man Standing," *Jihad Watch*, September 28, 2008, http://www.jihadwatch.org/archives/022867.php (accessed September 30, 2008).

252. George Bush, "Remarks by George W. Bush on US Humanitarian Aid to Afghanistan," President Hall, Dwight Eisenhower Executive Office Building, Washington, DC, October 11, 2002.

253. "Obama's Inaugural Speech," *CNN*, January 20, 2009, http://www.cnn.com/2009/politics/01/20/obama.politics/index.html (accessed January 20, 2009).

254. McCarthy, "The Jihad in Plain Sight."

255. Bruce Bawer, *While Europe Slept: How Radical Islam Is Destroying the West from Within* (New York: Doubleday, 2006), p. 233.

256. "The Study of Political Islam"; Bill Warner, "The 'Good' in the Koran," *Political Islam.com*, November 13, 2008, http://www.politicalIslam.com/blog/the_good_in_the _Koran (accessed November 13, 2008).

257. Chua, *Day of Empire.*

258. "63% Believe Bible Literally True," *Rasmussen Reports*, April 23, 2005, http:// www.rasmussenreports.com/2005/Bible.htm (accessed May 2, 2007).

259. "Religion in America: Non-dogmatic, Diverse and Politically Relevant," *Pew Research Center*, June 23, 2008, http://pewresearch.org/pubs/876/religion-america-part -two (accessed July 20, 2008).

260. Julia Oliver, "Graduate Enrollment in Science and Engineering Programs Up in 2003, but Declines for First-Time Foreign Students," *InfoBrief*, August 2005, http:// www.nsf.gov/statistics/infbrief/nsf05317/ (accessed March 2, 2007); Ernie Tretkoff, "Percentage of First-Year Foreign Graduate Students Falls to 43%," *American Physical Society*, November 2005, http://www.aps.org/publications/apsnews/200511/foreign-grad.cfm (accessed May 2, 2007).

261. Richard Dawkins, *The God Delusion* (Boston: Houghton Mifflin, 2006); Sam Harris, *Letter to a Christian Nation* (New York: Knopf, 2006); Christopher Hutchins, *God Is Not Great: How Religion Poisons Everything* (New York: Twelve Book, 2007).

262. This statement is attributed to Sam Harris.

263. Ken Adelman, "Troubles from Thailand," *Washington Times*, April 27, 2007, http://www.washingtontimes.com/commentary/20070426-082753-6067r.htm (accessed April 28, 2007).

264. William Broad, "U.S. Is Losing Its Dominance in the Sciences," *New York Times*, May 3, 2004, http://query.nytimes.com/gst/fullpage.html?res=9405E7DA133DF930 A35756C0A9629C8B63 (accessed March 15, 2007).

265. Robert Spencer, *Religion of Peace?: Why Christianity Is and Islam Isn't* (Washington, DC: Regnery, 2007), pp. 175–77.

266. Will Marshall, "Obama Needs a Strong Foreign Policy," *Wall Street Journal*, November 7, 2008.

267. "Libel Tourism," *Wikipedia*, http://en.wikipedia.org/wiki/Libel_tourism (accessed July 8, 2008).

268. "Libel Tourism Protection Act," *FrontPage Magazine*, April 25, 2008, http:// frontpagemag.com/articles/Read.aspx?GUID=972685B8-E881-4421-A1C4-55101D279 D7B (accessed July 20, 2008).

269. Associated Press, "FBI Eyes Profiling in Terrorist Inquiries," *Commercial appeal.com*, July 3, 2008, http://www.commercialappeal.com/news/2008/jul/03/fbi-eyes-profiling-in-terrorist-inquiries (accessed July 20, 2008).

BIBLIOGRAPHY

Abdo, Geneive. "A More Islamic Islam." *Washington Post*, March 17, 2007. http://www
.washingtonpost.com/wp-dyn/content/article/2007/03/16/AR2007031601941.html
(accessed April 5, 2007).

Abrashi, Fisnik. "Afghanistan Accuses Pakistan of Supporting Taliban." *Associated Press*, July
14, 2008. http://news.yahoo.com/s/ap/20080714/ap_on_re_as/afghan_pakistan
(accessed July 20, 2008).

Adamo, Marilyn. "Then vs. Now." *Fortune*, February 4, 2008.

Adams, Jonathan. "In Basilan, Philippines, a US Counterterrorism Model Frays." *Christian
Science Monitor*, December 11, 2008. http://www.csmonitor.com/2008/1211/
p04s04-wosc.html (accessed December 30, 2008).

Adas, Basil. "Al-Qaida 'Leaving Iraq for Sudan, Somalia.'" *Gulfnews.com*, July 11, 2008.
http://frontpagemag.com/Articles/Read.aspx?GUID=2E4B3901-F66A-47FA-A4F8
-F231DFC59D24 (accessed July 20, 2008).

Adelman, Ken. "Troubles from Thailand." *Washington Times*, April 27, 2007. http://
www.washingtontimes.com/commentary/20070426-082753-6067r.htm (accessed
April 28, 2007).

Ahmad, Mukhtar. "J&K Assembly Passes Shariat Bill." *Rediff.com*, February 9, 2007. http://
www.rediff.com/news/2007/feb/09mukhtar.htm (accessed March 8, 2007).

Ahmad, Munir. "Pakistani Scientist Accuses Military." Associated Press, July 5, 2008. http://
www.sfgate.com/cgi-bin/article.cgi?f=/c/a/2008/07/05/MN1H11K73C.DTL
(accessed July 20, 2008).

Ahmed, Aijazz. "Pakistan's Wonderlands with Little Wonder." *Asia Times*, February 19, 2003.
http://www.atimes.com/atimes/South_Asia/EB19Df02.html (accessed July 8, 2008).

Akhlaque, Qudssia. "Dialogue to Start Next Month: Joint Statement on Musharraf-Vajpayee

Meeting," *Dawn*, January 7, 2004. http://www.dawn.com/2004/01/07/top1.Htm (accessed February, 2007).

Akram, Ayesha. "Lashkar-e-Taiba Draws Well-Educated Youths." *Washington Times*, December 25, 2008. http://www.washingtontimes.com/news/2008/dec/25/lashkar-e-taiba-draws-well-educated-youths/ (accessed December 30, 2008).

Alexander, Paul. "The Generals Speak." *Rolling Stone*, November 3, 2004. http://www.rolling stone.com/politics/story/6593163/the_generals_speak/ (accessed July 20, 2008).

Ali, Hirsi. "Blind Faiths." *New York Times*, January 6, 2008. http://www.nytimes.com/2008/01/06/books/review/Ali-t.html (accessed March 5, 2008).

———. *Infidel*. New York: Free Press, 2008.

Allott, Daniel. "Islam and Violence." *Washington Times*, December 4, 2006. http://www.washtimes.com/op-ed/20061203-100623-9818r.htm (accessed March 2, 2007).

Altaf, Anjum. "View: Democracy—What Mr Jinnah Said." *Daily Times* (Pakistan), November 28, 2004. http://www.dailytimes.com.pk/default.asp?page=story_28-11-2004_pg3_2 (accessed July 24, 2008).

Anurag, K. "61 Killed in Serial Blasts across Assam." *Rediff.com*, October 30, 2008. http://www.rediff.com/news/2008/oct/30blasts.htm (accessed November 3, 2008).

Aslan, Reza. *No God but God: The Origins, Evolution, and Future of Islam*. New York: Random House, 2005.

———. "The War for Islam." *Boson Globe*, September 10, 2006. http://www.boston.com/news/globe/ideas/articles/2006/09/10/the_war_for_islam/ (accessed January 3, 2009).

Atal, Subodh. See Fotedar.

Atri, Akbar. "Solidarity with Iranian?" *Wall Street Journal*, October 15, 2007.

Ayoob, Muhammad. "Political Islam: Image and Reality." *World Policy Journal*, Fall 2004. http://worldpolicy.org/journal/articles/wpj04-3/ayoob.htm (accessed July 15, 2008).

Bagchi, Indrani. "Mumbai Attack: US, Western Pressure Worked." *Times of India*, February 13, 2008. http://timesofindia.indiatimes.com/India/Mumbai_attack_US_western_pressure_worked/articleshow/msid-4120445,curpg-1.cms (accessed February 12, 2009).

Baker, Aryn. "India's Muslims in Crisis." *Time*, November 27, 2008. http://www.time.com/time/world/article/0,8599,1862650-2,00.html (accessed December 5, 2008).

———. "A Taliban Spokesman's Confession." *Time*, January 17, 2007. http://www.time.com/time/world/article/0,8599,1579979,00.html (accessed March 2, 2007).

Balakrishnan, S. "Attacks Retaliation for Gujarat Riots?" *Times of India*, July 13, 2006. http://timesofindia.Indiatimes.com/articleshow/1742854.cms (accessed March 2, 2007).

Barrett, Ted. "War Costs Could Total $1.6 Trillion by 2009, Panel Estimates." *CNN*,

November 14, 2007. http://www.cnn.com/2007/POLITICS/ 11/13/hidden.war .costs/index.html (accessed July 20, 2008).

Baruah, Amit. "India Has Proof of ISI Hand in Mumbai Attacks." *Hindustan Times*, December 4, 2008. http://www.hindustantimes.com/StoryPage/FullcoverageStory Page.aspx?id=9537b8c1-3fcb-452b-b424-0baffb3e47a2 (accessed December 5, 2008).

Bawer, Bruce. *While Europe Slept: How Radical Islam Is Destroying the West from Within.* New York: Doubleday, 2006.

Belien, Paul. "In Bed with Islamists." *Washington Times*, April 11, 2007. http://www .washingtontimes.com/op-ed/20070410-100624-4394r.htm (accessed April 27, 2007).

———. "Islamization of Antwerp." *Washington Times*, March 14, 2007. http://www .washingtontimes.com/op-ed/20070313-090315-9588r.htm (accessed March 22, 2007).

Bender, Bryan. "White House Threatens Nuclear Retaliation to Attacks on U.S." *Government Executive*, December 11, 2002. http://www.govexec.com/dailyfed/1202/121102gsn1 .htm (accessed November 15, 2008).

Ben-Israel, Isaac. See Beres.

Benkin, Richard. "No Outrage over Ethnic Cleansing of Hindus." *Analyst-network.com*, October 16, 2008. http://www.analyst-network.com/article.php?art_id=2500 (October 18, 2008).

Beres, Louis. "The Limits of Deterrence." *Washington Times*, November 21, 2007. http:// www.washingtontimes.com/apps/pbcs.dll/article?AID=/20071121/EDITORIAL/ 111210011 (accessed December 2, 2007).

Bergen, Peter. "Afghanistan Testimony before the House Committee on Foreign Affairs." *New American Foundation*, April 7, 2007. http://www.newamerica.net/publications/ resources/2007/peter_bergens_afghanistan_testimony_before_the_house _committee_on_foreign_affairs (accessed April 28, 2007).

Berman, Ilan. "Detente with Tehran?" *Washington Times*, April 9, 2007. http://www .washingtontimes.com/op-ed/20070408-101851-9786r.htm (accessed April 20, 2007).

Berntsen, Gary. *Jawbreaker: The Attack on Bin Laden and Al Qaeda: A Personal Account by the CIA's Key Field Commander.* New York: Crown, 2005.

Bhadrakumar, M. "US, Saudi Arabia Revive Taliban's Comeback." *Rediff.com*, October 7, 2008. http://www.rediff.com/news/2008/oct/07guest.htm (accessed October 7, 2008).

Bhaduri, Aditi. "Erased from Memory: Kashmir's Forgotten." *Kashmir Herald*, November 9, 2008. http://www.kashmirherald.com/main.php?t=OP&st=D&no=288 (accessed November 10, 2008).

Bhandari, Mridu. "In Booming India, Hunger Kills 6,000 Kids Daily." *IBNLive.com*, March 29, 2008. http://www.ibnlive.com/news/in-booming-india-hunger-kills-6000-kids-daily/ 62220-17.html (accessed July 20, 2008).

Bhatia, Kishan. "Flawed Democracies." *IVarta.com*, June 27, 2008. http://www.blogs .ivarta.com/india-usa-blog-column126.htm (accessed July 20, 2008).

Bhatt, Sheela. "14–16 Indians Involved in 26/11 Attack, Says Mumbai Police." *Rediff.com*, February 12, 2009. http://www.rediff.com/news/2009/feb/12mumterror-26-11-had-local -help-mumbai-police.htm (accessed February 12, 2009).

Bhattacharyya, S. *Genocide in East Pakistan/Bangladesh*. Houston: A. Ghosh, 1987.

Bokhari, Farhan. "Pakistani Army's Ties to Islamists under Scrutiny." *Financial Times*, December 12, 2008. http://www.ft.com/cms/s/0/6032d200-c84d-11dd-b86f-000077 b07658.html (accessed December 30, 2008).

Borchgrave, Arnaud. "Afghanistan Quandary." *Washington Times*, July 17, 2008. http:// www.washingtontimes.com/news/2008/jul/17/afghanistan-quandary/ (accessed July 20, 2008).

———. "Al Qaeda on the Ropes?" *Washington Times*, September 28, 2007. http:// www.washingtontimes.com/article/20070928/COMMENTARY/109280001/1012/ commentary (accessed October 15, 2007).

———. "'Long War,' Not WW IV." *Washington Times*, February 28, 2007. http://www .washtimes.com/commentary/20070227-0847316067r.htm (accessed March 2, 2007).

———. "Pakistan, Saudi Arabia in Secret Nuke Pact." *Washington Times*, October 22, 2003. http://www.washtimes.com/world/20031021-112804-8451r.htm (accessed March 2, 2007).

Bostom, Andrew. "Apocalyptic Muslim Jew-Hatred." *American Thinker*, July 17, 2006. http://www.americanthinker.com/2006/07/apocalyptic_muslim_jewhatred.html (accessed October 20, 2008).

———. "Confused Islamic Apologetics." *FrontPage Magazine*, August 10, 2004. http:// www.frontpagemag.com/Articles/ReadArticle.asp?ID=14578 (accessed July 20, 2008).

———. "Jihad in the Hadith—Vol. 4, bk. 52, nos. 42 & 48." In *The Legacy of Jihad: Islamic Holy War and the Fate of non-Muslims*. Amherst, NY: Prometheus Books, 2005.

———. *The Legacy of Islamic Antisemitism: From Sacred Texts to Solemn History*. Amherst, NY: Prometheus Books, 2008.

———. *The Legacy of Jihad: Islamic Holy War and the Fate of non-Muslims*. Amherst, NY: Prometheus Books, 2005.

———. "The Muslim Mainstream and the New Caliphate." *American Thinker*, April 27, 2007. http://www.americanthinker.com/2007/04/the_muslim_mainstream_and _the.html (accessed July 20, 2008).

———. "The 9/11 Commission and Jihad." *FrontPage Magazine*, July 30, 2004. http:// www.frontpagemag.com/Articles/ReadArticle.asp?ID=14439 (accessed January 15, 2007).

———. "A Study in Contrasts." *National Review*, April 23, 2008. http://article.national review.com/print/?q=MGNjNGU4OGE2OWVjMDQ1NDY3NmM1OGRlNGI4Z DBjMmY= (accessed September 22, 2008).

———. "Sufi Jihad?" *American Thinker*, May 15, 2005. http://www.americanthinker .com/2005/05/sufi_jihad.html (accessed July 20, 2008).

Brittain, Becky. See Barrett.

Broad, William. "Eye on Iran, Rivals Pursuing Nuclear Power." *New York Times*, April 15, 2007. http://www.nytimes.com/2007/04/15/world/middleeast/15sunnis.html (accessed April 20, 2007).

———. "U.S. Is Losing Its Dominance in the Sciences." *New York Times*, May 3, 2004. http://query.nytimes.com/gst/fullpage.html?res=9405E7DA133DF930A35756C0A9 629C8B63 (accessed March 15, 2007).

Bronner, Ethan. "A Year Reshapes Hamas and Gaza." *New York Times*, June 15, 2008. http://www.nytimes.com/2008/06/15/world/middleeast/15gaza.html (accessed July 20, 2008).

Brown, Stephen. "Pakistan vs. the Taliban." *Frontpage Magazine*, September 4, 2008. http://www.frontpagemag.com/Articles/Read.aspx?GUID=F3F48A82-6B59-4D6A-9CA5 -CBB008ACED34 (accessed September 4, 2008).

Burns, John. "How Afghan's Stern Rulers Took Hold." *New York Times*, December 31, 1996.

Byman, Daniel. *Deadly Connections: States That Sponsor Terrorism*. New York: Cambridge University Press, 2007.

Carter, Ashton. See Perry.

Chellaney, Brahma. "Words Are All We Have." *Hindustan Times*, December 30, 2008. http://www.hindustantimes.com/StoryPage/StoryPage.aspx?id=4b9d0a27-ecb4-4c9b -8bd9-fc2f3720fdc0 (accessed January 1, 2009).

Chua, Amy. *Day of Empire: How Hyperpowers Rise to Global Dominance—and Why They Fall*. New York: Doubleday, 2007.

Colby, Elbridge. "The New Deterrence." *Weekly Standard*, April 10, 2008. http://www .weeklystandard.com/Content/Public/Articles/000/000/014/959tnykn.asp?pg=1 (accessed November 15, 2008).

Comras, Victor. "Treasury Designates Major Saudi Charity—Al Haramain—for Financing Terrorists." *Counterterrorismblog.org*, June 19, 2008. http://counterterrorismblog .org/2008/06/treasury_designates_major_saud.php (accessed July 20, 2008).

Conetta, Carl. "Resolving Iraq: Progress Depends on a Short Timeline for US Troop Withdrawal." *Project on Defense Alternatives Briefing, Memo #40*, January 18, 2007. http:// www.comw.org/pda/0701bm40.html (accessed March 30, 2007).

Cooper, Helene. "Unfriendly Views on U.S.-Backed Arabic TV." *New York Times*, May 17, 2007. http://www.nytimes.com/2007/05/17/washington/17hurra.html (accessed July 28, 2008).

Curtis, Lisa. "After Mumbai: Time to Strengthen U.S.-India Counterterrorism Cooperation." *Heritage Foundation Backgrounder #2217*, December 9, 2008. http://www.heritage .org/Research/AsiaandthePacific/bg2217.cfm (accessed January 18, 2009).

Das, Gurcharan. "The India Model." *Foreign Affairs*, July/August 2006.

Dasgupta, Swapan. "Asia's Other Maoist Threat." *Daily Times*, April 25, 2006. http:// www.dailytimes.com.pk/default.asp?page=2006%5C04%5C25%5Cstory_25-4-2006 _pg4_22 (accessed March 2, 2007).

————. "Treason Can't Be Made Respectable." *Pioneer,* October 19, 2008. http://www
.dailypioneer.com/128749/Treason-can't-be-made-respectable.html (accessed October 19, 2008).

Dastidar, Sachi. *Empire's Last Casualty: Indian Subcontinent's Vanishing Hindu and Other
Minorities.* India: Firma KLM, 2008.

Dawkins, Richard. *The God Delusion.* Boston: Houghton Mifflin, 2006.

Dhar, Maloy. *Fulcrum of Evil: ISI, CIA, Al Qaeda Nexus.* New Delhi: Manas, 2006.

Dighe, Shine. "The Life and Times of HEH." *Times of India,* July 3, 2006. http://timesof
india.Indiatimes.com/articleshow/msid-1702680,prtpage-1.cms (accessed March 2,
2008).

Dikshit, Bhabani. "Free Flow of Funds Sustains Terrorism." *Daily Excelsior,* April 17, 2002.
http://www.dailyexcelsior.com/02apr17/edit.htm#3 (accessed July 20, 2008).

Dombey, Daniel. See Bokhari.

Downey, Sarah. "A Safe Heaven." *Newsweek,* September 30, 2002. http://www.hvk.org/
articles/1002/69.html (accessed March 2, 2007).

Dreazen, Yochi. "US Mulls Talks with Taliban in Bid to Quell Afghan Unrest." *Wall Street
Journal,* October 28, 2008.

D'Souza, Dinesh. "Bin Laden, the Left and Me." *Washington Post,* January 28, 2007.
http://www.washingtonpost.com/wp-dyn/content/article/2007/01/26/AR2007
012601624.html (accessed March 2, 2007).

————. *The Enemy at Home: The Cultural Left and Its Responsibility for 9/11.* New York:
Doubleday, 2007.

Dvali, Akaki. "Will Saudi Arabia Acquire Nuclear Weapons?" *Monterey Institute of International Studies,* March 2004. http://www.nti.org/e_research/e3_40a.html (accessed
March 2, 2007).

Eads, Brian. "Saudi Arabia's Deadly Export." *Australian Reader's Digest,* February 2003.

Ehrenfeld, Rachel. "The Cure for the Wahhabi Virus." *FrontPage Magazine,* October 24,
2005. http://www.frontpagemag.com/Articles/ReadArticle.asp?ID=19853 (accessed
March 2, 2007).

————. "Saudi Dollars and Jihad." *FrontPage Magazine,* October 24, 2005. http://www
.frontpagemag.com/Articles/ReadArticle.asp?ID=19938 (accessed March 2, 2007).

Elst, Koenraad. *Negationism in India: Concealing the Record of Islam.* New Delhi: Voice of
India, 1992. http://koenraadelst.bharatvani.org/books/negaind/index.htm (accessed
March 10, 2007).

Emerson, Steven. "Expert on Radical Islam Fired from Pentagon." *Fox News,* January 11, 2008.
http://www.investigativeproject.org/article/584 (accessed July 20, 2008).

————. *Jihad Incorporated: A Guide to Militant Islam in the US.* Amherst, NY: Prometheus
Books, 2006.

————. "National Commission on Terrorist Attacks upon the United States: Third Public

Hearing." *U.S. Govt. Press*, July 9, 2003. http://www.9-11commission.gov/hearings/hearing3/witness_emerson.htm (accessed March 2, 2007).

Erlanger, Steven. "Israel Warns of Hamas Military Buildup in Gaza." *New York Times*, April 1, 2007. http://www.nytimes.com/2007/04/01/world/middleeast/01gaza.html (accessed July 20, 2008).

———. "Israeli Officials Say Hamas Damaged but Not Destroyed." *New York Times*, January 13, 2009. http://www.nytimes.com/2009/01/14/world/middleeast/14mideast.html (accessed January 13, 2009).

Fabian, K. See Barrett.

Fassihi, Farnaz. See Higgins.

Feder, Don. "Were There Muslims in Mumbai?" *GrassTopsUSA.com*, December 4, 2008. http://www.frontpagemag.com/Articles/Read.aspx?GUID=284B7E05-7736-42E8-9351-E3FA3984AE98 (accessed December 6, 2008).

Feldman, Noah. "Weighing the Threat of an Islamic A-Bomb." *International Herald Tribune*, October 28–29, 2006.

———. *What We Owe Iraq: War and the Ethics of Nation Building*. Princeton, NJ: Princeton University Press, 2006.

Fessler, Pam. "DHS Seeks Radiation-Sensing Gear Despite Critics." *PBS*, April 17, 2007. http://www.npr.org/templates/story/story.php?storyId=9626755 (accessed November 12, 2007).

Fighel, Jonathan. "The Saudi Connection to the Mumbai Massacres: Strategic Implications for Israel." *Jerusalem Center for Public Affairs*, February 12, 2009. http://www.jcpa.org/JCPA/Templates/ShowPage.asp?DRIT=1&DBID=1&LNGID=1&TMID=111&FID=442&PID=0&IID=2854&TTL=The_Saudi_Connection_to_the_Mumbai_Massacres:_Strategic_Implications_for_Israel (accessed February 15, 2009).

Filkins, Dexter. "Right at the Edge." *New York Times*, September 5, 2008. http://www.nytimes.com/2008/09/07/magazine/07pakistan-t.html?pagewanted=1&ref=magazine (accessed September 6, 2008).

Fotedar, Sunil. "Living under the Shadow of Article 370." *Kashmir Herald*, January 1, 2002. http://kashmirherald.com/featuredarticle/article370.html (accessed April 23, 2007).

Gabriel, Brigitte. *Because They Hate: A Survivor of Islamic Terror Warns America*. New York: St. Martin's Press, 2006.

Ganguly, Sumit. "India Watch." *Commentary Magazine*, April 2008. http://www.commentarymagazine.com/viewarticle.cfm/india-watch-11284?search=1 (accessed July 10, 2008).

Gartenstein-Ross, Daveed. "Descent into Appeasement." *Weekly Standard*, June 9, 2008. http://www.weeklystandard.com/Content/Public/Articles/000/000/015/169cxzga.asp (accessed July 20, 2008).

Gerstein, Josh. "Legal Judgments Soaring against Iran." *New York Sun*, April 3, 2006.

http://www.nysun.com/national/legal-judgments-soaring-against-iran/30230/ (accessed November 14, 2008).

Gertz, Bill. "Caughlin Backed." *Washington Times*, January 11, 2008. http://washington times.com/news/2008/jan/11/inside-the-ring-99910007/ (accessed July 20, 2008).

———. "Military Report: Terms 'Jihad,' 'Islamist' Needed." *Washington Times*, October 20, 2008. http://washingtontimes.com/news/2008/oct/20/report-says-terms-jihad -islamist-needed/ (accessed October 20, 2008).

Gettleman, Jeffrey. See Simons.

Ghildiyal, Subodh. "Muslim Recruitment Up in Central Forces." *Times of India*, October 12, 2007. http://timesofindia.indiatimes.com/Muslim_recruitment_up_in_central _forces/articleshow/2450770.cms (accessed October 20, 2007).

———. "We Are Pakistanis, Says Syed Geelani." *Times of India*, August 19, 2008. http:// timesofindia.indiatimes.com/We_are_Pakistanis_says_Geelani/articleshow/3378137 .cms (September 1, 2008).

Gilani, Iftikar. "Saudi Arabia, India Fail to Sign Anti-terror Accord." *Daily Times*, January 27, 2006. http://www.dailytimes.com.pk/default.asp?page=2006%5C01%5C27%5Cstory _27-1-2006_pg7_46 (accessed March 2, 2007).

Girard, Philippe. *Paradise Lost: Haiti's Tumultuous Journey from Pearl of the Caribbean to Third World Hotspot*. New York: Palgrave Macmillan, 2005.

Goldhagen, Daniel. "A Manifesto for Murder." *Los Angeles Times*, February 5, 2006. http:// articles.latimes.com/2006/feb/05/opinion/op-goldhagen5 (accessed October 20, 2008).

Goradia, Prafull. "Roots of Extremism Lie in India." *Pioneer*, January 21, 2009. http:// www.dailypioneer.com/151282/Roots-of-extremism-lie-in-India.html (accessed January 21, 2009).

———. "Waxing the Crescent." *Pioneer*, July 4, 2008. http://www.dailypioneer.com/ archives2/default12.asp?main_variable=oped&file_name=opd2%2Etxt&counter_img =2&phy_path_it=D%3A%5CWebSites%5CDailyPioneer%5Carchives 2%5Cjul408 (accessed July 20, 2008).

Gorman, Siobhan. See Dreazen.

Gul, Pazir. "Waziristan Accord Signed." *Dawn*, September 6, 2006. http://www.dawn .com/2006/09/06/top2.htm (accessed March 23, 2007).

Gupta, O. "Hindu Youth Reduced to Second-Class Status." *Organiser*, March 25, 2007. http://www.Organiser.org/dynamic/modules.php?name=Content&pa=showpage &pid=176&page=3 (accessed April 20, 2007).

———. "O Hindu Parents! O Students! Wake Up, Wake Up." *Organiser*, February 1, 2009. http://www.organiser.org/dynamic/modules.php?name=Content&pa=showpage&pid =275&page=12 (accessed January 30, 2009).

Habeck, Mary. *Knowing the Enemy: Jihadist Ideology and the War on Terror*. New Haven, CT: Yale University Press, 2006.

Hakakian, Roya. "Persian . . . or Iranian?" *Wall Street Journal,* December 28, 2006.

Halloran, Richard. "SEA Terror." *Washington Times,* April 21, 2007. http://www.washington times.com/commentary/20070420-080426-8307r.htm (accessed April 25, 2007).

Halper, Stefan. "Generals Dodge a Bullet on Iraq War." *Washington Times,* April 23, 2007. http://www.washingtontimes.com/commentary/20070422-110538-9555r.htm (accessed April 25, 2007).

Hammer, Joshua. "Freedom Is Not Enough." *Newsweek,* November 14, 2005.

Haq, Zia. "Jumps in Jobs for Minorities." *Hindustan Times,* December 24, 2008. http://www.hindustantimes.com/StoryPage/StoryPage.aspx?sectionName=Cricket&id=02aa 7935-ad63-4848-a5e7-039a70092adb&&Headline=Jump+in+jobs+for+minorities (accessed December 30, 2008).

Hardy, Robert. "Indonesia: The Shadow of Extremism." *BBC,* February 21, 2005. http://news.bbc.co.uk/1/hi/world/asia-pacific/4283357.stm (accessed November 15, 2008).

Hariharan, R. "War against Terror: ICJ Ruling on State's Role in Genocide." *SAAG,* March 11, 2007. http://www.southasiaanalysis.org/papers22/paper2163.html (accessed April 25, 2007).

Harris, Lee. *The Suicide of Reason: Radical Islam's Threat to the West.* New York: Basic Books, 2007.

Harris, Sam. *Letter to a Christian Nation.* New York: Knopf, 2006.

Harrison, Selig. "Pressuring Pakistan to Curb the Taliban." *Boston Globe,* February 19, 2007. http://www.boston.com/news/globe/editorial_opinion/oped/articles/2007/02/19/pressuring_pakistan_to_curb_the_taliban/ (accessed March 20, 2007).

Hasan, Khalid. "Swiss Documentary on Afghanistan: Pakistani, Saudi Engineers Helped Destroy Buddhas." *Daily Times,* March 19, 2006. http://www.dailytimes.com.pk/default.asp?page=2006%5C03%5C19%5Cstory_19-3-2006_pg7_38 (accessed November 3, 2008).

Helmand, Christina. "War on Taliban Cannot Be Won, Says Army Chief." *Sunday Times,* October 5, 2008. http://www.timesonline.co.uk/tol/news/uk/article4882597.ece (accessed October 5, 2008).

Higgins, Andrew. "Muslim Land Joins Rank of Tigers." *Wall Street Journal,* August 6, 2008.

Hinsliff, Gaby. "Gordon Brown: 75% of UK Terror Plots Originate in Pakistan." *Guardian,* December 14, 2008. http://www.guardian.co.uk/world/2008/dec/14/mumbai-terror-attacks-india (accessed January 2, 2009).

Hitchens, Christopher. *God Is Not Great: How Religion Poisons Everything.* New York: Twelve Books, 2007.

Hoge, Warren. "Dismay Over New U.N. Human Rights Council." *New York Times,* March 11, 2007. http://www.nytimes.com/2007/03/11/world/11rights.html (accessed April 5, 2007).

Hoodbhoy, Pervez. "The Saudi-isation of Pakistan." *Newsline.com,* January 2009.

http://www.newsline.com.pk/NewsJan2009/cover2jan2009.htm (accessed February 1, 2009).

Hornick, David. "Israel's Growing Internal Threat." *Frontpage Magazine*, July 23, 2008. http://www.frontpagemag.com/Articles/Read.aspx?GUID=16D5BAA0-40E3-4E29 -BA9E-94588BBC9FB8 (accessed July 25, 2008).

Hughes, Thomas. *The Dictionary of Islam*. Ottawa: Laurier Books, 1996.

Hussain, Zahid. *Frontline Pakistan: The Struggle with Militant Islam*. New York: Columbia University Press, 2007.

Idris, Kunwar. "The Brutalizing Laws." *Dawn*, August 3, 2008. http://www.dawn.com/ 2008/08/03/op.htm (accessed August 14, 2008).

Ignatius, David. "Young Anger Foments Jihad." *Washington Post*, September 6, 2006. http://www.washingtonpost.com/wp-dyn/content/article/2006/09/12/AR2006 091201298.html (accessed April 5, 2007).

Issac, C. "For Hindus in Kerala It's Now or Never." *Organiser*, October 32, 2004. http:// www.hvk.org/articles/1104/25.html (accessed April 5, 2007).

Iype, George. "Why Chidambaram Hiked Defense Outlay." *Rediff.com*, July 9, 2004. http:// ia.rediff.com/news/2004/jul/09spec1.htm (accessed May 1, 2007).

Jagmohan. *My Frozen Turbulence in Kashmir*. New Delhi: Allied, 2002.

Jain, Sunil. "Sachar Report: Myth and Reality." *Rediff.com*, December 11, 2006. http:// www.rediff.com/news/2006/dec/11sachar.htm?zcc=rl (accessed May 1, 2007).

Kandula, Ramesh. "Terrorism Most Dangerous Threat, Says Manmohan." *Tribune*, October 26, 2006. http://www.tribuneindia.com/2006/20061027/main1.htm (accessed May 1, 2007).

Kapila, Subhash. "South Asia's Conflict Generation and Its External Inputs." *SAAG*, November 22, 2004. http://www.southasiaanalysis.org/papers12/paper1170.html (accessed March 20, 2007).

Karsh, Efraim. *Islamic Imperialism: A History*. New Haven, CT: Yale University Press, 2006.

Khalidi, Omar. *Khaki and the Ethnic Violence in India*. Gurgaon, India: Three Essays Collective, 2003.

———. *Muslims in Indian Economy*. Gurgaon, India: Three Essays Collective, 2006.

Khare, Harish. "Manmohan Seeks $150 Billion U.S. Investment." *Hindu*, September 23, 2004. http://www.hindu.com/2004/09/23/stories/2004092308921101.htm (accessed May 1, 2007).

Khomeini, Ruhollah. "Islam Is Not a Religion of Pacifists." *Danielpipes.org*, 1942. http:// www.danielpipes.org/comments/95189 (accessed December 30, 2008).

Khosa, Aasha. "PDP Works Hand in Glove with Terrorists: Ex-Governor." *Rediff.com*, July 14, 2008. http://www.rediff.com/news/2008/jul/14inter1.htm (accessed July 20, 2008).

Kilcullen, David. "'Twenty-eight Articles': Fundamentals of Company-Level Counterinsurgency." *Military Review*, May 1, 2006. http://www.d-n-i.net/fcs/pdf/kilcullen_28 _articles.pdf (accessed July 29, 2008).

Kinsley, Michael. "It's Not Apartheid: Carter Adds to the List of Mideast Misjudgments." *Washington Post*, December 12, 2006. http://www.washingtonpost.com/wp-dyn/content/article/2006/12/11/AR2006121101225.html (accessed May 1, 2007).

Koelbl, Susanne. "Terror Is Our Enemy, Not India." *Spiegel*, January 6, 2009. http://www.spiegel.de/international/world/0,1518,599724,00.html (accessed January 24, 2009).

Koul, Lalit. See Fotedar.

Krauthammer, Charles. "Tolerance: A Two-Way Street." *Washington Post*, September 22, 2006. http://www.washingtonpost.com/wp-dyn/content/article/2006/09/21/AR2006092101513.html (accessed May 1, 2007).

Krishnakumar, K. "A Silent Genocide Is Taking Place in Bangladesh." *Rediff.com*, November 21, 2006. http://www.rediff.com/news/2006/nov/21rights.htm (accessed May 1, 2007).

Krishnaswami, Sridhar. "Pak Admits Having Helped Insurgency in J&K." *Rediff.com*, October 6, 2006. http://www.rediff.com/news/2006/oct/06pak.htm (accessed May 1, 2007).

Kumar, Hari. "Faiths Clash, Displacing Thousands in East India." *New York Times*, August 28, 2008. http://www.nytimes.com/2008/08/29/world/asia/29india.html (accessed September 12, 2008).

Labott, Elise. "Official: Saudis to Back Sunnis If U.S. Leaves Iraq." *CNN*, December 13, 2006. http://www.cnn.com/2006/WORLD/meast/12/13/saudi.sunnis/index.html (accessed January 22, 2007).

Lal, Kishori. *The Legacy of Muslim Rule in India*. New Delhi: Voice of India, 1992.

———. *Theory and Practice of Muslim State in India*. New Delhi: Aditya Prakashan, 1999.

Lall, Rashmee. "Islam Body to Guide UK Govt." *Times of India*, July 19, 2008. http://timesofindia.indiatimes.com/World/Islam_body_to_guide_UK_govt/articleshow/3251847.cms (accessed July 20, 2008).

Lamont, James. See Bokhari.

Lane, Edward. *An Arabic English Lexicon*. London, 1865.

Laskar, Razaul. "India Denies Troop Build-up Along Border with Pak." *PTI*, December 27, 2008. http://www.rediff.com/news/2008/dec/27mumterror-india-denies-troop-build-up-along-border.htm (accessed December 30, 2008).

Lavakare, Arvind. "The Woes of Jammu and Ladakh." *Rediff.com*, July 17, 2002. http://www.rediff.com/news/2002/jul/17arvind.htm (accessed April 3, 2007).

Lee, Matthew. "White House Bars Loaded Labels from Words of War." *San Francisco Chronicle*, April 25, 2008. http://www.sfgate.com/cgi-bin/article.cgi?f=/c/a/2008/04/24/MNVJ10BAEJ.DTL (accessed July 20, 2008).

Lehman, John. "We're Not Winning This War." *Washington Post*, August 31, 2006. http://www.washingtonpost.com/wp-dyn/content/article/2006/08/30/AR2006083002730.html (accessed May 1, 2007).

Levinstein, Joan. See Adamo.

Levitt, Mathew. "The Political Economy of Middle East Terrorism." *Middle East Review of International Affairs*, December 2002. http://meria.idc.ac.il/journal/2002/issue4/jv6n4a3.html (accessed May 1, 2007).

Levy, Janet. "The Erosion of Free Speech." *Frontpage Magazine*, July 4, 2008. http://frontpagemag.com/Articles/Read.aspx?GUID=1CAC2897-674D-44AB-ADF4-BA77930F421E (accessed July 20, 2008).

Lewis, Bernard. *The Crisis of Islam*. Waterville, ME: Thorndike Press, 2003.

———. *The Middle East: A Brief History of the Last 2,000 Years*. New York: Scribner, 1995.

Lewis, John. "'Gifts from Heaven': The Meaning of the American Victory over Japan, 1945." *Objective Standard*, Winter 2007–2008. http://www.theobjectivestandard.com/issues/2007-winter/american-victory-over-japan-1945.asp (accessed July 29, 2008).

Loudon, Bruce. "Pakistan Shuts NATO Supply Line." *Australian*, November 17, 2008. http://www.theaustralian.news.com.au/story/0,25197,24660347-2703,00.html (accessed November 17, 2008).

Luttwak, Edward. "Dead End: Counterinsurgency Warfare as Military Malpractice." *Harper's Magazine*, March 5, 2007. http://www.harpers.org/archive/2007/02/0081384 (accessed March 15, 2007).

Luxenberg, Steve. "U.S. Spied on Iraqi Leaders, Book Says." *Washington Post*, September 5, 2008. http://www.washingtonpost.com/wp-dyn/content/article/2008/09/04/AR2008090403160.html (accessed September 5, 2008).

MacKenzie, Warner. "Understanding Taqiyya—Islamic Principle of Lying for the Sake of Allah." *Islam Watch*, April 30, 2007. http://www.islam-watch.org/Warner/Taqiyya-Islamic-Principle-Lying-for-Allah.htm (accessed July 20, 2008).

Majumdar, Diptosh. "Whose UPA? 98 Letters Show Sonia's the Boss." *CNN-IBN.com*, August 3, 2008. http://www.ibnlive.com/news/whose-upa-98-letters-show-sonias-the-boss/70334-3.html?xml (accessed August 30, 2008).

Maogoto, Jackson. *Battling Terrorism: Legal Perspectives on the Use of Force and the War on Terror*. Hampshire, UK: Ashgate, 2005.

Marlowe, Ann. "Madrassas Built with Your Money." *New York Post*, July 15, 2008. http://www.frontpagemag.com/Articles/Read.aspx?GUID=1310110E-0079-4549-871E-CA8A5FFFD251 (accessed July 20, 2008).

Marshall, Will. "Obama Needs a Strong Foreign Policy." *Wall Street Journal*, November 7, 2008.

Masood, Eshan. "British Muslims." *Britishcouncil.org*, 2006. http://www.britishcouncil.org/spain-society-british-muslims-media-guide.pdf (accessed November 14, 2008).

May, Michael. See Perry.

Mazzetti, Mark. "C.I.A. Outlines Pakistan Links with Militants." *New York Times*, July 30,

2008. http://www.nytimes.com/2008/07/30/world/asia/30pstan.html (accessed July 30, 2008).

———. "U.S. Study Is Said to Warn of Crisis in Afghanistan." *New York Times*, October 9, 2008. http://www.nytimes.com/2008/10/09/world/asia/09afghan.html (accessed October 9, 2008).

McCarthy, Andrew. "The Jihad in Plain Sight." *Hudson Institute*, June 4, 2008. http://www.hudson.org/files/pdf_upload/2008_Bradley_Symposium_McCarthy_Essay.pdf (accessed July 20, 2008).

McElroy, Damien. "Mumbai Attacks: How Indian-Born Islamic Militants Are Trained in Pakistan." *Telegraph*, December 15, 2008. http://www.telegraph.co.uk/news/world news/asia/india/3741868/Mumbai-attacks-How-Indian-born-Islamic-militants-are-trained-in-Pakistan.html (accessed December 30, 2008).

Mir, Hamid. "'We Can Hit Any Soft Target in India.'" *Rediff.com*, January 9, 2007. http://ushome.rediff.com/news/2007/jan/09inter.htm (accessed March 13, 2007).

Mishra, Manjari. "Produce Babies, Get Reward." *Times of India*, January 23, 2007. http://timesofindia.indiatimes.com/articleshow/1386975.cms (accessed April 20, 2007).

Mondics, Chris. "A Former Al Qaeda Fighter Accuses a Saudi Charity." *Philadelphia Inquirer*, May 31, 2008. http://www.philly.com/philly/hp/news_update/20080531_A_former _al-Qaeda_fighter_accuses_a_Saudi_charity.html (accessed July 20, 2008).

———. "Pinning the Blame for 9/11." *Philadelphia Inquirer*, May 31, 2008. http://www.philly.com/philly/hp/news_update/20080531_Pinning_the_blame_for_terror.html (accessed July 20, 2008).

Mozumder, Suman. "India Occupying Kashmir, Says Newsweek's Zakaria." *Rediff.com*, June 25, 2001. http://www.rediff.com/us/2001/jun/25us6.htm (accessed March 22, 2007).

Mueller, John. *Overblown: How Politicians and the Terrorism Industry Inflate National Security Threats, and Why We Believe Them.* New York: Free Press, 2006.

Mukherjee, Andy. "India's Fiscal Advance, Sadly, Is an Illusion." *International Herald Tribune*, June 3, 2005. http://www.iht.com/articles/2005/06/02/bloomberg/sxmuk.php (accessed March 2, 2007).

Murari, Charisma. See Dighe.

Muthuswamy, Moorthy. "American Policy Advice in South Asia: Fatal Flaws." *SAAG*, June 2, 2004. http://www.southasiaanalysis.org/%5Cpapers10%5Cpaper914.html (accessed July 20, 2008).

———. "Bring Democracy to Iraq." *Washington Times*, July 19, 2003.

———. "Certain Koran Verses Threaten World Safety." *Washington Times*, October 2, 2001.

———. "Conquest Model of Islamic Terrorism." *Frontpage Magazine*, March 20, 2008. http://frontpagemag.com/Articles/Read.aspx?GUID=85447CC0-5BC0-4B50-BD31-7718A136D661 (accessed July 20, 2008).

———. "Jihadist Threat in India." *Washington Times*, December 21, 2006.

————. "Muslim War Criminals." *Washington Times*, December 6, 2008.

————. "New Ideas for a New War." *Sulekha*, April 2, 2003. http://news.sulekha.com/news analysisdisplay.aspx?cid=2651 (accessed March 2, 2007).

————. "A New Paradigm for the War on Terror." *Washington Times*, December 8, 2003.

————. "Pakistan and Militant Islam." *Washington Times*, September 25, 2004.

————. "Pakistan's 'Irrational Jihad Factory' a Threat to Global Stability." *Washington Times*, July 18, 2001.

————. "Pakistan's Undemocratic Underpinnings." *Washington Times*, November 22, 2002.

————. "Religious Apartheid in India and American Policy Response." *IVarta.com*, July 4, 2005. http://www.ivarta.com/columns/OL_050704.htm (accessed July 20, 2008).

————. "Talks with Pakistan: Overcoming Prithiviraj Syndrome." *SAAG*, January 23, 2004. http://www.southasiaanalysis.org/papers10/paper901.html (accessed March 2, 2007).

————. "Waffling on Islamic Ideology." *Washington Times*, December 8, 2002.

————. "Why the EU Does Not Want Turkey." *Washington Times*, December 18, 2002.

Naik, Yogesh. "Many Cops Would've Died Had SRPF Not Opened Fire: Bhujbal." *Times of India*, October 1, 2008. http://timesofindia.indiatimes.com/Mumbai/Many_cops _wouldve_died_had_SRPF_not_opened_fire_Bhujbal_/articleshow/3547102.cms (accessed October 16, 2008).

Nanjappa, Vicky. "How Fake Currency and Terror Are Related." *Rediff.com*, August 13, 2008. http://www.rediff.com/news/2008/aug/13beng.htm (accessed August 14, 2008).

————. "How to Tackle Economic Terrorism?" *Rediff.com*, September 30, 2007. http:// ia.rediff.com/news/2007/sep/30vicky.htm (accessed October 8, 2007).

————. "An Urdu Poem Keeps Terrorists Going." *Rediff.com*, December 15, 2008. http:// www.rediff.com/news/2008/dec/15mumterror-urdu-poem-keeps-terrorists-going.htm (accessed December 30, 2008).

Naqvi, Haider. See Pachouly.

Narayan, S. "Not a Rosy Picture Anymore." *Livemint.com*, June 22, 2008. http://www .livemint.com/2008/06/22222811/Not-a-rosy-picture-anymore.html (accessed July 20, 2008).

Nasr, Vali. "The Iran Option That Isn't on the Table." *Washington Post*, February 8, 2006. http://www.washingtonpost.com/wp-dyn/content/article/2007/02/07/AR2007 020702136.html (accessed March 2, 2007).

Niaz, Tahir. "Pakistan to Ask EU to Amend Laws on Freedom of Expression." *Daily Times*, June 8, 2008. http://www.dailytimes.com.pk/default.asp?page=2008%5C06%5C08 %5Cstory_8-6-2008_pg7_14 (accessed July 20, 2008).

Nomani, Asra. "Islam and Women: Clothes Aren't the Issue." *Washington Post*, October 22, 2006. http://www.washingtonpost.com/wp-dyn/content/article/2006/10/20/AR 2006102001261.html (accessed March 2, 2007).

Norfolk, Andrew. "Our Followers 'Must Live in Peace until Strong Enough to Wage Jihad.'"

Times, September 8, 2007. http://www.timesonline.co.uk/tol/comment/faith/article 2409833.ece (accessed July 20, 2008).

Oberoi, Surinder. "Ethnic Separatism and Insurgency in Kashmir." *Asia Pacific Center for Security Studies*, Spring 2004. http://www.apcss.org/Publications/Edited%20 Volumes/ReligiousRadicalism/PagesfromReligiousRadicalismandSecurityinSouthAsia ch8.pdf (accessed July 25, 2008).

Ohri, R. "The Other Side of Sufism." *Organiser*, April 27, 2008. http://www.organiser .org/dynamic/modules.php?name=Content&pa=showpage&pid=234&page=38 (accessed July 20, 2008).

Oliver, Julia. "Graduate Enrollment in Science and Engineering Programs Up in 2003, but Declines for First-Time Foreign Students." *InfoBrief*, August 2005. http://www.nsf.gov/ statistics/infbrief/nsf05317/ (accessed March 2, 2007).

Pachouly, Manish. "26/11 Planning Started a Year Ago, and We Had the Evidence." *Hindustan Times*, December 5, 2008. http://www.hindustantimes.com/StoryPage/Full coverageStoryPage.aspx?id=ecd15cbe-5d40-4af4-87ec-af32afa330b1 (accessed December 5, 2008).

Parekh, Virendra. "The Way Out: Do a 'Pakistan' to Pakistan." December 19, 2008. http://www.vijayvaani.com/FrmPublicDisplayArticle.aspx?id=295 (accessed December 30, 2008).

Parthasarathy, K. "Health Effects at Hiroshima, Nagasaki." *Hindu*, September 6, 2001. http://www.hindu.com/thehindu/2001/09/06/stories/08060003.htm (accessed March 2, 2007).

Patel, Aakar. "Jinnah after August 11, 1947." *News*, September 28, 2008. http://the news.jang.com.pk/daily_detail.asp?id=138344 (accessed September 28, 2008).

———. "Where Indian Muslims Have Gone Wrong?" *Mid-Day*, September 5, 2004. http:// ww1.mid-day.com/news/city/2004/september/91708.htm (accessed March 2, 2007).

Patel, Anjali. "Revenues from Temples Diverted for Haj Subsidy and Madrassas In Karnataka." *IVarta.com*, October 29, 2003. http://www.ivarta.com/columns/OL_031029.htm (accessed July 20, 2008).

Perlez, Jane. "Pakistan Mired in Brutal Battle to Oust Taliban." *New York Times*, November 10, 2008. http://www.nytimes.com/2008/11/11/world/asia/11pstan.html (accessed November 14, 2008).

Perry, William. "After the Bomb." *New York Times*, June 12, 2008. http://www .nytimes.com/2007/06/12/opinion/12carter.html (accessed July 20, 2008).

Phanda, K. "Balkanizing India." *Pioneer*, April 14, 2006.

Phares, Walid. "How to Measure Al Qaeda's Defeat." *American Thinker*, June 4, 2008. http:// www.americanthinker.com/2008/06/how_to_measure_al_qaedas_defea.htm (accessed July 20, 2008).

Pipes, Daniel. "The Moderation of American Muslims." *FrontPage Magazine*, April 8, 2004.

http://frontpagemag.com/Articles/Read.aspx?GUID=F9C71B00-156C-48EF-A3DC
-A7E61162C89D (accessed April 5, 2008).

———. "More Survey Research from a British Islamist Hell." *Danielpipes.org*, July 26, 2005.
http://www.danielpipes.org/blog/483 (accessed March 2, 2007).

———. "Next Steps in Israeli-Palestinian Peace Process: Hearing of the Subcommittee on the
Middle East and South Asia of the House Foreign Affairs Committee." *U.S. Govt. Press*,
February 14, 2007. http://www.danielpipes.org/article/4322 (accessed March 2, 2007).

Pocha, Jehangir. "India Erecting a Barrier along Bangladesh Border." *Boston Globe*, May 30,
2004. http://www.boston.com/news/world/articles/2004/05/30/india_erecting_a
_barrier_along_bangladesh_border (accessed March 2, 2007).

Polgreen, Lydia. See Simons.

Polgreen, Lydia. "Africa's Crisis of Democracy." *New York Times*, April 23, 2007. http://
www.nytimes.com/2007/04/23/world/africa/23nigeria.html (accessed July 20, 2008).

Price, Joshua. "Emerson Interview Part II." *Conservative Beacon*, September 27, 2007.
http://www.investigativeproject.org/article/490 (accessed July 20, 2008).

Punj, Balbir. "Hindu-Muslim Dishonesty." *Organiser*, May 22, 2006. http://www.organiser
.org/dynamic/modules.php?name=Content&pa=showpage&pid=79&page=9 (accessed March 2, 2007).

———. "Islamists Block Social Reform." *Pioneer*, October 31, 2008. http://www.daily
pioneer.com/131270/Islamists-block-social-reform.html (accessed October 31, 2008).

———. "Realpolitik: In Defence of the Rashtriya Suraksha Yatra." *Organiser*, April 2, 2006.
http://www.organiser.org/dynamic/modules.php?name=Content&pa=showpage&pid
=124&page=7 (accessed May 2, 2007).

———. "The Two-Regiment Theory." *Outlook India*, March 20, 2006.

Rabasa, Angel. "The Lessons of Mumbai." *RAND Occasional Papers #249*, January 16, 2009.
http://www.rand.org/pubs/occasional_papers/2009/RAND_OP249.pdf (accessed
January 18, 2009).

Raghavan, Sudarsan. "Iran Said to Support Shiite Militias in Iraq." *Washington Post*, August 15,
2006. http://www.washingtonpost.com/wp-dyn/content/article/2006/08/14/AR
2006081400477.html (accessed July 29, 2008).

Rahman, Mashuqur. "The Demons of 1971." *Rediff.com*, January 4, 2007. http://www
.rediff.com/news/2007/jan/04spec.htm (accessed March 2, 2007).

Rahn, Richard. "Economic Liberty and Islam." *Washington Times*, March 5, 2007. http://
www.washingtontimes.com/commentary/20070304-094010-8712r.htm (accessed
May 2, 2007).

Rajgatta, Chidanand. "Bush Keeps His Word on Nuke Deal, Assures Fuel Supply and Reprocessing Rights." *Times of India*, October 9, 2008. http://timesofindia.indiatimes.com/
articleshow/3575312.cms (accessed October 19, 2008).

Raman, B. "Bosnia and Hyderabad." *SAAG*, March 9, 2001. http://www.southasia
analysis.org/papers4/paper306.html (accessed September 9, 2008).

———. "India & Pakistan: Can Mindsets & Perceptions Change?" *SAAG*, December 10, 2006. http://www.southasianalysis.org/papers21/paper2057.html (accessed March 2, 2007).

———. "National Security: My Jaipur Musings." *SAAG*, February 6, 2007. http://www.southasiaanalysis.Org/%5Cpapers22%5Cpaper2123.html (accessed March 2, 2007).

———. "Waziristanization of Southern Thailand—International Terrorism Monitor." *SAAG*, February 22, 2007. http://www.southasiaanalysis.org/%5Cpapers22%5Cpaper2148.html (accessed March 2, 2007).

Rashid, Ahmed. "Accept Defeat by Taliban, Pakistan Tells NATO." *Telegraph*, November 30, 2006. http://www.Telegraph.co.uk/news/main.jhtml?xml=/news/2006/11/29/wafghan29.xml (accessed March 2, 2007).

———. "Musharraf at the Exit." *Washington Post*, March 22, 2007. http://www.washingtonpost.com/wp-dyn/content/article/2007/03/21/AR2007032101786.html (accessed May 2, 2007).

———. See Rubin.

Rice, Condoleezza. "National Commission on Terrorist Attacks upon the United States: Ninth Public Hearing." April 8, 2004. http://govinfo.library.unt.edu/911/archive/hearing9/9-11Commission_Hearing_2004-04-08.htm (accessed March 2, 2007).

Rifkin, Ira. "Complexities of the Koran Make Mastery a Challenge." *Washington Post*, January 17, 1998. http://www.iol.ie/~afifi/BICNews/Islam/islam30.htm (accessed November 12, 2008).

Right, Lawrence. *The Looming Tower: Al Qaeda and the Road to 9/11*. New York: Knopf, 2006.

Right, Robin. "Iranian Unit to Be Labeled 'Terrorist.'" *Washington Post*, August 15, 2007. http://www.washingtonpost.com/wp-dyn/content/article/2007/08/14/AR2007081401662_pf.html (accessed September 2, 2007).

Rizvi, Sayyid. *Shah Wali-Ullah and His Times*. Canberra, Australia: Ma'rifat, 1980.

Roberts, Kristin. "Pentagon Chief in Afghanistan as Al Qaeda Regroups." *Reuters*, December 3, 2007. http://www.reuters.com/article/topNews/idUSN0328131520071203 (accessed July 20, 2008).

Roggio, Bill. "US Targets Compound in North Waziristan." *Long War Journal*, November 14, 2008. http://www.longwarjournal.org/archives/2008/11/us_targets_compound.php (accessed November 14, 2008).

———. See Gartenstein-Ross.

Rohde, David. "U.S. Officials See Waste in Billions Sent to Pakistan." *New York Times*, December 24, 2007. http://www.nytimes.com/2007/12/24/world/asia/24military.html (accessed July 20, 2008).

Roul, Animesh. "Student Islamic Movement of India: A Profile." *Jamestown Foundation*, April 6, 2006. http://www.jamestown.org/terrorism/news/article.php?articleid=2369953 (accessed July 20, 2008).

Roy, Amit. "7/7 Report Links Bombers to Pak." *Telegraph*, May 11, 2006. http://www
.telegraphindia.com/1060512/asp/foreign/story_6214208.asp (accessed May 2,
2007).

Rubin, Barnett. "Ending Chaos in Afghanistan and Pakistan." *Foreign Affairs*, November/December 2008.

Sageman, Marc. *Understanding Terror Networks*. Philadelphia: University of Pennsylvania
Press, 2004.

Sanger, David. "Bush Adds Troops in Bid to Secure Iraq." *New York Times*, January 10, 2007.
http://www.nytimes.com/2007/01/11/world/middleeast/11prexy.html (accessed
March 23, 2007).

———. "Obama's Worst Pakistan Nightmare." *New York Times*, January 8, 2009. http://
www.nytimes.com/2009/01/11/magazine/11pakistan-t.html (accessed January 10,
2009).

Sareen, Sushant. "Islamists Taking Over Pakistan." *Pioneer*, January 8, 2008. http://
www.dailypioneer.com/archives2/default12.asp?main_variable=oped&file_name
=opd3%2Etxt&counter_img=3&phy_path_it=E%3A%5Cdailypioneer%5Carchives2%
5Cjan808 (accessed January 20, 2008).

Sarkar, Sonia. "St. Stephen's to Have 50% Christian Quota." *NDTV.com*, June 9, 2008. http://
www.ndtv.com/convergence/ndtv/story.aspx?id=NEWEN20080052488 (accessed
July 10, 2008).

Schelling, Thomas. "Dynamic Models of Segregation." *Journal of Mathematical Sociology* 1
(1971).

Schifferdecker, Arnie. "The Taliban–Bin Laden–ISI Connection." *American Foreign Service
Association*, December 1, 2002. http://www.afsa.org/fsj/Dec01/schiff.cfm (accessed
May 2, 2007).

Schmitt, Eric. See Mazzetti.

Schwartz, Stephen. "Ground Zero and the Saudi Connection." *Spectator*, September 22, 2001.

———. "The Saudi Arabia Accountability Act of 2005." *Weekly Standard*, June 8, 2005.
http://www.weeklystandard.com/Content/Public/Articles/000/000/005/703
azlsf.asp (accessed March 2, 2007).

———. "The Senate Holds a Hearing on the Saudi Arabia Accountability Act." *Weekly Standard*, November 10, 2005. http://www.islamicpluralism.org/articles/2005a/05senate
judiciarycom.htm (accessed November 14, 2008).

Sciolino, Elaine. "Our Saudi Allies." *New York Times*, January 27, 2002. http://www.sullivan
-county.com/identity/saudi_support.htm (accessed July 28, 2008).

Sengupta, Somini. "Terrorist Attacks Unsettling India." *New York Times*, July 29, 2008.
http://www.nytimes.com/2008/07/29/world/asia/29india.html (accessed November
10, 2008).

Shah, Pir. See Perlez.

Shahin, Sultan. "Manmohan's Kashmir Dreams." *Asia Times,* November 14, 2004. http://www.atimes.com/atimes/South_Asia/FK19Df02.html (accessed May 2, 2007).

Sharan, Abhishek. "Money Came from the Gulf, Claim Police." *Hindustan Times,* September 22, 2008. http://www.hindustantimes.com/StoryPage/FullcoverageStoryPage.aspx?sectionName=&id=f5f2b286-cf12-4705-91c8-b769b654d2ceTerrorStrikesDelhi_Special&&Headline=Money+came+from+the+Gulf%2c+claim+police (accessed September 22, 2008).

Sharma, Somendra. "Nariman House, Not Taj, Was the Prime Target on 26/11." *Daily News & Analysis,* January 5, 2009. http://www.dnaindia.com/report.asp?newsid=1218869&pageid=0 (accessed January 6, 2009).

Sharma, Vikram. "IT Cos to Keep Tabs on Techies." *Express Buzz,* October 8, 2008. http://www.expressbuzz.com/edition/story.aspx?Title=IT+cos+to+keep+tabs+on+techies&artid=tJitjVcLSbc=&SectionID=b7ziAYMenjw=&MainSectionID=b7ziAYMenjw=&SectionName=BUzPVSKuYv7MFxnS0yZ7ng==&SEO=IT,+multinational,+companies (accessed October 12, 2008).

Shavit, Ari. "Judgment Day—Israel Facing Apocalypse." *Ha'aretz Magazine,* October 6, 2000. http://christianactionforisrael.org/isreport/septoct00/landau.html (accessed July 20, 2008).

Shivhare, Varun. "Minority Rights: The Judicial Approach." *Legalservicesindia.com.* http://www.legalservicesindia.com/articles/judi.htm (accessed July 20, 2008).

Siddique, Mohammed. "Don't Link Terror to Religion, say Clerics." *Rediff.com,* November 8, 2008. http://www.rediff.com/news/2008/nov/08dont-link-terror-to-religion-say-islamic-clerics.htm (accessed November 15, 2008).

———. "'The MIM Has Been Given Rs 5,000 Crore.'" *Rediff.com,* July 20, 2008. http://www.rediff.com/news/2008/jul/20inter1.htm (accessed November 10, 2008).

Simon, Bob. "Killing in the Name of Islam Is a Cancer." *CBSNEWS.com,* March 27, 2005. http://www.cbsnews.com/stories/2007/03/23/60minutes/main2602308_page2.shtml (accessed May 2, 2007).

Simons, Marlise. "Arrest Is Sought of Sudan Leader in Genocide Case." *New York Times,* July 15, 2008. http://www.nytimes.com/2008/07/15/world/africa/15sudan.html (accessed July 20, 2008).

Sina, Ali. "Yes, Study the Quran!" *FaithFreedom.org,* January 21, 2004.

Slackman, Michael. "In Algeria, a Tug of War for Young Minds." *New York Times,* June 13, 2008. http://www.nytimes.com/2008/06/23/world/africa/23algeria.html (accessed July 20, 2008).

Smith, Michael. "British Government 'to Pull Troops Out of Iraq by Mid-2009.'" *Sunday Times,* July 13, 2008. http://www.timesonline.co.uk/tol/news/politics/article4322710.ece (accessed July 20, 2008).

Soloman, Jay. See Dreazen.

Spencer, Robert. "The American Muslim, Terrorism, and Islamic Supremism." *Jihad Watch*, October 6, 2008. http://www.jihadwatch.org/archives/022992.php (accessed October 6, 2008).

———."'Jihadist' Booted from Government Lexicon." *Jihad Watch*, April 24, 2008. http://jihadwatch.org/archives/020777.php (accessed July 20, 2008).

———. *Religion of Peace? Why Christianity Is and Islam Isn't.* Washington, DC: Regnery, 2007.

———. *Stealth Jihad: How Radical Islam Is Subverting America without Guns or Bombs.* Washington, DC: Regnery, 2008.

———. "SUNY-Stonybrook: Manufactured Outrage." *Jihad Watch*, October 27, 2008. http://www.jihadwatch.org/archives/023239.php (accessed October 28, 2008).

———. *The Truth about Muhammad: Founder of the World's Most Intolerant Religion.* Washington, DC: Regnery, 2006.

Spindle, Bill. "Crude Reality: Soaring Energy Use Puts Oil Squeeze on Iran." *Wall Street Journal*, February 20, 2007.

Sridhar, N. "Ethnic Cleansing in Pakistan during Partition: A Preliminary Statistical Analysis." *Bharat Rakshak Monitor*, September/October 2003. http://www.bharat-rakshak .com/MONITOR/ISSUE6-2/sridhar.html (accessed July 2, 2008).

Srinivasan, Rajeev. "India, the Kashmiri Colony." *Rediff.com*, November 9, 2002. http://www .rediff.com/news/2002/nov/09rajeev.htm (accessed May 2, 2007).

Srivastava, Siddarth. "India and Saudi Arabia Move beyond Oil." *Asia Times Online*, January 28, 2006. http://www.atimes.com/atimes/South_Asia/HA28Df02.html (accessed July 20, 2008).

Stalinsky, Steven. "The 'Islamic Affairs Department' of the Saudi Embassy in Washington, D.C." *MEMRI*, November 26, 2003. http://www.memri.org/bin/articles.cgi?Area =sr&ID=SR2303 (accessed July 20, 2008).

———. "Saudi Arabia's Education System." *FrontPage Magazine*, December 30, 2002. http:// www.frontpagemag.com/Articles/ReadArticle.asp?ID=5243 (accessed July 20, 2008).

Stenhouse, Paul. "Muhammed, Quranic Texts, the Sharia, and Incitement to Violence." *Jihad Watch*, August 31, 2002. http://www.jihadwatch.org/archives/Muhammad%20and %20Incitement%20to%20Violence.pdf (accessed September 30, 2008).

Steyn, Mark. *America Alone: The End of the World as We Know It.* Washington, DC: Regnery, 2006.

———. "Who Will Raise the Siege of Paris?" *Washington Times*, November 7, 2005. http:// www.washingtontimes.com/commentary/20051106-102157-9880r.htm (accessed May 2, 2007).

Stout, David. "Iraq Seems on Verge of Deal on American Presence." *New York Times*, October 17, 2008. http://www.nytimes.com/2008/10/18/world/middleeast/17 forcescnd.html (accessed October 18, 2008).

Straziuso, Jason. "US Think Tank: Pakistan Helped Taliban Insurgents." Associated Press, June 9, 2008. http://www.breitbart.com/article.php?id=2008-06-09_D916OJLG0 &show_article=1&cat=breaking (accessed July 20, 2008).

Suroor, Hasan. "A Question of Identity." *Hindu*, August 17, 2004. http://www .hindu.com/2004/08/17/stories/2004081701341000.htm (accessed May 2, 2007).

Swami, Praveen. "A Bend in the Road." *Outlook India*, March 18, 2008. http://www .outlookindia.com/fullprint.asp?choice=1&fodname=20080318&fname=simi&sid=1 (accessed July 20, 2008).

———. "Understanding Pakistan's Response to Mumbai." *Hindu*, January 26, 2009. http://www.hindu.com/2009/01/26/stories/2009012650570800.htm (accessed January 28, 2009).

Swamy, Subramanian. "A Strategy to Combat Terrorism in India." *Organiser*, October 8, 2006. http://www.organiser.org/dynamic/modules.php?name=Content&pa=showpage&pid =151&page=25 (accessed May 2, 2007).

Taher, Abul. "Revealed: UK's First Official Sharia Courts." *Times Online*, September 14, 2008. http://www.frontpagemag.com/Articles/Read.aspx?GUID=90E44A37-79BF-435D -B0F1-682392A1C633 (accessed July 22, 2008).

Taheri, Amir. "A Dubious Mission." *New York Post*, July 22, 2008. http://www.frontpagemag .com/Articles/Read.aspx?GUID=90E44A37-79BF-435D-B0F1-682392A1C633 (accessed July 22, 2008).

Takeyh, Ray. See Nasr.

Taleb, Nassim. *The Black Swan: The Impact of the Highly Improbable*. New York: Random House, 2007.

Tavernise, Sabrina. "Shiite Militia in Baghdad Sees Its Power Ebb." *New York Times*, July 27, 2008. http://www.nytimes.com/2008/07/27/world/middleeast/27mahdi.html (accessed July 20, 2008).

———. "Violence Leaves Young Iraqis Doubting Clerics." *New York Times*, March 4, 2008. http://www.nytimes.com/2008/03/04/world/middleeast/04youth.html (accessed July 20, 2008).

———. See Erlanger.

Thomas, Presley. See Pachouly.

Thompson, Mark. "Where Are the New Recruits?" *Time*, January 10, 2005. http://www .time.com/time/magazine/article/0,9171,1015898,00.html (accessed March 2, 2007).

Trager, Robert. "Deterring Terrorism: It Can Be Done." *International Security* 30, no. 3 (2005/2006).

Tretkoff, Ernie. "Percentage of First-Year Foreign Graduate Students Falls to 43%." *APS*, November 2005. http://www.aps.org/publications/apsnews/200511/foreign-grad.cfm (accessed May 2, 2007).

Ullman, Harlan. "Divided 'They' Fall." *Washington Times*, April 4, 2007. http:// www.washingtontimes.com/op-ed/hullman.htm (accessed May 2, 2007).

Upadhyay, Ramashray. "Anti-terrorism Conference Dar-ul-Uloom Deoband—A Failed Exercise?" *SAAG*, March 27, 2008, http://www.southasiaanalysis.org/%5Cpapers 27%5Cpaper2646.html (accessed July 20, 2008).

———. "Islamic Institutions in India—Protracted Movement for Separate Muslim Identity?" *SAAG*, February 6, 2003. http://www.southasiaanalysis.org/papers6/paper599.html (accessed March 2, 2007).

———. "Islamic Terrorism in Bangladesh—A Threat to Regional Peace." *SAAG*, May 10, 2007. http://www.southasiaanalysis.org/papers23/paper2242.html (accessed March 2, 2007).

———. "Restive Muslims—Impact on Internal Security?" *SAAG*, October 27, 2008. http://www.southasiaanalysis.org/papers29/paper2897.html (accessed October 27, 2007).

———. "SIMI and Its Alarming Growth." *SAAG*, April 22, 2008. http://www.southasia analysis.org/%5Cpapers27%5Cpaper2676.html (accessed July 20, 2008).

Varshney, Ashutosh. *Ethnic Conflict and Civic Life: Hindus and Muslims in India*. New Haven, CT: Yale University Press, 2002.

Verma, Bharat. "Take the War to the Enemy." *Rediff.com*, December 22, 2008. http://www.rediff.com/news/2008/dec/22mumterror-take-the-war-to-the-enemy.htm (accessed December 30, 2008).

Vijay, Tarun. "A Secular Protocol." *Times of India*, October 11, 2008. http://times ofindia.indiatimes.com/Opinion/Columnists/Tarun_Vijay/The_Right_View/A _secular_protocol/articleshow/3584631.cms (accessed October 14, 2008).

Warner, Bill. "The 'Good' in the Koran." *PoliticalIslam.com*, November 13, 2008. http://www.politicalislam.com/blog/the-good-in-the-koran/ (accessed November 13, 2008).

Warraq, Ibn. *Why I Am Not a Muslim*. Amherst, NY: Prometheus Books, 1995.

Warrick, Joby. See Wright.

———. "Smugglers Had Design for Advanced Warhead." *Washington Post*, June 15, 2008. http://www.washingtonpost.com/wp-dyn/content/article/2008/06/14/AR200806 1402032.html (accessed July 16, 2008).

Watson, Paul. "In Pakistan's Public Schools, Jihad Still Part of Lesson Plan." *Los Angeles Times*, August 18, 2005. http://articles.latimes.com/2005/aug/18/world/fg-schools18 (accessed July 20, 2008).

Wehner, Peter. "The War against Global Jihadism." *RealClearPolitics.com*, January 8, 2007. http://www.realclearpolitics.com/articles/2007/01/the_nature_of_our_enemy.html (accessed July 20, 2008).

Whitlock, Craig. "Al Qaeda's Growing Online Offensive." *Washington Post*, June 24, 2008. http://www.washingtonpost.com/wp-dyn/content/story/2008/06/23/ST200806 2302295.html (accessed July 20, 2008).

———. "Al Qaeda Masters Terrorism on the Cheap." *Washington Post*, August 24, 2008. http://www.washingtonpost.com/wp-dyn/content/article/2008/08/23/AR2008 082301962.html (August 25, 2008).

————. "U.S. Network Falters in Mideast Mission." *Washington Post,* June 23, 2008. http://www.washingtonpost.com/wp-dyn/content/article/2008/06/22/AR2008 062201228.html (accessed July 20, 2008).

Wilders, Geert. "America as the Last Man Standing." *Jihad Watch,* September 28, 2008. http://www.jihadwatch.org/archives/022867.php (accessed September 30, 2008).

Wilson, Graeme. "Young, British Muslims 'Getting More Radical.'" *Telegraph,* March 1, 2007. http://www.telegraph.co.uk/news/main.jhtml?xml=/news/2007/01/29/nmuslims29 .xml (accessed March 2, 2007).

Wonacott, Peter. "Lawless Legislators Thwart Social Progress in India." *Wall Street Journal,* May 4, 2007.

Woodward, Bob. *State of Denial: Bush at War, Part III.* New York: Simon & Shuster, 2006.

Wright, Robin. "U.S. Steps Up Unilateral Strikes in Pakistan." *Washington Post,* March 27, 2008. http://www.washingtonpost.com/wp-dyn/content/article/2008/03/27/AR 2008032700007.html (accessed July 20, 2008).

Zagorcheva, Dessislava. See Trager.

Zakaria, Fareed. *The Future of Freedom: Illiberal Democracy at Home and Abroad.* New York: Norton, 2003.

————. "India Rising." *Newsweek,* March 2, 2006. http://www.msnbc.msn.com/id/ 11564364/site/newsweek (accessed March 2, 2007).

————. "Vengeance of the Victors." *Newsweek,* January 8, 2007. http://www.msnbc .msn.com/id/16409404/site/newsweek (accessed March 2, 2007).

Zumwalt, James. "Nuke Forensics: No 'Cold Cases.'" *Washington Times,* March 8, 2007. http://www.Washtimes.com/commentary/20070307-091631-2252r.htm (accessed May 2, 2007).